W9-AUH-318

NO PARADISE
FOR WORKERS

Capitalism and the Common People
in Australia 1788–1914

NO PARADISE FOR WORKERS

Capitalism and the Common People in Australia 1788–1914

Ken Buckley and
Ted Wheelwright

Melbourne
Oxford University Press
Oxford Auckland New York

This work is dedicated to the memory of Brian Fitzpatrick, pioneer who laid the foundations for the study of class struggle in Australian history

OXFORD UNIVERSITY PRESS AUSTRALIA

Oxford New York Toronto
Delhi Bombay Calcutta Madras Karachi
Petaling Jaya Singapore Hong Kong Tokyo
Nairobi Dar es Salaam Cape Town
Melbourne Auckland
and associated companies in
Beirut Berlin Ibadan Nicosia

Oxford is a trade mark of Oxford University Press

National Library of Australia Cataloguing-in-Publication data:

Buckley, Ken.
No paradise for workers.

Bibliography.
Includes index.
ISBN 0 19 554622 9.
ISBN 0 19 554621 0 (pbk.).

1. Capitalism—Australia—History. 2. Labor and labouring classes—Australia—History. 3. Australia—Economic conditions—1788–1900. 4.?Australia—Economic conditions—1901–1914. 5. Australia—Politics and government—1788–1900. 6. Australia—Politics and government—1901–1914. I. Wheelwright, E. L. (Edward Lawrence). II. Title.

994.02

Edited by Shirley Purchase
Designed by Lynda Patullo
Typeset by Abb-typesetting Pty Ltd, Collingwood, Victoria
Printed by Impact Printing, Melbourne
Published by Oxford University Press, 253 Normanby Road, South Melbourne, Australia

Contents

CONTENTS

Preface

This work is not a general history of Australia in the conventional sense; the approach is not sequential, but deals with critical periods in the evolution of capitalism and its relation to the common people. Anyone who expects to find, for example, an account of the gold rushes of the 1850s, will be disappointed. However, such material can easily be found elsewhere. The work has had a long gestation; in 1975 we considered that the time was ripe for writing a 'History of the Political Economy of Australian Capitalism from the Earliest Times to the Present Day'. We also observed that before this could begin it would be necessary to provide some bricks and straw. This was attempted in the five-volume series we edited, under the title, *Essays in the Political Economy of Australian Capitalism*, published by the ANZ Book Company, 1975–83.

We acknowledge those contributors to these volumes on whose work we have drawn. We also wish to acknowledge the work of Toula Markos and Truce Timmer in transforming difficult manuscripts into immaculate typescript, the constructive comments of a referee, and the excellent editing skills of Carla Taines, of Oxford University Press, who helped us to produce a better book.

Ken Buckley
Ted Wheelwright
Sydney, April 1987

In the nineteenth century Australians enjoyed the reputation of being in the vanguard of human progress; they were often the pioneers in the introduction of bourgeois democracy, and rather boastful about it. By contrast, in the twentieth century Australians seem to have missed the bus carrying humanity into the future . . . We had the institutions and the values to promote the use of parts of our country as quarries for foreign powers, but neither the institutions, nor the inclination, nor the belief to make our country a paradise for the people.

Manning Clark, *A Discovery of Australia*
1976 Boyer Lectures

Introduction

The origins of capitalism in Australia are unique. In no other country were the elements of the social relations of the system transplanted by force of arms over such a vast distance, in the embryonic form of a military prison, which initially contained no capitalists, no free labourers, and no peasants. Yet within a generation the colony was essentially capitalist, free labourers were on the increase, there was an incipient peasantry, and the original inhabitants had been dispossessed, their culture fatally weakened at its material base by the seizure of their land.

As capitalism expanded from its point of origin in Europe, using superior military technology, the indigenous peoples of many parts of the world had their lands expropriated and their culture destroyed. In some cases the officer class of the occupying armies became the nucleus of a landed oligarchy, as in parts of South America, the conquistadores being the prototype. In others, slavery, second cousin to convict labour, ensured that the fruits of such labour accrued to the slave owner, thereby expediting capital accumulation as in parts of North and South America and the Caribbean. Only in Australia, however, did colonial capitalism begin with the combination of expropriation of the original inhabitants, the forced labour of convicts in a military prison farm, and the transformation of the overseeing officer class into one of nascent capitalists.

Once the essential basis of capitalism has been transplanted—a   1 particular class structure, ideology, and technology—its development, although subject to the 'general laws of motion' of the system as a whole, takes on a life of its own, certainly in its earlier years. It assumes distinctive forms shaped by the configuration of its economy, its relation to world capitalism, and the social classes emerging from this interaction. These forms or stages have often been given labels such as 'colonial', 'neo-colonial', 'pastoral', 'mercantile', 'industrial', and 'monopoly' in the past, and, today, 'national', 'international' or 'transnational', 'state', and 'client, or crony' capitalism. However they may be categorized, the purpose of this book is to trace the origins and evolution of various significant phases in the development of capitalism in Australia and their relationship to the common people. The themes include: the destruction of Aboriginal society, seizure of the means of production; the genesis of capital accumulation, formation of social classes, class struggle, the emancipation of women, the use of state power; economic crises, imperialism and racism, the impact of foreign capital and immigration; the rape of the environment, the concentration and centralization of capital and attempts to regulate it, alienation, the fetishism of commodities and its effects on human relationships; unemployment and the industrial reserve army, neo-fascism, transnational capitalism, repression and the client state.[1]

Capitalism presupposes two main classes, those who own the means of production, and need to employ labour to make it productive and profitable; and those who own no means of production, have nothing to sell but their labour, and therefore must seek employment to survive. For millennia the means of production for most of mankind was the land. If capitalism was to function, people must be driven off the land so that capitalists could own it, and be able to employ landless labourers.

State power is necessary to do this, which is why in the first instance capitalism had to be created by force, hence Proudhon's aphorism, 'Property is theft'; and hence the emphasis by some of the very early political economists, such as Boisguillebert, on crime and violence as a common way of getting access to the means of production.[2] Much of the great international migration in the nineteenth century was caused by capitalism in Europe uprooting masses of people and turning them into a landless proletariat. Most migrants were 'voluntary'; although most of those who came to Australia in the beginning were not.

Land was the pivot on which the origin of capitalism turned. In Australia the first common people were the Aborigines, and they experienced the fatal impact of state power using superior technology. There were no land rights for the First Australians: no treaties were signed between governments and Aborigines, and land was taken from them without compensation, the act being sanctioned by British laws. This seizure of Aboriginal land was not effected without resistance. Henry

Reynolds has documented this, pointing out that at times 'it appeared to threaten the general prosperity of colonial society'. In the nineteenth century, much of Australia was a frontier society, bristling with guns. Besides the slaughter of Aborigines, about 3000 white settlers died and another 3000 were wounded, stations were deserted all over the country, and in South Australia several towns were nearly abandoned. Fears were expressed that the flow of capital and immigrants would dry up. ' "We want capital and capitalists", the editor of the *Port Denison Times* proclaimed ... but he doubted if capitalists would invest in so unsettled a community.'

There was also humanitarian opposition to the 'relentless economic, political and intellectual currents which engulfed Aboriginal society'. Much of this opposition came from missionaries relying on the Christian view of all mankind being God's creatures; they were all extremely unpopular, faced threats of banishment and suffered loss of employment and social ostracism.

They appreciated too that the conflict over ideas grew out of and was shaped by the struggle over land, that racism was as functional for the frontier squatter as the Colt revolver. One cleared the land, the other cleared the conscience.

... The pastoral industry was the single most important agent in the destruction of Aboriginal society and the squatters were often the most persistent advocates of racist theories.[3]

Land was *the* major means of production in the first century of capitalism in Australia; changes in its ownership played a key role in the development of the rural economy. It became the property of the crown, which then proceeded to alienate large tracts of it, first by land grants of small areas to emancipated convicts, thus forming the nucleus of a peasantry. This practice soon stopped, and very much larger areas were then given to members of the officer class, forming the nucleus of an Australian landowning oligarchy. By mid-century even larger areas had been acquired by the practice of 'squatting'; forty-two squatters held 13.6 million acres out of a total of 73 million occupied in New South Wales alone, which must have been one of the largest concentrations of land ownership with dubious title anywhere in the world.[4]

From the 1830s, land was sold by the crown on a large scale, leading to substantial revenue used to subsidize the import of labour through immigration. The price of this land was deliberately kept high enough to prevent small holding and subsistence farming, on the advice of the prominent British theoretician of colonial capitalism, E. G. Wakefield. Otherwise, he said, larger-scale capitalist farming would be impossible as the supply of landless labourers willing to work for others would be

3

inadequate. The adoption of this policy is probably unique in the history of colonial capitalism, as was the extent and rate of privatization of the land. Long before the privatization vogue of the 1980s, Australian governments were past masters in the art of selling off publicly owned national assets to defray the costs of essential government expenditure.

The 1790s were a speculators' paradise, and the uncertain and irregular arrival of cargoes meant that anyone with capital could make big profits. The capital and the market were provided by the British government. The officers ensured their monopoly by ruling that only they could be admitted on board supply ships, and they pooled their resources to take shares in incoming cargoes, thus creating the first import cartel in Australia. Fortunes were made in the early decades of forced labour. In 1820 there were only 30 000 whites in New South Wales, and officers and officials formed a tight group controlling the state machine. None was wealthy to begin with: their social origins— petty bourgeois—were similar to those of contemporary British industrial capitalists.

The government of the colony was under constant pressure from the imperial power to keep the costs of running the prison farm as low as possible. Land was granted initially to ex-convicts. When land grants were made to officers, pressure to privatize farming increased and public farming was neglected. It is not surprising that Francis Greenway was to write later: 'I have generally found it that people consider that government and the public may be duped and plundered without crime: that every man has a right to do so who can do it *neatly.*'[5]

The genesis of capitalism in Australia demonstrated the quintessence of the system, state power being the prime road to private wealth. The public sector provided the officer class with free land, 'costless' labour, and the market for the produce, so putting public money and resources into private hands in the crucial early years. Forced labour and land seizure were the basis of capital accumulation, effected under the auspices of a military dictatorship accustomed to inflicting the most draconian punishments on transgressors of its regime.

The first Australian colonies began as prisons without walls. Special prisons were built, such as those at Norfolk Island and Port Arthur, designed for the particularly cruel punishment of recalcitrant convicts. These gaols were hell-holes which would rival the torture chambers of modern military dictatorships. As Robert Hughes points out, these places 'held a minority of the convicts but they were absolutely integral to the System; they provided a standard of terror by which good behaviour on the mainland of New South Wales ... would be enforced'.[6]

4

With such a repressive state machine, there was little convict resistance. Also, many police and magistrates were corrupt, making profit out of the control of state power. There was also ideological control. Some was religious in form, some cultural in the sense that the colonial culture was dominated by the desire to make money, and convicts desired their freedom not to overthrow the system but to join it. Sentences could be shortened, tickets of leave granted for good conduct, and convicts did have some rights. Forced labour rather than confinement behind bars was the essence of the system, which had developed into the provision of a cheap and mobile labour force.

These convicts formed the basis of the proletariat in Australia. They were drawn from the British working class, had a variety of skills, were predominantly young men, and came mostly from the cities, although a third were Irish with a peasant background.[7] The crime of which most were convicted (usually more than once) was theft. Many were dangerous when arrested, and probably more were brutalized by the convict system, but the laws under which they were sentenced were made by and for the men of property with the objective of protecting it. Noting that the final aim of the transportation system was 'less to punish individual crimes than to uproot an enemy class from the British social fabric', Robert Hughes regards it as a forerunner of the Gulag, although he is not the first to do so.[8]

The formation of a working class is a nodal point in the development of capitalism; the ideology and culture adopted at that time played a dominant role in working-class consciousness for decades. Convicts could be assigned to the outback pastoral industry, whereas free workers were inclined to stay closer to towns. There were far more convicts in the squatting areas of New South Wales than there were closer to Sydney and many of them preferred to remain bushworkers after emancipation. Hence the working-class culture which developed in the outback was an amalgam of Anglo-Irish traditions and the effect on them of frontier conditions. The Irish component was fundamental; for most of the nineteenth century at least one-third of the working class was of Irish origin. Most of those transported from Ireland were not political prisoners in the strict sense, but they were victims of English oppression. This collective memory

survived most tenaciously as one of the primary images of working class culture . . . the legacy of sectarianism in Australian politics, the sense of a community divided between English and Protestant 'haves' and Irish Catholic 'have-nots' . . . influenced the patterns of power in Australian life for another 150 years.[9]

A major contribution from Russel Ward was to show how the outback culture, which dominated Australia for so long, emerged from the　5 'convictism' of an unequal society on which frontier conditions had a levelling effect. The expression 'a fair go' may well date from this time, indicating the view that even such an oppressed class as convicts should have some rights or opportunities, and in fact *needed* to be given them if labour in such remote locations was to be able to fulfil its functions—free or unfree. If so, it could be described as a triumph of environment over ideology. For many years most free workers were ex-convicts, and there was no serious segregation of free and unfree workers. Robert Hughes agrees that bush comradeship was real, but 'so was the defensive, static, levelling, two-class hatred that came out of convictry'. Tasmania was the colony which had the highest density of convicts and their descendants, but its legacy was 'a malleable and passive working class, paternalistic institutions, a tame press, and colonized Anglophile values. The idea that rebels are the main product of oppression is a consoling fiction.' [10]

As the pastoral economy expanded there was a shortage of labour. By 1831 emigration from Britain was being promoted with assisted passages, and free labourers began to outnumber convicts, especially after 1840 when transportation to New South Wales ceased. These were the crucial formative years of the Australian working class, which began to flex its muscles, to form trade unions, and to demonstrate in the streets against the proposed restoration of convictism, which it saw as unfair competition driving down the wages of free men. Sixteen years after transportation ceased, organized labour achieved its first major victory, the eight-hour day in the construction industry, which was naturally protected from overseas competition and involved relatively large numbers of stonemasons engaged on public works. Unions of workers in the building and construction industry have played a key role in the evolution of Australian capitalism, from the achievement of the world's first eight-hour working day in 1856, to the important environmental contribution of the 'Green Bans' imposed by the NSW Builders Labourers Federation in the 1970s, led by Jack Mundey. [11]

Economic crises, in the sense of periodic slumps in output, employment, wages, profits and capital values, to which capitalism has been prone since its inception, increased in severity, owing partly to the larger scale of unco-ordinated production in relation to demand, and partly to the growth of capitalism on a world scale. If severe enough, such crises can cause a restructuring of the economy, and the rise of new social classes who may demand that state power be refurbished and used more in their interest. This was the case in the first severe crisis of colonial pastoralism in the 1840s, which showed that Australia had become linked to the world textile industry, through Britain and the USA. During the 1830s wool production for Britain increased five-fold as squatters spread their ever-increasing sheep runs over vacant crown land. However, by the end of the decade, the sale to the USA of British cloth, made from Australian wool, began to decline and the price of wool dropped sharply. This, combined with economic difficulties in Britain causing a cut in its investment outflow, led to Australia's first slump.

It provided Australia's first lesson in dependent development, showing the dangers of excessive reliance on export markets and foreign capital, which encouraged overproduction of a few commodities, in this case a virtual monoculture. The sharp contraction of capital inflow and credit had catastrophic effects on the common people, causing unemployment and poverty on an unprecedented scale, and even significant emigration. Men of property invented means of retaining control of their assets whilst fobbing off their creditors, through the device of voluntary bankruptcy, allowed by the NSW Insolvency Act of 1842. In 1987 much more sophisticated schemes enabled creditors to be defrauded of millions of dollars, using a similar principle.[12] Some of the propertied classes of the 1840s were caught by bank failure or foreclosure, which led to the first expressions of hostility to what came to be called 'the money power', in the form of verbal attacks on British-based banks, Jews and usurers.

Government revenue was also affected, especially that derived from the sale of crown land used to finance immigration. Alternative sources of funds were sought, squatters being an obvious target as they had not bought land and paid only a minuscule annual licence fee unrelated to the size of their runs. Governor Gipps proposed to alter this state of affairs to the 'user pays' principle: the more land squatted on, the higher the licence fee. This provoked a strong reaction from squatters, landowners and merchants who successfully mobilized against him in both the imperial and colonial governments. However, feeling that the imperial government was too remote from them, they strove to secure colonial governments which would give *them* control over the use of crown land and decisions about allocations of the revenue therefrom. Hence there were links between the first economic slump, government attempts to raise revenue, and the emerging political dominance of the colonial ruling class.

The ruling class has always seen the function of government to provide as much assistance to private capital as possible, which is to say, to themselves. Australian governments have never been, and could not have been, laissez-faire in character. By the 1860s public investment accounted for about one-third of total investment, a proportion which remained more or less constant for the next hundred years at least. This relationship between government and private enterprise has been called a 'partnership' between the state and the private sector, but we regard this as misleading and prefer the term 'state capitalism', which is taken to mean that, although the state had a degree of autonomy in decision making, most of the time sections of the capitalist class used the state for their own purposes. In Australia the end result was not quite so vicious as it was in America, mainly because the relative strength of the Australian working class was greater. This assessment is borne out by comparisons with other 'white dominions', such as Canada and Argentina.[13]

Nevertheless, private capital formation was very important, and after most of the rural land had been locked in by big landlords and squatters, the main private investment was in the growth of cities, especially in housing. Here, land values grew apace but accrued to an urban bourgeoisie as most rural landowners held little in the city. The 'squattocracy' put its stamp on Australia through its anti-liberal thought, its aping of the British landed aristocracy, its effect on the private educational system and the professional classes, and its negative political role through conservative upper houses of parliament. However, it did not constitute the leading force in the bourgeoisie. This role was taken by the mercantile class, which dominated the lucrative trade in imports and exports. Fortunes were made, some of which were invested in mining, manufacturing, shipping and share-broking. Here was the seedbed of Australian capitalism in which family dynasties were founded, many of them lasting until well into the next century, including well-known names of what came to be 'the establishment' in various capital cities. Such family dynasties have played a crucial role in the development of capitalism in Australia, which has not received the attention it deserves.

Mid-nineteenth century society was fluid. There was considerable upward mobility leading to the formation of a large middle class, consisting of those in the professions such as doctors and lawyers, senior officials in public and private bureaucracies, small businessmen, farmers and gold-diggers. Radical sections of these middle classes combined with working-class urban forces and some liberal elements among the merchants and landowners to push for popular democracy. This was boosted by the armed uprising at Eureka, which was essentially a revolt against an arbitrary tax on small capital that stood in the way of the ambitions of the gold-diggers to get rich quickly. It had nothing to do with working-class solidarity, but it did give a powerful impetus to political democracy, which was a real advance for the common people. This is a good example of how a particular incident can ignite a volatile mixture of the elements of different social classes, producing a result which no-one could foreseè. Although the bourgeoisie was alarmed and took steps to ensure that popular democracy would be more formal than real for several decades, there was no threat to capitalism. Most of society was infused with its ideology and acquisitive ethos: as long as this appeared to work for the majority of the population, it went unchallenged.

8   The years 1850 to 1890 may be termed the Long Boom, and are

comparable to the Age of Growth almost a century later, 1940 to the early 1970s. Both had a profound impact on the class structure, and through it on the political scene. In the late 1850s, pressure to 'unlock the land' grew, especially in Victoria. The driving force was small business people, such as shopkeepers and craftsmen who, apart from a desire to 'improve themselves', could see more prosperity and personal independence in a community of small producers than in one dominated by a few big graziers. Legislation from 1861 removing the political barriers to small farmers was not very successful. Squatters had better access to land and could use 'dummies' and other devices; the economic situation did not favour small farmers as the internal market was limited; and access to the external market was available primarily to those producing a big clip of wool, which meant large properties. A successful unlocking of the land would have had to involve measures to prevent squatters gobbling up the best land, and to provide sufficient capital for small farmers to work it. By the 1880s, 500 holdings of at least 10 000 acres accounted for half the alienated land in New South Wales, and in Victoria ten families owned 2 million acres.

Hostility to the near-monopoly of land by a few remained strong for a long time, as the response to the visit of Henry George indicates. George was an American political economist who saw the causes of inequality and depressions in the monopoly of land ownership by a few, the remedy being to remove all taxes on labour and its products, and have a single tax on the value of land: hence his sobriquet 'Single Tax George'. His appeal was much greater in America and Australia, where land grabbing and speculation were quite recent in living memory, than in Europe where large-scale land ownership was sanctified by centuries of occupation and the bestowal of feudal titles on the owners.

The attempts to unlock the land were not a complete failure; by the end of the century a new rural petty bourgeoisie was emerging, and class alignments were changing. The position of selectors (small farmers) was shifting and ambiguous: some failed, some sold out, while many could not support large families on small farms and worked as shearers or miners in the off season. This affected the growing bushworkers' unions, such as the forerunners of the Australian Workers' Union (AWU), for there were many 'temporary shearers', often sons of selectors only concerned with earning enough to pay the next instalment on the debt incurred to buy the property. They were not interested in strikes, especially long ones. Such factors weakened these unions, and although the AWU became the biggest union in the country, it was not as strong as often thought, especially in the face of sustained repression in Queensland as the debacle of the shearers' strikes of the 1890s indicates. Even so, rural labour in Australia was far better organized than anywhere else in the capitalist world.

The formation of the working class is a crucial factor in the development of capitalism, for the conditions under which it is formed tend to set a 'floor' for the wage levels achievable. The conditions in Australia were very favourable. They included a perennial labour shortage, high productivity in rural industry because of abundant land and imported capital, and early trade unionization fostered by the British heritage of struggle by the common people. Consequently the wage levels achieved in Australia were amongst the highest in the world. The fact that these were well above subsistence meant that a worker could save enough out of wages to set up a small business such as printing, building or dressmaking. To some extent this higher level of wages was characteristic of all 'newer' capitalisms, distinguishing them from the old, and fostering a petty bourgeoisie. Nevertheless the labour movement was weakened by divisions within the working class, based on skills, sex, race and religion. Without these divisions it would have been in a much stronger position to reduce what was still a high degree of inequality.

Despite weaknesses, the ability of the Australian working class to extract a reasonable share of the total output of a highly productive economy in the years of the long boom led to claims of 'a workers' paradise'. These claims were exaggerated. It is true that the common people were less downtrodden in Australia than was the case in Britain, Europe and the USA, but unemployment was not properly measured, much work was of a casual or seasonal nature, and although there were labour shortages in the countryside, each city had its 'reserve army of labour'. The extent of house ownership by the working class was exaggerated, especially in the cities, where it was costlier—in the countryside many houses owned by workers were of very inferior quality. Public health was neglected; infant mortality was high; the sewering of the cities did not begin until very late in the nineteenth century; even as late as 1900 there was an outbreak of bubonic plague in Sydney.

Nevertheless average income per head in Australia was one of the highest in the world, so that colonial capitalism was successful in this respect. Indeed, given the virtually 'free' real estate of an enormous continent, at least for the first half century; 'costless' forced labour in the initial stages; the subsidized import of labour in the later stages; and open access to a growing imperial market, it would be surprising if such an economy were not in the front rank of production and consumption per head of a very small population. Furthermore, capitalism produces a national income account, but not a national capital account showing the nation's resources which have been used up, the forests that have been cut down, the land which has been eroded, the rivers polluted and silted up, and the minerals extracted. After the first hundred years forests had been depleted; much of the soil was showing signs of exhaustion; yields were declining; and large doses of superphosphate were necessary to restore fertility.[14] At the end of the next hundred years the situation was much worse, with a growing realization that much of the success of earlier Australian capitalism had come from exploiting its natural resources as well as its people. As both nature and humanity began to rebel, the system became less viable.

Long booms often carry the economy on to a new technological plane and change the composition of owners, managers, and the workforce, which affects social classes. Unions of skilled workers grew stronger and more aggressive than those of the unskilled, especially in secondary and building industries, which employed a third of the workforce by 1891, compared with less than a quarter in agricultural and pastoral industries. The distinguishing characteristic of highly skilled workers was the degree of control they had over their jobs and the work process. They were not, in the main, socialists, but real militancy came from them, primarily because they had a strong sense of their own worth, good organizations, and adequate financial reserves. Although most businesses were still small scale, working standards tended to be set by big establishments which were pushed by powerful unions such as the Amalgamated Society of Engineers, which had strong British links. Yet Australian unions were not simply replicas of those in the UK; they developed to meet local needs, were more flexible and less bureaucratic.

In the 1880s there was a ferment of new ideas, including a growth of class consciousness. Part of this was due to anxiety among craftsmen because of the dilution of skills, the erosion of apprenticeship, and the emergence of new semi-skilled workers. This gave rise to an upsurge in union militancy, leading to demands for more control over jobs and, in some unions, a closed shop. These unionists were the Australian counterpart of what Marx called the English working men, 'the first-born sons of modern industry—new-fangled men', who were 'as much the invention of modern times as machinery itself'.[15] Employers felt their managerial prerogatives were being challenged by these union advances, and formed their own organizations to reassert control. This new aggressiveness emerged towards the end of the boom and was a key factor in the most decisive confrontations of the nineteenth century in the maritime and pastoral industries. The trade unions overestimated their strength and were badly beaten when the full panoply of state power was arraigned against them. The result was cuts in wages and harsher working conditions.

The slump in the economy in the 1890s made the situation much worse. It was caused by the classic combination of vast uncontrolled overseas borrowing (especially for purposes unrelated to export growth or import replacement), and overproduction of wool for a declining world market. It affected all classes, undermining in particular the predominance of merchant capital, which was subdued for a decade, being preoccupied with problems of insolvency and bankruptcy.

The chain of payments due at certain times is broken in a hundred places, and the disaster is intensified by the collapse of the credit system. Thus, violent and acute crises are brought about, sudden and forcible depreciations, an acute stagnation and collapse of the process of reproduction . . .[16]

The trade unions were decimated. Not surprisingly, as industrial action had failed so dismally, they turned towards political action, and created a Labor party. Initially in New South Wales this reflected a class standpoint, especially that of unskilled workers badly hit by the depression. In the early years radicals and socialists were prominent, but after 1895 the AWU became a dominant force in the party, as it could deliver a substantial number of parliamentary seats. It had connections with rural shopkeepers, small farmers and tradespeople, and reflected the needs of small producers in the bush. Hence it developed a petty bourgeois ideology. Also, with about a third of the working class being of Irish descent, it is not surprising that Irish Catholicism played a formative role in the early years of the ALP. In October 1890 when the Australian Socialist League was in the ascendant, pushing for a socialist Labor Party, Cardinal Moran told the faithful that 'socialists are the avowed enemies of all religion', and that 'the only hope of the success of Trade Unionism is to keep quite free from any Socialist movement'.[17] There is a sense, therefore, in which the ALP became a kind of Christian Democrat Party in Australia, and there was a line of descent from Cardinal Moran, through Cardinal Mannix to B. A. Santamaria and the 'Groupers' of the post-World War II period.

The trade unions used the Labor Party to play a major role in arbitration. Crippled by defeats and with no chance of using their industrial strength in the depression, the unions felt they could gain more—or lose less—by state intervention in industrial disputes. It was a historic decision: the Australian working class opted for a controlled wage system (including a minimum wage) as a method of determining their standard of living. Their counterparts in Europe were opting for a welfare system to supplement their wages—a system which later developed into assistance for those who could not, for various reasons, participate in the wages system. As capitalism developed in the latter part of the twentieth century and was manifestly incapable of providing employment for all, doubts have been raised about whether the approach chosen by Australian workers is appropriate today.[18]

In the early years of the twentieth century, protection and arbitration were linked, as some kind of bargain began to be struck between unions and manufacturers desiring protection. Older forms of protection had made good wages possible, but a new form of protection was emerging which could ensure that good wages were paid as a result of compulsory arbitration. This 'class alliance' between manufacturers and unions laid the foundation for the industrialization of Australia to supply much of the home market for the next half century. It involved some redistribution of income from capital in the rural sector, which could not set its own prices on the world market. In the 1970s this alliance began to break down and be replaced by a new one linking rural exporters, giant foreign-controlled mineral companies, and a growing middle class producing services rather than traded goods. Both protection and arbitration, the foundation stones of Australian industrialization, then came under attack as the economy began to base itself on the shifting sands of volatile transnational finance capital.

The longer-term response to the depression and the balance of payments crisis of the 1890s was considerable restructuring in ways which required little new investment, such as the diversification of rural production, involving more wheat and meat, which created more small farmers and hence a challenge to the dominance of the big graziers and their mercantile allies. Governments promoted closer settlement, this policy being intended in part to reduce the polarization of the 1890s by building up a block of yeoman farmers who might help to stabilize the class structure by strengthening the middle ground. This process gave a boost to incipient populist ideas based on the ideal of a community of small producers striving to provide security and independence for themselves.

Many sharefarmers, tenants and leaseholders, shopkeepers and small business people who were sympathetic to the ALP and the labour movement, were receptive to populist ideas, especially when the depression receded and more workers could start small businesses. Consequently the labour movement absorbed populist ideas through its political party. Parasitic ruling elites of big landowners linked with big banks and big business in general, associated with big government, were seen as the barrier to this small business utopia. In this view of society, class distinctions were blurred, and the state and its apparatus was portrayed as neutral; there was support for state intervention to make the system work, especially for the small producer. This was a far cry from socialism, which should not be confused with trade union militancy. Australian capitalism had not yet exhausted its possibilities: 'No social order is ever destroyed before all the productive forces for which it is sufficient have been developed ...' [19]

Populism was also linked to nationalism, and Australian federation was brought about through a curious amalgam of commercialism and nationalism, fused in a colonial crucible. The result was a constitution which could only be described as a colonial relic, created by and for the

13

men of property in both colony and empire. Commerce needed an Australian common market which only some form of federation could provide, and the push was led by the bourgeoisie in Victoria, a state with a relatively small area and a large labour force, which tended towards manufacturing and more intensive agriculture. Victoria also had tariffs, but their effect has been exaggerated; hidden protection, through non-tariff barriers such as government contracts for locomotives, was probably more important. Bankers and merchants also favoured federation as a means of facilitating trade and payments.

The workers were far less sure that the types of proposed federation would work to their benefit, and they were right; the eventual structure was loaded against New South Wales, which had the strongest labour movement. Nationalism probably secured labour acquiescence, especially as there was a clear need for a unified approach on defence, foreign policy and immigration. In addition, nationalism had earlier been fuelled by anti-British imperialism and republicanism, which had understandable appeal to that section of the working class which was of Irish origin.[20] There were also elements of racism, especially with respect to the immigration of black or Asian labour. The employers of such labour in Queensland, on the other hand, feared the White Australia policy emerging from federation proposals, and demanded higher sugar prices and protection as part of the compensation for that policy, which would increase their costs.

The conservative nature of the constitution was evident in certain features: the powers given to the High Court, an institution rarely composed of persons reflecting the interests of the common people; the restrictive procedure for amendment by referendum, designed to make changes extremely difficult if not impossible; the equal representation given in the Senate to States with widely disparate populations; and the safeguard to imperial investors and overlords provided by the powers of the Governor-General and provision for appeal to the Privy Council in London.

The complexity of the working class was growing, as the economy developed and changed. Up to about 1890, the emphasis of economic development had been on building the infrastructure for an industrial society. This created a demand for relatively unskilled labour, but for much of the next two decades there was a drastic reduction in construction, the pastoral industry and mining, and a substantial growth in manufacturing. This involved less demand for unskilled labour, and greater demand for skilled workers, whose resort to arbitration was really to get official recognition of what had already been won in the market place.

Workers gained little from the arbitration system, and female workers remained particularly poorly paid. Certainly, arbitration affected the growth of unions: by 1914 there were half a million union members and over 400 unions. A large number of these were quite small unions with little industrial muscle, seeking industrial awards. They were dependent on arbitration; heavy legal costs kept them poor, and their growth created barriers to amalgamation which inhibit the union movement to this day. Hence many of them lost any fighting efficiency they may have had. Part of the growth, however, came from old established unions such as the Amalgamated Society of Engineers, and the growth in militancy after 1907 had little to do with arbitration; it was partly to do with such well-established unions of skilled workers, and partly with the colourful Industrial Workers of the World (IWW), and the socialists. Militancy and class consciousness grew apace in the years immediately before World War I, but it should not be exaggerated: conservatives, by and large, were still in control of the labour movement, a large part of which had really been incorporated into the state apparatus, a development which, in Marxist terms, had institutionalized the rate of exploitation.

There was no real prospect of revolution. Nevertheless the bourgeoisie were worried, and the growing inequality of wealth and income was officially documented for the first time by a war census in 1915. This showed that the top 10 per cent of male income earners received 40 per cent of the total income; and that the ownership of wealth was far more unequal—5 per cent of the population owned two-thirds of the wealth, and the vast majority of the common people owned little more than their clothes and their furniture. No such official estimates have been made since, although the Hawke government promised such an investigation.

This census was perhaps the earliest statistical demonstration in any country of the power of the capitalist system to create wealth and poverty at the same time: 'Capital grows in one place to a huge mass in a single hand, because it has in another place been lost by many.' [21] The capacity of the system to concentrate and centralize capital in relatively few hands was clearly shown in the early years of the twentieth century in Australia. There was substantial debt redemption, less capital inflow, the maturation of a local capital market through stock exchanges and similar institutions, and a resumption of significant assisted immigration. The area under wheat doubled and there was also considerable diversification into sugar and dairy products. These farmers spent more of their income on locally made goods, especially agricultural machinery, than did most pastoralists. The economy became more articulated as the requirements of a diversified agricultural sector were met by an expanding manufacturing industry, using metal processed from the ores produced by the mining industry. Nevertheless, the resultant boom saw big profits, the accumulation of capital and its centralization and concentration in key sectors such as sugar refining, meat exporting, coal production, shipping and 15 importing, buttressed by diverse restrictive trade practices such as price fixing, cartels and virtual monopolies. These practices also involved foreign combines, as in the case of tobacco.[22]

Attempts were made to deal with such concentrations. For example, in 1910, the ALP federal government unsuccessfully prosecuted the Newcastle Coal Vend. The ALP Fisher government also tried to amend the constitution to enable it to nationalize such combines. This too failed. Shipping was exempted from such efforts for most of the twentieth century—a tribute to the power of British capital. The Colonial Sugar Refining Company (CSR) was the first strong home-grown industrial monopoly, and in 1912 a Royal Commission found 'a virtual abeyance of competition in the sugar industry'. It recommended public control of prices by a system of area boards comprising farmers and millers with independent chairmen, with wages boards to cover sugar workers. This was the first attempt at 'planning and control' of an industrial monopoly by state capitalism, put into effect in 1915, when CSR was to refine and distribute sugar in Australia on behalf of the Commonwealth government for a negotiated fee, subject to the import of sugar into Australia being totally prohibited. In the process of inquiry into its affairs, CSR refused to supply the Royal Commission with certain information on production and finance, on the grounds that such disclosure would adversely affect its profitability and standing in relation to the general public and rival businessmen. The refusal was subsequently upheld on appeals to the High Court and Privy Council.

This, together with the failure of previous anti-monopoly legislation, set the pattern for the next half century. Mammon was to be inviolate: the state was not to be allowed to meddle in the affairs of reputable companies. Henceforward state capitalism was to mean the use of state power to facilitate the making of profits and the accumulation of wealth, not to circumscribe these activities. Apart from wartime, the next attempt to control concentrations of capital and anti-competitive practices was not until 1965 when ineffectual trade practices legislation was passed, strengthened momentarily in the mid-1970s, then emasculated so that in the frenetic take-over years of the mid-1980s it was virtually powerless.

Unhampered by regulations, and fostered by protection, CSR was to grow into a large conglomerate involved in chemicals, building materials, pastoral properties, oil and alumina, with a special relationship to the state. Its chief executive officers served as chairmen of governmental committees of inquiry into aspects of the economy on two occasions, the Vernon Committee in the 1960s for the Menzies government, and the Jackson Committee for the Whitlam government in the 1970s. In the early 1980s CSR attempted to 'buy back some of the farm'. It had come a long way from the 1880s when it moved into Fiji, importing cheap Indian labour for its plantations and engaging in transfer pricing by charging its refinery in New Zealand low prices for sugar imported from Fiji. In Queensland in 1911, the company regarded new indentured white labour from Italy as potential strikebreakers. There is good reason to regard CSR as Australia's first transnational company, but it was forced to divest itself from its Fijian operations when the colony became independent later in the twentieth century.

In the early twentieth century, most capital imported into Australia still came from Britain. A good example of such investment is Lever Brothers Ltd (later Unilever) which opened an office in Sydney in 1888 to repack and distribute its British-made products, and to purchase tallow as well as copra from the Pacific islands. By 1899 it had built a soap manufacturing plant in Balmain; by 1914 it was one of the three major producers of soap in Australia, and later in that year it took over the other two. Half a century later, having swallowed up other local firms, it dominated Australia's soap and detergent industry and the production of edible oils, food and icecream, and toilet preparations.[23] These pre-World War I investments cast long shadows before them of the domination of the economy by foreign capital which was to occur at an increasing rate in the latter half of the twentieth century. World War I signalled the beginning of the decline of British imperialism, foreshadowing the accelerated industrialization of Australia, and its movement into the American orbit thirty years later, with momentous consequences for the common people.

1

White on Black:
Expropriation of the Original Australians

> They live in a Tranquillity which is not disturb'd by the
> Inequality of Condition: the Earth and sea of their own accord
> furnishes them with all things necessary for life, they covet not
> Magnificent Houses, Household-stuff etc., they live in a warm
> and fine Climate and enjoy a very wholsome Air, so that they
> have very little need of Clothing ... they set no Value upon any
> thing we gave them, nor would they ever part with any thing
> of their own for any one article we could offer them; this in my
> opinion argues that they think themselves provided with all the
> necessarys of Life and that they have no superfluities.[1]

For some 40 000 years, all the people of Australia were black.
However, the basic difference between these first-comers and the
immigrants of the last two hundred years lay not in skin pigmentation
but in social organization. White immigrants brought in their baggage
the seeds of plants, a knowledge of agriculture and an advanced technology. They also imported a class structure and the ideology of
capitalism. Aborigines, on the other hand, were basically hunters and
gatherers: the men went after game and fish, while the women collected fruit, nuts and plants or dug up edible roots. There was some
trade in items such as cloaks and ochre, but the planting and harvesting
of crops was unknown before the arrival of white settlers, so that
Aboriginal labour produced virtually no surplus beyond daily needs.
Nevertheless, it was not arduous labour and in some ways the average

Aborigine was at least as well off as the average inhabitant of Europe around the year 1800. Aboriginal diet often included items which would have been regarded as rare delicacies by European workers or peasants, and Aborigines worked fewer hours per day in winning their food.

Europeans generally had better clothing and more durable housing but of course these accessories were necessary in a cold climate. In Australia, a hot sun and nomadic life made such shelter much less appropriate. Aborigines were usually able to go naked in comfort, although in some areas, such as Victoria, cloaks made out of possum or kangaroo skins were worn to keep out the cold. Yet, despite Aboriginal ability to harmonize with the environment, it would be wrong to idealize this situation as a bush paradise. There was famine from time to time. Medical knowledge was scanty, violent conflict between bands of Aborigines was common and life expectations were low. There were also some divisions within Aboriginal clans or groups of extended families. Older men were accorded a degree of authority, which extended to the allocation of young women in marriage.

Although women in Aboriginal society were obviously important as food-gatherers and child-bearers, it is customary to portray them as submissive to men, in much the same way as in European society. However, Diane Bell challenges this concept of the role of Aboriginal women. She describes them as 'autonomous, independent ritual actors who actively participate in the creation, transmission and maintenance of the values of their society . . . Aboriginal women are the proud nurturers of people, land and the complex of relationships which flow from the *jukurrpa* [dreaming]'. If this be accepted, it reinforces the view of Aboriginal society as being egalitarian and lacking 'bosses'.[2]

Certainly, the big distinctions between black and white Australians related to class structure, culture and technology. Comparison of the living standards of the average Aborigine and average European two centuries ago leaves out of account the sharp class differences in white society. In Europe, ruling classes lived in luxury while poor peasants and workers barely eked out a living. The unequal distribution of the fruits of labour was made possible by the creation of a surplus, which was appropriated by the ruling class, first in feudal society and then under capitalism. The other side of the coin was the tremendous growth of production in the nineteenth and twentieth centuries as capitalism flowered. In this progressive phase, workers in capitalist societies won some benefits for themselves, through trade unions and other organizations.

As against this, the low level of technology among Australian Aborigines meant that there was little surplus of production over simple consumption, and this precluded the development of a ruling class based upon accumulation of wealth. Further, there was the remarkable 19 importance of sharing and reciprocity among Aborigines. In their eyes, white settlers were mean and greedy in hoarding tobacco or livestock in quantities which could not possibly be consumed in the next day or so. The acquisitiveness and competitive spirit of capitalism were alien to Aboriginal values. Those same values were flouted repeatedly when white men took black women for sexual purposes. Such union was often sanctioned by Aborigines but it was in anticipation of continuing reciprocal obligations due from the white man. The latter, however, was interested only in short-term gratification in return for a once-for-all transfer of some food or clothing.

When white settlement of Australia began in 1788, there were about 750 000 Aborigines. This figure is more than double the estimate of 300 000 which has been generally accepted since 1930. Indeed, N.G. Butlin suggests that there were approximately 300 000 Aborigines in New South Wales and Victoria alone in 1788.[3] Half a century later, there were probably fewer blacks than whites in the continent. The number of whites in 1840 was about 190 000, a figure which rose sharply to 405 000 in 1850. What happened to Aboriginal numbers is unknown—they were simply not counted in most censuses in the nineteenth century. Undoubtedly there was a big drop in absolute as well as relative numbers. The decline continued and it is estimated that by 1921 there were only about 62 000 Aborigines left. The impact of European capitalism upon the Aboriginal subsistence economy was catastrophic.

The two cultures were widely at variance. Typically, the white graziers' livestock occupied the waterholes and drove off the game upon which Aborigines depended. For their part, graziers were enraged when their sheep or cattle were killed by Aborigines for meat: the capitalist concept of the sacredness of private property was challenged. Conflict was inevitable as white settlement spread during the nineteenth century. In one area after another, whites took possession of land, blacks resented disruption of their traditional way of life, fighting developed, and a number of the blacks—together with a much smaller number of whites—were killed. Aboriginal spears were no match for guns. The standard result was that part of each tribe moved farther inland. Not only was Aboriginal culture ruined in its material base: it was also devastated by the attraction which Aborigines felt towards some products of white culture, notably tobacco, flour and alcohol. A number of Aborigines became dwellers on the fringe of white society. They were demoralized, although it may be noted that begging, for Aborigines accustomed to sharing, did not have the degrading connotation prevalent in white society.

Whites, including convicts, were contemptuous of those they regarded as black savages. Actually, few Aborigines were wholly black, and few Europeans lacked pigmentation. Nevertheless, indigenous Australians were the first victims of the racism which was later associated with the White Australia policy. True, at the level of British official policy in the first half of the nineteenth century, there were some well-meant attempts to provide for the welfare of Aborigines, but these efforts were ineffective. They were often inspired by Christian missionary zeal, which also contributed to the disintegration of Aboriginal spiritual and social life. In more immediate terms, guns and imported diseases such as smallpox decimated or wiped out Aboriginal peoples. Perhaps equally important in depopulation was the starvation which faced Aborigines as they were forced to move from their customary areas to less hospitable regions where game was scarce. Birth rates fell to very low levels.

Many white men found Aborigines useful. In outback conditions, where males heavily outnumbered females in white society, many whites sought sexual services from female blacks. Aboriginal knowledge of the bush also proved very useful to whites. Explorers whose exploits figured largely in later school textbooks owed much to black guides who received no comparable recognition. For the rest, the prime white interest in Aborigines was the land which the blacks roamed over and from which they were expelled.

By the eighteenth century, European imperial powers acknowledged certain conventions in establishing clear title to a colony. The main requirement was to get there first, to forestall other powers by mounting an expedition to take formal possession through proclamation, raising a flag and so on. If the territory were uninhabited, and the expedition established effective control over it, a new colony was recognized. Alternatively, if there were indigenous inhabitants, imperial overlordship could be established by 'persuading' the indigenes to accept the situation or by buying land from them. This was on the assumption that the indigenes held property rights in the land, as evidenced by their engaging in crop production or animal husbandry. In the case of Australia, it seemed obvious to visitors from Europe that the Aborigines had no such rights: they were not agriculturists but nomads with no permanent dwellings. Actually, recent research indicates that Aborigines were not as nomadic as was supposed. Periodically they occupied regular camp sites and sometimes they constructed durable huts. However, the fact that Aboriginal groups had close ties with a fairly well defined area of land passed unremarked by settlers.

Aborigines were thus considered to have no land rights. Land was taken from them without compensation, and British law formally bolstered this brutal fact. The situation was rather different in North America, where a number of American Indian tribes led settled village lives, practising agriculture. White American authorities signed treaties with such tribes, conceding rights to them, especially if the   21 tribal chiefs exhibited a dangerous capacity for organized warfare. Maoris in New Zealand were also formidable warriors. Admittedly, treaties with indigenes were often broken later, rights being whittled away, but the documents established a legal basis for argument in court and negotiation with governments. In Australia no treaties were signed between governments and Aborigines. The closest approximation occurred when the area around Melbourne was being opened up in the 1830s: one settler, John Batman, persuaded unsuspecting Aborigines to put their marks on what purported to be a treaty ceding an enormous amount of land to Batman in exchange for some blankets and other articles. The procedure was transparently fraudulent, and representatives of the British government repudiated the 'treaty'.

Both in practice and theory, all rights to land in Australia were assumed by Britain in the name of the crown. Colonial governments then granted or sold land to whites. Later, particularly in the twentieth century, a number of Aboriginal reserves were established but they were administered by white superintendents, the black inhabitants were placed in a subservient position and they had no real security of tenure over land in the reserves—especially if minerals were found there by white prospectors. It was not till the 1960s that a campaign for Aboriginal land rights began to achieve substantial results. It failed to gain court recognition of the injustice of the original decision concerning land ownership: the prospect of total upset of existing property relations was too horrifying for white Australians to contemplate. Nevertheless, there was a growing admission that Aborigines had always been treated badly and that, whatever the past legal position, there was no valid reason for not giving them some compensation through legislation or executive policy. Aboriginal Land Rights Acts were thus passed by the Commonwealth and some State parliaments from the 1970s. Much land thus came under the control of Aborigines, and particularly in the Northern Territory some groups of blacks succeeded in extracting large royalty sums from mining companies.

The struggle continues. Most Aborigines have not yet gained anything from land rights legislation. This is notably the case in urban areas. In an inner-city suburb such as Redfern in Sydney, compensation in the form of land for the Aboriginal residents is not practicable. The real need there is for cash compensation, jobs and welfare services. Yet even in urban areas the land rights campaign serves a useful purpose in sustaining black pride and dignity. Aborigines have been left with little else.

Advancement of Aborigines in the past two or three decades came partly through their own efforts and organizations (such as the Aboriginal Legal Service) and partly from supportive action by sympathetic whites (for example, through Commonwealth provision of funds for the Aboriginal Legal Service). There was a hostile reaction from many other whites with no concern for history or human dignity. They complain: why should Aborigines be given land rights which are not available to other Australians? Why shouldn't Aborigines, if they want land, buy it on the open market, as whites do? The plain fact that Aborigines have no means of obtaining funds for such purchase is irrelevant to ideologues like the Western Australian mining magnate, Mr Lang Hancock. To him, the solution is simple: the blacks should work, stay away from alcohol and save money. The associated fact that poverty is not peculiar to blacks—that, for example, most white Australians own little property outside their homes—does not present difficulties to advocates of laissez-faire capitalism. The explanation is unvarying: if individual whites as well as blacks have not prospered it is basically their own fault. It must be due to laziness or lack of responsibility and initiative.

On a more thoughtful plane of argument, it is sometimes suggested that there should be definite limits to the amount of land returned to Aborigines, because whites have proved that they can use land much more effectively than blacks can. Effective use, in this context, means taking no account of intangible costs of exploitation such as destruction of forests, erosion of soil or pollution of air and water resources. Leaving these matters aside, the argument is that the replacement of white control by black over vast expanses of land would entail lower production and a decline in living standards for many Australians besides those immediately involved. In particular, it is claimed, a major extension of land rights beyond existing Aboriginal reserves would be detrimental to the mining and oil industries. Incidentally, a parallel argument in terms of rational use of resources is often used as a justification of monopoly.

There are two answers to this line of approach. One is that, although Aborigines on their own land can be expected to be more concerned with preserving the natural environment than ripping fertility out of it, Aboriginal attitudes have been profoundly modified by two centuries of contact with capitalism. Aborigines today, when they have access to suitable land, farm it and produce for a market. They lack capital but that is available from white sources when there are prospects of high profits. Thus the effect of granting Aborigines land rights in the Northern Territory, amounting to well over 20 per cent of the region, has been to delay certain mining operations but not to prevent them. Indeed, capitalist ideology has been quite successful in penetrating Aboriginal society. Some small groups of traditional owners, in negotiations with mining companies, have held out for sums of money which are enormous in per capita terms. It seems unlikely that these benefits will be shared equally with less fortunate Aborigines elsewhere.

Secondly, even if it is conceded that ownership of more land by   23

Aborigines would result in a fall in production of some commodities, the standard assumption that this would be undesirable needs to be questioned. It ignores the question of distribution of benefits. Who gains? Mining companies through profits? Do employees also gain to some extent, and if so how? These matters are never raised by the mindless advocates of greater production regardless of consequences to human beings. Whilst growth in output can be a desirable end in a society where the common people live in poverty, it is not an absolute necessity in a rich, developed economy where problems concerning the quality of life and the use of leisure time loom larger. There is also the question of the social usefulness of production of certain commodities such as uranium and armaments.

Aborigines as a Labour Force

It is remarkable that whites in Australia in the nineteenth century made so little effective use of Aborigines as a labour force. This was a settler society in which labour was generally scarce and Aborigines obviously had potential as a workforce. Failure to employ Aborigines was certainly not due to objection by employers to colour of skin. Cheapness of labour was the main criterion in the eyes of employers, and graziers in New South Wales as early as the 1840s urged the importation of labour from India as a means of cutting labour costs. Later in the century, thousands of black South Sea islanders were brought to Queensland to work in the cane fields.

There were some instances of Aborigines being employed by whites. For example, blacks were used to good effect as oarsmen in whaling boats, and graziers in some areas found that Aborigines worked quite well for them in tending sheep, especially if these workers were paid more than merely an occasional handout of rations and clothing. On the whole, however, white settlers reckoned that the customary ways of Aborigines, particularly their habit of absenting themselves from work without notice, were too deeply ingrained for them to be considered a permanent labour force. They were written off as unreliable. As C.D. Rowley puts it, the Aborigine was seen as 'a pest rather than as a potential labourer'.[4]

Ironically, a comparable lack of discipline in the labour force applied also to many workers in Britain and other parts of Europe at the time of the Industrial Revolution: they had been accustomed to irregular patterns of work in homes or small workshops. They often worked very long hours for several days consecutively and then took time off for carousing or other activities. The advent of expensive machinery and factories necessitated the regular work rhythm and hours of capitalist production—invested capital could not be left idle unnecessarily. This

24

more rigid work regime was not to the liking of employees and it took a generation or more to train them to accept the new beat of labour discipline. The ultimate spur in the case of industrial workers in Europe was the alternative of starvation. In Australia, on the other hand, Aborigines had another possibility open to them: they could go on with their traditional way of life in the bush, though it became increasingly difficult in the face of the white advance.

The transplantation of European capitalist work habits to Australia was made easier by the fact that New South Wales and Van Diemen's Land (Tasmania) were initially convict colonies, where discipline was enforced by the lash. It is conceivable that if this convict labour force had not been available to free white settlers they would have been impelled to train labour from Aboriginal sources. As with any capitalist labour force, that would have required employers to provide for the survival, if not the reproduction, of the wage labourers. Instead, employers resorted to convict labour and employed Aborigines only on a casual basis. The crux of the matter was that Aborigines felt no desire or compulsion to adapt to capitalist society, while prospective employers provided no incentive for them to do so. For most whites, Aborigines were irrelevant, although sometimes there was a paternalist attitude, as in a slave society.

The record of white settlement in Australia is streaked darkly with the use of unfree labour, due in part to a shortage of free labour. First there were white convicts, then black Melanesians working in the Queensland sugar industry as indentured labourers. The question arises as to why there was no large-scale attempt by employers to use Aborigines as an unfree labour force by making them enter into indentured service. It would have been easier to instil labour discipline into such workers, who were not free to change employers. To some extent, the explanation for failure to develop an unfree labour force from Aborigines lies in the type of agriculture practised. Indentured servants, like slaves, require more supervision than do free workers, and the cost of supervision is lower per head when numbers are concentrated in a relatively small area. Thus plantation agriculture is generally more adapted to the use of unfree labour than is crop-growing on a small scale. Further, labour requirements are likely to be more seasonal in nature on a wheat farm than on a tropical plantation. Yet the owner of slaves or master of indentured servants must feed or supply them—he cannot sack them—so that, for maximum profit, he must keep them usefully occupied with work all the year round.

This was the background to the initial development of sugar plantations in Queensland, using indentured rather than free labour. The canefield workers were mainly blacks imported from South Pacific islands. These Melanesians constituted a cheap and compliant labour force, whereas there was already a fixed European view of Aborigines 25 as unreliable workers. Certainly, whether indentured or not, Aborigines were able to disappear into the bush very easily. This was not true of Melanesians in Queensland in the late nineteenth century: their homes in the New Hebrides and Solomon Islands were far across the ocean, and they had prospects of being shipped back there at the end of the term of indenture.

Plantations and Internal Colonialism

There was one industry and region in which Aborigines played a vital role in the late nineteenth and twentieth centuries. This was the cattle industry in northern and central Australia, regions where Aboriginal people still lived upon land which they regarded as their own, no matter what the white man's law decreed. There was an extreme shortage of white labour for the cattle industry in frontier regions, so Aborigines were used as stockmen. They found this kind of work congenial and they had skills for it. They were able to maintain kinship identities, although the other side of reality was that they were not free to do as they pleased: they were effectively bound to work—for little or nothing in wages—for the white station-owners.

Thus in parts of northern Australia there developed a system of exploitation which may be termed internal colonialism. In other words, the labour of these Aborigines was used in a fashion similar to employment in a standard type of colony. In the latter case, relationships of dominance and repression were imposed externally on a geographically separate country, whereas in Australia such relationships were established within the borders of a single sovereign state. Internal colonialism meant much worse conditions for Aboriginal workers than could be expected from the classic position of free wage labour in a capitalist society.

This point is perhaps best understood against the background of the general expansion of European powers overseas from the fifteenth century. The lead of Spain and Portugal in establishing empires was soon followed by the French, English, Dutch and others. For a long time the favourite targets were wealthy old civilizations which had little capacity to resist well-armed invaders. In Asia, particularly India, this meant heavily populated areas which were most easily exploited through trade, supported by armed force at strategic points. In other tropical regions, notably the West Indies, Europeans set up tobacco and sugar plantations, using slave labour from Africa. As Karl Marx wrote:

26 The discovery of gold and silver in America, the extirpation, enslavement and

entombment in mines of the aboriginal population, the beginning of the conquest and looting of the East Indies, the turning of Africa into a warren for the commercial hunting of black-skins, signalised the rosy dawn of the era of capitalist production.[5]

Temperate regions of North America and the southern hemisphere were much more sparsely inhabited by indigenous people and were less attractive to European powers. In these parts of the world, the prospect was not so much one of imposing a European merchant-planter elite on the existing social structure as of bringing in large numbers of Europeans to develop resources themselves. Australia came into this category of settler society in the nineteenth century, as did New Zealand, together with large parts of America and South Africa.

Settler societies had certain features in common. Virtually from the outset, they embodied the social relations of production characteristic of capitalism, with few feudal hangovers to impede progress. These societies depended for growth upon large transfers of capital and labour from Europe, they participated strongly in international trade and they made large quantities of land available cheaply for settlers. Also, wages and living standards were generally higher in the new countries, this being in effect a prerequisite for the attraction of free immigrants.

Settler societies are clearly differentiated from the older type of colony by the numbers of colonizers relative to the original inhabitants, and the ruthlessness with which the whites pushed aside, walked over or wiped out the indigenes. In Tasmania, genocide of the Aboriginal population was almost total. However, in other parts of Australia, particularly the arid interior, Aborigines endured, as did the Maoris in New Zealand, in rather better shape.

Elsewhere in the islands of the South Pacific region, colonialism and capitalist relationships arrived late and not in the form of settler societies. For example, Fiji became a crown colony of Britain in 1874, following an offer of cession by Fijian chiefs—an act which preserved certain land rights for Fijians. Soon after this, an important sugar industry was established by CSR, an Australian company. However, with this exception in Fiji, the prime South Pacific commodity which interested Europeans was copra, the dried meat of coconuts. There was a big European market for copra in the vegetable oils industry, producing raw material for soap-making and margarine.

Initially, Europeans organizing the copra trade in the Pacific islands took their profits as merchants, shippers and moneylenders. Then, around the turn of the nineteenth century, European capitalists—German, French and British—developed plantations of their own. The 27

British interests involved in copra production were mainly Australian, with the important exception of the English firm of Lever Brothers. One major problem for planters in the South Pacific was a serious shortage of labour. It was not so much that island populations were quite small as that a high proportion of islanders had access to land of their own and were bound up with traditional societies. In other words, there was virtually no proletariat dependent upon working for wages for its livelihood.

In Fiji, CSR met this problem by importing large numbers of indentured labourers from India for sugar cane production. In other areas, copra plantations were built up by using local indentured labour—generally from other islands with a view to keeping the workers docile. Plantation labourers were recruited for periods of three years or so, after which they generally returned to their villages. Planters complained about the difficulty of recruiting labour but they paid very little for it. For example, a plantation labourer in the British Solomon Islands in 1910 was paid at an annual rate of six pounds sterling in addition to rations and primitive accommodation.

The plantation system was not conducive to reproduction of island populations and labour supply. Families were split up, as wives and children were not permitted to live on the plantations—planters were interested only in the labour of adult males. Consequently, when recruitment of labour was concentrated on a particular area there was a tendency for its population to decline. This was not in the long-term interests of white rulers, including planters themselves, and colonial governments in the South Pacific laid down detailed regulations for the conduct of the labour trade. Ration scales, standards of accommodation and wages for indentured workers were prescribed; employers were made responsible for repatriating workers to their home villages at the end of the period of indenture; and sometimes whole areas were temporarily closed to recruitment.

Although this bureaucratic intervention restricted the power of planters to exploit labour mercilessly, the regulations had the effect of conserving both labour supply and traditional village society alongside the spread of capitalist relations of production on plantations. Village organization, for example in New Guinea, customarily performed functions of social security such as supporting a member of the community in old age, sickness or unemployment. Thus the state was relieved of considerable costs which are borne by governments in advanced capitalist societies. Individual planters derived benefit by being able to pay a wage deemed sufficient to support only an adult male without a family. Indeed, even this low wage was usually paid only at the end of the period of indenture, when it was spent on commodities such as knives and cloth to take back to the village. Such a display of wealth was calculated to encourage other young men to put their marks on indenture forms.

28

Clearly, there was a sharp contrast between the maintenance of traditional forms of society in black colonies in the South Pacific and the position in the white settler society of Australia where the previous hunter–gatherer mode of production employed by Aborigines was virtually destroyed. Nevertheless, there were elements of similarity in labour regulations for blacks. Thus in the colony of Western Australia, an Aborigines Protection Act of 1886 was aimed at conserving a labour force for the pastoral industry in the north. The Act formally stipulated official supervision of the signing of work contracts by Aborigines and it provided that each such worker should receive medical attention, rations, a blanket and a pair of trousers. However, unlike the situation under labour legislation in the Pacific islands, Western Australian employers were not obliged to return workers to their own areas at the end of a period of contract—probably because the Aborigines commonly belonged in the station area where they were employed. Indeed, the Act did not specify any limit to the term of service, so that the Aborigine could be held to work for an indefinite period for the master, although it was understood that in practice the Aborigine would disappear and go walkabout from time to time.

In other parts of Australia besides the West, pastoralists secured black labour at virtually no cost apart from providing rations. In effect, resident Aboriginal communities, continuing to provide some of their own sustenance by traditional methods, subsidized the wage costs of employers in much the same way as did villages in New Guinea. Indeed, the Western Australian Act of 1886 did not provide for payment of any cash wage to Aborigines. This was internal colonialism with a vengeance: no employer would have dreamed of being able to exploit white labour without paying a money wage. The treatment of Aborigines in Western Australia was justified officially in contemptuously racist terms, as when an Attorney-General, S. Burt, stated in Parliament in 1897:

Some persons do not understand what is the condition of natives in Australia, for they seem to class them with the natives of South Africa or the natives of India, where the natives are really far more like men than are the natives of this colony.[6]

In Queensland, policy was directed to the same end but a markedly different system was adopted in the twentieth century. Under an Aboriginals Protection Act of 1897, the government made a concerted effort to round up Aborigines and move them to mission stations or reserves controlled by white superintendents. Some Aborigines escaped the net but most were segregated on these settlements, especially in northern Queensland, where the cattle industry developed. Aborigines under this form of control could be employed as migrant labour outside the reserve under individual contracts, the terms of 29 these annual contracts being subject to official supervision, usually by a local policeman acting as 'protector' of Aborigines. Mission stations themselves engaged in economic activities, using the unpaid labour of residents, and the product of this labour was supplemented by supplies from government sources. Thus the state and charitable sources, together with Aborigines themselves, subsidized a system which enabled pastoral employers to pay no more than a single person's wage to a black worker.

Despite these questionable features, it is a fact that Queensland was ahead of all other Australian frontier regions in providing by law for a minimum cash wage for Aboriginal workers in the pastoral industry. The wage rates, specified for the first time in Queensland regulations in 1919, were well below those which applied to whites doing comparable work, but the innovation was an important one. However, its effect was vitiated by other regulations which meant that only a small part of the prescribed wage was received by the Aboriginal worker in cash, in the form of pocket money. The rest of the wage was paid by the employer to the local policeman who was designated protector of Aborigines. The policeman put the money into a savings bank account for the Aborigine. Not only did this compulsory investment return a low rate of interest but the bank pass book was retained by the policeman. Thus Aborigines, lacking reliable records and being unable to withdraw and spend their own money without police permission, were often swindled. Furthermore, a proportion of their earnings was lawfully deducted both for income tax and for transfer to a Welfare Fund for use on reserves. The system of police control of Aboriginal wages was maintained intact in Queensland until the 1960s.

Outside Queensland there was a growing practice of paying small cash wages to Aborigines in the pastoral industry in the first half of the twentieth century. This was because of a shortage of outback labour, the smallness of the wage paid being excused on the ground that pastoralists also supplied rations to local dependants of the workers. No minimum wage was prescribed for Aboriginal pastoral workers in South Australia or Western Australia, although there was a turning point in wage rates in the latter State when Aborigines went on strike for the first time in the late 1940s. They were advised in this novel procedure by Donald McLeod, a white whose experience included work as a wharf labourer. Predictably, McLeod was attacked by pastoralists as a Communist agitator. Less expected was the Aboriginal reaction in Western Australia. They were reported as saying: 'We talk about wages and place to stay, and squatters and police keep saying Communist. We say "What's this Communist?"'[7]

In the Northern Territory, under Commonwealth administration, rates of wages for Aboriginal pastoral workers were regularized for the first time by government Ordinance in the 1950s. The set rates were far below the minimum rates provided for white workers under the Cattle Station Industry (Northern Territory) arbitration court award, besides which substantial over-award payments were made to white workers. It is an extraordinary fact that *nowhere in Australia did the arbitration system acknowledge the existence of Aboriginal pastoral workers until 1965*, when the North Australian Workers' Union successfully applied to the Commonwealth Arbitration Commission for inclusion of Aborigines in the Northern Territory award. Subsequently, this decision was extended to other parts of Australia.

Besides being starved of economic rights, Aborigines in the twentieth century remained subject to severe restrictions upon civil liberties. This was particularly the case on reserves, where authoritarianism and petty tyranny were rampant. In Queensland, for example, under the Department of Native Affairs, there was a proliferation of regulations aimed at controlling the everyday lives of Aborigines. They could not leave reserves without official permission, nor could non-residents (including Aborigines) enter reserves to see what was going on. Reserve superintendents and police protectors had arbitrary powers of arrest and of trial in kangaroo courts on reserves, followed by punishment. As Rowley gently notes, a 'somewhat unusual feature of the Queensland Christian mission was the mission gaol'.[8]

Historically, what Aborigines most needed was protection against whites, including the self-appointed white protectors. Equality or, more precisely, equality of opportunity, has always had an unstated qualifying condition in Australia: it refers to white people and more particularly to white men with capital. What the Aborigines got was expropriation. They were robbed of their means of production, a process which Marx called the 'secret' of the primary or initial accumulation of capital, when 'masses of men are suddenly and forcibly torn from their means of subsistence ... The expropriation of the agricultural producer ... from the soil, is the basis of the whole process'. Although not writing about Australia, Marx made a very pertinent comment: 'the history of this ... expropriation is written in the annals of mankind in letters of blood and fire'.[9]

2

The Genesis of Australian Capitalism: A Police State with Vice-Regal Trappings[1]

In times long gone by there were two sorts of people: one, the diligent, intelligent, and above all, frugal elite; the other, lazy rascals, spending their substance, and more, in riotous living ... Thus it came to pass that the former sort accumulated wealth, and the latter sort had at last nothing to sell except their own skins. And from this original sin dates the poverty of the great majority that, despite all its labour, has up to now nothing to sell but itself, and the wealth of the few that increases constantly although they have long ceased to work.[2]

In this way Marx adopted the idiom of a religious fairy tale to pour scorn on the crude apologists for property of his own time. The defendants of property a century later have not changed their basic explanation of its origin. The clichés have been modified, of course: nowaways, we hear of entrepreneurial attitudes and skills, initiative, innovation and so on. The Liberal Party of Australia in 1987 invented a bastard composite, 'incentivation'. Yet the reality, as Marx remarked, was that capital came into the world 'dripping from head to foot, from every pore, with blood and dirt'.[3]

Capitalism presupposes the existence of a proletariat. For capitalist accumulation to work, two different kinds of people must be brought together, in the market and in the production process. There must be, 'on the one hand, the owners of money, means of production, means of subsistence ...; on the other hand, free labourers, the sellers of their own labour-power, and therefore the sellers of labour. Free labourers in the double sense that neither they themselves form part and parcel of the means of production, as in the case of slaves, bondsmen, etc., nor do the means of production belong to them, as in the case of peasant-proprietors'.[4]

Since the historical establishment of these conditions, the capitalist system has maintained the separation of the labourers from ownership of the means of production and has reproduced that separation on a continually extending scale. This was notably so in the nineteenth century, when there was a very rapid increase in population in Europe and America. Yet initially the creation of a proletariat was due not so much to a natural increase in numbers as to an institutional process in which force and the use of state power played major roles. For capitalism to develop, the small peasant had to be divorced from landholding and transformed into a 'free' labourer.

To Marx, this early process was the crux of primary accumulation — an original stage of capital when a bourgeois class concentrated property into fewer hands, partly at the expense of the old landowning elite but mainly through the dispossession of the peasantry. In the process, capital and labour matured jointly, capitalists employing the newly-created free labourers. However, investment in industry on any considerable scale was not attractive until a sizable body of such labour was available for hire. In the interim, there was a long period of primary accumulation which in the classic case of England extended from the sixteenth century to the Industrial Revolution.

On the face of things, the early history of the colonization of Australia has little relevance to the Marxist concept of primary accumulation. The first settlement, at Sydney in 1788, was made at a time when the Industrial Revolution was well under way in Britain. The imperial country's era of primary accumulation was largely over: a proletariat already existed in critical numbers. Indeed, in an important sense the development of capitalist industry and urbanization in Britain was responsible for the establishment of the colony of New South Wales, for these processes in Britain were accompanied by an increase in crime — or at least in the types of offence, such as housebreaking and burglary, which led to sentences of transportation. Earlier in the eighteenth century the North American colonies had been the dumping ground for Britain's transported criminals, but when those colonies achieved independence in the 1770s a new disposal area had to be established.

Getting rid of convicts was not the only motive in establishing a colony in New South Wales. The British government, intent upon rebuilding a shattered empire following loss of the colonies in North America, developed a strong interest in trade and bases related to India, China and the Pacific region. Tea from China was an important 33 commodity. In recent years, Australian historians have speculated on the relative importance of such strategic and commercial considerations in the decision to set up a colony at Botany Bay. Without entering into this complex debate, it suffices to say that the discussion is inconclusive. No doubt imperial factors were taken into account in London, yet the need to dispose of convicts still appears paramount as a motive. Botany Bay was designed primarily as a gaol.

The new colony had no capitalist class, no free labourers, and no peasantry. In fact there were no free settlers in the First Fleet. Yet there were incipient capitalists among those who arrived in the first few years. Elizabeth Macarthur, in a note to her mother before embarking in England, referred to New South Wales as a place 'from which we have every reasonable expectation of reaping the most material advantages'.[5] In this sentiment she undoubtedly took a cue from her husband, Lieutenant John Macarthur, whose eye for profit and personal advancement was most acute.

Such aspirants to wealth entertained the prospect of grabbing an enormous Australian productive resource—land. The use of force to dispossess Aboriginal occupiers was of little concern to the invaders; and the absence of compensation meant that the government could grant land freely to ambitious white settlers, who were thus given a fine start on the path to accumulation. These were the spoils of colonization. In contrast, land in Britain and other parts of Europe was expensive. There, the absorption of land and other property into private ownership had occurred long before, prompting the celebrated saying of P. J. Proudhon: 'Property is theft'.

State Power and Early Fortunes

Despite the origins of New South Wales as a gaol, the new colony had an organic connection with its imperial progenitor and it was inevitable that a capitalist economy would develop after the first few years of struggle for sheer survival. Free labourers came into being and so did a peasantry. Yet the early circumstances did not seem very propitious for a capitalist. In fact, for more than a decade nobody brought a substantial amount of capital into the colony with them. Not till the 1820s were there appreciable numbers of such moneyed immigrants. Nevertheless, quick fortunes were made in the first few decades, and New South Wales provides an ideal field for study of the ways in which it could be done. Thrift and abstinence, the economists' traditional explanation, had nothing to do with it. The essentials were social status and patronage, which entailed access to modest amounts of initial capital, plus a certain degree of intelligence or low cunning. Luck played a part and ruthlessness was another useful attribute, especially in the case of ex-convicts who started with nothing but were able to make their first gains through petty trading which was beneath the dignity of their social superiors.

The picture can be discerned with unusual clarity in New South Wales, where a small white community started virtually from scratch. The First Fleet transported about 730 convicts and 250 marines and officials and their families. Five years later, the total white population had risen to 4000, but the figure was still below 5000 in 1800. Then there was a rise to some 10 500 in 1810 (plus 1300 in Van Diemen's Land), followed by a sharper growth to 30 000 (plus 7000 in Van Diemen's Land) in 1820. Only from 1814 did the number of convicts transported each year rise into the thousands. In this microcosmic society, the members of the ruling class knew each other personally. They were small in number—for example, there were about thirty officers and officials who were landowners in 1800—and they were remarkably quarrelsome and litigious.

A handful of free farmer-settlers arrived in the 1790s but they, like the ex-soldiers who remained in the colony, were of no particular significance. They had no capital, they were given small land grants and little is known about them. The important elements in the population were the convicts—and, as time passed, the ex-convicts—and those set in authority above them: the Governor and his officials, and the officers of the New South Wales Corps which replaced the marines as a guard force in 1790. Although it is customary to refer to the officers of the 'Rum' Corps as a collective elite, the civilian officials were practically indistinguishable from them in their economic activities. In fact some officials, especially those who ran the commissariat, were in key positions for the advancement of their own and colleagues' interests. Officers and officials together formed a tight group controlling the state machine—military, administrative and judicial—in the colony. Nominally, the Governor had absolute power (subject to instructions from distant bureaucrats in London) but in practice he was generally unable to exercise such power in ways which conflicted with the interests of the ruling group. Only through this group could orders be made effective.

None of the officers and officials were wealthy at the outset. They were dependent upon their salaries which in the case of the officers ranged from about £80 a year for a lieutenant to £171 for a captain and £257 for a major. These were hardly the kind of incomes from which substantial savings could be made for investment purposes. It seems doubtful whether any of these men had more than a few hundred pounds to his name when he arrived in the colony. John Macarthur is said to have arrived as a lieutenant £500 in debt and to have transformed this into a fortune of at least £20 000 in the space of eleven years. The latter sum should not be taken too literally, for it was an   35 estimate by a hostile critic, Governor King. However, King was undoubtedly correct in adding that Macarthur's main efforts in that short period were devoted to 'making a large fortune, helping his brother-officers to make small ones'.

The reference to Macarthur having originally arrived in debt may be related to no more than the common practice whereby officers invested a little capital in the purchase of goods to be transported with them for speculative sale in the colony. Meagre salaries did not mean that officers were penniless—at the very least, they needed social connections to obtain a commission in the first instance, even in such a low-rated military unit as the New South Wales Corps. Macarthur's father was a draper in Plymouth, and John Macarthur himself was typical of the ruling group in New South Wales in his lower middle class origins. The one exception, in family background though not wealth, was D'Arcy Wentworth, who was related to the Lords Fitzwilliam of Yorkshire. However, Wentworth was clearly the black sheep of the family: after being tried several times at the Old Bailey on charges of highway robbery, he found it advisable to go to Botany Bay as an assistant surgeon. Family influence may have played a part in his four acquittals at the Old Bailey. Certainly it was preferable to go to Botany Bay as a free man—and part of the official establishment—than as a convict. Splitting skulls was more rewarding, if not more congenial, than breaking stones.

The prevalence of surgeons in the colonial establishment is interesting. Some, like William Balmain, had received their training in the navy; others travelled as civilian surgeons on convict transport ships and then remained in New South Wales. Naval ships' doctors did not rank as commissioned officers. Rather, they were warrant officers, on a par with chaplains. The medical profession had not yet attained full respectability, and surgeons in New South Wales had much the same origins in the lower middle class as officers of the NSW Corps. Like the latter, who did well out of guard duty in a penal colony, surgeons were concerned to make money. Indeed, they were so involved in economic activities that it is difficult to see how they found time for the medical duties for which they received salaries. For instance Thomas Jamison, who arrived as a surgeon's mate in the First Fleet, was heavily engaged in trade in wheat, pork and sandalwood in the 1790s. He amassed a capital of some £4000 by 1800, and his son, John Jamison, was one of the biggest landowners in the colony in the 1820s and 1830s.

There was a close similarity in origins between the embryo capitalists of New South Wales and the new industrial capitalist breed in Britain. The people who took the lead in developing factory industry in Britain in the Industrial Revolution were largely of humble descent. Typically, they were former master craftsmen or small farmers with a little capital which they expanded through partnership with more substantial merchants. In New South Wales, officers, surgeons and other officials disguised their own relatively humble origins and had no interest in factories or machinery, but in fact they possessed the basic vigour, greed and ambition of the petty bourgeoisie. Their problem was to find ways of expanding very small capitals into large ones in a short space of time.

Initially their hopes rested on the prospect of obtaining large grants of land from the crown and developing estates with labourers and tenant-farmers. This remained the long-term aim but it could not be achieved immediately. Time was needed to prepare land around Sydney for farming, and the only labour available was convict—cheap but in limited supply and inefficient, especially in the case of convicts from London slums. Furthermore, the market for agricultural produce was very limited: the colonial population was tiny and exports were out of the question.

In any case, no land grants were made to officers until 1793. Before this, Governor Phillip allowed officers the use of small plots of ground with two convict servants each to cultivate them, but Phillip's original instructions from London did not permit him to make land grants to anyone other than emancipated convicts—on a scale of 30 acres for an unmarried and 50 for a married man, plus 10 acres for each child in a family. In 1790, Phillip was authorized to make land grants to ex-marines wishing to settle in the colony. However, although the Governor wrote to London asking for permission to make grants to civil and military officers—and he implied that this would be effective only when they ceased to be officers—specific authority to make such grants was not received in the colony until after Phillip had left.

It was a penal colony, not one of the traditional sort. To the British government, the obvious way of keeping costs down was for the Governor to develop public agriculture, using convict labour and regarding the end product as a 'public stock'. In effect, the convicts would produce food for themselves and their gaolers. The provision for making land grants to ex-convicts was simply a device to cope with the immediate problem of what to do with such men. The last thing the British government wanted was for them to return home after their period of servitude, so they were offered land grants, together with a few primitive tools, seeds, and enough subsistence by way of rations to keep them going until they were able to raise a crop. In this way, as an incidental effect rather than by deliberate design, a peasantry was created.

Although the officers importuned the Governor for land grants at the outset, in 1788, they were probably not particularly disappointed at having to wait several years, for it was soon evident that the returns from arable farming were very low. The relative failure of harvests in   37

Sydney, together with shortage of supplies coming into the colony by sea, entailed near-famine conditions in the first four years. Rations were drastically reduced to a point where convicts were too weak to do much work and it was questionable whether the colony would survive. Apart from small windfall gains made by officers who brought commodities with them to the colony, it seems likely that the only people who profited in this period were the ships' contractors in Britain who transported convicts for the government and scurvily supplied short rations.

Yet it was precisely comparable conditions of an isolated and hungry market which had been the basis for the accumulation of merchant capital in mediaeval times. It was the very lack of development of markets, the simultaneous occurrence of a glut in one and a shortage in another, which gave merchants an opportunity to buy cheap and sell dear. Theoretically, such a situation invited the participation of more and more merchants, with the effect of lowering the average rate of profit, but such ideal conditions of competition were inhibited by poor communications and by various regulations fencing in a particular market against outsiders. In these ways merchant capital was able to influence the terms of trade to exploit producers and consumers.

For a decade or so there were no professional merchants resident in Sydney. The colony was a speculators' paradise in the 1790s, and the officers were not slow to take advantage of this. Dependence upon the uncertain and irregular arrival of ships' cargoes, and the consequent high price of goods locally, meant that anyone on the spot with capital could make big profits. At first glance, a major difficulty would seem to be the question of who would buy imported commodities. It might be expected that luxuries and semi-luxuries would be imported by the officers for their own use, but if that were all there would be no capital accumulation. The officers had to find a market for their commodities and apart from themselves there were only convicts and ex-convicts with very low purchasing power. This situation might be likened to that on slave plantations in the old South of the USA: the slaves grew their own food but their poverty limited imports into the plantation to luxury items for the owners.

However, a crucial difference in the case of New South Wales was the role of government. The British government had the prime responsibility of feeding and clothing the convicts and their guards. Ration scales were laid down and it was the duty of the Governor to obtain supplies to meet them. As it was anticipated that some time would elapse before the new colony became self-sufficient, the Governor was empowered to buy goods and to pay for them with bills of exchange drawn on the British Treasury. Thus, given the fact that supplies sent directly on government account from England were insufficient, the colonial government provided both a market and the internationally acceptable currency which importers needed. Indeed, the economic importance of the government was much more widespread and complex than this, as will be indicated later. The first milch-cow for capitalists in Australia was the British government.

The main initial problem for officers in New South Wales was not so much the market as their lack of capital with which to exploit it. Operating as a merchant was not a matter of investment of a few pounds only, and the officers had no business experience or credit links with established mercantile houses in Britain. Until Phillip received an official consignment of about 4500 Spanish dollars from London in 1792, the only coins in the colony were those brought in the purses and pockets of the officers and some of the convicts.

The officers found two ways out of the dilemma. One was to pool their resources and take shares in the purchase of a cargo of incoming goods. This became a regular procedure in the 1790s, Balmain apparently being the main organizer of such pools. The shares taken by officers were not equal; the amount invested by each officer was related to rank and available capital. Nevertheless, these rings were comprehensive and constituted the first cartels in Australian history.

Second, and more important, was access to public money in the form of regimental funds. Pay for both officers and men of the NSW Corps was credited to them monthly in London. In addition there were substantial sterling funds, such as subsistence allowances, which were at the disposal of company commanders. Through the Corps paymaster, the officers were able to draw bills on these resources held by the regimental agent in London; and these bills paid for commodities purchased by the officers on their own private account. John Macarthur was Corps paymaster between 1793 and 1800.

With initial capital derived from such sources, the officers were all set to make great profits once the first few bad years of the settlement were over. On a couple of occasions they chartered ships themselves to bring goods to the colony, but usually they were content to present a monopolistic front to any ship's captain arriving in Sydney. As Governor Hunter remarked, 'every vessel, British or neutral, was expressly *prohibited* admitting any other than an officer on board, by which means, as they were all combined together, every shilling's worth of private trade was engrossed by those who were in the pay of the crown'. Fearing the development of competition, the officers and some of the other 'principal inhabitants' in 1798 formally bound each other, under penalty of £1000, not to purchase goods from incoming ships except through two officers chosen to act as agents for all of them. As a further sanction, this time of a social nature, they agreed to 'avoid the company of any individual, and to consider him an infamous character, who shall be convicted of a breach of these articles'.[6]

It is ironic that the officers attempted to justify their practices by asserting that without them a ship's captain would be in a position to demand monopolistic prices for his cargo. As Elizabeth Macarthur put it, the united front of the officers 'prevents monopoly, and the impositions that would be otherwise practised by the masters of ships'.[7] This was true enough, but in reality the officers were two-faced: their monopoly was directed against the shipmasters from whom they bought and against the great majority of the colonists to whom they sold directly or indirectly. It is not possible to make any realistic calculation of the rate of wholesale profit in the colony but such records as have survived indicate that it was remarkably high.

The standard approach of the business historian is often used to exculpate the officers. Since they were the only colonists with any capital, 'the officers' virtual monopoly of the early import trade was the fruit of circumstance rather than contrived'; and these men, together with some ex-convicts, 'helped to create a colony out of a prison by erecting a business community and a commercial structure suitable to a colony but increasingly unsuitable to a prison'.[8] Actually they were parasites. As Margaret Steven comments about the first decade in New South Wales,

> market conditions were so favourable that anyone, regardless of ability, with a command of capital was capable of producing a profit. Practically no degree of business acumen, except at the most primitive level, was necessary to make a profit in such a monopolistic situation . . . Even in retailing they cut risks to a minimum. Goods were passed to convict 'dealers'.[9]

Ex-convicts were used as dealers and agents, partly because the officers, with few exceptions, were tyros in business matters but mainly because of social inhibitions: a gentleman could engage in wholesale but not retail trade. Besides the social stigma of being a shopkeeper or huckster, such lowly dealings would have advertised too openly the contrast between the officers' economic interests and the employment expected of the wearer of the king's uniform. Although some officers sold imported goods such as liquor directly to their soldiers, and others used as agents the women with whom they lived, most officers sold to ex-convict middlemen—publicans, storekeepers and the like—who engaged in retail trade. This process rather than small land grants is the explanation for the economic rise of some ex-convicts. For example, Simeon Lord, who was transported to Sydney in 1791 and was emancipated early, appears to have been set up in business as a baker and licensed victualler by Captain Rowley, who probably used him as a cloak for his own trading activities. Before long, however, Lord was able to branch out independently as a trader on a growing scale. By 1800 he had moved into importing and wholesale trade, shipowning and seal-hunting, whilst retaining a big retail network.

Only a very small proportion of convicts ever came anywhere near achieving this kind of economic independence. Nevertheless, Lord was not alone. There were others such as Kable and Underwood who became prominent, particularly in shipbuilding, the hunt for seal skins and oil, and small manufacturing and building. This remarkable phenomenon of economic opportunity for some of the lowest on the social scale arose mainly from the extraordinary circumstances of the colony: that is, the absence of middlemen in the first instance, together with the officers' reluctance to venture themselves outside the cosy spheres of monopolistic wholesale trade and grazing. Needless to say, men like Lord charged their customers very high prices for goods by adding extortionate margins to wholesale prices.

The phenomenon was short-lived. Once rigidities of structure set in, there was little opportunity for the likes of Lord or Samuel Terry to blossom. In Van Diemen's Land, which was settled later—from 1803 —there was little development of emancipists comparable to New South Wales' wealthy ex-convicts. Actually, not all of the latter arrived penniless in the colony. Robert Cooper, when he was sentenced to transportation in 1812 for receiving stolen goods, was a London publican with a trade turnover of £17 000 per year. He may be presumed to have transferred capital to Sydney where he was granted a conditional pardon in 1818 and opened a general store in George Street. He became a merchant on a large scale and one of the principal shareholders in the Bank of New South Wales; by 1827 he was operating a distillery and a few years later he established a brewery.

Dealers who were mostly ex-convicts sold goods to farmers, soldiers, convicts and emancipated workers. Because there was little money in the colony, these deals took the form mainly of barter, with such commodities as sugar, alcohol and flour being swapped for equivalent values. Wheat had a special importance in trade, as it was the main commodity for which the government commissariat store provided a market. The commissariat issued store-receipts in payment for its purchases. These receipts served as a form of paper money within the colony and, when consolidated into substantial sums, they could be presented to the colonial government for exchange into bills on the British Treasury. In turn, Treasury bills, which were as good as gold, could be used to pay for imports.

Thus the officers were links in a commercial chain which extended from themselves as importers, through dealers and producers, to the commissariat and Treasury bills which paid for more imports. Having utilized regimental funds as their initial source of capital, the officers

41

grew fat on colonial government funds. For instance, in the three years 1798 to 1800, Governor Hunter issued Treasury bills to a total of about £94 000. Not all of this was made available to the officers—the government itself bought some goods from ships—but a large proportion certainly came into their hands.

Agriculture and the Labour Market

Social relations in agriculture were of critical importance. The original intention of minimizing costs to the government by developing public agriculture on the basis of convict labour was subject to an obvious difficulty: if ex-convicts were to be given land grants to keep them in the colony, then a market must be made available for their produce. The only feasible market in the circumstances was that which could be provided by the commissariat, which had the task of feeding large numbers of convicts and others. In this way there developed a conflict of policy between public and private farming: if public farming were extended, the market for the produce of settlers was narrowed. The commissariat could not waste public funds by giving an unlimited guarantee to buy all that farmers could produce.

This problem was only beginning to appear when the colonial government received authority to make land grants to officers in 1793. For the next two years, between the departure of Governor Phillip and the arrival of his successor Hunter, the officers held nominal as well as real power. In point of fact, they did not make large grants to themselves in this period of military government. Rather, they were concerned to bring about a change in policy concerning public agriculture and the use of convict labour. Public farming was substantially reduced, and convicts were switched to work on the officers' own farms as assigned servants. The officers were now allowed not merely two but ten convicts each to cultivate their land, these convicts being still maintained with rations and clothing by the public stores.

The officers tapped an additional source of labour among those convicts who were still in direct government service, being employed on public works as well as agriculture. This point is related to the fact that convicts in government service were generally not set to work for the maximum number of hours possible; they were allowed a certain amount of time in which to work 'on their own hands'—that is, for wages paid by private employers. On the face of it, this procedure seems surprisingly enlightened but the explanation is one of practical necessity. Until a big convict barracks was built at Hyde Park in 1819, the government could not accommodate most convicts in Sydney. They were therefore left to find private lodgings for themselves in the town and they were allowed to work privately to earn the rent for lodgings. Those who could not find work had to sell part of their rations for the purpose; but generally a compulsory work-day of 'only' nine or ten hours for the government (spent doing as little as possible) was an actual working day of twelve or thirteen hours, the extra time being put in on paid work for officer-employers.

At first this source of part-time labour was not effectively mobilized by the officers—the convicts were used inefficiently on odd jobs. However, when the officers secured land grants they realized that they could use this pool of labour to supplement the full-time work of the convicts assigned to them. Indeed, during the period of military government the official hours of work for government convicts were deliberately reduced in order to give these men more time to work for private employers. The work of government was neglected in the interests of the officers. In 1793 John Macarthur was appointed Inspector of Public Works at Parramatta, a key position which gave him control over both public agriculture and the allocation of convicts. Two or three years later, although he had received only 200 acres of land by way of grants from the crown, he had 130 acres of his own land under crop, worked by thirty or forty servants. As Captain Waterhouse noted, Macarthur had 'remarkable fine farms of his own but I cannot say so much for Government's'.[10]

Public farming was sharply curtailed at this time. Later, on instructions from London, it was expanded to some extent but was then virtually ended in the 1810s. This is in no sense to be regarded as a failure of what a conservative historian termed 'the economic last ditch, communism':[11] public agriculture based on convict labour was no more socialist in content than Newgate prison or the British Army. Nor should the growth of emphasis towards private farming be attributed exclusively to the officers' activities in 1793–5. They precipitated the movement but it was inevitable once the concept of a mere gaol began to give way to a capitalist economy. The real significance of these developments was two-fold. First, British government expenditure on the colony rose substantially, through the purchase of grain and meat produced on private land—and the flow of Treasury bills went mainly to the officers. Second, the officers had found a permanent source of profit, not subject to the vicissitudes of wholesale trade: surplus value from the labour of convict and ex-convict workers.

For a time the officers were in a better position than slave-owners, for they did not even have to feed and clothe the convicts assigned to them—the colonial government accepted responsibility for that. This singularly profitable position could not be maintained indefinitely in face of the imperial government's realization that it was being swindled all round: not only was a large part of the unfree labour force diverted from public to private farming, with the government buying the product of the latter, but the government was still committed to maintaining assigned convicts from the commissariat stores. In 1798, Governor Hunter tried to return to the original practice of allowing each officer only two assigned servants maintained by the stores. His orders were ignored initially, but by about 1804 the great bulk of assigned convicts were 'off the stores'—that is, fed and clothed by their masters rather than by the government. It was still, of course, a very cheap supply of labour for those who were in a position to exploit it. In addition, the officers and their civilian allies had at their disposal several other sources of labour: the part-time labour of convicts retained in government service; ticket-of-leave men, a semi-free form of labour with wages depressed by the fact that these men were not free to move out of their particular police district; and finally a growing pool of free wage-labour consisting of ex-convicts who had served out their sentences or been emancipated for other reasons.

The use of unfree labour was a basis for rapid capital accumulation within the colony by the first generation of employers. Officers grumbled about the quality of convict labour—it was reckoned to be about two-thirds as efficient as free labour—but it had the great advantage of being dirt cheap in real terms. However, the conventional assumption that New South Wales remained primarily a gaol until about 1820 overlooks the importance of free (including ex-convict) labour. Actually in 1805 there were 800 free male workers, compared to 650 male assigned convicts. True, there were also 500 female convicts, mainly used as domestic servants, and 1000 male government convicts. However, part of the labour of the latter group—time spent working on their own hands—was available to private employers, although most of it was utilized on building and other government work which was not directly profitable to employers.

In terms of labour, then, as well as other respects, the economy is to be regarded as essentially capitalist after the first couple of decades. In course of time, the proportion of convicts in the labour force declined as sentences expired, children born in the colony grew up and free immigrants arrived. This was not a smooth progression, for these factors were offset to some extent by the growth in numbers of convicts imported from 1814.

Convict labour, especially for big employers, remained very important until the 1840s. However, it would be wrong to characterize the economy as pre-capitalist for that reason, or to describe it as a slave economy. Slaves almost invariably remain slaves all their lives, as do their children. Convicts generally secured their freedom after a period of years, and their children were born free. On the other hand, it would be misleading to draw a very sharp dividing line between free workers and assigned convicts. They often lived under the same employer's roof together and were expected to work hard in return for food and clothing, the value of their labour above this level being in the main appropriated by their employers. Much the same could be said of free labourers in England, the capitalist homeland. It may be further remarked that in the free colony established in Western Australia in 1829, most labourers were under indenture to private employers. 'Freedom' is a relative term.

In New South Wales from the 1790s, wages for free workers were nominally high because of the labour shortage. Even assigned convicts were paid wages by their masters: £10 per annum for a male convict and £7 for a female. Of these amounts, £3 in the case of a male and half that sum for a female was reckoned to be for clothing to be supplied by the master. The rationale for making the payment was that it was unfair to expect assigned convicts to work all day for their masters without a wage whilst government convicts were allowed to work for wages outside the regular government hours. However, the extraordinarily high level of colonial wages by comparison with Britain is deceptive. Prices were also high in New South Wales, and wage rates were expressed in a debased colonial currency. Moreover, wages were generally paid in kind, not cash. Workers drew their wages either in the form of 'indulgencies' such as tea, tobacco or alcohol, or in commodities such as wheat which they could barter for such comforts, over and above bare rations.

As always with payment in kind, the goods supplied to workers were heavily over-priced. On top of this, the officers as employers paid for labour in the very commodities which they themselves imported at great profit. This command over goods for wages also gave the officers an advantage in competing for labour against small employers. As Hunter observed about the use of rum as an incentive: 'Much work will be done by labourers, artificers and others for a small reward in this article . . . which money could not purchase'. It amounted to trading on the misery of the many to whom grog represented the one obvious way of securing temporary enjoyment or forgetfulness—and a befuddled labour force was less likely to plan revolt.

Another section of the population open to exploitation consisted of the growing number of ex-convicts who obtained land grants. They lived a poverty-stricken existence, scratching over the soil, and many were dispossessed of their small holdings within a short time. This was due partly to such factors as their ignorance of and unsuitability for farming, lack of capital and subjection to flood and drought. However, there were other reasons related to the officers' control over political power in the colony. Small farmers were squeezed between (a) low prices received for their produce and (b) high costs of production in the form of imported commodities and relatively high wages for free labour. The high costs of production were mainly attributable to the officers' wholesale monopoly, while low producer prices for grain flowed from the officers' influence over the operations of the commis- 45 sariat as the main purchaser. In the case of a good harvest, the commissariat stores were opened for the purchase of only as much grain as the government needed and could store, and in the ensuing competition to have grain accepted by the public stores there was never much doubt that the officers and traders would be favoured as sellers. Small farmers who failed to get into this market were forced to sell their produce at low prices to private dealers (ex-convict middlemen) or to officers.

The economic importance of the commissariat underlines the role of government and of the civilian officials who were accepted as part of the officers' ring. Actually, the officers did not produce very much grain on their own land, preferring to concentrate on meat production which was more profitable. Nevertheless, wheat came into their hands, sometimes as rent paid by small farmers, more generally because wheat was a substitute for money. Consequently, the officers relied upon sales of grain and meat to the commissariat in exchange for more negotiable forms of money.

A peasantry was barely established in New South Wales before the emerging bourgeoisie was busy dispossessing peasants of their land and turning them into wage workers. The attitude of the officers towards small farmers is typified by the comment made by Macarthur in 1796, that it would have been better 'had these men, instead of being permitted to become settlers, been obliged to employ themselves in the service of an industrious and diligent master'. Two years later, a group of farmers reciprocated the feeling in a statement complaining about the high price of imported goods and about being forestalled at the public stores in the sale of their grain. They declared:

The Farmer is branded as an infamous, idle drunken and abandoned character —the Trader on the other hand who has the opportunity of getting Money and is in fact only a nuisance and pest to the Colony not doing any one thing for the support or welfare of it ... meets with respect, enjoys all the comforts of life, and in a very few years makes his Fortune out of nothing at the expense of the distressed and industrious Farmer, and ... Government on whom they so grossly impose.[12]

Certainly by 1800 many ex-convict peasants had lost their land through foreclosure of mortgages. The point should not be exaggerated, for in the following two decades a number of small farmers were able to acquire and hold on to land and to prosper in a small way. The use of convict labour was not confined exclusively to the officers and wealthy immigrants and there was economic differentiation within the peasantry: a bourgeoisie was developing on agricultural land. Around 1820, when Commissioner Bigge investigated the situation, he found that small farmers, mostly ex-convict, still held by far the greater part of the *cultivated* land in the colony, although many of them were only tenants.

Nevertheless, the extent to which land originally held by ex-convicts and soldiers passed into the hands of the ruling elite is remarkable. In 1802 John Macarthur owned nearly 4000 acres at Parramatta, only 320 of which had been acquired by way of grants from the crown; the remainder had been bought (some of it from other officers). In 1820, W. C. Wentworth, in addition to land received by grant, owned 23 880 acres of purchased land. Such cases represented primary accumulation in the classic Marxist sense. Even more ruthless was the amassing of 22 000 acres by emancipist Samuel Terry, mainly from small settlers who were unable to pay their debts to him.

Merchants and Graziers

From about 1800 a new element was introduced into the colonial situation with the arrival of the first professional merchants, mainly representing British mercantile firms established in India. Foremost was Robert Campbell, who settled in Sydney and built up a permanent base for importing. Unlike the officers, Campbell was not limited in his operations by commissariat expenditure and the consequent supply of Treasury bills: as a professional, he had access to external sources of capital and credit, immediately in India and ultimately from Britain. For some years at the beginning of the nineteenth century, Campbell was the largest importer of goods into New South Wales. At last the officers had to face some competition in this sphere. Yet although Campbell initially represented a challenge to the officers' import monopoly, the ring was not really broken—rather, it was widened to accommodate him and his ilk. Campbell was soon playing the same game of obtaining favours from the colonial government. He depended heavily upon government contracts to import spirits and cattle from India and he was closely associated with the commissary, John Palmer.

In the first decade of the nineteenth century, the officers continued on the whole to trade profitably. Governor King made some efforts to restrict the quantity of spirits imported into the colony but he made no attempt to control the retail price of grog, with the result that the position of those who controlled imports remained privileged. In the long run, however, the appearance of Campbell on the scene signalled the opening up of trade with the outside world. Without severely restrictive conditions of trade, the occupation of merchant could be hazardous, subject to big losses as well as profits. It was a field for skilled full-time professionals, not part-time speculators.

In 1812–15 there was a serious commercial depression in the   47 colony, associated with credit difficulties in Britain which spread to mercantile firms in India. Such connections brought even Campbell to the brink of ruin, while men like Macarthur had their fingers badly burned. Macarthur, on hearing that a cargo which he had despatched from London had fared badly in the Sydney market, declared: 'It is ... *the last mercantile project* in which I will ever try my fortune'.[13]

This was virtually the end of the officers' activities in wholesale trade. Their functions were taken over by representatives of merchant houses from India such as Richard Jones and William Walker. The older elite concentrated its attention upon land and grazing. For them, big speculative trading profits were over, but they had accumulated capital and now faced a bright prospect of further solid accumulation by exploiting labour and accelerating their grab for land—in which they were joined by new immigrants with capital.

The process of establishing large estates began long before this, of course. The officers learned very early that animal husbandry, for both meat production and the breeding of stock, was more profitable than arable farming—and grazing was an occupation more suited to a gentleman. Officers invested profits from wholesale trade in building up flocks and herds and in 1800 they owned about 80 per cent of all the sheep in the colony, and nearly all the cattle in private ownership. Yet at the same time the officers' landholdings amounted in aggregate to only 14 500 acres. Certainly, that was more than one-third of the total land granted by the crown but it was not much in absolute terms.

Transfer of land from the crown to private ownership was speeded up in the following decade, for example through the grant of 5000 acres at the Cowpastures to Macarthur. The first few free immigrants with capital (men who were neither officers nor officials) arrived in New South Wales and were given fairly large land grants, together with convict labour. Later, Governor Macquarie was generous in making grants, and by 1821 a total of about 380 000 acres had been alienated from the crown in New South Wales, about 60 per cent of this being owned by only eighty individuals out of the 1665 landholders. The Blue Mountains had been crossed and the real rush for grazing land was beginning.

The amount of land alienated from the crown in the 1820s greatly exceeded all previous transfers. In addition to land leased out or licensed by the crown, a total of nearly three million acres was alienated by 1829—one million acres of it in a single grant to the Australian Agricultural Company. The main incentive now was profit from production of wool for the London market and this attracted to New South Wales a growing number of free immigrants with capital. At the same time the system of small land grants to ex-convicts was effectively ended and replaced by grants which varied in size according to the amount of capital possessed by the applicant: the bourgeoisie needed a proletariat, not a peasantry. Restriction upon access to land, except for men of capital, was made virtually watertight in the 1830s by the cessation of all grants. Instead, crown land was alienated only by sale, at a price which kept small men out but allowed ample profits for big graziers.

Government, as a source of landownership on a large scale, together with the continuing flow of convict labour, remained the prime road to greater private wealth. Yet although a growing number of fresh capitalist immigrants took that road, 'old colonials' were well up in the race. Some retired to England but others stayed where the money was, in land and wool. For example, in 1837 James Macarthur and his brothers (sons of John) owned 50 000 acres, 18 000 of which had been acquired by crown grants. Even the first generation of professional merchants, men like Jones and Walker, invested heavily in grazing from the 1820s onwards. Robert Campbell re-established himself as a merchant and received large land grants in the area which was later the site of Canberra. In the 1830s Campbell bought more crown land in the area, giving him a total of 19 000 acres; and he squatted on large runs such as Delegate which comprised 38 000 acres. His biographer does not explain precisely how Campbell made such dramatic gains after being paralysed by debts in 1815, but it may be remarked that throughout the nineteenth century the Australian bourgeoisie displayed a remarkable facility for surviving times of depression, often by concealing assets from creditors.

Primary accumulation was the genesis of a number of family fortunes which, as in the case of the Wentworths, are still evident in Australia. Once the initial stage of accumulation was over, more sophisticated methods were devised to exploit labour, which came increasingly in the form of free immigrants. It should never be forgotten, however, that the initial stage of accumulation is crucial and that it was accomplished in Australia by a form of police state, or military dictatorship, which extracted the surplus over subsistence from unfree labour. The use and control of state power was absolutely central to the process. Attempts to portray the genesis of capitalism in conventional terms of the growth of the market are false.

3

Forced Labour:
The Convict Basis of the Proletariat

I'm old	I am he	I split the rock;
Botany Bay;	*Who paved the way,*	*I felled the tree:*
Stiff in the joints,	*That you might walk*	*The nation was—*
Little to say.	*At your ease to-day ...*	*Because of me!*[1]

I'm old
Botany Bay;
Stiff in the joints,
Little to say.

I am he
Who paved the way,
That you might walk
At your ease to-day ...

I split the rock;
I felled the tree:
The nation was—
Because of me![1]

In early Australian white society, the most common people were convicts. Apart from their bondage and certain other distortions, these convicts mirrored the working classes in the country of origin. One gross distortion was the imbalance between sexes: out of a total of about 160 000 convicts transported to Australia between 1788 and 1868, only 15 per cent were female. Employers and masters deplored the 'moral evils'—prostitution and homosexuality—associated with the numerical disparity, while welcoming any growth in the size of the male labour force. Female convicts were desired mainly as domestic servants and for sexual purposes.

The convict population also differed from the poor of Britain in characteristics of age and work habits. The average age of convicts on arrival in New South Wales or Tasmania was twenty-six years, so that they constituted a ready-made workforce; and a relatively large proportion of convicts came from urban areas, whereas agriculture still employed more people than any other sector of the economy in Britain in the first half of the nineteenth century. More than one-third of the transported convicts were Irish, and their background was probably more peasant in character than was that of the English convicts.

Some groups of convicts were exceptional. They included 'gentle-men', such as the architect Francis Greenway, who was transported to Sydney after being caught forging a document. In the class-based colonial society, the social origins of these convicts were recognized: they were allocated to soft jobs as government clerks and the like, and they were generally allowed tickets of leave at early stages of their sentences. Other groups consisted of political prisoners of various descriptions: Luddites, Chartists, Canadian rebels, agricultural labourers who revolted against poverty and degradation in southern England, and so on. The essence of the crime for which such men were transported to Australia was the threatened destruction of property belonging to their employers. Resort to the breaking of knitting frames or burning down hayricks was often the only available form of protest in the absence of labour unions. Unions were no longer illegal in England in the 1830s, but when six farm labourers in the Dorsetshire village of Tolpuddle formed a union in 1834 they were convicted and transported to Australia. Nominally, their offence was that of administering unlawful oaths at an initiation ceremony—a procedure deemed useful, by friendly societies as well as trade unions, against potential embezzlers or police informers. Actually, the crime committed by the Tolpuddle martyrs was to aim for an increase in wages.

Nevertheless, the convicts in these particular categories represented no more than one per cent of the total number transported to Australia. The most common offence recorded was theft of one kind or another, not offences against the person. Nowadays, the orthodox view among Australian historians is that the bulk of the convicts were more or less professional criminals. L.L. Robson concludes:

The convicts were neither simply 'village Hampdens' nor merely 'ne'er-do-wells from the city slums'. But if the Hampdens were placed on one side of a scale and ne'er-do-wells on the other, the scale must tip towards the ne'er-do-wells.[2]

Yet 'ne'er-do-well' is an imprecise term, unrelated to a historical context. In this case, the particular context was eighteenth-century England, accurately characterized as 'a society with a bloody penal code, an astute ruling class who manipulated it to their advantage, and a people schooled in the lessons of Justice, Terror and Mercy'. Legal terror and punishments were made more systematic. The number of criminal offences for which the death penalty or transportation was prescribed multiplied. At the same time there was increasing resort to transportation instead of hanging. This was on the recommendation of judges, who used their discretion in such a way as to make men of property appear merciful. In this way, respect for the law was maintained while the deference or gratitude of poor people was invoked.   51

The operation of the law was both coercive and ideological in function: it punished, yet it helped to create a spirit of consent and submission, binding the poor to the rich. It also 'allowed the class that passed one of the bloodiest penal codes in Europe to congratulate itself on its humanity'.[3]

It is generally acknowledged that the Irish convicts were exceptional in some ways, their offences reflecting to a greater degree the depth of poverty in that country and the feelings of hatred towards the English ruling class. Theft or assault in Ireland, when directed against landlords or the state, could be deemed political in nature. The perpetrator, far from being considered a criminal, might be looked up to by ordinary folk in the same way as bushrangers often were in Australia: admired, so long as they did not rob the poor. Certainly the Irish men and women, convict and free, represented a distinct element in the nascent proletariat in the colonies. They brought with them their national pride, their Catholicism and the knowledge that their homeland had been the first victim of British imperialism centuries earlier. The most serious uprising by convicts in Australia, at Castle Hill near Sydney, was the work mainly of Irishmen. It came only six years after the national rebellion of 1798 in Ireland.

Despite the existence of diverse elements in the convict population, commentators in England at the time reckoned that the great bulk of those transported to Australia formed an undiluted mass of scoundrels, the dregs of society. Even those observers who could appreciate the nexus between economic and social circumstances and the law and crime regarded the Australian convicts as a debased element, a lumpenproletariat which was parasitic on the working classes from which its members came. Frederick Engels, in a letter of 23 September 1851 to Marx, referred to the recent gold discoveries in Australia and thought that, before long,

the British will be thrown out and the united states of deported murderers, burglars, rapists and pickpockets will startle the world by demonstrating what wonders can be performed by a state consisting of undisguised rascals. THEY WILL BEAT CALIFORNIA HOLLOW. But whereas in California rascals are still lynched, in Australia they'll lynch the *honnêtes gens* [honest folk].[4]

Undoubtedly there were many unpleasant, dangerous characters among the convicts transported to Australia and it would be romantic nonsense to portray these as innocent victims. Furthermore, the convict system was calculated to brutalize nearly everyone, both those who suffered under it and those who administered and benefited from it. Yet it should be remembered that the laws which provided for transportation to Australia were drafted and interpreted by parliaments and courts which took no account of the interests of the common people, except where they coincided with those of the propertied classes. Thus murder was demonstrably contrary to public interest, whereas vagrancy was always a class offence, being directed only against the poor. In Ireland, vagrancy was punishable with transportation.

Engels, writing on a different occasion about conditions of which he had personal knowledge, noted the indulgence of English workers in alcohol and unrestrained sexual relations. 'The bourgeoisie has left the working-class only these two pleasures', he observed. As a gloss upon this point, Engels also stated the class origins of complaints about such working-class habits. 'Drunkenness, sexual irregularities, brutality, and disregard for the rights of property are the chief points with which the bourgeois charges them.'[5] Little is known about the views of workers themselves on these matters, as they rarely left any written record. Judged by actual behaviour, there were sharp differences between bourgeois morality and the working-class culture. As E. P. Thompson comments, contemporary estimates as to the number of criminals in England 'reveal as much about the morality of the propertied classes . . . as they do about the actual criminal behaviour of the unpropertied'. A classic example was a calculation made in 1797 by P. Colquhoun, a police magistrate, that among a very large number of criminals in London were 50 000 harlots. However, Colquhoun's definition of the latter was that they were 'lewd and immoral women', including 'the prodigious number among the lower classes who cohabit together without marriage'.[6]

Colquhoun's revelation of middle-class values has relevance for white society in Australia, which derived its law, customs and ideology from Britain. Female convicts in the colonies were widely regarded as prostitutes. No doubt this was correct in a number of cases. In circumstances where there were few economic opportunities available to women, the sale of sexual services could ensure a modicum of independence, however degrading the practice might appear to moralists then and later. The alternative might be that of being yoked to a male brute through marriage. On the other hand, an unattached woman in a violent, male-dominated society was often at risk, so that she might seek protection with one man. Cohabitation outside marriage (and without the connotation of sexual promiscuity) was common among working-class people in both Britain and Australia, especially as a marriage licence cost as much as £4 and divorce was available only to the wealthy.

Cohabitation without the benefit of clergy was acceptable conduct among workers. Nor was it restricted in Australia to convicts or ex-convicts, despite railings by middle-class males such as the Reverend Samuel Marsden against what he termed concubinage. Later, from the 1840s, when middle-class females such as Caroline Chisholm were 53 extolling the virtues of marriage and the family, these institutions took deeper root. Moralists were then able to concentrate upon the narrower definition of prostitution, and Australian wowserism grew.

Divergencies between bourgeois and working-class values were not confined to sexual relations, and some of the differences were carried over into the twentieth century. For example, pilfering by workers on wharves has been traditional. Pinching a few bottles of Scotch whisky from a cargo was deemed to be all right: it was thieving from the capitalists, who could afford it. Yet in some ways life on the waterfront was highly moral. Wharf labourers pitched in to support one of their own down on his luck, in a spirit of co-operation alien to the individualist ethic of middle-class society.

A similar kind of camaraderie may be glimpsed under the surface of convict life in the Australian colonies. There was a bond of hatred of harsh authority, of hypocrisy and social pretension. A delightful story is told of one official visit to a female factory at Hobart, where about 500 convict women were held. They were addressed as a body by the Governor of Van Diemen's Land and his wife, after which a parson named Bedford had his turn. As reported by another chaplain present:

These women had had quite enough of Mr. Bedford; they were compelled to listen to his long stupid sermons, and knew his character, and that he loved roast turkey and ham with a bottle or two of port wine much better than he loved his Bible, and when he commenced to preach they with one accord endeavoured to cough him down, and upon the warders proclaiming silence they all with one impulse turned round, raised their clothes and smacked their posteriors with a loud report. The Governor was shocked, and the parson was horror struck ... and even the ladies could not control their laughter.[7]

Collective gestures of this sort were rare: so were open individual acts like that of James Murray who, as reported to a court at Bathurst in New South Wales, told his master that 'he might go and fuck himself'.[8] The ever-present threat of severe punishment meant that convict resentment was generally passive in form, expressed as sullenness, dumb insolence and reluctance to work. In practice, the common front of silence towards authority was frequently undermined by informers. Major George Druitt, chief engineer in charge of public works in New South Wales, told the Bigge Commission of Enquiry in 1819 that in his opinion there was no danger of concerted escape by convicts, as they 'invariably give information to me, as they term it "split upon each other"'.[9]

There were other divisions in convict ranks as some of their number were singled out for favoured treatment. Overseers of gangs of government convicts were themselves convicts. Policemen were initially recruited from trusted convicts because of a shortage of free men available for such lowly jobs—although there were compensations from the fruits of corruption and the assertion of authority. The Bigge Enquiry learned that on one occasion constables at Parramatta had beaten up William Parkes for replying 'Ask my arse', to their call 'Who goes there?' This was a raw, heavy-handed environment and the most hated of all in it were those who carried out sentences of flogging. They too were selected convicts.

As already noted, some convicts were very successful in material terms. One of them, Samuel Terry, conspicuously sided with authority at an early stage: in 1804, while still a convict, he enrolled in the Parramatta Loyalist Association against the uprising of convicts at Castle Hill. Terry prospered greatly, leaving a personal estate of £250 000, together with much landed property, at his death in 1838. He personified the spirit of individual acquisitiveness which permeated capitalist society—an ideology which embraced convicts and ex-convicts as well as the unconvicted. Indeed, Humphrey McQueen argues that it was the desire for self-improvement which led to most of the convicts being transported in the first place!

It remains a fact that the great majority of convicts transported to Australia were from working-class or peasant backgrounds and they came to form part of those same classes in the colonies. To portray them as a collection of sub-human thugs is to adopt the warder mentality of their gaolers. Even that part of the stereotype which assumes that the convicts had very few skills other than that of picking pockets is wide of the mark. Recent research suggests that there was a remarkable variety of work skills among the convicts and that they may well have been broadly representative of the British working classes in this respect. Undoubtedly the convicts were the basis for the creation of a proletariat in Australia. Their fundamental importance as a labour force was expressed very well by Edward Gibbon Wakefield, despite his own preference for free colonies. In words purporting to come from a settler in New South Wales in 1829, Wakefield wrote:

We owe everything, over and above mere subsistence, to the wickedness of the people of England. Who built Sydney? Convicts. Who made the excellent roads from Sydney to Parramatta, Windsor and Liverpool? Convicts. By whom is the land made to produce? By convicts. Why do not all our labourers exact high wages, and, by taking a large share of the produce of labour, prevent their employers from becoming rich? Because most of them are convicts. What has enabled the landowner readily to dispose of his surplus produce? The demand of the keepers of convicts.[10]

Of the total number of convicts transported to Australia, about half (80 000) went to New South Wales between 1788 and 1840, and

55

another 67 000 went to Tasmania up to 1852. However, only about 14 000 of all these people were transported to Australia before 1814, when the Napoleonic wars in Europe ended. Thereafter, the flow of convicts rose dramatically to a peak level in the 1830s, when an average of more than 5000 convicts per year went to the two colonies. These increases reflected conditions in Britain where rapid structural changes in the economy meant better conditions for some workers and unemployment for others such as handloom weavers. Masses of those who were termed the redundant poor emigrated from Britain, some voluntarily, others as convicts bound for Australia.

The flow of convicts into New South Wales was so strong that in 1828 they constituted 47 per cent of the total population in that colony. Thereafter, as the regular process of emancipation or expiration of sentence took effect, the proportion declined to 40 per cent in 1835, followed by a rapid drop in the next six years or so as the number of free immigrants grew. Clearly, consideration of the formation of working classes in Australia requires initial focus upon the convicts, though they did not compose a class in themselves. Rather, their legal position made them low-caste workers in status—a status which their social superiors sought to maintain after emancipation.

The first Australian colonies began as gaols without walls. The openness was feasible (and cheap) because of isolation from the outside world. If a convict escaped into the bush he was likely to die there. In the course of time, some buildings were erected to hold government convicts; and some special penal establishments were set up at outlying points such as Norfolk Island and Port Arthur. These special places were terrible spots, designed for cruel punishment of those convicts who committed serious offences after arrival in the colony or were potential rebels. They were dreaded hell-holes within a colony-wide prison. However, most convicts who transgressed were simply punished with floggings, which interfered less than imprisonment with their ability to work for the employers to whom they were assigned. Even the government convicts, apart from particular groups such as chain gangs working in shackles, enjoyed an astonishing degree of freedom of movement. For example, the convict barracks built at Sydney's Hyde Park in 1819 housed 700 convicts but they were normally let out after church on Sundays—whereupon they 'run immediately to the part of the Town called the Rocks, where every species of Debauchery & villainy is Practised'.[11] In short, pubs and brothels were open to convict as well as free customers. Although government convicts wore a distinctive uniform, this was not true of assigned convicts whose occasional participation in bawdy, boozy activities (outside working hours) was thus less easily remarked—which was just as well for them, as they were not supposed to leave the employer's property without a permit. As in South Africa today, there was a system of

56

passes, to be carried by people who moved about, so as to make it easier for police to spot suspicious characters. The colonial pass laws were sometimes irksome to the free population as well.

Relatively favourable aspects of life in an open gaol ought not to obscure the reality that on the whole convicts led harsh, painful lives. Most of them were assigned by colonial governors to work for individual settlers; and although this meant variations in the convict experience, assigned servants remained under very close control. Despotic governors like Arthur, who ruled Van Diemen's Land from 1824 to 1836, tightened regulations and tried to stamp out the allowance to convicts of 'indulgencies' such as tobacco and alcohol. Whippings were commonplace for both assigned and government convicts. An assistant surgeon at Sydney Hospital, who regularly attended floggings, told the Bigge Enquiry that these punishments were not as severe as in the army and navy. Perhaps so, but it may be doubted whether the incidence was so high in the armed forces. Out of a total of 8800 convicts in Tasmania in the year 1830, one in six was flogged. In the same colony, a Lieutenant Barclay boasted to some visitors that a group of convict coalminers was known as

Barclay's Tigers—for their backs were striped in so symmetrical a manner that visitors had often remarked on the extraordinary regularity and he was warmly congratulated on his able flagellator—it being often necessary to administer 500 lashes apiece.[12]

It was not permissible to flog female convicts, although no doubt many were cuffed or kicked by their masters and mistresses. Other forms of punishment were available, such as confinement to female factories, which served as prisons within a prison for colonial offenders. The factories also served as labour bureaus and maternity hospitals. Although there was a relatively high infant mortality rate at the factories, the prospects for women giving birth there were probably better than at Sydney Hospital, which was known to patients as the Slaughter House. On the other hand, in Tasmania a pregnant convict woman, expecting an illegitimate child, faced the prospect of six months' hard labour after the child was weaned.

There was remarkably little organized convict resistance to the system. This was partly the result of a repressive state machine. At the apex was military force, seen in the smashing of the Castle Hill rebellion. For sixty years after the return of the original NSW Corps to England in 1810, regular troops were stationed in Australia. They were not there for defence against foreign foes: the enemy was within. There were also police. Linking these forces were magistrates, who performed a variety of administrative and judicial functions. A few were paid stipends and known as police magistrates. Their reputation was not enviable: of the nine Sydney police magistrates appointed between 1832 and 1849, five had to be removed for corruption or immorality. In country districts, magistrates were generally local landowners. Their appointments were honorary but they and their class derived considerable benefit, especially in relation to labour discipline. The connection between private profit and control of state force was particularly evident on the large estate of the Australian Agricultural Company at Port Stephens, north of Newcastle in New South Wales. Not only was a detachment of soldiers stationed there in 1830 to guard a large body of assigned convicts but the officer commanding this detachment was also a resident magistrate, in which capacity he was paid by the company.

Besides force, there was ideological control, some being religious in form. Ironically, although Catholicism was detested by colonial governments, they came to view the Roman Catholic church as an important adjunct to convict discipline. As a Governor of Tasmania wrote in 1841, more priests were needed in the colony, for they would 'exercise a powerful influence in the moral improvement of this class of offenders'.[13] On the other hand, there is no evidence that non-Catholic convicts were much impressed by the clergymen whose services they were compelled to attend. One Presbyterian minister, J.D. Lang, saw a connection between this and the fact that some clergymen also functioned as magistrates and ordered whippings. Lang's caustic comment was that:

In other countries the clergy have often been accused of taking the *fleece*; but New South Wales is the only country I have ever heard of, in which they were openly authorized, under His Majesty's commission, to take the *hide* also, or to flay their flock alive.[14]

In broad terms, colonial culture was dominated by the desire to make money. Individual convicts desired their freedom but there was no thought of a radically different social system. There was thus no revolutionary focus for opposition to the *status quo*. Groups such as the Tolpuddle martyrs, who might be assumed to differ from established authority on political or ideological grounds, were mainly concerned to get back to their old lives in Britain as soon as possible. They played no real part in colonial politics. Apathy and disinclination to rebel were particularly marked in Tasmania, where shortage of convict labour was much less pronounced than in New South Wales.

One important factor in convict submission was that most felons were not bereft of hope for the future. Sentences of seven or fourteen years expired, pardons at an earlier stage were possible and even 'lifers' might eventually be emancipated, while tickets of leave (comparable to the modern prison parole) were freely granted for good conduct. In 1832 about 10 per cent of all the convicts in Tasmania held tickets. Such variations in expectations militated against the organization of resistance among convicts. Moreover, the legal system did not strip a convict of all rights. Indeed, the shortage of free persons meant that convicts were accepted as witnesses in colonial courts, which was contrary to the position in England. Ticket-of-leave convicts in New South Wales were permitted to sue for recovery of debt (including wages owed) in civil courts until 1832, when the House of Lords in effect prohibited the practice. Even floggings were formally not the responsibility of employers: they could be imposed only on the order of magistrates, although this nice distinction was a highly dubious protection for convicts.

The widespread existence of convict 'rights', often unacknowledged by authority, is crucial to an understanding of this extraordinary society. Forced labour rather than confinement behind bars was the essence of the convict system. Coercion and fear drove convicts to work, but they had some defences of their own. 'Go slow' labour practices in present-day Australia have antecedents in convict times, and some employers found it more effective to give their assigned servants the incentive of more food or 'indulgencies' than to have them flogged. As one settler expressed it, 'the belly is far more vulnerable and sensitive than the back'.[15] There were regulations and conventions governing the assignment of convicts, and customs concerning hours of work and payment were extremely important. Allocation of tobacco and alcohol might be an indulgency from the employer's viewpoint, but in convict eyes the allowance became a right in the course of time. Cutting it off was likely to arouse resistance which could extend to withdrawal of labour—the ultimate weapon, short of violent reprisals, against an employer.

In other words, while convicts were more or less resigned to their loss of freedom, they retained a sense of being entitled to 'a fair go' within the limits of the system. Law and custom were not necessarily the same. For example, by 1831 in New South Wales, employers were no longer required by government to pay their assigned servants wages of seven or ten pounds per year, although there was an obligation to supply them with stipulated amounts of food and clothing. Yet the earlier wage payment was also generally made in the form of goods rather than cash, and many employers found it expedient to continue the practice in the 1830s, especially in the case of skilled workers whose services were particularly valuable.

Convict protests were usually directed against withdrawal of 'rights'. For example, six assigned men at Bathurst on one occasion refused to leave their huts to go to work, 'as they had not got their beefs' (meat as part of weekly rations). James McLaughlin, a convict assigned to a priest, told an overseer: 'I shall not work a bloody stroke, 59 for you or bloody Father Terry until I get a jacket'.[16] There was a violent incident at the Parramatta Female Factory in 1827, after rations had been reduced by the matron as a punishment. One hundred of the female convicts, wielding pickaxes and other implements, broke out of their prison and were persuaded to return only after troops were called out.

Convict refusal to work was seldom successful in achieving its immediate objective. Masters held the whip-hand. In the longer term, however, employers were forced to take account of convict reaction to arbitrary repression. Incidentally, the pattern can still be seen in prison populations, which remain predominantly working-class in origin. In 1970 there was a disturbance at Bathurst Gaol, which ended when the prisoners involved agreed to return to their cells. The following day, these men were savagely bashed by prison warders armed with rubber truncheons. The action was unprovoked and amounted to illegal assault, depriving the convicts of a primary right. Three years later, vengeful prisoners at Bathurst rioted and burned the gaol down. After this a Royal Commission was appointed, bad conditions were exposed in a number of gaols and some improvements were effected.

Earlier, in the convict colony of New South Wales, a perennial labour shortage was a powerful aid to workers, both convict and free. It meant that employers, especially on distant stations, sometimes turned a blind eye to breaches of labour discipline; and standards of living, at least in terms of food, were quite high as early as 1820. A standard scale of weekly rations issued to assigned convicts consisted of twelve pounds of wheat or flour and seven pounds of fresh beef or mutton (plus a few ounces of salt and soap), which was little different from the normal diet of agricultural workers in England. Those in the latter group probably ate more potatoes, but meat was more plentiful and cheaper in Australia as flocks and herds expanded. Tea was the customary non-alcoholic drink in both countries. It was often asserted that a colonial convict was better off than his contemporaries in England, although the comparison ignored the basic differences in freedom. How many pounds of meat were worth fifty lashes?

Employers, despite their repeated complaints about the costs and defects of the convict system, never as a class advocated an end to transportation. Forced labour was not only cheap: it was highly mobile. This was very important for the development of the outback pastoral industry. Free workers were inclined to stay in or close to towns—they disliked the loneliness and boredom, the flies and other irritants, of bush life. A convict, on the other hand, had no choice but to go where his master wanted him. Indeed, many convicts were happy enough to be located on a remote station. The life was relatively free, it was good to be out of sight of the employer, and a convict with a mind dulled by years of imprisonment could be an ideal shepherd. John Macarthur put the point rather differently: 'When Men are engaged in rural occupations their days are chiefly spent in solitude—they have much time for reflection and self examination, and they are less tempted to the perpetration of crimes'.[17]

In the squatting districts of New South Wales in the 1830s, white males outnumbered white females by about four to one, partly because there were few small family holdings there. Among the males, the proportion of assigned convicts was far higher than in urban or agricultural areas closer to Sydney. Furthermore, many of these men preferred to remain as bushworkers after being emancipated. They were the stockmen, bullock-drivers, cedar-cutters etc. of a pastoral economy—rough, adaptable, egalitarian in spirit and accustomed to hard work interspersed with periodic bouts of heavy drinking. Later, writers such as Henry Lawson and Joseph Furphy, largely ignoring the claims of urban life, evoked an ethos of mateship, resourcefulness and group solidarity in the outback. They fashioned an image with which Australians could identify. There were some undesirable aspects of the picture—mateship was only for whites (primarily males) and racism was acceptable—while practice often failed to measure up to the myth; yet the stereotype of the typical Australian, endowed with manly characteristics, was potent.

The culture which developed in the outback was the product both of Anglo-Irish origins and traditions (as evidenced by contemporary ballads) and frontier conditions in Australia. The influence of the frontier was apparent among free as well as unfree people and it was not peculiar to the convict period. Nevertheless, as Russel Ward shows in *The Australian Legend*, the outback image emerged primarily from convictism, from an unequal society on which 'the new Australian conditions had a levelling effect'.

Significantly, one feature of the convict experience became an abiding element in ruling-class consciousness: the value of forced labour as an offset to shortage of free labour. This is exemplified by a letter written by James Burns, chairman of the mercantile firm of Burns, Philp & Co. Ltd, at a much later date, 7 March 1960. Addressing himself to A. R. Downer, federal Minister for Immigration, Burns expressed support for a policy of restricting immigration to Europeans only. Admittedly, this would not contribute to the development of under-populated northern Australia, but Burns had a suggestion for that:

if long-term prisoners were sent up there they could grow a lot of their own food and develop roads and settlements. This probably would cost less than keeping such prisoners in the many jails throughout Southern Australia. As there is a very large stretch of desert country between the Kimberleys and the

61

south of Western Australia, I do not suppose there would be much chance of prisoners escaping. After all, the whole of the southern part of Australia developed in this way in the early days . . . it appears to me that something will have to be done to populate the north, otherwise somebody may come down and populate it for us.

In the convict colonies, forced labour shaded into free labour. For many years, most of the free workers were ex-convicts. When an influx of free workers from Britain developed strongly in the 1830s, there were some signs of tension between them and the assigned convicts. 'Old hands' were inclined to jeer at 'new chums', while the latter were reluctant to associate with convicts. Nevertheless, there was no sharp segregation of convicts and ex-convicts from the rest of the workforce. Economic prosperity and shortage of labour had the effect of masking differences and inhibiting the development of caste distinctions. On colonial newspapers such as the *Sydney Gazette*, convict compositors exercised their skills alongside free workers and were paid similar rates of wages. Indeed, the two groups joined in the formation of an early printers' union.

One important difference between convict and free workers was that only convicts could be flogged. This did not protect free workers from other kinds of punishment for offences against labour discipline. The convict milieu encouraged employers to impose penalties even heavier than were permissible in England under the imperial country's Masters and Servants Act. A local New South Wales Act of this type in 1828 provided for sentences of up to six months' gaol for male servants (twice the maximum sentence applicable in England) and three months for females, as well as forfeiture of wages by servants. The offences which attracted such penalties included neglect of work or leaving a job unfinished, misconduct, or damaging the master's property. The law was tailor-made for tyrannical or capricious employers, and female domestic servants were prominent among those who suffered for insubordination. Masters and mistresses accustomed to being spoiled by the availability of convict servants were not inclined to tolerate cheekiness from free servants, although working-class girls were noted for their freedom from the servility which was common in domestic service in England.

Colonial Masters and Servants Acts were not entirely one-sided. For example, an employer might be charged with ill-treating a servant or failing to pay wages due. If this were proved, the employer could be ordered to make financial restitution. Yet no penalty of imprisonment was provided against employers in such cases, and the legislation—which was implemented summarily in the magistrates' courts—was mainly used against servants. In New South Wales, selective operation of the legislation was modified by an amendment in 1857 which removed the primary penalty of imprisonment for workers, but if male employees were unable to pay fines they could still go to gaol in default. The Australian Masters and Servants Acts are still on the statute books in all states except two, although the use of the legislation has been overtaken by arbitration court awards.

It was one thing to punish employees for unsatisfactory work, but what of workers who were disinclined to take jobs and managed to eke out a living without them? This ultimate nightmare for the capitalist class was countered by the law on vagrancy. For centuries it was used in England to force the poor to work. The idle rich were safe, for the offence was that of having no lawful visible means of support, which was interpreted as meaning no money or no job. For this crime the penalty was imprisonment. The English legislation was imported into Australia and in 1835 a specific colonial enactment was passed in New South Wales—quaintly entitled 'An Act for the more effectual prevention of Vagrancy and for the punishment of idle and disorderly Persons Rogues and Vagabonds and Incorrigible Rogues'. Other Australian colonies followed suit. The Vagrancy Acts also proscribed offensive or indecent language or behaviour. This too was used as a class weapon against workers.

Historically, Vagrancy Acts have been used by police and courts to terrorize the unemployed. However, during the quarter century of virtually full employment in Australia following World War II, attention was directed more towards nonconformists such as hippies and the beat generation. Moreover, charges of offensive behaviour were laid by police against political protesters, notably those who demonstrated against Australian participation in the Vietnam War. Ironically, many of these were middle-class people, who realized through experience that police and the state were not as impartial as they had supposed. The new perception helped to bring about some changes in the law, although Vagrancy Acts remain in existence in most Australian states. Modern governments, though they accept no legal obligation to provide jobs for all, acknowledge that an unemployed person in receipt of dole payment should not be convicted of vagrancy; yet it is still, in the eyes of the law, a crime to be penniless in the greater part of Australia.

4

Land and Labour:
Transporting the Social Relations of Capitalism

*It is the great merit of E. G. Wakefield to have discovered ...
in the Colonies the truth as to the conditions of capitalist
production in the mother-country. As the system of protection
at its origin attempted to manufacture capitalists artificially
in the mother-country, so Wakefield's colonisation theory ...
attempted to effect the manufacture of wage-workers in the
Colonies ... property in money, means of subsistence, machines,
and other means of production, does not as yet stamp a man
as a capitalist if there be wanting the correlative—the wage
worker, the other man who is compelled to sell himself of his
own free-will.*[1]

Free Labour

In the nineteenth century, the advance of capitalism in Europe
uprooted masses of people and transformed them into proletarians.
Their numbers were augmented as a result of improvements in medi-
cine and sanitation which cut down the death rate. Institutional barriers to the mobility of capital and labour were swept away, and as part
of the process millions of people emigrated—first from Britain and
Ireland and then from Germany, Italy, Russia and other countries. The
main attraction was America, where the prospects for land or jobs
were brightest. Between 1821 and 1850, more than two million

64

immigrants arrived in the USA, and this was far from being the peak of the movement.

Australia played a relatively minor role in this international migration, even after allowance is made for an odd feature of official statistics. Although convicts were counted as they were transported, they were regarded in effect as non-persons rather than emigrants. Disregarding the plain meaning of the word 'emigrant', British governments and subsequent historians classified as such only those people who left their native country of their own free will. Thus the emigration statistics show a total of about 195 000 people going to the Australian colonies between 1831 and 1850, whereas the actual figure, including convicts, was approximately 280 000.

However, it remains true to say that far more people emigrated from the United Kingdom to the USA than to Australia. Indeed, in the first half of the nineteenth century, the number of free emigrants to British North America alone (distinct from those who went directly to the USA) was appreciably greater than the number to Australia. The reasons were simple. The journey across the Atlantic was much shorter and cheaper than a voyage to Australia, and the American economy offered more opportunity. The USA, with a population of nearly ten million people as early as 1820, had a large internal market for produce and a vast amount of fertile land which could be bought from the government for as little as one hundred dollars for an 80-acre block. In the circumstances, special inducements were necessary to attract free immigrants to Australia. However, although the number was small in international terms it was high as a proportion of Australia's total white population.

Before 1831 the British government did virtually nothing to promote the emigration of free workers to Australia. There was little point in doing so while there was an adequate flow of cheap convict labour to New South Wales and Tasmania. In the 1820s imperial policy in relation to these two small colonies was mainly aimed at reducing the cost to government of the increasing number of convicts transported, so there was pressure to get them off government hands through assignment to private employers, who fed and clothed the convicts. For some years in the decade there was a ludicrous system of making land grants conditional upon agreement by the beneficiaries to take a number of convicts proportional to the size of the grant—as if assigned convict labour were a burden rather than a boon!

Along with the policy of minimizing government expenditure on convicts went official encouragement for small capitalists to emigrate to Australia. Such emigrants were tenant farmers from England and Scotland, army officers retired on half pay, younger sons of landowners and a sprinkling of lawyers and other middle-class people. Some hundreds of them went to Australia with their families each year. The 65 bait offered to them consisted of grants of crown land, which from 1818 varied in size according to the amount of capital possessed by the recipient. The land itself was virtually free, the capital being regarded simply as an indication of ability to develop the landholding. Thus the official scale in New South Wales in 1828 provided for a grant of 640 acres for an approved applicant with £500 capital, and proportionately larger grants for richer people. By then, too, the old system of making small land grants to ex-convicts had practically ceased. Incidentally, few women received land grants, whether as ex-convicts or as free immigrants, although there were some exceptions based upon class status: Governor Darling made a number of land grants as marriage-portions for 'the Daughters of Men of Respectability', especially clergymen's daughters, to improve their marital prospects. Daughters of ex-convicts were left to fend for themselves.

Although the emphasis in the 1820s was on the emigration of small capitalists, some British investors of greater substance also eyed Australian land. In particular, the Australian Agricultural Company was established in London in 1824 by a group of merchants and bankers. The company was based upon an official promise of a huge land grant with convicts to work it, and the venture represented the first resort to the London capital market to finance pastoral development in Australia. Most of the shares were held in Britain and thirty of the shareholders were members of Parliament. Actually, a number of years passed before much profit from the company accrued to its absentee investors—but one colonial capitalist, John Macarthur, who acted as local agent for the company in New South Wales, made an early personal profit by selling his own flocks of old or mangy sheep to the company at inflated prices.

Another instance of a big capitalist with interests in Australia had wider significance for the process of colonization. Thomas Peel, an English landowner, in 1829 developed grandiose plans in connection with the British government's decision to establish a new colony in Western Australia. The government intended to keep its own costs down as much as possible, and no convicts were to be transported to the new Swan River area. Consequently the onus was on would-be settlers to provide a labour force for themselves. As an inducement, they were offered generous land grants proportionate to their capital, including 200 acres in relation to each labourer shipped to the colony at the settler's own expense. In these terms, Peel initially envisaged financing the despatch of 10 000 people, together with provisions, in exchange for a grant of four million acres of land. In the event, these figures were whittled down to the point where Peel was responsible for about 500 people reaching Western Australia, in return for which he and his partner, a wealthy emancipist from New South Wales, received a grant of 250 000 acres. Peel, who emigrated to Western Australia himself, located the grant on poor land.

Peel's name has gone down in history, yet actually a number of other settlers in the new colony followed his example, on a smaller scale. They paid the cost of passages from Britain for workers who were indentured to work for a specified employer in the colony. In Peel's case the term of indenture was five years. Although each such employer secured some labour for himself, nobody had any idea as to the overall availability of labour in relation to capital. Unlike the familiar scene in Britain, workers did not materialize on demand as jobs were offered. There was an imbalance between colonial labourers and employers: labour was scarce and wages were high for those workers who were free to change employers. Furthermore, there was no imperial government subsidy, despite previous indications that state expenditure of one kind or another was essential for the success of any new colony. In Western Australia there was neither convict labour nor the expanded market for foodstuffs which such labour provided. By 1832 about 2000 white people had arrived in the colony and a million acres of land had been alienated from the crown, but only a few hundred acres were actually being cultivated.

The initial influx of people dried up, the economy stagnated and employers like Peel used up capital in procuring supplies for themselves and their indentured workers. Some masters, unable to feed or pay workers, voluntarily released them from their indentures. Other masters were taken to court to secure cancellation of indentures, on the ground that the employer was not fulfilling the terms. Indentures generally specified wages at rates lower than those obtainable on the open market so that it was in the interest of workers to break the agreements. Peel himself was sued by workers for wages which he had guaranteed to pay. It was a nightmarish situation for capitalists. Conversely, workers were well pleased, and this should be borne in mind before writing the colony off as a failure, as is customarily done by historians. One labourer wrote 'home' in 1832:

We bless the day we left England . . . I am at work brick-making . . . we work eight hours . . . we have no rent to pay, no wood to buy, we just go out of doors and cut it down . . . It is not here as in England, if you don't like it you may leave it—it is here, pray do stop, I will raise your wages.

This was the authentic voice of the common people. The viewpoint of the capitalist was expressed by E. G. Wakefield, who realized that the large grants of crown land in Western Australia were of little use to the grantees without labour to work them. Landowners wishing to sell land privately found that there was such a glut of it on the market that prices were very low, which presented opportunities to some workers. Wakefield saw that this kind of situation was a universal problem in colonies of settlement where there was an abundance of land. In the USA, one solution had been the institution of slavery. As Wakefield noted in his book, *England and America*, in 1833, 'where land is very cheap and all men are free, where everyone who so pleases can easily obtain a piece of land for himself, not only is labour very dear . . . but the difficulty is to obtain combined labour at any price'. In referring to 'combined labour', Wakefield urged the need to have a class of free wage-labourers, as he deplored the alternative of slavery. Nevertheless, the labour market must be regulated.

In developing these views, Wakefield used the situation in Western Australia to good effect. In that colony, he wrote, 'there never has been a class of labourers'; and Peel had been 'left without a servant to make his bed or fetch him water from the river'. Karl Marx later reproduced this last quotation from Wakefield and added his own mocking comment: 'Unhappy Mr Peel who provided for everything except the export of English modes of production to Swan River! . . . Think of the horror! The excellent capitalist has imported bodily from Europe, with his own good money, his own competitors! The end of the world has come!' Marx also remarked that Wakefield, whom he regarded highly as an economist, had found that

capital is not a thing, but a social relation between persons, established by the instrumentality of things . . . the means of production and subsistence, while they remain the property of the immediate producer, are not capital. They become capital, only under circumstances in which they serve at the same time as means of exploitation and subjection of the labourer.[2]

The apparent fiasco in Western Australia may have made a contribution to decline in general use of the indentured labour system, both there and in the other colonies. More important in the decline was the fact that from the 1830s the immigration of workers was subsidized by the state for the benefit of employers as a whole. Such free workers could seek work as they pleased. However, this was not to the liking of all colonial masters, and a brief reference to the later history of indentured labour is instructive.

A number of employers preferred the more comprehensive control over labour which an indenture provided, and they paid the passage cost for immigrants who agreed to work for a stated period for the employer, at wages specified in the indenture. Breaches of indenture could be dealt with in court under the Masters and Servants Acts. This legislation was biased against workers, yet there were legal requirements which often provided loopholes. One instance of this occurred in 1840, when the Australian Agricultural Company shipped a hundred Irish labourers to New South Wales for employment on its own estate. When these men arrived in Sydney they realized that they could obtain from other employers better wages than those fixed in their indentures, so most of the immigrants refused to travel up to the company's property at Port Stephens. The company took court action for breach of contract but the prosecution was lost on a technicality—the difficulty of proving signatures of witnesses to engagements entered into a long way off in the United Kingdom.

Undeterred, the A. A. Company tightened its labour recruitment procedures and continued to import indentured workers into New South Wales. Among them were coalminers needed for the colliery which the company operated at Newcastle. Thus one Welsh miner in 1853 bound himself to obey and serve the company diligently until he had repaid, through deductions from wages, the cost of £66 for passages to the colony for himself, wife and four children. As usual in such cases, the wages stipulated in the indenture were substantially below prevailing colonial rates, with the result that this worker and others like him proved to be 'difficult' employees. There was a related miners' strike at Newcastle in 1855.

Other employers experienced similar problems with indentured labour. Many such workers simply absconded, leaving employers bemoaning uncollected debts. There remained one set of circumstances in which employers found it useful to resort to tied white labour occasionally: this was when they were used as strikebreakers. An example of this was seen in Sydney in 1860 when a big engineering firm, P. N. Russell & Co., reduced the wages of employees. In reaction, a body of ironmoulders went on strike. Anticipating this, Russell had already arranged to import twenty-seven moulders from Britain on contract to him. The arrival of these men in Sydney had the effect of breaking the strike there, and the local Moulders' Club or Society collapsed. Of course the effectiveness of such action by employers depended upon planning and timing, and the outcome was not always as expected. Russell's imported moulders were not strikebreakers by inclination—they were simply ignorant about the colonial situation. They soon had grievances of their own, and moulders in 1861 joined members of the Amalgamated Society of Engineers in another strike at Russell's workshop. Many years later, Russell, who was childless, ensured the perpetuation of his name by donating £50 000 to the school of engineering at the University of Sydney, on condition that it be called the Peter Nicol Russell School of Engineering.

To say that, with such exceptions, the indentured labour system declined in the latter part of the nineteenth century, is subject to a further large qualification. It is not true of black labour, notably Melanesian islanders who were imported to work as indentured labour in the sugar industry of Queensland. Even in the case of Aborigines, who played only marginal roles in the capitalist workforce, the practice of indenturing was often adopted in Western Australia. The aim was not so much to keep wages low—in fact, little or nothing was paid to Aborigines—as to bring these blacks within the coercive scope of 69

Masters and Servants Acts if they ran away. Not only were Aborigines more easily deceived as they put their marks on documents, but they could be punished more severely than white workers. In Western Australia a white might be imprisoned for breaking an indenture, whereas a black could be sentenced to whipping instead of, or in addition to, imprisonment. This discriminatory treatment for blacks was covered by an Aboriginal Native Offenders Act of 1849, and there are cases on record of Aborigines being sentenced to twenty-four lashes each for absconding from employment. This was in a colony regarded from inception as being for free persons, although from 1850 to 1868, at the request of propertied colonists, it took in 10 000 transported convicts as a supply of labour.

Land

Labour creates value. Capital has component parts which, as Marx expressed it, 'are creations of labour, products of labour, accumulated labour. Accumulated labour which serves as a means of new production is capital.' Land is obviously a major natural resource for production, yet it yields little without the use of labour on it. In the circumstances of the Australian colonies, where Aboriginal landholders were dispossessed, a great expanse of land was available and its initial owner was the imperial state in the name of the crown. This sovereignty over land gave the state a dominant position in the process of settlement of the country but the price of undeveloped land was inevitably low—there was so much land relative to labour.

An intimate connection between land and labour was acknowledged freely in the colonies. Francis Forbes, Chief Justice of New South Wales, declared in 1829: 'Without labour, land in this Colony is useless'.[3] The nexus was institutionalized in the establishment of an official Land Board in Sydney in 1826—a body which was to handle both land grants and the assignment of convicts. The corollary was a system of conserving the free labour force by preventing workers from acquiring land for their own use. Such a policy was effectively in force before 1829, when E. G. Wakefield published *A Letter from Sydney*. He wrote the work in London's Newgate Gaol, where he served a three-year prison sentence in the comparative comfort available to convicts who could afford to pay for good food and facilities. Wakefield had abducted a 15-year-old heiress from her school, persuading her under false pretences to go through a form of marriage with him at Gretna Green. Money was the motive, not passion: the marriage was not consummated. Nevertheless, the anger of the girl's father resulted in Wakefield being put on trial and convicted.

70   Wakefield's criminal record seemed to preclude him from the

political career as MP which he had in mind. Accordingly, he turned his attention to colonies, seeking to enhance their attractions for ambitious, educated gentlemen of modest fortune like himself. He envisaged British colonies of settlement as extensions of the class structure of English society. In particular, civilization and the accumulation of capital required the formation and continued existence of a body of wage labourers. Wakefield elaborated his views within the framework of a systematic theory of colonization which put the economic interests of the imperial country foremost. Colonies were desirable for three reasons: first, because they offered an extension of markets for British manufactured goods; second, as providing greater scope for the employment of capital, the investment possibilities being more promising in the colonies than in England; and third, as providing a safety-valve from the dangerous pressure of population upon the means of subsistence in Britain.

Thus Wakefield presented a rounded, methodical justification for colonization, and his writings caught the attention of many influential people. The core of his argument was insistence upon the need to bar colonial workers from early access to landownership, to ensure that they remained available for hire, at least for a substantial period of time. Events in Western Australia bolstered the argument. In relation to New South Wales, Wakefield believed that free workers there too were securing land for themselves; and furthermore he reckoned that it was better for the government to sell land openly than to dispose of it by a system of grants which was inefficient and susceptible to corruption. The price to be charged for crown land should be fixed at a level high enough to prevent a labourer from acquiring land until he had worked, and saved from his wages, for a period of years. Wakefield was quite explicit about the aim. 'The object of the restriction on land, of a price being put upon land, is to prevent the labourer from being a freeholder too soon', he said.[4] Actually, there were great difficulties in deciding upon a precise figure for such a 'sufficient price', especially as theoretically it should vary from time to time in accordance with an appropriate balance between land, labour and capital. Wakefield avoided specifying a particular price per acre for crown land, although he once suggested that a figure of £2 per acre would be appropriate. In practice, he generally reckoned that the contemporary price, whatever its level, was too low.

Wakefield's views accorded very well with an important change in British colonial policy in 1831. This arose partly out of the fact that there was no longer any doubt about the future expansion of the wool industry in Australia. The industry could be relied upon to produce a valuable raw material for British manufacturers as well as employment in the colonies for both labour and capital. Thus continued emphasis upon official encouragement of emigration of capitalists to Australia

71

was quite unnecessary—the obvious prospect of profit was enough for them. A more important factor was recognition by the British government of a vital need to encourage the emigration of labourers. The social disruption attendant upon the Industrial Revolution in Britain produced such a surplus of labour that it became a heavy burden upon the state. Keeping paupers alive—even if only barely so in workhouses —meant quite high contributions from ratepayers. Beyond that was fear of the social menace represented by common people. In 1830 rural poverty led to serious riots by agricultural labourers in southern England, as a result of which 481 people were transported to Australia as convicts. In 1833 Wakefield drew the appropriate lesson with reference to free emigrants: 'one chief end of colonization is to prevent tumults, to keep the peace, to maintain order, to uphold confidence in the security of property'.[5]

The riots provided a background to the decision by the British government in 1831 to promote the emigration of labourers rather than capitalists—a policy which dovetailed neatly with the interests of colonial capitalists. As part of the plan, the Colonial Secretary, Lord Goderich (better known as Ripon) ended the old land-grant system in the Australian colonies. Henceforth, land was to be alienated from the crown by sale only, through auction at a minimum price of five shillings per acre. More was involved than the elimination of abuses in the land-grant system. It was acknowledged that it was not enough simply to arrange for labourers to go to Australia: in the interests of capital, they must remain labourers. The influence of Wakefield's views is evident in Goderich's instructions on the new land regulations. Goderich believed that in New South Wales there had been an

extreme facility of acquiring land, by which every man has been encouraged to become a Proprietor, producing what he can by his own unassisted efforts ... what is now required is to check this extreme facility, and to encourage the formation of a class of labourers for hire, as the only means of creating a Market for the Agricultural produce of the Colony, of effecting various improvements ...[6]

Wakefield considered that a price of five shillings per acre for crown land was too low for the purpose. As it happened, both Wakefield and Goderich, lacking any personal experience, were wrong about crucial facts concerning the situation in New South Wales. Without evidence they assumed that reported shortages of colonial labour were due to workers becoming landowners, whereas the basic reason was that the rapid expansion of the pastoral industry was demanding more workers. The primary importance of the pastoral industry also meant that land was needed in large units, and crown land was usually put up for sale in sections of 640 acres. In the 1830s, the cost of such a block was £200 or more on average. The real cost per acre to the big settlers who were the main buyers was much lower, because they bought river-frontages commanding back runs which they were then able to use without payment. However, this does not affect the point that a low price per acre for a large area of land was just as effective in keeping out prospective buyers with small means as was a high price for a small amount of land. Alexander Harris, who knew about colonial wages and land prices, wrote in 1847: 'If any one wish to be a servant for twenty years first, and then begin to farm, Australia is his ground'.[7]

The decision to charge a price for all crown land was naturally expected to produce a new source of revenue. This was welcome to the British government, which was then considering ways of subsidizing the emigration of labourers to Australia—preferably ways which did not entail extra costs for the imperial government. However, it was not anticipated initially that much money would be raised from the sale of land in the colonies. Consequently, in 1831 the Colonial Office, at the same time as it despatched the new land regulations to the colonies, put forward several suggestions as to how the emigration of labour to New South Wales might be materially encouraged. For example, revenue for the purpose could be raised from a tax upon colonial employers according to the number of assigned convicts they employed; or employers could themselves advance passage money to immigrants on seven-year indentures, recouping the cost by deductions from the immigrants' wages; or revenue from sales of land could be used to subsidize passages. As might have been expected, the New South Wales Legislative Council disliked the idea of a tax upon the assignment of convicts. Instead, the Council in 1832 appropriated £10 000 from the land fund, to be used to assist immigration.

In this way, revenue from sales of crown land came to be associated with the subsidization of immigrant labour, and the connection became permanent as land sales grew rapidly in volume. Historians with a fine eye for the perils of class analysis have tended to ignore or gloss over Wakefield's fundamental concern for the creation of a colonial proletariat: instead, they have emphasized the connection between Wakefield's views and the policy of state assistance for emigration. Yet Wakefield himself left no room for doubt on the point. The revenue derived from the sale of crown land was 'a mere incident', he said:

The object of the price is not to create an immigration fund. You may employ the fund in that way if you please; but the object of the price is to create circumstances in the colony which would render it, instead of a barbarous country, an extension of the old country ... Therefore I see no relation (it is easy to see one which is of no consequence, but I can see no proper relation) between the price required for land and immigration.[8]

Transporting a Working Class

The decision to substitute sales for grants in the alienation of crown land applied to all British colonies in Australia. However, it made no practical difference in Western Australia where, against the background of earlier generosity in grants of crown land, sales were negligible, so that there was very little revenue from that source to subsidize immigration. Land sales in Tasmania were greater but there too the effect of large land grants, compounded by the relatively small size of the island, was apparent. Thus the impact of the new land policy was felt mainly in New South Wales, where about two million acres of crown land were sold between 1832 and 1841; and a large part of the land fund was devoted to assisting immigration. If poor British emigrants were to be persuaded to go to Australia, it was necessary to offset the fact that a steerage passage to Australia cost about £18, compared with £5 to New York.

Financial assistance for poor emigrants to Australia began with a modest scheme to grant about half the cost of passages to selected young women. The aim was both to redress the disproportion between the sexes in the convict colonies and to meet a colonial demand for domestic servants. In 1833 the amount of government grant was raised so as to cover the full fare, and about 3000 women travelled to Australia under the scheme. They were subjected to much criticism in the colonies, on the ground of supposedly poor quality. Some female emigrant ships were filled largely with paupers, as English local government authorities seized an opportunity to get rid of workhouse inmates at little or no cost to the parish. Colonists for their part disregarded a point made by a Colonial Office official, that the word 'pauper' meant 'a redundant labourer, who may be either a good or a bad character—the redundancy being determined by the demand for labour as compared with the supply, and not by the individual characters of the labourers soliciting employment'. Actually this was an attempt to create a good image for export—it was not the way that paupers were perceived in the United Kingdom itself. In the case of females there was a sexual form of abuse in addition to the stigma of pauperism. Many of these women, like their convict sisters, were derided as prostitutes. Censorious clergymen, such as J. D. Lang, asserted that assisted female immigrants in the early 1830s rendered 'the whole colony, and especially the town of Sydney, a sink of prostitution'. In even more sexist terms, Lang claimed that 'one bad woman let loose upon society does infinitely more harm than a dozen bad men'.[9]

Although the aim of increasing the proportion of women in the colonies remained, the separate scheme to assist the emigration of women was terminated in 1836. In its place, emphasis was given to the

74

emigration of families conforming to certain criteria as to age and occupation; and those selected were provided, in effect, with free passages. Heads of families were expected to be mainly skilled workers or agricultural labourers. Initially, most of these assisted emigrants were selected and looked after by a government agency. However, there was a variant form, known as the bounty scheme, whereby colonial employers (or their agents) could be authorized to engage workers for themselves in Britain and to arrange for their passages to the colony. On arrival, if such an immigrant was shown to conform to the established criteria, a bounty—equivalent to cost of passage—was paid to the employer responsible. Thus individual employers were able to make their own selection of workers, although the colonial government bore the cost of importing those workers. On the other hand, as such workers were not formally tied to a particular employer, the procedure should be differentiated from the old alternative whereby an employer personally bore the cost of a worker's passage in return for a lengthy indenture of service.

These were the mechanisms through which assisted immigrants entered Australia. In addition, there were many other immigrants who had financial resources of their own and received no government assistance. Nevertheless, the importance of state aid is evident from the fact that about three-quarters of all the free immigrants who arrived in New South Wales between 1832 and 1851 were classified as assisted. Further, a change in the ratio of free immigrants to convicts was clear by 1837, when the number of free persons arriving in New South Wales exceeded the inflow of convicts—the first year in which that occurred. In the next five years, 58 000 free immigrants entered New South Wales, 48 000 of them being assisted. The magnitude of these figures may be gauged by relating them to the size of the colony's total white population, which was 131 000 in 1841.

The land–labour nexus which developed in Australia in the 1830s amounted to land being sold cheaply to capitalists, while workers were kept out of landowning; and the price paid for the land was used primarily to import workers for the benefit of employers as a whole, particularly graziers. From the viewpoint of employers, there could be no better way of spending the money. In the process, the imperial government relieved itself, at little or no cost, of unwanted elements of the British population. Two factors contributed to the assisted emigrants themselves gaining better living standards. The first was that, even if free passages to Australia were provided, they did not necessarily induce emigrants to go there rather than to North America, so that general prospects in Australia had to compete in attracting people. The second was that labour in Australia remained scarce, so that colonial employers were unable to screw wages down as much as they wished. On the other hand, they could seek a better quality of labour, 75 and this partly accounts for the resort to the bounty system by big employers. Actually, the unofficial definition of quality was peculiar. As a contemporary writer noted, in the eyes of graziers the ideal shepherd was 'an able bodied single man from an agricultural county, humble, ignorant and strong'.[10]

The large increase in emigration of free working-class people was also a prerequisite for the British government's decision to end the transportation of convicts to New South Wales. British prison reformers, humanitarians and others played a part in that decision, but the context was recognition of a need to speed the emigration of the redundant poor, which embraced both free workers and convicts. The supply of assisted free emigrants was much more elastic than the number of convicts, and in *A Letter from Sydney* Wakefield foresaw that convict labour would be insufficient for future colonial development. In 1835 more than 20 000 convicts in New South Wales worked on assignment for private employers, yet requests by the latter for many more could not be met by the colonial government. Governor Bourke then decreed that no employer could have more than seventy assigned convicts.

In Britain in the 1830s, Wakefield was associated with a group of well-to-do, thoughtful people known as philosophical radicals. They had links with older intellectuals like Bentham and James Mill—men who, with their emphasis upon the greatest good of the greatest number of people, and the paramount importance of free trade, may be regarded as the ideologues of industrial capitalism in the struggle against big landowners. While the philosophical radicals argued inside and outside Parliament in favour of free institutions and an extension of the right to vote, the particular contribution of Wakefield and his supporters was a strong advocacy of capitalist colonies populated by free people. The group influenced the decision taken in London to stop transportation to New South Wales as from 1840.

Propertied settlers in the colony were almost unanimous in objecting to the decision. They were happy to see an expansion of free immigrant labour but they did not want their supply of convict labour to be cut off at the same time, especially in circumstances of economic boom. They were little impressed by assertions that the ill repute of the convict system deterred emigration of respectable people to the colony. However, that argument was persuasive in London, where a British parliamentary Select Committee on Transportation considered the subject in 1837. One of those who gave evidence to this committee was a prominent settler, James Macarthur, who produced a thoughtful variant on the question of whether continuation of transportation was compatible with free immigration. Macarthur's opinion was particularly interesting because little hard evidence was produced by other witnesses to support the general argument based on morality.

Macarthur was in a good position to make judgements about different kinds of labour. As he told the committee, he and his two brothers employed 186 people on their estates in New South Wales. Of these employees, 130 were convicts and the other fifty-six were free or ticket-of-leave. Probably most of the free employees were immigrants rather than native-born, as the Macarthurs were quick to use the bounty system. Presumably some of the employees were married. James Macarthur made no mention of women but his brother William referred to thirty women working on the estate at Camden, together with 'ten to twenty children, from five and six years old, employed at wages from 3d. to 1s. per diem'.[11] Against this background of experience, James Macarthur reckoned that 'convict labour and free labour could not be combined on one establishment to any extent'. He said that the status of New South Wales as a penal colony 'has a tendency certainly to discourage respectable well-conducted families going to the colony'; and if free immigrant workers were not respectable in character, then 'not having the same power of restraining and coercing them as you have over the convicts, the evils resulting from such an emigration might be greater even than those of the present system of transportation'. The outcome would be 'either to render the situation of the convict such as would be no punishment, or to punish the free servant'.[12]

Evidently Macarthur's prime interest was in labour discipline. He was less concerned with the question of compatibility of convict and free labour within the bounds of one colony than with the feasibility of simultaneous control over both kinds of labour by a big employer. The growing shortage of convict labour, relative to employers' needs, made the problem more acute, and Macarthur concluded that 'free labour must be cheaper in the end than slave or forced labour'. He was almost alone among the landowners of New South Wales in supporting the proposal to end transportation of convicts, even though he did so reluctantly and with the qualification that it should be brought about gradually over a period of five years, so as not to dislocate the supply of labour. Other influential colonists also pleaded that, in the event of an official decision to end transportation, it should be implemented over a lengthy period of time. In practice this procedure was adopted. In 1838 the British government gave public notice of its intention to cease transportation to New South Wales in 1840, thus allowing time for colonial employers to step up the inflow of free immigrants, and convicts already assigned were not withdrawn from private employers when transportation stopped. They were left to work out their sentences, so that the effect upon the supply of labour was cushioned to protect employers.

Transportation of convicts from Britain to Tasmania continued. Indeed, there was a substantial increase in the number shipped to the   77 island in the 1840s. Even so, the flow was not strong enough to satisfy the requirements of the British government, which had second thoughts about its earlier decision concerning New South Wales and tried to reverse it. Attempts to renew transportation of convicts to New South Wales were greeted with approval by landowners and squatters, and James Macarthur himself adopted an equivocal position. He did not support transportation in principle but he favoured disguised versions of it, such as shiploads of 'exiles'—convicts who, after serving part of their prison sentences in Britain, were sent to New South Wales with conditional pardons. In reality Macarthur did not shift his position much, for even in 1837, while agreeing that transportation and assignment should end, he had said that it would still be desirable for the colonial government to use a large number of convicts on land clearance, road-building and other public works, because free labour would not engage in such irksome work except at high wages. He said that 'convicts so employed would become the pioneers to a better class of population'.[13]

Macarthur's day was almost over. There was a new radical element in colonial politics by 1850, when huge demonstrations by workers in alliance with middle-class people in Sydney induced the imperial government to drop plans to renew transportation. Macarthur fearfully noted the arousal of city 'mobs'. He told the New South Wales Legislative Council: 'The voice of the unthinking multitude is against me. There are amongst the working class some persons for whom the epithets mob and rabble are too good.'[14]

Free workers were objecting to the entry of convicts whom they regarded as competitors in the labour market—competitors who would be used by employers to depress wages. The urban masses protested and won. At last the weight of the working classes was beginning to be felt, a development which stemmed from the rapid growth of free immigration in the previous decade or so, coupled with the phasing out of the convict system. Employers were conscious of the implication of these changes for labour discipline, and the NSW Masters and Servants Act was amended in the 1840s. The main effect was to extend the scope of the Act to cover workers in squatting districts and to bring piece-workers such as shearers within the net of jurisdiction. Despite this, Macarthur and other capitalists remained caught up in an insoluble contradiction in their mode of production: while they were committed to expansion of capital and employment of more workers, in due course those workers asserted their own rights through class struggle.

5

Pastoral Capitalism: Locking up the Land

---

*If squatting lands are to be locked up under leases, this would
put an entire stop to Immigration; and would thereby prove
ruinous at no distant date, even to those who had acquired the
monopoly of the land; for, without a very extended and continued
introduction of fresh labour, what will the lands of the Colony
be worth? I will tell you. They will be worth nothing to any man.*[1]

Origins of the Squattocracy

In Britain from the 1830s there was rapid expansion of the woollen
manufacturing industry as machine-production spread and textile markets overseas were opened up. Consequently there was a great growth
in demand for wool as raw material for the English mills. Australia had
enormous expanses of land available for grazing purposes, and the
climate was favourable. Australian wool producers faced competition
in the English market, notably from German growers, but German
wool production declined as land there became relatively more valuable for arable farming and meat, while rents for pasture land rose. In
contrast, Australian pastoralists paid very little for their land, thanks to
benevolent governments. Thus there appeared to be no constraint
upon market demand for Australian wool, once the problem of quality
of fleece had been overcome by importing merino sheep and by 79

selective breeding from the stud flocks of such pioneers as Elizabeth Macarthur.[2] The volume of Australian wool exports rose from about 2 million pounds weight in 1830 to 4 million in 1835, 10 million in 1840 and 39 million in 1850. As a proportion of total British imports of wool, Australia supplied 20 per cent in 1840 and 53 per cent in 1850, while the German share in the British market declined correspondingly.

The massive growth of Australian wool production resulted not from technical change but from geographical expansion to fresh pastures and the multiplication of sheep. In 1829, for administrative convenience, the government of New South Wales proclaimed the existence of nineteen counties extending out from Sydney. Several other counties, notably including land around Melbourne in the Port Phillip district, were added to the list during the next decade or so. The counties were intended to establish the boundaries of location for the time being, as crown land could be granted or sold only in proclaimed counties. The aim was simply to facilitate the process of land surveying and to give the government some control over land settlement. The limitation of area was not intended to be permanent, nor did it appear unduly restrictive. Indeed, the boundaries of location comprised well over 20 million acres, and a substantial amount of this crown land was sold in the 1830s, mainly to established landowners. However, the pressure to profit from the wool boom impelled many graziers to move their sheep on to the inland plains beyond the boundaries of location.

The movement was extraordinarily rapid. Besides the general shift westwards, graziers pushed north from Sydney to the area later named Queensland; and they went south to the new Port Phillip district, later called Victoria. Also into Port Phillip flowed capitalists from Tasmania and Britain. By 1850 graziers were in occupation of the greater part of the usable land of eastern Australia. Most of the adventurers on the land were squatters, who simply took possession of unoccupied crown land beyond the boundaries of location. Initially they paid nothing for using the land, yet they did not act illegally, for the government of New South Wales did not prohibit grazing outside the counties—the government merely refused to sell crown land there. From 1836 Acts passed by the New South Wales Legislative Council regularized the position of squatters beyond the boundaries of location by requiring them to obtain government licences and by establishing a body of Crown Land Commissioners to supervise conditions. The cost of a licence was nominal—£10 per annum, irrespective of the size of the station—so that squatters paid practically nothing for use of the land. It was a tremendous bonanza, with the new landholders rendering no service to government or society in return. Capital accumulation was fast in these circumstances.

Yet grazing afforded no openings to poor men, apart from some stealers of livestock. Quite substantial sums of capital were necessary to enter the industry. To buy a flock of, say, 600 sheep cost about £1000 in 1838; and in addition there was a need for working capital, to pay wages and so on, until the wool was sold. Some capital might come through a partnership and some might be borrowed (though that usually required the borrower to have assets as security). Rural money wages of £20-£30 per annum, even if they did not go quickly into the pockets of storekeepers and publicans, were no basis for becoming a grazier. Most squatters seem to have come from the British gentry or tenant-farmer class: they were small capitalists, in much larger numbers than in the 1820s. For example, Niel Black was a Scots farmer who took over a run of 44 000 acres in the Western District of Port Phillip in 1840. In the name of Niel Black and Company, he represented a partnership of four men, one of whom was a Liverpool merchant, T. S. Gladstone (cousin of a future prime minister). The partners prospered greatly and Black was a diehard representative of squatters. He took advantage of Victorian land selection legislation in the 1860s to buy much freehold land, and he left an estate of £179 000 when he died in 1880.

Besides providing an incentive for such people to emigrate to Australia, the wool boom in the 1830s attracted the attention of bigger capitalist interests in Britain. One such group came to the fore in connection with proposals to establish a new colony in South Australia. E. G. Wakefield was influential in promoting this project. It was to be a free colony, untainted by convictism yet avoiding the mistakes of Western Australia. Land in South Australia was to be sold at a fixed price of twenty shillings per acre, and the revenue from these sales was to be used to ship working-class emigrants to the colony from Britain. The original plan provided for a colonization fund of £35 000 to be raised as a prelude to establishing a settlement at Adelaide. Actually, sales of South Australian land in Britain were languishing far below this minimum level, and the scheme was in danger of foundering, when G. F. Angas put up a new proposal. Angas, a merchant and shipowner, formed a syndicate of hard-headed businessmen. While supporting Wakefield's ideas in principle, these men had little concern for pure theory, especially if it conflicted with profit. Angas offered to buy sufficient land, though at a price of only twelve shillings per acre, to bring the colonization fund up to the required level of £35 000. The offer was accepted, and Angas's large purchase was transferred to a newly-formed South Australian Company, based in London, with Angas as its chairman. Then the price for future sales of crown land in the colony was restored to twenty shillings (one pound) per acre, and the first shiploads of settlers arrived in Adelaide in 1836.

81

Wakefield dissociated himself from the South Australian scheme. He considered the figure of one pound to be too low, and he described Angas's cut-price bargain as 'what is commonly called a job' (or, in modern parlance, a racket). However, this did not stand in the way of the South Australian Company becoming the most important force in the new colony. Its interests embraced land and wool, whaling, shipping and, through a subsidiary Bank of South Australia, finance. Between 1836 and 1840, 12 200 assisted emigrants were shipped to South Australia, many of them on vessels of the South Australian Company, together with 1600 emigrants who paid for their own passages.

British capitalist groups with interests in specific Australian colonies were sometimes in conflict with each other, as became apparent in 1838 when the British government decided to increase the price of crown land in New South Wales to a minimum of twelve shillings per acre. This decision was made in the context of ending the transportation of convicts and increasing the flow of free emigrants: in Wakefieldian terms, the Colonial Office argued that it was necessary to raise the price of crown land so as to prevent it from being acquired 'too soon' by the growing number of working-class immigrants. However, leading settlers in New South Wales, seeing no evidence or likelihood of workers moving into landownership, objected to the policy decision —they wanted to go on buying land cheaply. Their objections were overruled in London and there is reason to believe that this was because of the rival political influence of groups involved in South Australia. The South Australian Company wanted a higher price to be imposed upon crown land in New South Wales, fearing that otherwise the employers in the Port Phillip district of NSW would use their price advantage to offer higher wages to scarce labour, including workers initially brought from Britain to South Australia.

On the other hand, there were some important capitalists with interests in more than one Australian colony. For example, the Montefiore family was involved in a variety of business matters connected with several colonies, including New South Wales and South Australia. In particular, certain shipowners and merchants had strong connections with Australian trade. As emigration increased, so did the business of shipowners and brokers: in 1841 a prominent London shipowner, John Marshall, was advertising one large migrant ship sailing to Australia every month. Cargo business also grew rapidly as British merchants developed trade with Australia. The Australian market was small in volume but high in value per head of population, viewed as consumers of imported manufactured goods, as well as tea and sugar.

The wool trade gave the colonies heightened status in imperial eyes, as became evident in the struggle over squatting. A specific Australian interest group became established in London, constituting a powerful political lobby. As one historian comments:

Between 1835 and 1841, the Australasian trade suddenly broke through to maturity ... In 1836 the leading London merchants formed the N.S.W. and Van Diemen's Land Commercial Association. In 1835–7 the Bank of Australasia and the Union Bank of Australia were founded.[3]

These two English-based banks had substantially larger capital resources than existing colonial institutions such as the Bank of New South Wales, and it was mainly through the Union and Australasian Banks that capital was channelled into Australia to sustain the wool boom. British investors were attracted by the promise of high colonial rates of interest — 10 per cent on sound short-term loans and up to 20 or 25 per cent on less secure ones. Credit was thus readily available for graziers, although banks, regarding them as dubious risks, were very reluctant to lend directly to them, except in the form of mortgage on real estate. W.C. Wentworth, speaking as a director of the Bank of New South Wales in 1843, explained:

Mercantile paper is preferred in our bank, but ... [we] occasionally oblige settlers; not that they are in good odour with us ... they are certainly a very irritating set of persons, as regards the payment of their promissory notes and bills; they think if they pay them three or four months after they become due they behave tolerably well; the Bank is of a different opinion.[4]

Banks were indeed happier when dealing with mercantile paper, that is, making discounted loans on merchants' bills of exchange, which related to goods in transit. Such goods provided tangible security for a short-term loan. There was also some truth in the assertion that primary producers were slow payers. Yet there was another reason for the banks' preference for dealing directly with merchants: the bigger colonial merchants in this period were often directors of banks as well. In this capacity, merchants arranged bank loans for themselves and they then re-lent the money to graziers at higher rates of interest or commission. The advances to graziers covered purchases of supplies for stations, consignments of wool and so on. A large and growing number of graziers consigned their wool through merchants, to London or Liverpool; and until the wool was sold at auction there, it remained legally the property of the grazier. Consequently, there was a long interval of time before the grazier received the net proceeds of a sale, and merchants were important financial intermediaries in the process. Merchant capital provided crucial links in the wool trade. Colonial merchants themselves enjoyed commercial connections with firms in England and were thus able to draw upon the resources of the London capital market.

The Boom of the 1830s

As integral parts of the British Empire, the Australian colonies were affected by the British trade cycle, which itself was tied in to economic fluctuations on a global scale. As McMichael puts it, the Australian depression of the 1840s 'represented primarily a crisis in colonial pastoralism as a world-economic industry'.[5] The prosperity of the textile manufacturing industry in Britain depended upon exports of cloth, particularly to the USA; and a slowing of sales of British woollen goods in the American market in the late 1830s was reflected in a gradual decline in the price paid for Australian wool in London. From a peak of twenty-four pence per pound weight in 1836, wool prices dropped to only twelve pence in 1844.

The effect of the price fall was offset for a time by two important factors. The pastoral boom of the 1830s fed upon itself in certain respects. So long as geographical expansion continued, an influx of fresh squatters provided a strong demand for livestock. Established graziers derived considerable income from the sale of part of the natural increase in their flocks due to lambing. It was an ideal way of accumulating capital, requiring virtually no expertise. This was just as well, as many squatters knew little about the business of sheep-farming. One NSW grazier, E. Hamilton, remarked: 'What business have medical men, lawyers, or merchants, to become graziers? They rarely, if ever, visit their stations'.[6]

The wool trade was all-important in the colonies. As the scientist, Charles Darwin, noted: 'The whole population, poor and rich, are bent on acquiring wealth: amongst the higher orders, wool and sheep-grazing form the constant subject of conversation.'[7] Nevertheless, when the boom collapsed in the 1840s, it was the livestock market which was hardest hit, and to many graziers the loss of profit from sale of surplus stock seemed more important than the loss from declining wool prices. In part this was because the total value of wool exports continued to increase, because of a larger wool clip. This was the second main factor in the long continuance of the wool boom in the 1830s: in terms of income, a grazier could compensate for a fall in wool prices by producing more wool. Yet this might entail higher costs of production. As squatters pushed farther into the interior, transport costs grew heavier, both for wool hauled to a port and supplies carted to a station.

Labour costs also rose, as a result of increases in real wages during the boom and the ending of transportation of convicts to New South

84

Wales. Employers received encouragement from the concurrent increase in the number of free immigrants, but this source of labour was neither as cheap nor as reliable in outback areas as convict labour. Furthermore, the inflow of free labour was predicated upon revenue from sales of crown land to subsidize it; and the increase in the minimum price per acre of crown land in New South Wales after 1838 led to a sharp drop in the amount of country land sold. Initially this had no adverse effect upon total land revenue, as speculation was deflected into investment in town land allotments, which were relatively highly priced. This activity was linked to a further increase in the volume of credit on which the boom was based.

On top of these problems affecting the pastoral industry came the shock of a tightening in the London money market in 1839, due to economic difficulties in Britain. This led to an increase in interest rates and a check in the flow of credit for the Australian pastoral industry. Graziers' profits were squeezed; and when news of this reached Britain, investors there reacted by making heavy cuts in the export of private capital to Australia. Concurrently, owing to the ending of transportation of convicts, there was a substantial reduction in commissariat expenditure in New South Wales—in effect, a severe pruning of British government export of capital to the colony. Breaks in capital inflow undermined the colonial land boom and pastoral expansion. There is some uncertainty about the timing of changes in capital flow, as no official figures relating to capital transfer are available. There was normally a time-lag between developments in Britain and Australia, and a large excess in the value of NSW imports over exports until 1842 implies a continuing inflow of capital to balance the account. However, the trade figures were distorted by very large speculative imports of goods into New South Wales in 1839–41.

These particular imports were significant in themselves. Luxury items such as carriages, jewellery and alcohol (including champagne) featured prominently, and it seems that English merchants were dumping goods in Australia which they were unable to sell in depressed markets in Britain and the USA. Speculators miscalculated. A combination of drought in agricultural districts of New South Wales and the running down of the pastoral boom meant that colonial merchants were left with a glut of imported commodities which they could not sell at the prices on which their bills of exchange were based, so goods were sold at auction at very low prices, as colonial merchants were pressed by imperial merchants in Britain for payment. At the same time, colonial merchants in need of ready money turned to graziers for payment of overdue accounts.

These events signalled the end of the boom. In 1841 there was a liquidity crisis and a demand for cash, extending from merchants to graziers, and from banks to merchants as the banks in turn sought a 85 sharp reduction of outstanding loans. Pastoral expansion slowed and livestock prices crashed—which in effect meant a severe reduction of graziers' capital. Revenue from sales of crown land in New South Wales dropped from £324 000 in 1840 to only £18 000 in 1842, much to the embarrassment of Governor Gipps. Bounty permits issued by him were outstanding to the value of about £1 million. In other words, the colonial government had virtually promised to pay this sum for immigrants yet to arrive, although the land sales which were expected to provide the money had practically ceased. It was necessary to suspend assisted immigration for a time.

The Bust of the 1840s

Depression in the early 1840s affected South Australia and Tasmania as well as New South Wales. For the first time Australia was taught a major lesson about dependent development: the import of large amounts of capital encouraged rapid growth but the flow could be cut off suddenly for reasons which were beyond Australian control. Gipps reported to London: 'From a system, indeed, of nearly unbounded credit, the transition has been sudden to an almost total denial of it; and consequently persons, who can no longer get accommodation at the Banks, are obliged to dispose of such property as they may be possessed of at very depreciated prices'.[8] The loudest cries of anguish came from landowners and squatters, but the depression was felt most markedly in towns.

A peculiarity of sheep-raising was that, by comparison with arable farming, it provided employment for relatively few people in rural areas. Furthermore, barriers to crop production limited the growth of country towns. Many more jobs were created in the seaports where wool was handled and despatched: jobs for waterside workers, storemen and clerks, as well as sustenance for those with more prestigious occupations such as merchants, shopkeepers and lawyers. Thus the growth of such towns as Sydney and Hobart—originally administrative centres with good harbours—was reinforced by the wool trade. By the middle of the nineteenth century Australia was one of the most urbanized countries in the world. Most of the free working-class immigrants who arrived in the port towns in the 1830s stayed there and a number of small manufacturing industries developed. One important feature of the economic boom of that decade was a thriving building industry as towns grew. Artisans such as carpenters and cabinet-makers found work readily and a number of trade societies were formed by skilled workers.

Up to one hundred trade societies came into existence in the Australian colonies between 1830 and 1850. Membership was small—between twenty and sixty in each case—and none of the societies was long-lived. They were generally concerned with providing sickness and other benefit payments for members, although some societies also functioned as trade unions, engaging in collective bargaining and strikes. In the circumstances of the 1830s, the societies had some success and real wage gains were made. However, these were cut back in the following depression, when most trade societies, weakened by the depression, collapsed. Caroline Chisholm, famous for her efforts to place female immigrants in jobs during the depression, is less well known in her capacity as a critic of 'combinations' (trade unionism). She encouraged women workers to take jobs at low wages. Naturally she was lauded by employers.

The severity of the slump is indicated by the extent of unemployment and poverty in Sydney. There was an increase in begging on a scale not seen before, and there was one report of children eating potato parings found in the streets. In general disillusion, several hundred people used their meagre savings to emigrate to Chile in 1843: cheap passages to South America were available in ships which had brought grain and would otherwise have left Sydney in ballast. This extraordinary reversal of roles for a colony which traditionally depended upon immigrant labour jolted the local ruling class into the realization that official acknowledgement of the problem of unemployment was necessary. Further pressure came from a newly-formed Mutual Protection Society in Sydney, which collected more than 3000 signatures to a petition urging relief for the unemployed. Although most of the members of this Society were workers, some small employers were prominent in it, indicating the virtual absence of independent working-class organization as yet. The Legislative Council responded in 1843 by appointing a Select Committee on Distressed Labourers, which found that in Sydney alone there were at least 1243 people unemployed, with 2500 dependants. Thus about 10 per cent of the town's population were affected, including many building workers.

The colonial government provided some relief through public works and a special grant to the Benevolent Society of NSW. This body was a private charitable organization run mainly by middle-class ladies who doled out aid to the 'deserving poor'—in other words, hand-outs for those people whose misfortune was deemed not to result from any moral failing. In practice some of the undeserving also received crumbs to keep them alive, especially if they bowed and scraped sufficiently. A strong element of ideology infused philanthropic activities. Obedience to masters and acceptance of a lowly station in life were enjoined upon female servants, as shown by a book written by Lady Eliza Darling and published in Sydney in 1837. This work rationalized differences between rich and poor in the following terms:

God himself has appointed it, and therefore when we know a thing to be *His will*, we ought to be sure it is all for the best whether we understand why it should be so or not ... God ... gives different abilities to render some capable of serving others, and to some he gives wealth to enable them to purchase the good offices of those around them ... When you are in service ... Obey the orders which your masters and mistresses give you ... always remembering that it is their place to command and your duty to obey.[9]

Political Remedies for Men of Property

Among men of property—there were few women who could be so described—the main problem in the depression of the 1840s was to retain control over assets and avoid disaster as creditors pressed for payment. The problem was eased by a new Insolvency Act which came into effect in New South Wales in 1842. It permitted voluntary bankruptcy; and those debtors who were expected to be able to pay their debts in course of time were allowed to continue using their property. Dishonest debtors were often able to conceal their assets or dispose of them to wives and other relatives before going through a court. One of the biggest crashes involved the Sydney mercantile firm of Hughes & Hosking, which became insolvent in 1843, owing £155 000 to the Bank of Australia. However, both partners in this firm had earlier married into the family of Sam Terry, the wealthy ex-convict; and although Sam himself was dead by 1843, his widow Rosetta was a clever business-woman with an eye to the interests of her daughters. Despite the collapse of the mercantile firm, Hosking 'ended up no pauper': his wife had money of her own, and he was also saved by 'Rosetta's shrewd purchasing of properties before they were sequestrated as a result of his bankruptcy'.[10]

In its failure, the firm of Hughes & Hosking dragged down with it the Bank of Australia. The bankruptcy of this institution (not to be confused with the bigger Bank of Australasia) posed a serious threat to shareholders of the bank, as they did not have the privilege of limited liability: in law, they were responsible for the bank's debts, to the full extent of their own property. Among the shareholders were members of the Legislative Council—including merchants such as J. Lamb and landowners such as W. C. Wentworth and Hannibal Macarthur. In attempting to meet its own debts, the Bank of Australia foreclosed on some estates mortgaged to it, but if these properties were to be sold by the bank on a depressed land market they would inevitably fetch low prices. Wentworth had an alternative plan: in 1844 he piloted through the Legislative Council a bill which would permit the bank to dispose of its properties by a public lottery—a gamble which was expected to raise much more money. The imperial government, on moral grounds, vetoed the bill—although five years later some of the real estate holdings of the Bank of Australia were actually sold by lottery, without legal sanction.

Other banks also foreclosed or took harsh action during the depression, giving rise to considerable public criticism. One observer referred to 'the smashers (banks as they are called) of this place'.[11] Wentworth tried to turn the hostility to his own advantage by promoting a bill designed to force banks to reduce their rates of interest on loans to a maximum of 5 per cent per annum, with retrospective effect. This would benefit colonial debtors, including Wentworth himself. Although Wentworth was self-seeking and hypocritical in this proposal (especially in the light of his remarks in another context concerning the unreliability of landed debtors), he directed his action specifically against the English-based banks and overseas investors. He made emotive statements about 'Jews and usurers' having poured money into New South Wales in the 1830s. Wentworth's bill was defeated in 1843—banks had their own means of exerting pressure on members of the Legislative Council—but interest rates were in fact reduced voluntarily soon after. Overseas financiers were affronted by Wentworth's manoeuvre. When the Sydney manager of the Scottish Australian Investment Company reported to Aberdeen concerning Wentworth's bill, the company directors wrote back: 'You seem to have a pretty Legislative Assembly! resembling for the most part, in your description, the "Forty Thieves".'[12]

Many leading merchants and settlers were caught in the depression of the 1840s. Some survived after a fashion by resort to an old stand-by of the privileged classes: patronage. Thus Hannibal Macarthur, president of the Bank of Australia and nephew of old John Macarthur, succumbed to bankruptcy in 1848, but four years later he secured appointment as police magistrate at Ipswich, Queensland, on a salary of £250 per year. Others, such as Wentworth, rode out the storm. Wentworth's position is indicative of shifting interests and alliances among graziers. On the one hand he owned much land within the boundaries of location—yet it was heavily mortgaged, so that his equity in it was diminished. On the other hand Wentworth held stations covering more than one-quarter of a million acres in squatting districts. He occupied this land on annual licences, but was unable to mortgage it, as he did not own it. By the same token, however, the squatting land represented future security if he could hold on to it, even if he lost estates within the boundaries of occupation. There were many other landowner–squatters in a similar position.

Landowners versus Squatters

Differently situated was a body of old conservative landowners such as the Macarthur family. They had only marginal involvement in squatting and their interests centred upon estates within the boundaries of location. These interests were substantial: well over one-quarter of all   89 the sheep in New South Wales still grazed on land within the boundaries when the squatting crisis developed in the 1840s. Such landowners viewed the squatters (about 900 of them) with some distrust. Certainly the squatters were capitalists, like the landowners, but most squatters owned no land and had made no contribution towards subsidizing working-class immigration—despite which, as employers, they had equal access to the pool of labour. This factor influenced the proposals which Governor Gipps advanced to reform the squatting system in 1844. Revenue from crown land sales having dried up in the depression, it was imperative to tap an alternative source of funds from which to assist immigration. The squatters were an obvious target, not only because they paid so little in licence fees but because of the inequality and inefficiency which characterized the squatting system: some runs were much larger and more valuable than others, although each paid the same licence fee; and many runs were badly under-occupied, relative to their carrying capacity for livestock.

Gipps proposed to define a station or run in the squatting districts as an area of not more than 12 800 acres capable of carrying up to 4000 sheep; and a fee of £10 per annum would be charged for each station as so defined. A squatter who occupied a larger area would be charged proportionately more. Further, in order to give squatters more security of tenure, they would be given the option of *buying* a homestead block of 320 acres on each station, and such a purchase would guarantee the squatter's occupation of the whole station for a period of at least eight years.

These proposals, quite reasonable in themselves, provoked a storm of protest from the colonial ruling class, which operated partly through the Legislative Council and partly through a powerful Pastoral Association. To some extent the opposition to Gipps was due to the fact that the colony was only just beginning to recover from the depression. Even those settlers who acknowledged that it was a simple matter of equity for squatters to be charged more for their runs felt that the move was badly timed and would retard economic recovery. Leading these people on were large squatters such as Wentworth and Ben Boyd. If Gipps's proposals were implemented, these big men would be obliged to pay substantially more in annual licence fees: for example, Boyd squatted on about a million acres, which translated into well over sixty stations under the new definition. Even more serious, Boyd and the others would have to buy a homestead block on each station; and the price at auction was likely to be high, as the successful bidder would acquire not only 320 acres but the contingent right to occupy the whole station. The thought of vigorous competition made every squatter fearful. The Pastoral Asssociation advocated long leases instead, with an implied right to renew them in due course.

90

Crown Land and Privatization

Underlying the greed which was manifest in the struggle between the squatters and Gipps was a long-term question concerning the future disposal of crown land in Australia. Gipps aimed to maintain government rights to ownership of the great expanse of land in the squatting districts, as against the growth of customary rights on the part of squatters. Already squatting runs were being 'sold' privately—that is, occupation licences were traded with expectations of permanency. The imperial authorities did not object to such trading or to the use of the land for grazing purposes, provided that it was understood that at some future time the land would be required for crops, when it would be sold at a relatively high price, to the benefit of public revenue. The interests of future generations needed to be considered.

Thus the imperial authorities took a long-sighted view of crown land, in contrast to the squatters' concern to seize the land for themselves. Ironically, Gipps's plans came unstuck on the question of the official price for crown land. In 1842, some time before the squatting crisis erupted, the British Parliament passed an Australian Land Sales Act, which prescribed a minimum price of £1 per acre for crown land. The NSW auction system was extended to South Australia, but more important was the application of the South Australian price to New South Wales. Settlers there protested strongly against the increase. They argued that no land was worth so much for grazing purposes (a point which Gipps acknowledged) and that there would inevitably be a big fall in land sales and, consequently, in immigration. There certainly was such a fall. Gipps attributed it primarily to the general depression but landowners asserted that government policy was responsible. They went on demanding a reduction in the minimum price of crown land, not so much because they wanted to buy more land themselves as because they believed that the high price of crown land deterred prospective immigrants with capital. An influx of such immigrants was considered necessary as a boost to the depressed livestock market which affected all graziers.

Merchants, Graziers and State Power

The question of the minimum price was the most serious of several grievances which landowners voiced against Gipps. The significance of this became apparent when the squatters objected to Gipps's proposals in 1844, for the landowners joined them in a united front against the Governor. Antagonisms and divergencies between sections of the landed interests were set aside temporarily in a broad onslaught on

91

imperial land policy. Ordinarily Gipps might have expected support from landowners, but he did not receive it on this occasion. The Pastoral Association adopted opposition to a high minimum price for crown land as part of its policy, along with opposition to Gipps's proposals concerning squatting.

Apart from some muffled remarks from common people about 'land monopoly', squatters and landowners also received strong support from urban people in the struggle against Gipps. In particular, mercantile capital threw its weight behind its landed clients. Through the dominance of the wool trade, merchants were inextricably tied to the fortunes of graziers: if the latter were in economic difficulties, then so were the merchants. Gipps was isolated politically. His proposals were attacked in the colonial press and at meetings throughout New South Wales. In the process, there was some wild talk about arbitrary taxation and oppressive government, but this was in no sense a revolutionary situation. The colonial ruling class was accustomed to getting more or less what it wanted from the imperial government—there was a general convergence of interests—and if a strong-willed Governor insisted upon going his own way, the standard recourse for squatters, landowners and merchants was to make it clear to the British government that there was overwhelming opposition to that Governor.

That was done. More insidiously, Gipps's influence at the heart of the empire was undermined by lobbying from a pressure group. Representatives in London of firms engaged in wool manufacturing and trade, banking, shipping and other elements of 'the Australian interest' made approaches to the Colonial Secretary. The general theme was that it would be a mistake to force squatters to buy homestead blocks of land, as this would tie up capital which could be better employed in producing more wool. It would be preferable, it was suggested, to offer squatters long-term leases over the stations they occupied. Additionally, squatters favoured a resumption of transportation of convicts, which was engaging the attention of the Colonial Office at the time. New South Wales was emerging from the depression, and wages for free workers were rising again. For example, Ben Boyd, who was able to employ shepherds for as little as £10 per annum (plus rations) in 1843, was paying £30 in 1846.

After a bitter struggle, Gipps was defeated. His proposals for homestead purchase were abandoned. In their place, decisions by the Colonial Office in 1846–7 provided for squatters to be granted, without competition, leases of eight or fourteen years for their runs. At the same time the alliance between squatters and landowners in New South Wales disintegrated. Landowners realized, too late, that they had been outmanoeuvred by big squatters in negotiations in London. There the commercial associates of the squatters, who dominated proceedings, virtually ignored the question of the minimum price of crown land. In the upshot, that price remained unchanged at £1 per acre. The net result, to the landowners' consternation, was a likelihood of squatting land being 'locked up' permanently: not only were the squatters to receive long leases but if a future government decided to put squatting land up for sale, nobody was likely to buy at such a high price.

Triumph of the Squattocracy

This set the scene for a struggle to unlock the land in the following decades. For the time being the squatters were secure. The big men among them had good reason to rejoice. In 1849 there were in New South Wales five squatters who each held more than half a million acres of land and there were thirty-seven others who held more than 200 000 acres each. Between them, these forty-two squatters held 13.6 million acres of the total of about 73 million acres of land occupied by squatters in the colony. Squatters claimed that their efforts as pioneers entitled them to such broad domains. Actually, while some squatters were genuine pioneers, others pioneered by proxy, leaving the hazards and discomfort to overseers and employees. Ben Boyd 'bought' all his stations, already in existence; and many squatters spent much of their time in Sydney or Melbourne. There were others who preened themselves, like the squatter of whom it was said: 'He had only to go forth in the morning and get upon his horse-back and superintend, and fancy that he was very busy and take credit to himself for enduring the hardships of the bush.' [13]

For squatters, landowners, and others regarded as gentlemen, establishment institutions such as the Melbourne Club already existed, functioning with the traditional system of blackballing prospective members who did not measure up to conventional standards. Needless to say that included all those people who did the real work on stations — in New South Wales, some 16 000 shepherds and stockmen, comprising about 20 per cent of the total workforce in that colony at the census of 1851. Others beyond the social pale included a somewhat larger number classified as craftsmen or labourers (together, about 23 per cent of the workforce); and domestic servants, mainly female, constituting another 13 per cent. These groups, despite the difficulties they laboured under in the depression of the 1840s, were already noted for their levelling, democratic tendencies. One gentleman in the Port Phillip district, provoked by a servant's complaint that 'there ain't no pudding after dinner', noted in a letter that this 'scoundrel had precisely the same food as I eat myself'.[14]

Besides miscellaneous professional and other categories, the census noted two other sections of the workforce: people engaged in commerce, trade or manufacturing (15 per cent of the total), and a similar proportion occupied in agriculture other than grazing. The number of farmers was thus quite large. In terms of hard work and low standards of living, most of them should be counted as 'common people', and in the depression of the 1840s they seem to have suffered more severely than the graziers. For many graziers, a subordinate body of small farmers had uses: farmers produced grain and other commodities which graziers bought largely as rations for the workers employed on stations. The cost of this portion of wages could be kept down by exploiting a considerable number of farmers willing to produce at very low rates of return, using mainly family labour. So long as the growth of a proletariat (through immigration and natural increase in population) was not materially hindered, this position was to the advantage of graziers. Moreover, in the 1840s a number of landowners found it profitable to lease out part of their land to tenant farmers, who paid relatively high rents for it.

The growth of small farming was particularly noticeable in South Australia in the latter part of the 1840s, a phase of economic recovery. In contrast to the other Australian colonies, South Australia placed more emphasis upon wheat-growing. Suitable land lay close to the coast, so that transport costs were relatively low, as was the cost of clearing land in South Australia. Also, it was a general practice there to sell crown land in 80-acre lots, not blocks of 640 acres as in New South Wales. Thus a price of £1 per acre for crown land in South Australia— land used for agricultural purposes—was much less restrictive than in the other colonies. Many people with little capital were able to become farmers in South Australia. Wool-growing, while important there, was less so than in New South Wales, and the same was true of squatting.

The prospects for small farmers in South Australia played a part in the first substantial emigration of non-British people to Australia. This new strand consisted of German Lutherans, people of hard-working peasant stock who were subject to religious pressures in Prussia. They looked abroad for a new home for their community and Australia seemed a possibility, except that these Lutherans were poor and in-eligible for the British subsidy for emigrants to Australia. The gap was bridged by G. F. Angas of the South Australian Company, who per-sonally advanced a loan of £8000 to enable an initial body of 200 of the Lutherans to reach Adelaide. Angas may have had some sympathy for the group's religious dilemma (though he was himself a Baptist), but there was a very practical side to his action. In the first place, it was a case of 'philanthropy and five per cent', that being the interest rate charged by Angas on his loan. More strategically, Angas aimed to use the Germans either to bring down wages in South Australia or to work Angas's own land there.

Other groups of German Lutherans followed in the footsteps of the early immigrants, and many of them settled on land owned by Angas near Adelaide. Angas sold land to them 'on terms which bound them to him as tenants for more than thirty years'.[15] In one instance, Angas charged German immigrants £10 per acre for land which he had bought for £1 per acre. Spiritual support was also available: when some of the Lutherans were slow in repaying Angas's advances they were threatened with excommunication by their leader, Pastor Kavel, who supported Angas. The latter himself emigrated to South Australia in 1851 and towards the close of his life there he was said to be making charitable donations of £10 000 per year. An obvious point about such philanthropy is usually overlooked: heavy donations come only from those who can well afford them, and the means employed by the donors to accumulate such capital are often suspect.

By 1844 there were 1500 Germans in South Australia, and thousands more arrived in the next six years. Through unremitting hard work over many years, they were successful on their farms and in their close-knit village communities. As an ethnic rural minority, they led quiet lives, as did their Australian offspring until the First World War, when they were subjected to mindless abuse and discrimination by jingoists. Official chauvinism went to the length of altering all but one of the German place names in South Australia. The one exception was the capital city, named after Adelaide of Saxe-Meiningen, wife of William IV. Royalty, with its international ramifications, was in a class of its own.

In the later years of the 1840s, there was a return to stable economic conditions in Australia. Rapid pastoral expansion was resumed in New South Wales, and a novel feature was the exploitation of copper and other mines in South Australia. Growing demand for labour was reflected in a big wave of emigrants to both these colonies—a movement comparable in size to the earlier one around the end of the 1830s. As before, most of the emigrants were poor people who received government financial aid (funds were raised by pledging future land revenues), although there was also a strong element of encouragement to skilled workers and middle-class people. Inspiration for this came from private philanthropic organizations in Britain, such as Caroline Chisholm's Family Colonisation Loan Society which had links with London merchants interested in trade with Australia. Additionally, many newcomers around 1848 were Irish, victims of the potato famine and the callousness of the British government. Some were not free: a number of Irish female convicts were transported to Tasmania. One historian comments: 'Courting transportation was not unusual in Ireland especially during the famine. For many the gaols became a refuge where at least they would be fed.'[16]

Some convicts transported to Australia at this time were political prisoners: for example, 'physical force' Chartists found guilty of involvement in riot or conspiracy. Paradoxically, some police spies and informers who were instrumental in securing the conviction of such Chartists were given assisted passages and sums of money to enable them to emigrate to Australia. This was done for their own safety, their cover having been blown in court cases in England. It was the height of irony that the planned refuge for some of these undesirable characters was New South Wales, where people who betrayed their mates were generally regarded as utterly despicable.

Irrespective of the character of immigrants, they contributed most to the growth of white population in Australia in the first half of the nineteenth century. In 1851 that population totalled 405 000, more than double the figure for 1841. Incidentally, the squatters of the 1840s were very fortunate in the timing of their bid for control over land. They acted before the rapidly growing working classes—soon to be reinforced by a great number of gold-diggers—were able to establish strong organizations of their own. Up to this point the evolution of political institutions was designed basically to suit the interests of wealthy colonists. Thus the Legislative Council of New South Wales, originally consisting of persons appointed by the Governor to advise him, became a part-elected body in 1843: two-thirds of its members were elected on the basis of a property franchise. This was the forum through which Wentworth and other landowner–squatters attacked Gipps. At the same time the landed interests remained conscious of the British government's crucial role in upholding class relations in the Australian colonies. For well-to-do colonists there was little to be gained, and much to be lost, from demanding outright independence.

In constitutional terms, the local ruling classes sought to achieve responsible government—that is, government answerable to their interests. A widespread feeling that the imperial government was too remote to comprehend colonial conditions fully was exacerbated by the events of the 1840s. In particular, the decision to increase the minimum price of crown land to £1 per acre seemed perversely wrong to prominent settlers in New South Wales. Indeed, their prime concern was to secure a transfer, from imperial authorities to colonial parliaments, of control over crown land and decisions as to the use of revenue derived from it.

The British government accepted such dilution of its power in the 1850s. However, the changes arising out of the gold discoveries of that decade meant that the new colonial legislatures signified not only self-government but much more democratic forms of government than Wentworth, Macarthur and their cronies had anticipated.

6

The Rise of the Bourgeoisie

Changes in British Imperialism

Until well into the twentieth century, Australia remained firmly within
the orbit of British imperialism, and this fact calls for consideration of
Britain's position in the world. Britain transformed production and
trade in the third quarter of the nineteenth century. World trade
increased 260 per cent between 1850 and 1870; and Britain, as the
chief exporter, especially of capital goods, was the main beneficiary.
British capital organized a great outflow of iron and steel products,
while British labour and skills contributed to the spread of industrial-
ism to many parts of the world. Railways and steamships shrank the
boundaries of distance and time.

Britain's leading position as the 'workshop of the world' could not be
maintained indefinitely. In the last quarter of the nineteenth century,
competition from the USA and Germany developed. Britain's exports
expanded at a much slower rate than previously and her manufacturers
complained about falling profits. In the 1880s, British concentration
upon exports and overseas investment tended to switch from the more
difficult markets of Europe and America to parts of Asia, Africa and
Australia.

Class relationships in Britain were affected. Britain's early economic
prominence in the world was associated with the doctrine of free trade
and economic liberalism, the essence of which was that, if institutional

barriers to international trade were removed, Britain as the first industrialized country stood to gain. Further, the repeal of the Corn Laws in 1846, by lowering restrictions upon the import of grain into Britain, helped other countries to pay for their purchases of British manufactured goods.

This decisive victory of industrial capital against the landed interests was reinforced from the 1870s onwards, when reductions in transport costs made it possible for American wheat and meat to pour into Britain. British agriculture was badly affected: farmers' profits fell, and landowners were accordingly forced to reduce the rents charged for agricultural land. As against this, industrial employers gained from a reduction in the cost of living in Britain, which could be expected to result in less pressure by workers for wage increases. Nevertheless, the old landed aristocracy, despite erosion of its economic position, remained a potent force. Its representatives maintained a prominence in politics, the civil service and government which the new class of industrial capitalists was unable to match in a class-conscious society.

There were parallel developments in the field of finance. Free trade meant benefits to British merchants and financiers as well as industrialists. In particular, London became the financial centre of world trade. Merchant bankers and the London Stock Exchange concentrated upon handling long-term loans for governments or large corporations, paying little attention to the investment needs of the typical British industrial firm. Thus City of London interests, including insurance and shipping companies, established a power base of their own, linked to politicians. Another important link was between the City and middle-class investors, mainly in southern England, who put their money into the home and foreign stocks which the City promoted. This rentier class included many landowners.

Although these processes might be characterized as a merger between industrial and finance capital, it seems more appropriate in Britain's case to note the weakness of organic connection between banks and industrial firms. The real merger was between big financiers, enjoying high social status, and the aristocracy and gentry. The connection was strengthened by intermarriage, education at exclusive private (misnamed 'public') schools and Oxbridge, and dealings through government, the bureaucracy and the professions. Possession of a 'pukka' ruling class accent, often accompanied by an effete manner, was the passport for entry to a privileged 'old boy' network; and these sections of the ruling class set the tone for the gentlemanly British culture which in a political context was both flexible and, on occasion, ruthless. Much later, in the 1970s and 1980s, the same elements in society presided with equanimity over the dismantling of large sections of British manufacturing industry, unmoved by the horrendous effects upon employment.[1]

Economic Impact on Australia

The relevance of the foregoing sketch to Australia in the latter part of the nineteenth century may be considered first in economic terms. The discovery and exploitation of gold in Australia in 1851 had a great impact upon both capital and labour. Hopeful immigrants poured into the country and the white population almost trebled in a decade, rising to about 1 115 000 in 1860. Nearly half this total number were in Victoria, the new colony where the main gold discoveries were made. The newcomers were consumers as well as producers, and the great enlargement of the Australian market for commodities of all kinds was seized upon by British merchants and manufacturers. An additional factor was that on average the Australian consumer was relatively prosperous, so Australia became much more important for British exporters. Whereas in the years 1844–50 only about 2.5 per cent of all exports from Britain went to Australia, in the years 1851–7 the proportion was 9 per cent. In the 1860s the value of imports into Australia per head of population fell substantially, but there was some compensation in the form of a continued growth in population. Moreover, the Australian colonies continued to obtain most of their imports from Britain. The trade relationship between Britain and Australia was much tighter than was that, for example, between Britain and the USA, though the US market was larger.

On the capital side, gold was itself an important item. Many of the immigrants who joined in the gold rushes brought small amounts of capital to Australia with them, and larger amounts flowed in as banking capital. The great bulk of the gold dug out of the ground was exported to Britain, and banks expanded to take control of gold dealings as well as to finance the increased flow of goods. In the 1850s three new English-based banks were established to conduct business with Australia—one of them being the English, Scottish and Australian Bank. In addition, several new banks were launched in Australia itself, and these ventures are indicative of the fact that gold was a general stimulus to business within the colonies. Capital was generated internally and these years saw solid foundations laid for many subsequent fortunes. Usually, those who made money steered clear of the risky and arduous work of digging for gold; instead they went for more profitable openings in activities associated with the goldfields. For example, F. G. Dalgety, a Melbourne merchant, made £150 000 in the three years from 1852 in dealings in gold and property; in Sydney, T. S. Mort's

99

fortune was firmly based on speculative gains and commission profits made during the inflation of the 1850s; Alfred Felton did well out of carting goods to the Victorian goldfields before establishing himself as a merchant and drug manufacturer; and James Tyson is said to have made £200 000 by droving his cattle to the Victorian diggings, to be slaughtered for butcher's meat. When he died in 1898, Tyson's pastoral estate realized £2 million.

Gold remained an important Australian export in the 1860s. Indeed, in that decade, as in the previous one, its value was greater than that of wool. Actually, that fact rather undervalues the continuing importance of the pastoral industry, as many pastoralists found good internal markets for their livestock on goldfields in the 1850s. In the following decade the emphasis returned to wool and there began a tremendous expansion of wool production, lasting until the 1890s. Initially this rapid growth was due mainly to an extension of the industry to fresh land and an increase in the number of animals pastured on it: livestock, through natural increase, provided a special form of capital accumulation for graziers. Then high wool prices in the 1870s provided an incentive for heavy capital investment on pastoral properties. A massive amount of fencing was erected on outback stations, while expenditure on wells, dams and artesian bores conserved water supplies. The number of sheep in eastern Australia (NSW, Victoria and Queensland) rose from about 17 million in 1860 to 104 million in 1891.

British Investment Flows

Wool as a raw material was needed for the mills of England, and this was undoubtedly the Australian commodity which most attracted British capital and made Australia part of the international division of labour. A great amount of capital from Britain poured into Australia for investment, both in the pastoral industry and in other sectors of the economy. The inflow resulted in part from conditions in the British capital market. The rate of return upon safe investments outside Britain was substantially higher than upon similar investments within that country. There was no shortage of capital in Britain, and profits and interest rates there were particularly low in the 1880s: British government consolidated bonds were converted from 3 per cent to 2.75 per cent interest in 1888. Thus Britain exported capital to various parts of the world; and the Australian colonies were specially favoured because of the strategic nature of the wool industry, strengthening their evident creditworthiness. Indeed Australia was the most important overseas borrower of British funds between 1877 and 1886. While the ordinary rate of interest paid on bank deposits in Britain was about 3 per cent per annum, Anglo-Australian banks and other financial institutions with offices in Britain were offering 4 or 5 per cent for fixed deposits — and the money could be readily lent in Australia at returns of between 8 and 10 per cent. Similarly, there was an appreciably higher rate of return on colonial government bonds issued on the London Stock Exchange than upon British government issues.

There were indirect as well as direct gains to be derived by British capital from investment in Australia. Investment and trade were intimately linked. To take a simple illustration, the colonial governments raised loans in London which were mainly used to finance the building of railways in Australia; and the iron and steel rails, as well as most of the locomotives, were imported from Britain. Important questions arise as to the nature of the connection between British capital and the Australian colonies. Was the nexus exploitative in the sense of being detrimental to the interests of Australians, both capitalists and workers? Was Australia a victim of British imperialism or simply an acquiescent junior partner? [2]

In considering these questions, it may be noted first that Australians were certainly not oppressed and hunger-driven in the way that was common in tropical areas of the British Empire. Despite the existence of notorious black spots, Australian standards of living were reckoned to be generally higher than those in Britain itself in the second half of the nineteenth century. Secondly, whilst approximately three-quarters of Australian imports at this time came from Britain, this was because that country was usually the cheapest available source of supply of manufactured goods. For the same reason the Australian colonies relied upon the London money market for imports of capital: loans could be raised there more easily and cheaply than anywhere else, especially after the British Parliament passed a Colonial Stock Act in 1877 which facilitated colonial access to the money market.

In the colonies, opportunities for profit were often limited by a shortage of capital from Australian sources, hence the resort to imported British capital. If that capital were used to produce benefits greater than its cost to the borrower — for instance, by increasing productivity in the pastoral industry — the use of the capital could be justified. Moreover, in cases where loans were not used wisely, the initiative and responsibility usually lay with the borrower, not the lender. In a broader setting, the major part of Australian borrowing overseas was invested in projects such as the construction of railways, bridges and buildings — that is, the provision of long-lived assets in which there was inevitably a considerable lapse of time before their operation provided an adequate return on the capital cost. There was a great amount of such investment in the Australian colonies, requiring long-term loans from Britain.

For the Australian economy as a whole, the practical effect of these developments was that the inflow of capital financed a high rate of 101 import of goods from Britain without need for a commensurate increase in the value of Australian exports. Severe balance of payment crises were thus avoided until the 1890s. Economic historians refer to the period from 1860 to 1890 in Australia as 'the long boom'—a period of sustained growth and capital accumulation. The characterization is primarily in terms of investment, and between one-third and one-half of all new investment during the long boom was accounted for by capital from Britain. Ironically, while British capital contributed much to the economic growth of Australia in the 1880s, Britain itself was in a depressed condition, with unemployment rising. Capital was highly mobile, though its possessors were unmoved by conscience.

The Age of Growth

Applying criteria wider than simply investment, the period of the long boom can be reasonably stretched to include the 1850s, so that there were four decades of rapid growth and comparative prosperity from 1851. The period more or less coincided in time with Britain's heyday as an industrial nation; and Britain could even afford to allow the Australian colonies, if they wished, to establish protective tariffs on imported goods—provided that such tariffs did not discriminate against goods from Britain in relation to goods from foreign countries. There were some colonial moves towards protection, especially in Victoria, where David Syme, editor of the *Age*, wrote in a leader:

The doctrine of 'Free Trade' is not science but cant, and cant of that kind which is meant to fill the pockets of its originators at the expense of its dupes . . . Let us beware of being bled to death like Ireland—of being any longer phlebotomized to fill the pockets of an oligarchy which treads down Englishmen as it does Irishmen when they stand in its way.[3]

Syme was not the only influential colonist to resent English dominance, and from time to time there were conflicts of interest between colonial and imperial capitalists. For example, many graziers were critical of heavy marketing charges imposed by London wool merchants; and on this point the graziers received some support from colonial merchants such as Richard Goldsbrough in Melbourne, whose interests lay in expanding wool sales in the colonies rather than at auction in London. Some antagonism also developed between local shipowners, mainly engaged in coastal trade, and the big British shipping companies which were primarily concerned with deep-sea trade between Britain and Australia but which also, as part of the process, carried goods and passengers from one Australian port to another. The picture was complicated by the fact that the main intercolonial shipper, the Australasian United Steam Navigation Company (AUSN), became a subsidiary of the London-based British India Steam Navigation Company in the 1880s.

British Immigrants

Despite differences, British and Australian interests on the whole complemented each other. On the Australian side there was a vital need to expand the workforce. Between 1861 and 1891 the population of Australia increased by about 160 per cent to a level of more than 3 million people. About 40 per cent of the increase was due to immigration, the proportion being substantially higher than this in the 1850s and 1880s. Most of the immigrants came from the British Isles, and most were single men and women who went straight into the Australian workforce. Thus the Australian colonies were still heavily dependent upon labour as well as capital from Britain.

British immigrants brought with them a network of values, customs and institutions. Some of these—notably trade unions—were not to the liking of Australian employers. Indeed, Benjamin Disraeli's perception of 'two nations' co-existing in England had meaning for Australia also. If the term 'culture' is used to describe a whole way of life, then there was more than one culture in each country. The rich had little conception of how the poor lived. Nevertheless, at all levels of Australian society, except among the Irish, there was a marked pro-British sentiment, which remained in evidence despite a growth of nationalism and republicanism towards the end of the nineteenth century. Support for the imperial country was underpinned by emphasis upon patriotism and 'the Empire' in Australian schools.

Sentiment found practical expression in a variety of ways. Officials in the NSW Railway Department were influenced in their habit of placing orders for locomotives in England rather than in the USA by their personal familiarity with British workshop conditions and products; and although Australian workers had less occasion than their social 'superiors' to exhibit a cultural cringe in relation to the imperial country, a broad sympathy for British people sometimes took unexpected forms. When London dockers in 1889 engaged in a historic strike against inhuman working conditions, Australian donations to support the strikers were extraordinarily generous: more money was collected in Australia than in Britain itself. Australian trade unions initiated the fund-raising, but the response was by no means confined to workers. It seems likely that for many donors sympathy was combined with an implicit expression of their own superiority: they felt that they had done better for themselves than had those people who stayed in the 'home' country.

103

In short, Australians did not regard themselves as victims of British imperialism. The feeling was justified: in terms of increased production and improved living standards, Australia on the whole benefited from the link with Britain. Without the capital from overseas the Australian colonies would not have developed as quickly and evenly as they did—at least until the 1890s. It was a different story in that decade, when British moneylenders called a halt and there was severe depression in Australia. Even so, a few years later most Australians were caught up in the jingoism of the Boer War, just as people in Britain were.

Public Capital Formation

Between the 1850s and 1890, economic growth in Australia signified far more than an extension of sheep-walks and goldmining. Railways were built, houses and other structures were erected in cities to accommodate the growth in population and trade, and manufacturing and service industries developed there also. In particular, the significance of extensive railway-building in such a vast country is obvious. The problem was to find the capital to finance railway construction, for there was usually a long period of time before traffic on a line grew to the point where the investment became profitable. Private enterprise tried to overcome the difficulty and failed. The first attempt was made by the Sydney Railway Company, established by a group of businessmen, including T. S. Mort and John Fairfax (proprietor of the *Sydney Morning Herald*), who visualized the importance of railways for expanding trade. They took the precaution of securing from the NSW government a guarantee that an interest rate of 5 per cent would be paid, from public funds if necessary, on about £100 000 capital raised for their project.

Construction began in 1851. The line was designed to run only a short distance initially, between Sydney and Parramatta, but before Parramatta was reached the company collapsed under the weight of construction costs much greater than expected: wages for construction workers rose sharply in the circumstances of the gold discoveries. In 1855 the colonial government took over and completed the line, while paying very generous compensation to the shareholders who had 'risked' their money. The railway was saddled with a big capital debt. This episode set the pattern for the railway future in all the Australian colonies. Apart from a few short lines, private railway projects were unsuccessful, even when they were not hamstrung by the abnormally high construction costs of the gold period. Colonial governments either took over or themselves initiated railway projects and then operated them as public enterprises. By the end of the nineteenth century, more than 10 000 miles of railway track had been laid down in Australia.

There was nothing 'socialist' about this. On the one hand capitalists generally recognized the advantages to themselves from the lowering of costs brought about by railways. On the other hand there was a lack of private capital for investment in a sphere which promised little direct profit to businessmen. Resort to the state and to public capital was an obvious solution, especially as colonial governments were able to raise loans on the London capital market at much lower rates of interest than private borrowers could. Australian authorities used their high credit standing to borrow at interest rates of only 3 to 4 per cent. About 70 per cent of all Australian borrowings through the London Stock Exchange were by colonial governments and munici-palities; and the outstanding public debt of the Australian colonies rose from £11 million in 1861 to £155 million in 1891. About two-thirds of the public borrowing was applied to railway building, the remainder going to such projects as telegraphs, tramways, water and sewer-age.

Public capital formation, then, was very considerable. As a propor-tion of total investment (derived from both domestic and overseas sources), the public sector accounted for about one-third in the 1860s and 1870s, and more than 40 per cent in the 1880s. This extensive involvement in the economy raises questions as to the role of the state in the Australian colonies. There was not a simple duplication of the British situation. In Britain the triumph of free trade led to the dis-mantling of much of the apparatus of bureaucratic regulation of the economy. Laissez-faire was the dominant doctrine, and the function of the state was regarded as little more than that of maintaining law and order—not an onerous task in the third quarter of the nineteenth cen-tury, when British workers were far from being a threatening force. In Australia the position was similar in some respects: for example, police and armed forces were small in size. Yet Australian governments were never laissez-faire. The ruling classes saw the proper function of gov-ernment as being to provide all possible assistance to private capital—that is, themselves.

Although the building of railways was done by private contractors working to government specifications, to operate the lines colonial governments had themselves to become large employers—of men in railway workshops as well as station staff and the like. The number of public servants also grew rapidly as governments concerned them-selves with the regulation of many other areas of the economy. This was apparent in the sphere of immigration. Even in the gold years of the 1850s, when hundreds of thousands of immigrants needed no encouragement for their journeys, colonial governments gave full or partial financial assistance to many thousands of others—including 500 navvies brought in to work on the Sydney railway project. When the colonies gained self-government, they no longer allocated a set proportion of revenue from land sales for the assistance of immigration. Nevertheless, governments continued to spend money from consolidated revenue for this purpose, and more than half the immigrants between 1861 and 1900 received public assistance in paying for their passages. Government aid, in the interest of employers, was usually greatest at times of severe labour shortage.

The extent of government involvement was indicated in Victoria by the commissioners on the civil service in 1859:

the Government of this country is compelled to conduct the business of a great landowner—to survey, to lease, and to sell its property ... to form railways and electric telegraphs; to assist municipalities, road boards, mining boards, and charitable institutions; to establish and supervise lighthouses, lunatic asylums, pounds, and cemeteries, and to do many other acts which in older countries possessing similar institutions are effected either through private enterprise or through local exertion.[4]

This feature of colonial life is characterized by N. G. Butlin as a 'partnership' between the state and the private sector, with governments supplying 'large scale overhead facilities and services designed to provide massive aid in the development of private enterprise, particularly in rural activity'.[5] However, this interpretation implies that the state was an independent force in its own right, that it chose to ally itself with private interests and could presumably break away from them if governments felt so inclined. This is misleading. It is true that various interest groups in the colonies conflicted with each other at times: merchants in conjunction with graziers were opposed to manufacturers over the question of free trade or protection; and squatters fought against other classes to preserve their privileged position. There were struggles for control of government policy and when opposed forces were evenly matched the state was required to perform a balancing act. Even the interests of workers were occasionally taken into account. Thus if trade unionists in times of depression demonstrated their objection to government aid for immigration loudly enough, the allocation of public funds for that purpose was reduced.

In effect, then, the state (using that term to comprise a set of administrative institutions, political parties and dominant classes, as well as police, army and judiciary) had some autonomy in decision making. Yet the underlying reality was that colonial society was capitalist. There was never any doubt about this, particularly at times of crisis, and sections of the capitalist class operated accordingly, using the state for their own ends. Most of the state endowment of land was ripped off, subsidies of public money were gained for a variety of private purposes, and political influence was at a premium. Most

106

obviously, decisions to build a particular railway line, where to locate it and where to establish stations, were of vital importance to local landowners, real estate agents and other businessmen.

Actually, despite repeated incidents of corruption, the history of government railway departments in Australia compares very favourably with privately owned railways in the USA in the latter part of the nineteenth century. Not content with subsidies in the form of grants of millions of acres of public land, American railroad magnates like Jay Gould proceeded to exploit both the farmers who were their customers and, through financial manipulation, shareholders in the railroad companies. Capitalism in Australia was triumphant but not so vicious, the difference being partly a reflection of the relative strength of the Australian working class.

Private Capital Accumulation

As noted earlier, capital imported into Australia from Britain up to about 1890 was directed primarily into the pastoral industry and railway-building. Emphasis upon the importance of this capital inflow is justified by the central significance of these two sectors of the economy, but this tends to obscure the obverse point that an even higher proportion of capital accumulation was generated domestically. Australian businessmen made profits and re-invested part of them. The pastoral industry was no exception: in the 1870s high wool prices meant high profits which were ploughed back into pastoral properties to the extent that the borrowing of capital from overseas was relatively small for most of that decade. By the 1880s Victorian capitalists were investing heavily in pastoral stations in western New South Wales and Queensland, as well as sugar plantations in the latter colony and silver–lead mines at Broken Hill.

At lower levels of capital formation, small farms and manufacturing plants developed mainly on the basis of the ploughing back of profits. Banks were generally unwilling to make long-term loans to them, although short-term overdrafts might be automatically renewed for those whose prospects seemed sound. Inheritance was important in some cases. In mining also, local investors were the main source of capital. Above all, Australian capitalists invested in the enormous growth of Australian cities. The proportion of Australian population living in the six capital cities rose sharply between 1861 and 1891. In the case of Melbourne, the increase was from 125 000 to 473 000, so that by 1891 four out of ten Victorians lived in the capital. Concentration of this nature called for a great amount of new building, especially in the outer suburbs of Melbourne and Sydney.

107

House-building was one of the main outlets for investment in Australia at this time. Most of the occupants of the dwellings were tenants, and the landlords were usually quite small capitalists, owning only a few houses each. Typically, landlords were builders, shop-keepers or small manufacturers. Besides a return of about 10 per cent on housing investment, there was a prospect of capital gain. Indeed, a large element in growth of capital in the colonies came simply from increase in urban land values, associated with the growth in population. This capital increment accrued to the bourgeoisie without effort, although it depended vitally upon the institution of private ownership of land.

The Mercantile Class: Leading Force of the Bourgeoisie

Money-making was the dominant motif of Australian society in the latter part of the nineteenth century. It affected all classes, being natu-rally more prominent among members of the bourgeoisie: a term which is useful in broadly denoting the owners of the means of produc-tion in capitalist society, marking them off from the proletariat. For purposes of class analysis it is necessary to look closer, to distinguish various sections of the bourgeoisie from each other, although this pro-cess can be confused by the common use of the term 'middle classes' as synonymous with 'bourgeoisie' or 'capitalist class'. Ambiguity arises from the fact that the middle classes are generally considered to include professional people such as doctors, some of whom (through investments) are capitalists, while others—especially the younger ones—are not.

'Middle class' of course implies the existence of a class above, as well as one below. In Europe the term had meaning in relation to the old aristocracy, but in Australia there was no such survival from feudal times. In the 1850s W. C. Wentworth argued for the creation of an Australian peerage whose representatives would constitute the upper house of the Parliament of New South Wales, but the proposal died in a deluge of public scorn poured on the idea of a bunyip aristocracy. There were jeers about My Lord Pinchgut, the Marquis of Woolloomooloo, Botany Bay magnificos and so on. Certainly, some wilting or dissolute offshoots of the British aristocracy found their way to Australia from time to time. Indeed the civil service of Victoria during the goldrush years was 'packed with drones . . . the hours [of work] were generally ten to three!' [6] The authoritarianism of officers and goldfield com-missioners bore much of the responsibility for the armed rising by resentful diggers at Eureka in 1854.

At the apex of polite society, the tone was set by the Governors and their entourages—well-bred parasites equipped with visiting cards who lorded it over the local barbarians. One old Harrovian, R. C. Gallop, wrote home in 1886:

I don't care much for Melbourne Society; they are a very young growth, having made heaps of money very fast. [At the Melbourne Club] they stink of money. They dress 'loud' talk 'loud' . . . and can drink nothing but champagne . . . In a London Club half the men would be 'barred' and nearly half the rest would be considered 'bad style'.[7]

Actually, Gallop's class-mates back in Britain at this time did not regard it as bad form to take seats on the London boards of Australian land companies: in effect, they lent their titles for directors' fees. On the whole, however, such decorative figures were of importance in colonial society only in reinforcing the position of landowners and squatters. Members of this landed class aped the manners of their counterparts in England. As Anthony Trollope wryly observed about sheep stations in New South Wales in 1873:

The number of sheep at these stations will generally indicate with fair accuracy the mode of life at the head station: 100,000 sheep and upwards require a professed man-cook and a butler to look after them; 40,000 sheep cannot be shorn without a piano; 20,000 is the lowest number that renders napkins at dinner imperative.[8]

Along with snobbery among landowners went a marked antipathy towards democracy. Niel Black, one of the most prominent graziers in Victoria, wrote privately in 1861 that 'a lazy, idle vagabond democracy is making war against capitalists, striving by political influence to become possessors of the wealth which others created by industry, toil and perseverance'. Black's forebodings were evidently unfulfilled, for ten years later he wrote that sheep men were 'wallowing in wealth not knowing what to do with their income'.[9]

Some squatters' money was invested in other sectors of the economy. Many invested in mining, for example. Members of the original board of directors of the Broken Hill Proprietary Co. Ltd (BHP) in the 1880s—people like Bowes Kelly—were essentially wool men. Some profits from landholding also went into banking and insurance. W. J. T. Clarke, one of the largest landholders in Victoria—where he was generally referred to as 'Big' or 'Moneyed' Clarke—was a large shareholder in, and director of, the Colonial Bank of Australia. When he died in 1874 he left an estate worth some £2.5 million, and his son was governor of the Colonial Bank for the following twenty years.

Despite such instances, capital usually flowed the other way, in the

109

form of loans from banks and pastoral finance companies to squatters to enable them to extend their operations and to buy land. Security for the loans came from mortgages on the land, with the result that a large proportion of graziers became heavily indebted. The extent of this was not evident before the depression of the 1890s, for in good times the financiers did not intervene in the management of stations. Nevertheless, the independence of squatters was basically undermined; and to this factor was added the broad public hostility towards the squatters for their greed in seizing control of great areas of land.

Unlike a number of landed aristocrats in Britain, Australian landowners, though they often had imposing residences in towns, were not urban landlords on a large scale. There were no rent-rolls of town property at all comparable with those of, say, the Duke of Westminster in London. A more significant difference between the two countries is that the Australian landed class contributed very little to the culture of its own country, except perhaps in the style of country residences. The political role of the landowner-squatters, especially through the conservative upper houses of colonial parliaments, was essentially negative and blocking. As one perceptive historian noted: 'They did not provide a governing class . . . in culture as in politics the majority held aloof from the new society that was being shaped so vociferously about them. They were indeed "men of yesterday".' [10]

If there was no old aristocracy in Australia and the landowners did not constitute a 'governing class' or ruling elite, what then was the leading force in the bourgeoisie? It was none other than the mercantile class. This was not always obvious with reference to full-time politicians, amongst whom professional people such as lawyers figured prominently, although it may be observed that two of the leading Victorian politicians of the late nineteenth century, James Service and James McCulloch, arrived in Melbourne initially in 1853 as representatives of Scottish mercantile firms. Certainly in the economic sphere, merchants dominated the Australian scene, and this accorded well with the increased importance of export–import trade. Profits from trade were reckoned to be substantially higher in Australia than in Britain, and this appears to have been particularly true of manufactured goods imported from Britain. Sometimes merchants combined wholesale and retail trade, as in the case of Burns, Philp & Co. operating in Queensland. At a more specialized level, James McEwan & Co. in Melbourne both imported a great amount of ironmongery and sold it retail.

Naturally, the wool trade was the basis for a number of fortunes. Thomas Elder, son of a Scots merchant, emigrated to Adelaide in 1854 and was later instrumental in the formation of the firm of Elder, Smith & Co., a very large wool-selling business. Elder and his partner, Robert Barr Smith, also financed big copper mines in South Australia, besides acquiring extensive pastoral properties. As that example suggests, merchants branched out from the buying and selling of goods into other spheres. J. B. Were, originally a merchant, established a prominent sharebroking business in Melbourne. Some merchants invested in manufacturing, the outstanding example being Edward Knox, who founded the Colonial Sugar Refining Co. (CSR) in Sydney in 1855. Other merchants were engaged in shipping and occasionally a merchant–manufacturer went into farming, as did T. S. Mort in developing butter and cheese-making (for the Sydney market) in southern New South Wales.

Mercantile contacts extended across the whole spectrum of business, including the supply of Melanesian indentured labourers to Queensland sugar planters. There were necessarily links between merchants and banks, and there was a particularly intimate connection between CSR and the Commercial Banking Co. of Sydney: Edward Knox and Henry Kater were simultaneously directors of both companies in the late nineteenth century and this dual role was maintained later through several generations of the two families. While this raises interesting questions concerning access by merchant–manufacturers to loan money, bankers themselves appear to have played only relatively minor roles, as financial intermediaries, during the long boom. They were either professional managers or directors whose prime interests were in the pastoral industry or commerce. Only one NSW banker left a very large fortune (Thomas Walker, president of the Bank of New South Wales for eighteen years until he died in 1886, left £938 000) but his origins lay in a mercantile family established in the colony more than half a century earlier.

On the matter of origins, some clarification is necessary. Neither wealthy pastoralists nor merchants came from the working class. Usually they began their careers with some capital from family sources. For instance, 'Big' Clarke brought a capital of more than £2000 with him when he arrived in Van Diemen's Land in 1829—whereupon he received a land grant of 2000 acres. Frederick Grimwade, when he went into partnership with Alfred Felton in a wholesale drugs business in Melbourne in 1867, borrowed £8000 from his own father. Edward Wienholt, an old Etonian who was one of the wealthiest squatters in the Darling Downs district of Queensland in the 1870s and 1880s, inherited a substantial capital from his father, a London merchant.

There were some cases of self-made entrepreneurs in Australia— windfall gains on goldfields could be important—but they were at lower levels of society. Another possibility was to marry into money. Edward Wienholt did this when he married the only daughter of Daniel Williams, a wealthy railway contractor and investor, who left £500 000 when he died in 1884. Yet Wienholt did not need the inheritance: the example goes to show that money generally married money. Businessmen were generally single-minded about building family dynasties and they brooked little opposition from sons or daughters. James Ewan, shipowner and bank director in Sydney, exercised tyranny over his family to the extreme of disinheriting his eldest son in 1902 and, when the vindictive old man died a year later, he asserted his will from the grave by leaving a large sum of money to his widow on condition that she did not remarry.

Mercantile capital, as a category, could be stretched to encompass some large urban contractors and manufacturers, such as brewers and newspaper proprietors. No doubt elasticity of personal description was enhanced by the social prestige and status accorded to merchants. There was a big distinction between being a merchant and, say, a shopkeeper. Furthermore, wealthy people—from landed as well as merchant classes—set about preserving such distinctions for the benefit of their offspring. While the bourgeois liberal creation of a secular state system of education was a striking achievement, the rich (often with the aid of government grants of money) established expensive private schools, modelled on the British 'public school' system. For example, Scotch College, Melbourne Grammar, Geelong Grammar, Geelong and Wesley Colleges were founded in Victoria in the 1850s and 1860s, followed by Xavier College for Roman Catholics in 1878. Beyond these boys' schools lay the University of Melbourne. There were also some prestigious girls' schools, such as the Presbyterian Ladies College, but their function was rather different, wealthy parents being less concerned about academic standards for their daughters: sons were given preferred treatment.

One important consequence of the private school system is indicated in the following quotation from a Melbourne historian (and the situation in other capital cities differed only in degree):

the professions remained securely in the keeping of Melbourne's upper middle classes. Of native-born doctors who commenced practice in Melbourne during the 1880s, three-quarters were themselves the sons of professional men though, by the early 1890s, a large number of merchants', squatters' and even builders' and estate agents' sons were coming forward. The law . . . may have been a little less inbred, though even here two-thirds were sponsored by professionals, businessmen and other 'gentlemen'.[11]

Diggers, Middle Classes and Democracy

'The middle classes' is an expression which in the Australian context can be taken as applying to several fairly distinct groups of people: professionals, along with senior officials in public and private bureaucracies; small manufacturers and contractors; self-employed business-men such as shopkeepers; and two other independent categories, farmers and gold diggers. These middle classes were large and mobile. Although tales about many Australians starting from nothing to acquire great wealth are mythical, it is a fact that a number of out-standing businessmen came from middle-class backgrounds, where modest amounts of capital were available to them. Much the same was true of their counterparts in the USA, men like Rockefeller. Australian examples are Benjamin Fink, notorious land-boomer in Melbourne in the 1880s, who arrived in that town originally as a boy with his small-draper father; and William Lawrence Baillieu, whose father is usually described as a lowly boatman and lighthouse-keeper. Actually Baillieu senior had become a hotel-owner in Melbourne by the 1880s, when the son began his meteoric ascent as a businessman—an ascent aided by marriage to the only daughter of wealthy Edward Latham, founder of the Carlton brewery. This is not to decry W. L. Baillieu's business ability: the point is that access to capital was usually a prerequisite for success in business.

Australian society was fluid, and this was particularly true of those people who poured into the country in search of gold in the 1850s. There were probably about 140 000 goldminers in Victoria in 1858, though the number dropped rapidly from that peak. These diggers were not wage-workers; rather, they were lower middle-class people. They were self-employed, mostly in small co-operative groups. Many were intent upon becoming full-fledged members of the bourgeoisie. Others were Chartists. The revolt at Eureka was not simply a protest against authoritarianism. It was also directed at the exorbitant licence fee of twenty or thirty shillings per month which diggers were required to pay whether they were successful or not. In effect, the fee was seen as an arbitrary tax on small capital, standing in the way of ambitions to get rich quickly.

It has been estimated that in practice only some 20 per cent of the Victorian diggers gained more than the equivalent of reasonable wages from their efforts, and one typical digger confided to his diary: 'I don't much like working for a "boss", but I think constant regular wages is preferable to what I have lately been engaged at'.[12] Perhaps 10 000 diggers in Victoria at this time, by saving several hundred pounds each, managed to set themselves up as small farmers—often as tenants. Some others established small businesses. Many went on prospecting for gold, moving from one field to another. However, most of the dig-gers in the next decade or two joined the ranks of the proletariat, working either in company-owned mines or in jobs in other indus-tries.

The diggers left an enduring mark on Australian society. Egalitarian   113 attitudes flourished in the 1850s as employers made bids for workers in a very tight labour market. One English gentleman, after experiencing Melbourne and the diggings, referred ironically to the 'hairystocracy':

It is a wonderful place to take the conceit out of men who expect much deference ... every servant in this Austral Utopia thinks himself a gentleman, and really is far more independent than his employer for the time being. He engages on his own terms ... His doctrine is ... 'Hard work would kill a man'; and he is a philosopher who carries out his theory to perfection.[13]

The independent diggers were also a strong force for political democracy. Their armed rising at Eureka was symbolic of willingness to die, if necessary, in a fight for freedom. The rising itself was quickly put down, about thirty diggers and five soldiers being killed, but the ruling classes were frightened into making concessions. In particular, the Victorian government replaced the licence system with an export duty upon gold and introduced a 'miner's right' which, for a fee of £1 per annum, entitled the holder to vote as well as to dig. Enfranchisement of the miners, coupled with outspoken opposition to squatters' dominance, gave a strong boost to the popular democratic movement in following years. Nor was this restricted to Victoria. In New South Wales a liberal section of the merchants and landowners sided with radical middle-class and working-class urban forces.

The general result was a breakthrough in forms of democracy. By 1860 most of the Australian colonies (including Queensland, newly separated from New South Wales) had instituted both manhood suffrage and voting by secret ballot. The only exceptions were Tasmania and Western Australia. The democratic advances were not all that they seemed on the surface. To some degree, they were designed simply to check the pretensions of squatters. More broadly, the political moves can be seen as both bourgeois recognition of the need to make concessions and of the confidence of the bourgeoisie in its own ability to keep change within proper bounds. Farsighted observers noted that in the Australian colonies there was a significant proportion of people with an actual or potential interest in property ownership. They had a stake in society and could be relied upon to pose no threat to capitalism.

It is a standard ruling-class strategy to give rights to people in order to contain them, to restrict them from further àdvance. The problem for those who employ the strategy is that those who are given the rights may transform them in course of time. They may, for example, use the vote to secure election of working-class candidates. In this sense, the institution of a democratic framework was a very real advance for the common people—a victory won long before it fell within the grasp of a more mature working class in Britain. Never-

114

theless, the Australian bourgeoisie of the 1850s, while bringing in the formal procedures of democracy, carefully limited its effects for decades to come. Appearances were deceptive. In the first place, nearly half the population—females—were automatically excluded from voting rights. For the rest, there was serious class discrimination. In New South Wales men were subject to a six-months' residential qualification for voting, which meant that many mobile workers were unable to exercise their rights. At the other end of the social scale there was plural voting: in all colonies except South Australia, a man who owned property in several constituencies could vote in each of them. Upper houses of Parliament, whose members were either nominated by the Governor or elected by holders of property, were fundamentally conservative.

In addition, payment of MPs was not instituted until the 1880s, apart from an earlier temporary provision in Victoria, so that Parliament was for the relatively well-to-do. Very few workers were elected before the 1890s. The bourgeoisie reigned supreme and its political representatives could afford the luxury of factions and private deals. Temporary alliances were the focal points of politics: articulation of disciplined parties was unnecessary whilst there was virtually no challenge from the working class in the political arena. Moreover, the weakness of challenge from working-class sources was a reflection not only of problems of organization but of the seductive capitalist ideology which pervaded the period of the long boom. As Humphrey McQueen put it:

For most of the nineteenth century Australia was an open-ended society, politically and economically. The working class that was formed in this circumstance accepted the acquisitive ethos of capitalism because it worked for them.[14]

The rush to get rich, and the accompanying corruption, became so commonplace as to be accepted even by those who did not benefit. The ethos was akin to that of Australia a century later, when a wealthy person who did not resort to artificial devices to dodge paying taxes was so unusual as to be regarded in business circles as odd or stupid. In the earlier period, by the 1880s, crooks and speculators like Benjamin Fink were publicly admired for their smart business coups. In sport, while polo was for the rich and football for the masses, all classes united around horse-racing, culminating each year in a gamble on the Melbourne Cup. Perhaps the most cynical calculation of the time came from a group of Melbourne businessmen who saw a good prospect for land speculation in the site of the half-built St Paul's Cathedral. They offered £300 000—and the proposal, made to a solidly bourgeois Anglican body, was rejected by only one committeeman's vote. If Mammon was a false god, he was nevertheless highly regarded.

7

Class War on the Land:
Farmers and Squatters

Beneath the facade of parliamentary politics, class struggle continued during the long boom. Besides the overarching conflict between employers and workers, there were problems arising out of the establishment of a petty bourgeoisie of farmers on the land in the face of hostility from squatters. There were some set battles in this agrarian struggle but for the most part it took the form of grim guerrilla skirmishes. Corruption was rife in the process; and enormous public assets were transferred into private hands. The 'privatization' policies of conservative political parties today had forerunners in Australia a century earlier. There was little ideological content in the earlier situation, but there is little enough today either.

It is impossible to calculate precisely the amount of crown land which passed into private ownership at this time, for much of the land acquired under selection legislation from the 1860s onwards was 'bought' through systems of deferred or conditional payment. Many selectors in fact never completed payment for their holdings. Subject to this element of uncertainty, some very broad figures can be given as to the amount of crown land virtually alienated in New South Wales. Compared with about 7 million acres over the whole period from 1788 to 1861, it amounted to 5 or 6 million acres between 1862 and 1871, and 44 million acres between 1872 and 1891. In Victoria, with its smaller area, the amount virtually alienated was naturally less but it nevertheless totalled some 20 million acres by 1881.

The revenue raised by colonial governments from the sale or leasing of crown land was very substantial. In New South Wales it came to a total of about £64 million between 1856 and 1900—more than was raised by customs duties. Most of this land revenue was once-only in nature, representing a squandering of capital assets for the sake of short-term relief from taxation or public borrowing. Thus politician Henry Parkes in 1869 was advised by the London managing director of the Bank of New South Wales to 'dispose of every acre of the Riverina Country, devoting the proceeds to the extinction of your debt'.[1] The main beneficiaries of massive land sales in New South Wales were graziers and merchants who stood to gain from continuance of free trade. Victoria, with a smaller revenue from land, depended upon import duties which were both protectionist and revenue-producing; and a mild tax on the capital value of land was introduced in Victoria in 1877. New South Wales, to the joy of the more wealthy of its inhabitants, imposed neither land tax nor income tax before 1896.

In the late 1850s there developed a popular demand to 'unlock the land' by depriving squatters of the privileges which they had gained from their victory in 1847. The campaign was particularly strong in Victoria, where a Land Convention was established. The Convention was described by W. Westgarth, a leading merchant of Melbourne, as 'a sort of People's Parliament'; and indeed the Convention met over the road from Parliament and aped that institution's forms of procedure to the extent of electing a Speaker. However, the first comprehensive land selection legislation was enacted in New South Wales in 1861, when John Robertson was Premier. With some variation, Robertson's Land Acts were used as models in other Australian colonies and are therefore singled out for attention here.

Various elements contributed to Robertson's Acts. The driving force came from radical craftsmen, shopkeepers and small businessmen: 'little men' who were ambitious and keen to remove obstacles to upward social mobility. Their ideal, like that of the gold diggers, was personal independence in a community of small producers, and the entrenched squatters were seen as standing in the way. Another reform element consisted of part of the established elite, particularly landowners resentful of the way in which squatters had won their victory in the 1840s. Robertson himself was not a squatter: he owned freehold land, much of it being let out to tenant farmers, and this gave Robertson an active concern for agriculture. More broadly, he embraced the liberal ideal of equality of opportunity. Rather than seeking to destroy pastoralism, he and other liberal reformers wanted to make land freely transferable, like other commodities in a capitalist society.

During the long boom, land and its productive uses were the major outlets for investment capital. Although this related mainly to grazing and wool production, selection legislation created markets for land in regions where squatters had previously been undisturbed in possession of long leases. Disruption of the pastoral lease system also facilitated penetration by financial interests into the pastoral sector. Moreover, many businessmen saw that in the long run a more intensive development of agriculture through small farming offered them more than the prospect of continued squatter dominance. For example, country storekeepers realized that a prosperous community of small wheat farmers would expand markets and provide more trade in a locality, whereas a big grazier might deal directly with a Sydney or Brisbane merchant. There were thus various reasons for breaking down the existing form of monopoly of pastoral occupation.

Robertson repeatedly claimed, with much justification, that his legislation was not anti-squatter in intent: he was only concerned to put prospective farmers on an equal legal footing with squatters. Nevertheless, embodiment of that aim in legislation inevitably entailed interference with the squatters' special privileges. The main bone of contention arose from the reformers' claim that a land selector should be entitled to choose a block of crown land anywhere in the countryside (except in settled districts) without waiting for it to be surveyed: the survey would come later. Squatters objected, arguing that, if changes were deemed necessary, it would be best to make them in an orderly fashion by defining agricultural districts and surveying land there, while leaving squatters in outside areas untouched. Unfortunately for this argument, there was no public confidence in the NSW Survey Department, which was interminably slow, with a deserved reputation for incompetence and dishonesty. Indeed, because of official delay in surveying stations, none of the pastoral leases promised by the Colonial Office in 1847 were issued until 1854 and most runs were still unsurveyed in 1860. Instead, the majority of squatters were given licences for eight or fourteen years from 1852, the rent being based largely upon the squatter's estimate of the area of the run. In 1861 there were about 3000 squatters in New South Wales, paying rents of less than one farthing per acre annually.

Apart from the practical difficulty over measurement of land, advocates of the principle of selection before survey pointed out that squatters had themselves chosen their holdings without prior survey: why not give farmers an equal opportunity? Squatters lost this particular argument. The Robertson Land Acts superseded the squatting regulations of 1847 and gave anyone the right to purchase a block of between 40 and 320 acres of crown land virtually anywhere in the colony. There were certain exceptions, such as urban land and land reserved for public purposes; and selectors could not choose land in squatting runs during the currency of existing leases, which meant that 118 most squatting land was not opened up in New South Wales before

1866. In effect, squatters were given time to re-arrange their affairs, to plan the frustration of the stated object of the legislation. This was even more markedly the case in Victoria, where Duffy's Land Act in 1862 gave squatters security of tenure until 1870.

Under the Robertson Acts in New South Wales, a selector was charged a fixed price of £1 per acre for purchase of land. Only one-quarter of the sum was required as a deposit. The balance was payable over the next three years—or alternatively the selector could defer payment indefinitely by paying interest on the amount outstanding. The selector was also expected to reside on the holding for a year or more. These provisions accorded with the ostensible aim of the legislation, to enable small farmers to gain access to the land. The government did not expect workers to benefit, however. Employers had no desire to see the numbers of the proletariat dwindle, and as D. W. Baker comments: 'Capitalism does not commit suicide during adolescence'. Robertson himself in 1861 said 'that it was not desirable that the poor man should free select, but he hoped that his bill would help those with £200 or £300 in their pocket'. In practice many hopeful selectors chanced their arms with much smaller amounts of capital, disregarding the fact that the acquisition of a small holding was only a minor part of the cost of farming. The costs of clearing the land, buying harvest machinery and draught animals and so on were much greater.[2]

Selection legislation removed political barriers to small farming yet at the same time it set the scene for a protracted class war between farmers and squatters. The latter were determined to retain control of their holdings against encroachment by selectors; and in the competitive struggle for land the squatter had the great advantage of access to bank credit and mercantile mortgage finance. Moreover, squatters remained in possession and had certain exclusive rights under the Robertson Land Acts. Notably, they had a pre-emptive right to buy a portion (one twenty-fifth) of a run, as well as sections on which they had made improvements. In addition, squatters and members of their families had as much right to make selections under the Act as anyone else. In any case, it was necessary to buy only part of a run in order to retain control of the whole: the prime consideration was to secure strategic areas, such as blocks with access to water—'peacocking' (picking the eyes out of the land), as it was termed.

Squatters used a wide range of devices to secure their position. Some methods, such as bribery and false declarations as to residence and the like, were plainly illegal. Others were within the letter, though not the spirit, of the law. Thus the use of dummies to make selections was quite legal, provided that the dummy fulfilled residence and improvement conditions before transferring the holding to a principal. Squatters used employees, paupers and children as dummies: the 119 minimum age at which anyone might legally make a selection was two years until 1874, when it was raised to sixteen years.

It may be remarked that dummying has a long and dishonourable history in Australia. As late as the 1920s, when the former German plantations in New Guinea were sold by the Commonwealth government, big Australian trading companies used ex-servicemen as dummy buyers, because ex-servicemen were given preferential terms by the government. Among the dummies employed by W.R. Carpenter & Co. at this time were two people named Howard, a father and son who ran a small garage and service station in suburban Sydney. No doubt their transaction with Carpenter was legal, though not one to boast about in public. Interestingly, the younger Howard was father of John Howard who became Commonwealth Treasurer in a federal Liberal government half a century later.

A different kind of parallel may be drawn between the 1870s and the 1970s. At the later date, the federal Whitlam government abolished fees for universities and colleges in the hope that this would make tertiary education more available to working-class students. In fact this has happened to a moderate extent only: students of middle-class and ruling-class background still predominate. A radical change would require more subsidies for working-class children at schools and through universities, coupled with changes in working-class family expectations about jobs. Comparing the role of government in this matter with the position concerning land settlement in the late nineteenth century, it may be said that a genuine attempt to settle a host of small settlers on the land presupposed two things. First, it would have been necessary not merely to make land available at a low price but to ensure that squatters could not seize the opportunity to gobble up the best land themselves. Second, the state would have needed to provide small farmers with capital to work their holdings until they became firmly established.

Neither of these propositions was within the realm of practical politics. Merchants and their allies derived some satisfaction from the curbing of squatting pretensions but they had no desire to cripple the squatters. Merchants were far from being a revolutionary force and there were close links between them and big graziers through trade and credit. As for the possibility of state provision of working capital for small farmers, the reality was that those in control were concerned to use selection legislation to increase government revenue, not reduce it.

Politics aside, economic realities were unfavourable to small farmers in Australia. Selectors might achieve a degree of self-sufficiency in production for a time, perhaps living on a diet of porridge, bread and dripping and corned meat plus tea, but they were not 120 peasants in the traditional sense. Rather, they worked in a capitalist market framework where the drive to get bigger or get out was already apparent. Access to market was of crucial importance. For example, in the 1850s it was several times more expensive to transport wheat by road from Goulburn to Sydney (a distance of less than 200 miles) than to ship a similar load by sea from South America. On the other hand, wool producers were less concerned about transport costs: their commodity was much more valuable than an equal amount of grain, and the cost of transport could be more easily absorbed.

The spread of railways and, to a lesser extent, of steamships changed this situation. It meant that the wheat frontier in Victoria could be pushed further inland in the 1870s, while South Australian farmers found an appreciable export market in Britain for their grain. Wheat farmers in New South Wales did not benefit much from railways for another decade or so. Much depended upon the narrowness of mesh of a railway system. Generally, farmers needed to be within about twenty miles of a railway siding for marketing purposes, yet many of them selected land farther away. To some extent this also happened in the USA, where the Homestead Act of 1862 gave ownership of a block of 160 acres of public land *gratis* to any family man who lived upon it for five years. In practice, many American settlers preferred to buy land from private railroad companies because proximity to the track provided easy access to market. However, the basic difference between American and Australian conditions at this time came from the enormous population and the even spread of internal markets in the USA. An American farmer on 160 acres of arable land had some prospect of success, whereas a selector on a similar-sized holding in Australia was much more likely to fail unless located close to one of the few big city markets.

There were certain agricultural areas of Australia where selection legislation appears to have had a measure of success in encouraging small farmers on to the land. This was so, for example, in the maize and sugar-growing district of northern New South Wales. A rather similar development of mixed farming took place in the Darling Downs region of Queensland, although there it took the form mainly of a combination of crop-growing and grazing on farms of between 5000 and 15 000 acres. The owners of such grazing farms were not typical selectors. Rather, they were small capitalists—boss cockies—who aimed at acquiring the necessary minimum area for commercial grazing. Under land legislation, the maximum permitted size of a selection was too small: it was increased to 640 acres in New South Wales in 1875, and 320- or 640-acre maxima applied in most other colonies, but several times that much land was required for a viable grazing property. Beginning with a selection, some aspiring capitalists bought additional land on the private market (often from less successful selectors) or leased it from the government. Others resorted to the same range of dirty tricks—sometimes used as blackmail—as the squatters themselves employed. Thus disputes between boss cockies and squatters ran parallel to the broader struggle between the bulk of the selectors and squatters.

In New South Wales, an official Inquiry by A. Morris and G. Ranken into land laws reported to the Legislative Council in 1883 that over the previous two decades there had been a 'class contest' for possession of public lands and that

It is manifest all through the mass of testimony, that the conservation and beneficial management of the Crown Lands as the heritage of the colony have been the last matters considered . . . The plain meaning of any existing Act is now of less weight than the caprice or bias of the Minister, and it is notorious that the most effective mode of getting business done at the 'Lands' [Department] . . . is to select a land agent who is a member of the popular branch of the Legislature.[3]

This was a pro-squatter report, designed to highlight defects in selection legislation. If the authors had been less partial, they might have noted administrative abuse at lower levels as well. At local land offices, which were open for selection business only one day per week, the crown land agent was also the clerk of petty sessions, in which capacity he was usually subservient to local squatter–JPs. Undoubtedly squatters received preferential treatment. Actually, most squatters would rather not have spent money on buying land in their runs: the interest on money borrowed for the purpose cost them about sixteen pence per acre, which was far higher than the leasehold rent paid by squatters for the same land. Nevertheless, squatters felt obliged to buy in order to forestall selectors who were eyeing choice blocks within runs. Purchase by squatters was speeded up considerably in the 1870s, when the government permitted millions of acres of crown land to be sold at auction, supplementary to the standard selection process. Blocks sold at auction were not limited to the maximum size prescribed for selectors and the auctioned land was bought by those who had cash available—the squatters. The price was only marginally more than £1 per acre on average.

It is impossible to determine how many small farmers were successfully established on the land during the long boom. Statistics relating to selection do not differentiate between small men and squatters or dummies using the legislation. In New South Wales, the Morris-Ranken report made a very rough estimate that less than 20 000 farm homesteads remained in existence in 1883 out of several times that number of purported selections over two decades. However, the authors of this estimate were biased against selectors. For Victoria, where the broad principle of free selection before survey did not apply before 1870, Serle suggests that 'perhaps half' of the selectors of the

1870s failed and abandoned their blocks; while Waterson reaches a similar conclusion concerning selectors on the Darling Downs over a longer period. However doubtful the statistics, it is clear both that a large proportion of the land made available through selection legislation was bought by squatters, and that despite this the number of small farmers grew steadily—though not necessarily as a result of the legislation.[4]

Squatters were not the only predators faced by farmers. Shortage of capital and lack of security for loans made farmers easy marks for grasping moneylenders and storekeepers. Following a drought in Victoria, a Royal Commission looked into the position of selectors in 1878. The Commission found that it was quite common for farmers to pay annual interest rates of 20–30 per cent; and in some country districts the prices of goods sold on credit by storekeepers were 50 per cent higher than in Melbourne. R. W. Bennett, a commission agent, brazenly testified that he charged risky borrowers up to 70 per cent interest. While acknowledging that he had overcharged a client on a particular account, Bennett explained: 'The fact is, I can give a man accommodation and pay his rent, but I cannot give him brains. If he is not sharp enough to see he is slated [cheated] that is his business.' Small wonder that another witness, a selector named Baker, when asked whether he had ever been in the hands of moneylenders, replied: 'No ... I know they are nothing but a lot of pick-pockets.' Baker evidently had resources of his own: many selectors had no choice but to borrow from blood-suckers like Bennett.[5]

Easy credit payments for crown land meant that many selectors were effectively encouraged to choose blocks of land which were beyond their financial ability to work properly. It was a form of speculation. In times of crisis, and under political pressure, colonial governments sometimes gave emergency relief to selectors, as in Victoria where, following the Royal Commission referred to above, the yearly payments (rent) due from selectors to the government were reduced. South Australia's land policy was different from that of the other colonies in important respects. Until the 1880s the expansion of wheat growing was much more marked in South Australia. Wheat farms in this colony were also relatively prosperous but the old 80-acre holdings gave way to much larger units as South Australian wheat found markets in the other colonies and Britain. The trend was further accentuated by growth in use of costly farm machinery. This reduced labour requirements so that farming became more capital-intensive.

Policy in South Australia was adapted to these circumstances. Selection before survey was not introduced there. Crown land was made available for farming through a modified auction system, rather than being sold at a fixed price; and it was not till 1869 that the South Australian government gave credit terms to purchasers. Eight years later the maximum amount of land which might be bought on credit terms was increased from 640 to 1000 acres. In short, the emphasis in South Australia was on selectors who possessed appreciable amounts of capital. The conventional picture of a more egalitarian society on the land in this colony is rather misleading: the 'small man' was not so small in reality. Certainly squatters were of limited importance in South Australia; but in 1891 there were 131 freehold estates of more than 5000 acres each, accounting for nearly one-third of all the freehold land in the colony.

On the other hand, figures for other colonies are indicative of grosser concentration of land ownership. In New South Wales by the 1880s, about 500 holdings in excess of 10 000 acres accounted for half the total of land alienated from the crown. Indeed there were eighty estates recorded as being over 40 000 acres, some of them covering more than 200 000 acres of freehold land. In Victoria at the same time, ten families owned almost 2 million acres between them; and it was notorious that the public lost valuable areas, particularly in the Western District of Victoria, which would have accommodated many more farmers than the handful of pastoralists who became their owners. As may be inferred from these figures, use of the term 'squatter' is increasingly less accurate from the 1860s, as such men bought land. Nevertheless, most of them purchased only parts of their runs, and it is still convenient to refer to them as squatters to distinguish them from genuine selectors. It is also useful in the Australian context to demarcate 'farmers' from 'graziers', although in other countries the latter are usually embraced in the broad category of farmers.

Certainly in the late nineteenth century the term 'squatter' continued to be used as one of opprobrium by most Australians. In the Victorian countryside in the 1870s, the activities of bushrangers, notably the Kelly gang, were symptomatic of hostility between selectors and squatters. Communities of poor farmers were sympathetic to the Kelly gang, which not only stole the squatters' livestock but robbed banks, 'where the burning of mortgage papers held against local men was not simply a capricious act'. Kelly also struck a sympathetic chord in his attacks upon constituted authority, particularly the police—seen as agents of squatters. In a statement of self-justification written in 1879, Ned Kelly referred to

the brutal and cowardly conduct of a parcel of big ugly fat-necked wombat headed big bellied magpie legged narrow hipped splay-footed sons of Irish Bailiffs or English landlords which is better known as officers of Justice or Victorian Police . . . The Queen must surely be proud of such heroic men . . . It takes eight or eleven of the biggest mud crushers in Melbourne to take one little half starved larrakin to the watchhouse.[6]

Besides individual resistance and the social banditry represented by the Kelly gang, small farmers formed a number of Selectors' Associations in the 1870s. These were not very effective as political pressure-groups and they tended to fall under the domination of country-town businessmen and boss cockies with holdings of 2000 acres or more. Along with the growth of this conservative element went recognition by many squatters that, once they had secured control of their own runs, it could be advantageous to have farmers as neighbours. Selectors often supplied labour, farm produce and carting services to local squatters. By the end of the 1880s, tensions between the two groups were declining, and the state was beginning to give tangible assistance to farmers, for instance to Queensland sugar-cane producers. By the turn of the century, to use Waterson's phrase, a 'new rural petit-bourgeois community with an apparently immutable pattern of society had been created'. The farmers who survived were 'essentially small business men bitterly opposed to any tampering with private property'.[7]

Class alignments were changing. Yet hostility towards land monopoly remained an important element in Australian political thought. It was given a strong boost in the 1880s by the ideas of the American, Henry George. In a seminal work, *Progress and Poverty*, George attributed social ills primarily to the growth of rent. The increase of raw land values, created by society through growth of population and other factors, represented great unearned increments in the hands of landowners. The remedy, according to George, was to institute a single tax on unimproved land values, which would replace all other kinds of taxation. This remedy appealed to public imagination, and the criticism of rent as unearned income had a respectable lineage among economists. Adam Smith wrote:

As soon as the land of any country has all become private property, the landlords, like all other men, love to reap where they never sowed, and demand a rent even for its natural produce. The wood of the forest, the grass of the field, and all the natural fruits of the earth, which, when land was in common, cost the labourer only the trouble of gathering them, come, even to him, to have an additional price fixed upon them.[8]

George's ideas were eagerly taken up in Australia, since they reinforced the popular antipathy towards squatters. Whereas in Europe the private ownership of land was sanctified by centuries of usage, in Australia it was within living knowledge and experience that the squatters had grabbed land for themselves and that speculators had made fortunes. Many workers, professional people and employers other than landowners, accepted George's explanation of the paradox of poverty amidst plenty. It was particularly appealing to advocates of free trade, for according to the single tax theory there would be no need for revenue from tariffs.

Land Nationalisation Associations were set up in Australia to 125 propagate George's views, which were widely adopted in the labour movement. Thus an Intercolonial Trades Union Congress meeting in Brisbane in 1888 expressed support for land nationalization and resolved grandly that

a simple yet sovereign remedy which will raise wages, increase and give remunerative employment, abolish poverty, extirpate pauperism, lessen crime, elevate moral tastes and intelligence, purify government, and carry civilization to yet nobler heights, is to abolish all taxation save that on land values.[9]

As a footnote to the story of George's influence in Australia, it may be remarked that there was an obscure connection between that country and another very prominent economist, the Englishman Alfred Marshall, who was the founder of the Cambridge School of Economics. Marshall dominated the teaching of economics in the British Empire between the 1880s and the 1930s. He began his work as an economist 'at a time when the scientific foundations of the subject were being knocked away, and its very survival was in doubt; a situation not unlike that facing economics today'. Marshall gave the subject a new authority—a conservative one, for he was strongly opposed to socialism and trade unionism. Of the big engineers' strike in Britain in 1897, he said: 'I want these people beaten at all costs: the complete destruction of Unionism would be . . . not too high a price'.[10]

Much later, J. M. Keynes commented upon a tenuous link between Alfred Marshall and Australia. According to Keynes, Marshall in his youth had 'a well-disposed uncle willing to lend him a little money . . . which . . . opened to him the doors of Mathematics and of Cambridge'. Before this, the uncle had sought his fortune in Australia and had become established as a pastoralist at the time of the gold discoveries. An eccentric man, he had

to the mirth of his neighbours refused to employ anyone about his place who did not suffer from some physical defect, staffing himself entirely with the halt, the blind, and the maimed. When the gold boom reached its height his reward came. All the able-bodied labourers migrated to the goldfields and Charles Marshall was the only man in the place able to carry on. A few years later he returned to England with a fortune.[11]

In the nineteenth century, it was not uncommon for British emigrants to Australia who accumulated capital there to repatriate themselves and adopt the style of English landed gentry. For example, F. G. Dalgety, while continuing to build up his Australian pastoral interests, lived in England from 1859 until his death in 1894. He built Lockerley Hall, a mansion and estate in Hampshire worth £238 000. At least it is to Charles Marshall's credit that he was willing to apply some of his Australian money to education, specifically the education of his clever nephew, Alfred. Indirectly, this led to the establishment of a very influential school of economists, some of whose followers in Australia in the depression of the 1930s provided intellectual foundations for attacks upon the living standards of Australian workers. No doubt Alfred Marshall would have been proud of their work, but kindly Uncle Charles can hardly be regarded as responsible for that distant outcome!

8

Class Struggle on the Land:
Miners and Shearers

In 1891 the proportion of the total working population of New South Wales engaged in agricultural and pastoral activities was around 24 per cent. In Victoria it was 20 per cent. Most of these people were in agriculture rather than grazing; but as the figures include employers and self-employed, besides workers, it is not easy to identify small farmers. Undoubtedly, selectors were strong in numbers by this time. In Victoria alone, there were some 35 000 farmers, whose produce was worth twice as much as that of the pastoralists. However, the average farmer depended upon family and seasonal labour. Large aggregations of workers were to be found only on pastoral properties.

The position of selectors in rural society was shifting and ambiguous. Some sold out for capital gains. Others failed and returned to their previous occupations. The two other classes on the land, landowner–squatters and workers, were clearly defined as well as being sharply differentiated from each other. The traditional story of hospitality for passing visitors at outback stations, and of social mixing, has elements of myth in it. Then, as now, station owners and managers, along with visiting gentlemen, ate their meals at the homestead, while station hands and the like ate in separate quarters. In fact, the practice of hospitality towards outsiders was largely dictated by the squatter's need for a pool of labour, especially in spring and summer: 'sundowners' were expected to earn their tucker by doing odd jobs around the homestead. Thus there was a fairly strict social hierarchy on pastoral stations.

Rural workers comprised a variety of people such as station hands, boundary riders and shearers. With the advance of fencing (a labour-saving improvement), shepherds were replaced by boundary riders who were usually permanent hands. Despite the great increase in numbers of livestock, permanent employment on pastoral stations rose only slowly in the 1870s and 1880s, but there was a large growth in the number of casual or itinerant workers. Many of these—shearers and fencers, for example—were engaged by squatters on a contract basis: payment of an agreed price for a task. Some, like bullockies and carters, were self-employed, owning their own teams of animals. Another prominent feature of the work situation was that many people worked for wages part of the year, having other occupations the rest of the time. Many selectors did this.

Surprisingly little is known about selectors in social terms, apart from the stereotypes of Dad and Dave, which at least have the merit of highlighting the desperate hardship and bucolic idiocy of the poorer selectors' existence. The stereotype pays much less attention to Mum, except to portray her (most favourably in the guise of a squatter's wife) as the bearer of civilized values in the bush. What the selector's wife actually bore was many children and the drudgery of everyday routine on a small farm, isolated from the amenities of civilization. The seldom asked question was not what women did for life in the bush, by way of softening its harshness, but what the bush did *to* them. Farm children also suffered, as schools 'emptied at harvest time, and children were forced into heavy farm duties at an early age without any choice'.[1]

No doubt many selectors were immigrants with farming experience, although such people were more likely to head for the USA than Australia. Certainly a number of Irish immigrants became selectors and they were probably familiar with agricultural life, though perhaps only as labourers. Selectors came also from the ranks of the working class in Australia, native-born as well as immigrant. Some selectors were labourers attracted by the countryside through which they built railways; others were tradesmen, artisans or miners. There were also some female selectors. Single women who wished to take up farming on their own were generally barred by official administrators, but there were numerous instances of adult females taking up selections alongside those of males in the same family, the selections being then worked as a whole. Recent research by Patricia Grimshaw and others indicates the important role of women and family units on farms. Women, besides doing their full share of farm work, reared large families, and the children as they grew up lightened the burden of work:

It is clear that the existence of extended family ties contributed to the prosperity . . . of those families which succeeded in establishing themselves securely on selections . . . Conversely, those who faced the most severe privation appeared usually to be couples with many young children but no neighbouring adult kin to rely on.[2]

Besides the females in selectors' families, many women were employed as wage-earners in the rural sector. In the second half of the nineteenth century, according to male statisticians and historians, females constituted 10 to 13 per cent of the total rural labour force in Australia. Female historians consider this figure to be a serious under-estimate due to bias: there was a 'hidden' female labour market, quite apart from the mass of women who were excluded from official stat-istics because they were not part of the *paid* labour force.[3]

There was considerable movement out of, as well as into, the ranks of selectors, not only because many gave up the struggle—although some made more than one attempt to farm—but because small farms could not support large families. Thus coalminers in the Illawarra dis-trict of southern New South Wales in the 1880s were often the sons of neighbouring selectors, such as dairy farmers (cow-cockies). Miners themselves lived in rural surroundings, in pit villages, and there was a connection between them and shearers through work patterns. Coal-miners were mostly piece-workers; they contracted to cut coal and convey it to the mine mouth for an agreed price per ton. Shearers, accustomed to piece-work rates of pay, often worked as miners in the 'off' season, which helps to explain the dominant position of W. G. Spence in both the Amalgamated Shearers' Union (ASU) and the Amalgamated Miners' Association (AMA) in the 1880s.

Many shearers were full-time wage-earners. Many others, how-ever, were selectors or their sons, who took paid work for part of the year, often as itinerants, leaving wives and children on the farm to do the best they could in the meantime. Sometimes the 'breadwinner' did not return. Kay Daniels comments that 'little attention has been paid to the great Australian male habit of wife desertion. Women often paid for the "mobility" of the "nomad tribe" '.[4]

It is commonplace to remark upon the unique phenomenon of strong trade unions covering rural workers in Australia: the ASU, formed in 1886 and claiming to have 16 000 members two years later; the sep-arate Queensland Shearers' Union; the Queensland Labourers' Union, covering shedhands; and the AMA, which began in 1874 as a grouping of Victorian goldminers and expanded in the 1880s to embrace coal-miners and metal miners in New South Wales and goldminers in Queensland. It is not difficult to relate these developments to the rapid growth of certain industries and the establishment of large companies, collieries and pastoral stations which brought together substantial numbers of workers and provided obvious bases for union organizing. For example, the Jondaryan woolshed in Queensland had fifty-two shearers' stands. Rather incongruously, the first South Australian branch of the Shearers' Union was established in a city, Adelaide, because shearers and shedhands gathered there at the outset of each season, to be hired by pastoralists through private labour bureaus before travelling out to the stations. There was a marked contrast between this sort of situation and the scattered isolation of agricultural labourers in other countries—and indeed on farms in Australia itself.

Yet the appearance of strength in Australian bushworkers' unions was deceptive. Numerous factors militated against sustained unity in a struggle against employers. The various divisions in the mining industry are clear examples of this. To start with the Victorian gold-mining industry, the establishment from the 1860s of mining companies, organized on a capitalist basis, meant a rapid decline in the number of independent diggers. However, they did not all become wage-earners. It was common for a company to let out part of a mine to a group of working miners, who were neither paid ordinary wages nor paid solely by piece-work: rather, they were paid a share of the value of the ore they mined. This tribute-system (which was particularly strong in South Australian copper mines) encouraged miners to continue to regard themselves as independent and to disregard trade unions. Even when miners were transformed into wage-earners, their thought-patterns and habits did not change automatically. Moreover, many of these workers speculated in the shares of mining companies, becoming 'little capitalists'. The Victorian No Liability Act of 1871 meant that a speculator could lose only the money he had originally invested: there was no contingent liability. As Blainey points out, 'Ballarat and Bendigo had busier stock exchanges than Melbourne's during mining booms'.[5]

A similar situation developed in Queensland mining areas, such as Charters Towers, in the 1880s. Outback miners were relatively well paid and the initial impetus towards trade unionism there seems to have come from the need for protection against a high level of mine accidents and diseases such as tuberculosis. Accident and sickness insurance funds thus featured prominently in mining union operations, including those of coalminers in New South Wales. Regulation of working conditions by governments, through Mining Acts, was a standard demand by such unions. In general, miners' unions were conservative in their attitudes. Yet although this accorded with a reputation for moderation in Queensland, the NSW coalminers and the metalminers at Broken Hill had a well-earned reputation for militancy in industrial disputes. To a large extent this was carried over from the British coal pits in which many Australian miners originally derived experience of class struggle. Miners tended to be isolated geographically, and their close-knit communities bred inner resources to sustain them in a fight against oppression.

131

Militancy on the part of coalminers, manifest from the formation of the first miners' union in the Newcastle district of New South Wales in the 1860s, was all the more remarkable in that the method used to determine wages promoted co-operation between miners and mine-owners. The 'hewing rate'—the price per ton of coal paid to the miner —was directly linked to the market price of coal. If the price of coal fell, so did the hewing rate (wage); and conversely, if the price rose. Under this sliding scale system, miners had a common interest with employers in ensuring a high price for coal. This was translated into union support for employers' attempts to maintain high coal prices through restriction of competition. In Newcastle, a mine-owners' cartel, known as the Vend, operated in this fashion from the 1870s, despite occasional breakdowns due to disagreement between members. Legal problems were not important. As one company lawyer wrote privately about the 1881 Vend agreement, 'the document is not worth the paper it is written on being in restraint of trade ... but of course a little illegality more or less won't matter'.[6] The miners' union co-operated with the Vend, initially no doubt because establishment of the first Vend coincided with high coal prices, which the union was concerned to maintain. The prime function of the union related to the setting of a minimum hewing rate and, through lodges (branches), negotiation of local variations in the rate due to unusual or difficult working conditions. Yet a degree of common interest with employers did not do away with the fundamental class aims of greater profits on one side and better wages on the other. At times, mine-owners tried to cut the minimum hewing rate, and this was guaranteed to cause trouble, as was the use of blacklegs in strikes. In the Maritime Strike in 1890, for example, employers brought in 'free labourers' to work pits in the Illawarra district, and strong objections by local workers resulted in a number of miners being prosecuted for assault and intimidation. Some miners' wives lay in front of a locomotive to prevent it from hauling a trainload of 'free labourers' to a pit.

On that particular occasion, the Illawarra miners—not previously noted for militancy—remained on strike for two or three months after their fellow-miners around Newcastle and Lithgow had returned to work. It is possible that the obduracy of the Illawarra men was due partly to the fact that many of them were able to live on family selections during the strike. If so, this is an interesting sidelight on the more general effect of the presence of such men among the members of trade unions: they were weak links at a time of crisis.

Finally with reference to the coalminers' union, it may be noted that it did not rely solely upon the employers' ability to keep coal prices up by restricting production. Recognizing the likelihood of future clashes with employers, in which the latter would have a decided advantage if stockpiles of coal were high, the union lodges commonly imposed 'dargs'—that is, limits on individual output per day. This policy had the further effect of reducing unemployment and minimizing rivalry between individual miners. Taking everything into account, it would be absurd to suggest that miners, because they worked under contract, were not really members of the working class. Certainly employers had no doubt about that fact. Nevertheless, the peculiarities of the miners' work situation, with each union lodge functioning as guardian of a multitude of local customs and rates, led to a clannish outlook. Lodges tried to preserve their autonomy within the union, and miners were slow to acknowledge themselves as part of a larger entity, whether it was the broad union movement or, from the 1890s, the Australian Labor Party.

The shearers' union had even more serious problems, resulting in divided loyalties. Shearers were recognized as 'aristocrats of labour', skilled men who earned several times as much as the rouseabouts (handymen) who also worked in woolsheds. Like other skilled workers, shearers had their own sense of superiority:

> For although your shearer is a mighty 'liberty, equality, fraternity' fellow as far as to those above him, don't think for a moment he believes in that trinity when dealing with those he regards beneath him, and looks upon a roustabout just as a skilfull citizen does upon a hod carrier. For a shearer to call another a roustabout there is only one resource—the backyard and blood from the nose.[7]

Although all members of the ASU were concerned to secure as high a piece-work rate for shearing as possible, plus good conditions, there was a strong potential difference of interest between two kinds of shearer. One might be termed a professional, following the seasonal migration of shearing, usually southwards from Queensland to Victoria. These men predominated on large stations in western New South Wales and central Queensland, and their style of work developed a strong sense of camaraderie, manifest in hostility towards squatters (and often in contempt for small farmers—'cockatoos'). Quite distinct from this group were those shearers who were also selectors or sons of selectors. Although the sons might be radical in outlook, the basic interest of the selector–shearers was in earning a sum of money to pay interest and instalments due to the government for their holdings. A long strike, even if the shearers won it, would imperil that aim, especially as shearers were usually paid only at the end of a job. In the 1880s members of selectors' families probably comprised the largest group of shearers. Many of them kept clear of the ASU but others joined it or followed the union's lead.

There is some truth in the claim that, to Australian bushworkers, unionism came 'as a religion ... bringing salvation from years of tyranny', to quote W. G. Spence. There was a proselytizing zeal and forthrightness, as shown by one ASU organizer, Arthur Rae, who was brought up on a charge of inciting shearers against pastoralists in 1890. He told a magistrate at Hay that he would 'just as soon go to hell to look for ice as come into that court and look for justice'. Nevertheless, ASU leaders were aware of the limitations imposed by the conservatism of union members with selector family connections. Consequently, short strikes on individual stations, taking advantage of the crucial importance of timing in shearing operations, figured prominently in union activities.[8]

ASU leaders noted with concern that, while non-union shearers on big stations in the west generally adhered to union decisions, the same non-unionists (and even some unionists) later in the season, in more closely settled areas, were often willing to shear under conditions which were contrary to union rules. The problem appeared mainly among selector–shearers, and an obvious remedy was to establish a closed shop in the shearing industry. However, the ASU did not have sufficient strength to impose a closed shop on its own, so other unions were asked to assist. This tactic was employed first in Queensland early in 1890, when maritime unions, in the interests of the Queensland Shearers' Union (QSU), blocked shipment of wool shorn under non-union conditions on the big Jondaryan station. The action was successful: Darling Downs pastoralists agreed to employ only union shearers in future.

Spurred on by this victory, Spence, as president of the ASU, arranged for a similar blockade of non-union work by waterside workers in New South Wales. This time the scheme backfired, for just as the plan to assist the ASU came into effect, a much larger strike began. This dispute, known as the Maritime Strike, centred on matters which were not connected with the wool industry, although the involvement of wharf labourers affected transport of wool. This suited the ASU, but a month later, when it was clear that the Maritime Strike was going badly, Spence came under pressure from leaders of other unions. They wanted reciprocal supporting action from shearers. Very reluctantly, the ASU leaders agreed to call their own members out on strike. The shearers' strike was a failure, terminated after one week. The timing was precipitate and disastrous: shearers were already working under agreements with pastoralists and were therefore exposed to the penalties provided by the Masters and Servants Act, whereas ordinarily a body of shearers would negotiate with a pastoralist before signing an agreement with him.

Defeat of Shearers

Spence has been criticized for miscalculating, but at bottom the fault lay with the internal weakness of the ASU which, as John Merritt notes, 'contained many indifferent and unreliable members'.[9] This weakness led to hopes that other unions would do the ASU's work for it, without the shearers themselves risking their jobs by strike action. The strategy failed in the course of the Maritime Strike in 1890. Nevertheless, shearers in Queensland the following year fought hard against graziers who were intent upon reasserting their authority. The graziers disavowed the closed shop principle ceded in Queensland in 1890 and they demanded some wage reductions. A long strike ensued, and hundreds of angry shearers, some of them armed, massed in camps at Barcaldine and Clermont. There were clashes with numerous scabs brought in from Melbourne by employers, and the Queensland government reacted dramatically by deploying troops and artillery. Many unionists were arrested, and nearly all the executive members of the two main unions involved, the QSU and the Queensland Labourers' Union, were sentenced to terms of imprisonment.

The bold temper of this struggle was later strikingly portrayed in 'The Ballad of 1891', written by Helen Palmer and immortalized in the musical play, *Reedy River*. Two stanzas of the 'Ballad' are reproduced here:

> From Clermont to Barcaldine the Shearers' camps were full,
> When through the west like thunder rang out the union's call:
> 'The sheds'll be shore union or they won't be shorn at all!'
> To trial at Rockhampton the fourteen men were brought;
>
> The judge had got his orders; the squatters owned the court—
> But for every one was sentenced, a thousand won't forget
> When they gaol a man for striking, it's a rich man's country yet![10]

The shearers' strike of 1891 was a clear manifestation of the use of state power against workers. The Queensland government, courts and pastoralists colluded in efforts to break the strike. For example, the secretary of the United Pastoralists' Association on one occasion penned a request to the government's Colonial Secretary: 'Would you be good enough to return the journal left with you today and also let us have Mr. Ranking's telegrams re the movements of military, etc. etc.?' Ranking was a police magistrate who had been appointed as government agent in charge of the strike-affected Rockhampton area. The government also drew the attention of magistrates to a British Act of 1825 which had been repealed in England but was still in force in Queensland. This Act related to conspiracy and intimidation, making peaceful picketing—such as attempts at verbal persuasion—unlawful. The Act was used effectively by Queensland courts to sentence strike leaders to harsh terms of imprisonment.[11]

After lasting some months, the strike collapsed, as unions ran out of money and felt the full force of the upholders of 'law and order'.

135

Ruling-class prejudice against the shearers was epitomized by Supreme Court Judge Harding. In the course of trials, he openly criticized police for acting too leniently, indicating that if he had been present he would not have hesitated to fire on the unionists to restore order. His attitude was redolent of the manner of colonial administrators when dealing with unruly 'natives'. Fortunately for Harding, it was not public knowledge that he was one of the speculators involved in heavy borrowing from the Queensland National Bank: dubious transactions which led to the bankruptcy of that bank in 1893-6.

Queensland has an extraordinary history of repression of the labour movement by reactionary governments. Control was institutionalized in 1938 when the State Transport Act empowered the Queensland government to exercise draconian powers following the proclamation of a State of Emergency. This device has been used both to break strikes, as at Mount Isa in 1964-5, and for more directly political purposes, as in imposing a ban on anti-apartheid demonstrations on the occasion of a tour by a visiting South African football team. More recently, the Bjelke-Petersen government smashed a strike by electrical workers by proclaiming a State of Emergency and passing legislation which provided for civil conscription in the electrical supply industry: under the Electricity (Continuation of Supply) Act of 1985, the Electricity Commissioner has authority to 'direct any person whatever who, in his opinion, is capable of carrying out the necessary work to provide, to maintain or to restore a supply of electricity'. The legislation also deprives such workers of any right to strike, as well as imposing severe restrictions upon freedom of speech.

Queensland's record of ruling-class contempt for civil liberties runs for a century from the 1890s. Landed capital has been the driving force. Also significant is the relative weakness of an industrial and professional bourgeoisie with potential for mediating in class struggles. The one thing that has saved the State from being classed as a police state is that its workers and their middle-class allies are equally renowned for refusing to recognize limitations upon the right to strike or the right to engage in political protest.

Metalminers at Broken Hill

In 1892 it was the turn of metalminers at Broken Hill to bear the brunt of onslaught by employers. The Amalgamated Miners' Association in 1889-90 had won several concessions from the Broken Hill silver–lead mining companies, notably a closed shop, a 46-hour week and a system of wage-rates based on the time worked. Further, the companies were induced to collect union dues from all employees on pay-days and to hand the money over to union representatives. These union gains were resented by company shareholders and directors, most of whom lived in Melbourne or Adelaide. In Broken Hill itself, the environment in which workers lived was harsh and isolated. The separation of capital and labour was accentuated by the employment as mine managers of some Americans, who were antipathetic to trade unions.

In 1892, with metal prices falling and unemployment rising, the Broken Hill companies attacked working conditions. Without negotiations, they announced their intention to introduce a contract system for the mining of ore, in effect substituting piece-work rates of pay for daily rates. The AMA saw this as a move to cut wages at the discretion of the mine managers, and a strike resulted, involving about 7000 employees. The mine owners despatched strikebreakers from Melbourne and Adelaide, the NSW government sent nearly 300 police to Broken Hill, and when the BHP company office opened to engage labour there, policemen with fixed bayonets marched up to perform guard duty. Three weeks after this, strike leaders were arrested and charged with seditious conspiracy. They were sent to Deniliquin for trial by a jury of farmers, 'since this once notoriously pro-selector area was by then so conservative as to give short shrift to striking miners'. This official calculation—itself significant of changing class alignments on the land—was proved accurate. Six of the strike leaders were sentenced to terms of imprisonment.[12]

The strike ended in ignominious defeat after an eighteen-week struggle. The AMA lost on the wage issue, hours of work were increased for those men who were re-employed, and the closed shop was no more. The AMA retained only a fraction of its previous membership at Broken Hill and was in no position to oppose the owners. 'Peace reigned on the Barrier for the ensuing decade', as BHP commented blandly many years later. For destitute and victimized unionists it was akin to the peace of the graveyard.[13]

The Shearers' Second Round

Defeat in strikes encouraged moves for greater co-operation between some unions. In 1893 the QSU and the Queensland Labourers' Union merged to form the Amalgamated Workers' Union, and two years later the ASU (whose main membership lay in New South Wales) absorbed a General Labourers' Union to form the Australian Workers' Union (AWU). However, these moves did not save the shearers and shedhands from further hammerings. In Queensland pastoral pay scales were first reduced and then, in 1894, the Pastoralists' Union devised a new form of shearing agreement which gave woolshed overseers the right to determine any dispute. Incensed at being thus excluded, the unions told their members not to sign the new contracts. A long, bitter

137

struggle ensued, spreading southwards from Queensland as the season progressed.

This particular shearers' strike was marked by more violence than any previous dispute, with 175 people being arrested in New South Wales alone. In one celebrated incident, unionists boarded and took over a steamer, the *Rodney*, while it was tied up in the River Darling one night. The *Rodney* was carrying a contingent of strikebreakers, whose swags were thrown into the river by the boarders. The unionists ordered everyone off the vessel, which was then burned. Some arrests were made, but there was insufficient evidence to convict any of the perpetrators.[14]

Despite such exploits, the strike was lost. Similarly, coalminers at Newcastle were defeated in 1895–6, and the same fate befell seamen a little earlier, in 1893. In the circumstances of a great depression in the 1890s, unions had little chance of winning industrial disputes. It was as much as they could do to remain in existence. In 1904 the Amalgamated Workers' Union in Queensland joined the AWU, thus establishing a truly national body, but actually the total of unionists involved was much smaller than in the 1880s. However, there was a strong growth in numbers from 1907, and by 1911 the AWU had 47 000 members.

The AWU

The legend of the militancy of bushworkers' unions remained potent, and AWU leaders constantly referred to it. In 1909 Spence dedicated his autobiography, *Australia's Awakening*, to 'the Tyrannical Employer and the Aggressive Fighting Trade Unionist'. Yet Spence had not always spoken in such terms. He was basically conciliatory, and in 1888 he said: 'He wanted the workmen to understand that the interests of capitalists and workmen were identical. There should be no friction or antagonism between the two; it was detrimental to the commonwealth.'[15] As it happened, renewed life was given to the legend of militancy early in the twentieth century, though Spence himself was not responsible. In 1907 the Amalgamated Workers' Association (AWA) was formed in Queensland. In an improved economic environment, this was a forceful body representing miners, railwaymen and sugar workers, particularly in the northern part of the state. Then, in 1913, the AWA merged itself in the AWU, as did several other unions in various States, such as the Rural Workers' Union of NSW, the Amalgamated Rabbit Trappers' Union, the Carriers' Union and, in South Australia, the United Labourers' Union which covered fruit pickers, railway navvies and labourers on public works projects. Thus

138

the AWU became the biggest union in Australia, spreading out to embrace unskilled workers in a variety of industries, urban as well as rural.

Yet the giant had feet of clay. True, a hard core of shearers remained the dominant element in the AWU, and shearers were prepared to strike to protect their interests, as happened in 1956—but shearers made up only about 12 000 of the 150 000 members at that time. In representing the bulk of members, AWU leaders in the twentieth century were very moderate. They were often verbally aggressive for the sake of appearances, while avoiding direct industrial action. From the 1890s they were strong supporters of compulsory arbitration and this attitude was carried over into the new Labor parties. Particularly in New South Wales, the AWU, through its ability to deliver votes in rural constituencies, was very influential in the Labor Party. The union had full-time organizers in rural areas.

As this twentieth-century development indicates, care is necessary in assessing the role of Australian bushworkers and their unions. Certainly they were remarkable by comparison with rural counterparts in other countries, yet the Australian organizations were neither as strong nor as important as is sometimes assumed. Despite the appearance of militancy in the 1880s, their involvement in big strikes in the 1890s was primarily defensive—and they lost. The really dynamic force of the labour movement lay elsewhere, among urban industrial workers and sections of miners. Even so, there is food for thought in Joseph Furphy's wry comment about drovers and other members of the 'nomad tribe' towards the end of the nineteenth century: 'The successful pioneer is the man who never spared others: the forgotten pioneer is the man who never spared himself, but, being a fool, built houses for wise men to live in, and omitted to gather moss.'[16]

9

Working-class Divisions:
Skills, Sexism, Racism and Religion

Of all the classes that stand face to face with the bourgeoisie today, the proletariat alone is a really revolutionary class.[1]

Cynics may argue that there has been little sign of revolution from the proletariat in capitalist democracies since Marx wrote his great polemic in 1848—that indeed workers have become increasingly conservative. Yet there is an essential core of truth in Marx's dictum. Historically, major reforms in capitalism, culminating in the era of the welfare state, have arisen out of struggle and pressure by the labour movement, even where the reforms appear to be the work of conservative governments. Such radical changes have not ended the exploitation of labour but they have altered the face of capitalism in a striking fashion, especially in the past half century. Nevertheless, there have been many twists and turns in the path, and it would be wrong to suppose that the labour movement, as an organized expression of the common people, was fully representative of them or of the working class. Many differences emerged.

Maurice Dobb, writing about Britain in the latter part of the nineteenth century, pointed out that the survival there of the old conditions of domestic industry and small workshops

meant that not until the last quarter of the century did the working class begin to assume the homogeneous character of a factory proletariat. Prior to this . . .

the horizon of interest was apt to be the trade and even the locality, rather than the class; and the survival of the individualist traditions of the artisan and the craftsman, with the ambition to become himself a small employer, was for long an obstacle to any firm and widespread growth of trade unionism, let alone of class consciousness.[2]

Dobb's point may be applied with still more force to Australia, where large-scale manufacturing and a factory proletariat were much less prominent. To say this is not to deny the existence of a working class during the long boom. Nor does it imply that workers constituted an amorphous mass still in process of formation into a distinct class. The class was there, with interests separate from those of employers. Taking the standard definition of a workforce as comprising employees, working proprietors and self-employed people (but not dependants), in 1890 around 40 per cent of the Australian population were in the workforce; and, of these, about 70 per cent were wage or salary earners. There were areas of uncertainty, for example, where salaried white-collar workers shaded into the lower middle class. There were also problems in defining the social position of white-collar workers such as junior clerks who, despite relatively low incomes, were highly conscious of status and regarded themselves as being a cut above manual workers. Yet despite such haziness at the margin—the middle class being an excellent example of an ill-defined mass—the large body of manual workers unquestionably constituted a working class.

Craftsmen and Labourers

There were very important dividing lines within the working class itself: lines which promoted discord and lack of unity. For a start, there was the basic distinction between skilled and unskilled workers. A craftsman could expect to earn around 50 per cent more than a labourer. This margin was small compared with that paid in Britain, the difference being related to the particularly heavy demand for unskilled constructional labour in Australia, in railway building and other projects. Indeed, N. G. Butlin reckons that the typical margin for skill in New South Wales fell to only about 25 per cent in the 1880s. The problem with all such calculations is that they relate only to *wage-rates*: the factors of overtime or, alternatively, lost time (including unemployment) are unknown, though they probably had a substantial effect upon *earnings*. John Merritt indicates that a competent shearer, working on piece-rates, could 'earn in a week perhaps three to four times as much as a shed hand and two or three times as much as an urban or rural labourer'—but only if the shearer was able to maintain continuity of employment, avoiding unproductive days and travel costs   141 due to moving from one station to another. On the other hand, unskilled workers were usually worst affected by insecurity of employment due to economic depression or the seasonal nature of jobs.[3]

In a big city like Melbourne, about 42 per cent of the workforce in the 1880s could be classed as skilled or semi-skilled manual workers, and 23 per cent as unskilled (other workers being regarded as white-collar). It may be that skilled workers were proportionately more numerous than in, say, London. In the case of the metalworking industry in Australia, about two-thirds of the workers were skilled. However, there were many gradations of skill. At one end of the scale were craftsmen, especially in the building and engineering trades, who had generally served lengthy periods of apprenticeship in their youth. Their ranks were often infiltrated by men without formal training who had picked up skills on the job, for example in carpentry or bricklaying. Such men, usually described as 'improvers', were used by employers as a form of cheap labour, undercutting trade union preserves of skill. There were other areas of semi-skilled work in mining (where coal-mining required more skill than goldmining) and in transport (e.g. tramway workers). Experience and the exercise of care counted for something, as in the case of stevedores stowing cargo economically in the holds of ships. Strategic positioning of workers in certain sections of industry was often important: on the railways, engine-drivers were able to command wages higher than those of skilled fitters and almost twice as high as those of labourers such as porters.

Even among labourers there were marked differences in earning capacity. Relatively high wages were paid to sturdy pick-and-shovel men, as indicated in a remarkable letter written by John Monash in 1891. At the time of writing, Monash had had several years' experience as an engineer in charge of construction of a railway on the outskirts of Melbourne. He wrote:

It is a mistake . . . to suppose that any ragamuffin can turn navvy. He must be a physical giant . . . Nine out of every ten are raw ignorant Irishmen, strong and muscular, intemperate, improvident . . . the wages are 10½d. per hour up to 1/- . . . This means £2/2/- per week and on this they keep a *wife and 5 children* and have a spree on pay day as well . . .
Where work is plentiful parties of navvies arrive from no one knows where like crows around a carcase, and when the work is over they vanish as mysteriously. Every man has one or more 'mates' and they travel, work, spree and fight together . . . In rainy weather no work proceeds and the men suffer. No work, no pay.[4]

Undoubtedly, wages paid to construction workers and builders' labourers were high compared with those paid to unskilled workers in manufacturing and other industries. Navvies building the Great

Northern railway line in New South Wales in the 1880s could earn twice as much as a farm labourer, although the navvies received their pay only once a month—a practice which saved the employer some money, probably at the cost of aggravating the problem of drinking bouts noted by Monash. Incidentally, the Great Northern navvies appear to have been mainly native-born Australians rather than Irish or English immigrants. Whatever their origins, they lived fairly well while the particular job (and their physique) lasted, and one historian suggests that they might well be described as 'the aristocracy of the unskilled'.[5]

Builders' labourers have never been noted as accumulators of capital. Over a wider grouping, probate records show that as late as 1908 in Victoria (and probably the whole of Australia), more than half of all the men and women who died each year left behind them no measurable wealth or property at all. As for incomes, inequality was extreme in the 1880s, even if wealthy pastoralists are left out of account: at the top end in Melbourne, a university professor received '£1,000 and a house, while many business and professional men earned between £1,000 and £3,000 a year'. The word 'earned' is perhaps inappropriate in this context, for as Twopeny noted at the time: 'It is very difficult to mix thoroughly in business without dirtying your hands; it requires no ordinary moral courage to keep them clean when there is so much filthy lucre about.'[6]

In comparison with these figures, a skilled worker earned between £150 and £180 a year. Clearly, the income differentials within the working class were relatively small, though they might make the difference between modest comfort and scraping through with difficulty. The real significance of the differences lay in their effect upon workers' attitudes. Status was an issue, and craftsmen were inclined to keep aloof from labourers, if not to regard them with contempt. Labourers sometimes responded with hostility towards trade union leaders. In the building industry, distinctions between craftsmen and labourers were quite marked, extending to refusal to engage in joint workplace industrial action. In Victoria, according to one observer, there was 'no real consolidation between skilled and unskilled labour';[7] and in 1892, in the midst of depression, a representative of an Unemployed Workers' Union alleged that the craft unions dominating the Melbourne Trades Hall Council were exclusive and indifferent to the plight of the unemployed.

Sexism

The degree of skill possessed by workers was also a factor in the depressed condition of women, although other reasons were more 143 important. Most women were occupied with work in the home, associated with child-bearing and care for the family. They received no wage for this work and were not officially counted as part of the work-force unless they had jobs for which they were paid. Bettina Cass comments: 'Women's unpaid domestic labour supports, like an infra-structure, the wage structures and profits of the industrial-capitalist economy.' [8] Actually, most females were in the paid workforce before getting married, whereas only about 10 per cent of married women were in this category. There were strong social and cultural forces leading to general belief that married women should remain at home; and women's assumption of responsibilities for child-care meant that most mothers were unable to go out to work anyway. There were also class differences. Some women had well-to-do husbands or relatives, and therefore felt no need for extra income: indeed they might them-selves employ female workers.

Statistically, one result was that, in the 1891 censuses, females constituted about 20 per cent of the total workforce in Victoria and 18 per cent in New South Wales. From a different perspective, and re-stricting consideration to women of working age in metropolitan areas, about 37 per cent of such women in Melbourne were in the workforce in 1891. In Sydney and other cities where manufacturing was less developed, the proportion was around 30 per cent. As for occupations, during the long boom between 40 and 50 per cent or more of all women in paid employment worked as domestic servants—housemaids, cooks and so on. Another large body of women was concentrated in the clothing, textile and footwear manufacturing industries. Smaller num-bers worked as shop assistants, nurses, teachers and governesses. Another source of income was accommodation of lodgers.

It was customary for domestic servants to 'live in' on the premises of the employer, which meant that the servants were constantly at beck and call and subject to petty tyranny. Partly for this reason, women developed a preference for factory work, even though wages and con-ditions were not necessarily better. Consequently, as more employ-ment opportunities appeared in manufacturing, the proportion of women in domestic service declined somewhat. Colonial governments, together with charitable institutions, did their best to maintain the supply of cheap labour for domestic service by assisting the immi-gration of single young women, especially Irish girls, and by directing hapless colonial girls into service. These latter were sometimes orphans, sometimes children abandoned or deemed to have been neglected or 'exposed to moral danger' by their parents, including Aborigines. Institutions took control and trained boys as farm-labourers and girls as domestic servants. In South Australia, records of a government department set up in 1887 show that in every single year between then and 1940 there were hundreds of young state wards who had been placed in 'respectable' foster-homes where they were treated more or less as unpaid servants. One such girl wrote to the secretary of the department in 1890:

I would rather be back in the school again than at service . . . You said it was better for me to write and let you know than it was to run away . . . I get eight shillings a week it is a good thing that I do as I brake so many things and I have to replace them again.[9]

Another depressed section of female workers consisted of those whose circumstances constrained them from living in as domestic servants or taking factory jobs entailing long or regular hours of work. Thus there were wives with young children, the husbands being itinerant or on low pay or unemployed; and there were widows and deserted wives with children to support. Many of these women took in washing or went out as charwomen. Alternatively, there might be work which could be done in the woman's own home, such as dressmaking. This was commonly termed outwork or domestic work, although as Marx noted it had very little in common with the traditional style of industry in the home, which presupposed independent urban handicrafts and peasant farming. 'That old-fashioned industry has now been converted into an outside department of a factory, the manufactory, or the warehouse.'[10]

Particularly in Victoria in the 1870s and 1880s, there was a considerable growth of such outwork in the clothing and footwear industries. Most of the outworkers were female, especially in needlework trades, and they either did the same work as in factories (cheap sewing machines were available for home use) or they supplied factories with their piece-work output for later stages of manufacturing. In effect, then, outwork developed as an adjunct to factories. Employers found it profitable to use domestic workshops to increase production without the need for additional investment in factory facilities, and conversely when trade conditions worsened the outworkers could be easily thrown aside or paid less. Outworkers are notoriously exploited through low piece-work rates of pay, which may be reduced in competition against factory workers' wages. There was a considerable pool of female labour, both cheap and flexible for employers' use. Ray Markey sums up as follows:

cheap female labour was an essential part of the process of capital accumulation in the developing manufactures, which were inefficiently structured, subject to price and quality competition from overseas, relatively labour intensive, and, unlike other sectors, relied largely on domestic capital formation even prior to the cessation of British capital inflow in the 1890s.[11]

Wages for women require consideration in the context of the question of wages in general. Wage levels are the product of various 145 factors. At bottom, wages in a capitalist society represent the minimum necessary to feed, clothe and shelter a worker and—because a worker's ability to labour needs to be reproduced from one generation to another—a spouse and children. The acquisition of work skills entails cost in training or education so that, as an inducement, a margin is payable for skill. In addition, there is the effect upon wages of the supply and demand for labour, which is affected by the state of the economy. Pressure from workers, usually through trade unions, is also important: employers do not pay increases of their own volition.

None of this is an adequate explanation of the fact that in the 1880s the wage of a labourer in Australia was about seven shillings a day while an Indian or Chinese plantation worker in the tropics received one shilling a day. Differences in productivity are part of the answer; and the cost of a worker's family was of little concern to employers who saw endless streams of Asians desperate for jobs. Yet it is evident that beyond all these factors there is an element of historical variation between one country or region and another. As Marx noted in *Capital*, a worker's wants, and the modes of satisfying them, 'are themselves the product of historical development, and depend therefore on the degree of civilisation of a country, more particularly on the conditions under which, and consequently on the habits and degree of comfort in which, the class of free labourers has been formed'. Australia, with its British heritage of struggle by the common people, its perennial labour shortage, high productivity and early union organization, was close to the top on the international scale.

Relatively low rates of pay for women in Australia were part of the cultural inheritance from Britain, reinforced in Australia by low productivity in manufacturing. The social environment, with strong ideological supports, was one in which women's work was regarded as marginal, as something to occupy their labour for a few years before marriage. Women themselves accepted this viewpoint, which provided little incentive for them to embark on training to acquire skills. Women in the workforce were generally less skilled than men. This was sometimes used to explain away the fact that average female wages in Australia were only one-third to one-half of those of males, but actually levels of skill accounted for only part of the difference. Institutional barriers were present even in acquiring skill, for male craft workers and their unions maintained a monopoly over entry to skilled trades through apprenticeship.

There was a clear sexual division of employment, whereby certain occupations were considered 'women's work' and were poorly paid precisely for that reason. In some other industries, where women were employed along with men, the female rate of pay for the job was lower than the male. As Desley Deacon notes, Australian women 'made important gains with regard to divorce law and access to higher

146

education in the 1880s, and in the 1890s and the early 1900s they won the vote'. Yet when men felt threatened by competition from female labour, moves were made to squeeze women out of those particular labour markets. In circumstances of depression in Victoria in 1894, the employment of married women as public schoolteachers was made illegal. Some trade unions in the early twentieth century supported the notion of equal pay for women, mainly in the expectation that, if this were implemented, the employers, finding female labour no longer cheap, would be prejudiced in favour of employment of males. More generally, male workers adopted a strategy of claiming that they as breadwinners needed higher wages than women. This false distinction was strengthened by agreement among all colonial statisticians, as from the censuses of 1891, to divide the population into the two categories of breadwinners and dependants—a classification described by Deacon as being 'in part a political act carried out in the interests of working-class men for the purpose of labor market closure'.[12]

Working women were part of the same class as working men: the labour of both was exploited by employers. Nevertheless, class analysis alone is not enough to explain the position of women in the workforce. Sexual discrimination was severe, and the differentiation presumably enabled male workers in some industries to secure higher wage margins for themselves. Employers, male and female, also gained in material terms; but from the viewpoint of the working class as a whole, the most important aspects of discrimination against women were the adverse effect upon unity in class struggle and the absence of the contribution which women could have made to the struggle.

Unions of male workers occasionally gave a helping hand to women, as in 1882 when the Melbourne Trades Hall Council helped to establish a Tailoresses' Union, but such gestures were rare and not always as altruistic as they seemed. The exclusion of women from working-class organizations reinforced the standard cultural pattern of poverty which was marked among women in the workforce: low expectations, timidity and hopelessness meant disregard for communal interests. There is very little evidence of women playing any active role in the great industrial disputes around 1890, which is not surprising since few women were members of labour unions. The membership of the Tailoresses' Union in Melbourne had declined to 100, compared with 2000 in 1883.

Racism

One important component of the cultural baggage which British immigrants brought to the Australian colonies was racism. Not that British people were unique in their feelings of superiority over the inhabitants of other countries—it was an inevitable concomitant of imperialism and was most easily focussed upon people with different skin pigmentation. In Australia that meant first Aborigines and then Chinese and Melanesians.

In New South Wales by the 1870s, white settlement on the land was so extensive as to make it impossible for most Aborigines to continue their hunter-gatherer way of life. They became a depressed segment of the working class, employed on a casual intermittent basis, mainly in the pastoral industry. They were treated with contempt and in all the Australian colonies they were 'underpaid, given no formal training, were rarely praised and often bashed and kicked and whipped'. Aboriginal women were doubly exploited. The 'jolly swagmen' of Australian bush mythology often 'at night became far from funny shagmen when they staggered into blacks' camps'.[13]

Some leading members of the Amalgamated Shearers' Union objected to discrimination against Aborigines, and W. Browne, a prominent member of the Queensland Labor Party, stated in Parliament in 1897: 'They have a right to be employed; a right to the first show to get a living, and if the aborigine does a day's work on a station, or a farm, or anywhere else he is entitled to a fair wage the same as a white man or anyone else.'[14]

Yet the reference to a 'day's work' indicates the marginal position of Aborigines in the white economy, and in practice the trade unions did no more than pay occasional lip service to racial equality. As Reynolds remarks, blacks developed bargaining skills of their own. 'They do not like working in the fields', noted a North Queensland missionary, and they considered that 'our issues of food and tobacco are not very generous'. The Aborigines asked him pointedly, 'Does the One up in Heaven tell you to give us so little?'.[15]

Racist attitudes were endemic. Often apparent only in the form of casual contempt, they became virulent when the 'inferior' groups became numerous and appeared to be a threat to the interests of the Anglo-Celtic majority. Chinese arrived in Australia in large numbers in the 1850s with the same goal as European immigrants: gold. By the end of that decade, there were about 40 000 Chinese in Victoria, the great majority of them being goldminers. Many of them worked poor areas abandoned by European diggers, but this did not prevent hostility from flaring up among the latter, especially as the average yield of gold per digger fell from the early 1850s. Competition from Chinese might be indirect but it could be argued that their efforts depleted a finite supply of gold in the ground. The fact that this was also true of the efforts of white diggers passed without comment. There were anti-Chinese riots in mining areas, and in 1855 Victoria legislated to restrict Chinese immigration by imposing discriminatory taxes on entry into the colony and on Chinese people resident there. South Australia and New South Wales soon followed suit.

These measures, coupled with the general decline in alluvial digging, proved effective. Actually censuses in 1861 showed that 9 per cent of the population of Victoria and 7 per cent of the population of New South Wales had been born outside the British Empire. Most of these were Chinese; and their proportion of the male population alone was much higher, as there were few Chinese female immigrants. However, many immigrants returned to China in the 1860s, and the colonial legislative restrictions were repealed.

The process was repeated a decade or so later, when the Palmer River gold discoveries in northern Queensland led to an influx of about 17 000 Chinese. Legislative barriers were re-introduced and, in the 1880s, Chinese immigration into Australia was virtually prohibited. The extension of this exclusive policy to people from other parts of Asia in the following decade meant that 'White Australia' became a foundation stone in the establishment of the Commonwealth. It was a policy with which most Australians agreed, partly because it was associated with a growth of nationalist feeling based upon an ideal of a free society, with high standards of living. It was difficult for racially prejudiced white Australians to fit Chinese immigrants into such a picture.

It is of some interest that violent anti-Chinese racism in Australia was first manifest among independent, self-employed diggers rather than members of the working class. However, workers were not slow to join in; and subsequently goldminers working for wages carried over their antipathy into trade unions. The general argument was that, given the historically low Chinese standard of living, *unrestricted* Chinese immigration into Australia would result in Australian wages being driven down close to Chinese levels. The fear of this was justified, and there was a parallel in working-class objections to financial assistance being given by colonial governments towards the immigration of European workers. On the other hand, Australian trade unions did not disapprove of unassisted immigration from Europe, nor were European immigrants (whether assisted or not) subject to specific disabilities after arrival in Australia. The contrast in the case of the Chinese was glaring, and racism was clearly a prime factor in it. Racism was also evident in the customary highly derogatory way of referring to the Chinese and their culture.

Outside mining, Chinese in Australia during the long boom were noted as market gardeners, cooks and merchants. Their trading activities roused some resentment among other small businessmen, and those Chinese who worked for wages showed a strong preference for 149 employers of their own nationality. The preference was understandable in the light of the racist attitudes of whites, but it reinforced those attitudes in the middle classes: Chinese were not readily available as a source of cheap labour for small employers. In the case of large employers, the position was rather different. Graziers often employed Chinese, as did sugar planters in Queensland. On the plantations there was a racial gradation among unskilled field labourers, with Chinese being paid much lower wages than Europeans but substantially more than the wages of a Melanesian, while Aborigines were usually given only their rations.

In urban areas also, Chinese occupied a particular segment of the labour market: menial, low paid work which was generally not directly competitive with the jobs of white workers. In this sense, the role of Chinese workers was similar to that of white female workers, both groups being subject to a higher degree of exploitation by employers. White workers were not unhappy about the segregation of Chinese workers but they objected violently in 1878 when a big employer, the Australasian Steam Navigation Company (ASN), imported Chinese crews from Hong Kong to replace Australian ships' crews at less than half the standard rate of wages. This development was new—a threat to displace white workers and to undercut wages generally. Trade unions representing ironworkers employed at the large ASN workshop in Sydney feared that imported Chinese seamen would soon be followed by shipyard workers from Hong Kong.

A strike was called by the Seamen's Union, which had been established in Sydney and Melbourne a few years earlier. Wharf labourers, engineers and other workers joined in sympathy and the strike spread to Queensland ports. It was probably the biggest strike in Australia up to that time, and a crucial factor in the success of the Seamen's Union was the support it received, not only from other trade unions but also from the middle class, motivated mainly by anti-Chinese prejudice. The Seamen's Union itself was probably as racially biased as any other organization in the community; it recognized the propaganda value of racist arguments and it welcomed support from any quarter, although to its credit the union voiced opposition to anti-Chinese violence in the streets of Sydney.

The strike ended after thirteen weeks. The ASN was isolated in public opinion as expressed at many mass meetings. Even newspapers (which can normally be expected to support any employer in a strike situation by arguing that strikes are never justified) either withheld support from the ASN or were half-hearted. The strike was concluded on the basis of agreement by the company to retain in its service no more than 180 Chinese, a number which was soon to be reduced. In effect, the ASN undertook not to persist in its cheap labour policy. Within three years in fact it ceased to employ Chinese.

This industrial dispute decisively discouraged any further attempts by employers to import cheap Chinese labour into New South Wales or Victoria. Ideally it might be said that the trade union campaign against the ASN in 1878 should have been fought on the principle that all workers, including the Chinese, should be paid the prevailing rate of wages. However, this would have been unrealistic: unions were much too weak to force such a solution upon employers. On the other hand, the actions of white cabinetmakers (craftsmen) organized in the United Furniture Trade Society in Melbourne in the 1880s were contemptible from the viewpoint of trade union solidarity. This union, along with white employers in the trade, objected to allegedly unfair competition from Chinese cabinetmakers, particularly in the form of longer hours of work. The union campaigned strongly and succeeded in having legislative restrictions placed upon the Chinese.

This was a fairly standard tactic but then the unexpected occurred: Chinese furniture workers formed a union of their own, demanding better wages and shorter hours from the Chinese employers in the trade. In 1885 this Chinese Workers' Union organized a strike in Melbourne. This stirring illustration of the ability of a good English tradition to take root in alien soil should have been welcomed by white workers. The question at issue was not the old one of stopping Chinese immigration: in this case, the Chinese concerned were established residents, although in fact the total number of Chinese in Melbourne was only about one thousand. The matter was really one of orthodox trade union action. The move by the Chinese Workers' Union held promise of benefits not only for its own members but also for white furniture workers who were complaining about unfair competition from the Chinese section of the trade.[16] Despite this, the Furniture Trade Society maintained hostility towards brother-unionists. An outrageous example of this occurred in 1890, when the white union heard that a broad-based union body had accepted a donation from the Chinese in aid of striking shearers. The white cabinetmakers then demanded that the money be returned, promising to make up the deficit from their own funds. Nor was this an isolated type of incident. When W. G. Spence wrote that unionism 'had in it that feeling of mateship which he [the Australian bushman] understood already, and which always characterized the action of one "white man" to another', he meant 'white man' literally. The Shearers' Union (later the AWU) recognized that 'all workers, no matter what their occupation or sex may be, have a common interest'; but the union specifically barred Chinese and Melanesians from membership.[17]

Racial antagonism divided and weakened the working class, although on some occasions, as in 1878, it had the contrary effect of attracting support for white workers from other classes. There were also divisions among white workers, stemming from ethnic differences. Apart from immigrants from the British Isles, there were sizable groups from Germany, Scandinavia and, by the 1890s, Italy.   151

The immigrants from northern Europe, together with a scattering from the USA, were fairly well accepted in Australia. This was particularly true of immigrants from the United Kingdom who constituted the great bulk of all immigrants. Actually the British contribution to Australian stock was by no means homogeneous in ethnic content: most of these immigrants were Anglo-Saxon in origin, but others (Irish, Scots, Welsh) were Celts. In practice there had been considerable intermixing long before their arrival in Australia.

Despite the common language used by immigrants from the British Isles, the Irish were distinct in a number of respects. They were generally poorer, less educated and more likely to be labourers or domestic servants. 'In the colonies those who make money are generally Scotchmen, and those who do not are mostly Irishmen', noted Anthony Trollope, the English novelist who travelled through eastern Australia in 1871. The only business occupation in which there were numbers of Irish people was that of publican. Along with drinking, the Irish had a reputation for violence and were generally regarded with contempt, as indicated by the quotation from Monash above. Despised as 'bog-Irish', they were allotted hard or unpleasant jobs which most other workers avoided if possible.

In this sense there was a division between many Irish and other British workers in Australia. Its importance is underlined by the fact that in 1891 nearly a quarter of a million people in Australia had been born in Ireland. They made up about 28 per cent of those residents of Australia who had been born in different parts of the United Kingdom; and this proportion was fairly constant over the preceding three decades. The percentage was higher still among workers. However, the barriers between Irish and other workers were by no means insuperable, and although the Irish tended to cluster in some areas—for example, part of the Melbourne suburb of Richmond was called Irishtown—there were no Irish urban ghettoes comparable to the concentration in Boston in the USA.

The separateness of the Irish in Australia was accentuated by religious differences. Most of them were Roman Catholics, and the fact that 26 per cent of the total population of New South Wales was Catholic in 1901 was largely a reflection of this. On the other hand, between 10 and 20 per cent of Irish immigrants in Australia came from Protestant Ulster, and their Orange Lodges fomented religious bigotry. Frederick Cato, a Melbourne Methodist and co-founder of the Moran & Cato grocery chain, could 'never properly trust an RC'—so he did not employ one.[18] In turn, Irish Catholics reacted to prejudice and a hostile Establishment by organizing themselves. One result was that in course of time their church institutionalized socio-religious divisions by setting up an educational system separate from the public one. More generally, the ethnic Irish became active in politics; and as the great majority of them were working-class until after World War II, their influence was felt mainly in and through the Australian Labor Party.

That particular development, coupled with an Irish 'Tammany Hall' style of machine politics and a strong Irish Catholic infiltration of the public service, was a twentieth-century phenomenon. Of the thirty-five Labor members elected to the parliament of New South Wales in 1891, only five were Roman Catholics—and three of those had been born in Australia. Nevertheless, it may be noted that, while the Irish were much better off materially in Australia than in their homeland, the memory of their oppressed origins was kept alive by the ever-present Irish Question: the fight for Irish home rule. Consequently, hostility towards British imperialism and a corresponding sympathy for Australian nationalism were prominent in the minds of the Irish and their offspring in Australia. It has been said (admittedly, by an Irishman) that 'Australia was Ireland's revenge upon England'!

The same thought may have occurred to employers in Australia, the great majority of whom were English or Scots in origin. The Irish reputation for convivial fecklessness was allied to a fiery fighting spirit. When this was channelled into trade union and labour activity, it provided a formidable force, as employers discovered in industrial disputes. Yet it is easy to exaggerate the strength of national characteristics. If anyone ever undertakes a serious study of the large number of blacklegs in Australian history, it may well be found that Irish were prominent among them. Irishmen also figured largely in the colonial police forces.

Nevertheless, when all ethnic differences have been explored, it must be said that the divisions between Irish and other groups of European origin in Australia were minor by comparison with those in other countries which took in large numbers of immigrants. This meant that the task of trade union organizers was much easier in Australia than in the USA, where the problems of uniting workers of many different nationalities, languages and cultures were overwhelming, and immigrants were repeatedly used as strikebreakers. Against this comparative background, the failure to combat racism in Australia shows up starkly. 'White Australia' was a shackle on the labour movement's progress to maturity.

Religion

Religion has divided social classes since the beginning of capitalism. Tawney and Weber have argued that the new social values inherent in capitalism necessitated changes in religious beliefs, and they linked the Reformation to the transition from feudalism to capitalism.[19] The working classes in Britain and most European countries were affected in one way or another by the religious schisms which developed, and it would be surprising if Australian capitalism had escaped them. It did not, and although there were manifestations in all social classes, the clearest illustrations of the divisions were within the working class, between Protestant and Catholic, the latter overwhelmingly of Irish origin.

The most concentrated expression of this is to be found in New South Wales at the time of the formation of the Labor Party there. Cardinal Patrick Francis Moran was Catholic Archbishop of Sydney then, and was instrumental in ensuring that it did not become a socialist party. From the inception of the Labor Party, Moran utilized his powerful position in the church to campaign for fifteen years against the possibility of any connection between trade unionism and socialism, and between Labor Party policy and socialism.

Here was a divisive influence on the Australian working class, exerted by religion, for Moran was telling his flock, in essence, that workers' organizations, whether industrial or political in form or purpose, must not embrace any ideology that is not Christian and/or is aimed at the overthrow of existing society. 'Socialists', he said, 'are the avowed enemy of all religion'. As most persons of Irish origin were Catholic, this was in effect a political directive to a very significant part of the Australian working class, from the highest religious authority available to them.[20]

Moran's biographer, Patrick Ford, records that in October 1890 the Australian Socialist League was in the ascendant in Labor circles in New South Wales. Its members had a share in strike leadership as well as editorship of Labor's official organ, and it was pushing for a socialist Labor Party. Moran, who was acting as a kind of mediator in the Maritime Strike, supported the workers on the basis of Catholic notions of social justice, including the right to a living wage, frugal though it might be. Yet Moran also said that the only hope for the success of trade unionism was to keep it quite free from any socialistic movement. Those words, Ford notes, were of historical significance because they represented the first major clash between a churchman and socialist leaders. They constituted a warning which the Labor leaders could not ignore, because they needed the Catholic electorate, and Moran was a national figure, supportive of workers and significant electorally. He led one-quarter of the population, and perhaps one-third of the workers:

Being mostly of Irish descent, they were politically conscious, and anxious to exercise the freedom denied them in their homeland ... A Labor party would be their normal channel of political expression. But Catholics, though very conscious of their freedom in political affairs, were in the main very loyal in matters of faith and morals, which were compromised by the philosophy and doctrines of Socialism. *This numerous, politically-conscious, ecclesiastically-loyal group would support the Labor party in matters temporal, but in matters spiritual it would, in numbers large enough to count, follow its popular and decisive leader.*[21]

R. N. Spann notes that, in the late 1890s, 'some Catholics were already starting to build hopes on the new Labor Party, once it was clear that the party was there to stay, was not likely to become extremely "socialistic", and was open to Catholic influence'. He suggests that, with its union substructure and its democratic branch organization, the Labor Party offered new channels to rising elites and hence a new career potential in politics.[22]

In the early 1900s there were eight or nine Catholic Labor MLAs in New South Wales, and they averaged 31 per cent of the parliamentary Labor Party; by 1910 the percentage was 37, and it rose at later elections. 'The major change followed the 1916 conscription crisis, which split the Labor Party in two, and "ushered in a period of hitherto unparalleled Irish-Australian ascendancy in the ALP"', for by 1920 over half the Labor MLAs in New South Wales were Catholic. A similar development took place in the federal Labor Party and in other States. In New South Wales a Protestant Labor Party ran nineteen candidates in the 1925 elections; it won one seat, obtaining 3.9 per cent of the votes in contested electorates. However: 'No work seems to have been done in Australia on Protestant political behaviour, which is a pity, as any account of religion and voting is one-sided that concentrates on the oddities of a single religious group.'[23]

Ford considers that, in the 1920s, when Labor embraced a socialist objective, the Catholic element ensured support for the moderate tradition in the party, an effect which continued up to the time of his writing—the mid-1960s. He concludes:

The voice of Moran was indeed the voice of Christian Democracy in Australia ... Moran can be said to have been not merely a Churchman opposing extremist Socialism, but a Cardinal Archbishop setting the course of Catholic social thought and action in Australia, and one of the makers of modern Australia.[24]

There is here a nucleus of evidence which suggests that the ALP in New South Wales became a kind of Christian Democrat party at a very early stage; and that there is virtually a direct line of descent from Moran, through Mannix, Duhig and Gilroy to Santamaria and the National Civic Council and the Democratic Labor Party (DLP), each in   155 their own way being architects of politico-religious alliances which have divided the working class and the parties purporting to represent it, using religious dogma to attack and proscribe socialism.

There is similar evidence for Queensland:

1899 saw the beginning of the Catholic-Labor nexus, which was to become so crucial in subsequent Queensland history . . . the way was being prepared for an alliance between the labour movement and the Catholic church, whose members comprised almost 24% of the Queensland population.[25]

The basis of this alliance was legislation allowing scholarships to be taken out at church schools. This represented a major revision of the Education Act of 1875 which had abolished state aid to church schools. The final obstacle to the alliance was removed in 1905 when Cardinal Moran and the Plenary Council of Bishops declared that the Labor Party was not socialist in the sense condemned by Pope Leo XIII. The partisan nature of the pro-conscriptionists in World War I—strongly anti-Irish and anti-Catholic—helped to consolidate the alliance, and in 1915 when the Ryan government was elected in Queensland, five of its front-benchers were Catholics. Ryan was said to be a close friend of Archbishop Duhig, colloquially known as 'the uncrowned King of Queensland', who remained Archbishop of Brisbane throughout Labor's entire period of office and beyond: 1917 to 1965.

Social and Working Conditions

In considering the conditions in which people lived and worked in the latter part of the nineteenth century, there is one obvious question: what did the long boom mean for workers? The standard answer is that this was a period of sustained and rapid economic growth, in which there was virtually full employment, and workers shared in the general benefits. The reality is more complex, even after allowance is made for the effect of the large growth in population, which brought the rate of increase in Australian economic output down from nearly 5 per cent per annum overall to 1½ per cent annually *per head* of population in the period 1861–90. These are statistical averages of gross domestic product, which say nothing about unequal distribution.

It appears that for both male and female workers, real wages improved modestly, hourly wage-rates rising more than sufficiently to offset any fall in the standard number of hours worked. As for unemployment, it is misleading to state simply that the economic recessions which punctuated the long boom and produced sharp rises in unemployment were relatively short in duration. A six-months' term of unemployment could be disastrous for a worker with no reserves to fall back upon and no unemployment pay from the state. Even skilled workers had to be highly mobile in search of work. For example, when there was a depression in Adelaide but not in Melbourne and Sydney in 1883, engineering workers moved out of South Australia, usually by ship. In other words, although shortage of labour was common during the period, which was to the advantage of workers, this was not so at all times and places. Employers were sometimes gratified. As Rachel Henning wrote about her brother Biddulph, a squatter in Queensland:

Now, owing to the failure of the Peak Down diggings and the tide of emigrants, the masters have their turn. Biddulph never gives more than 20s. a week, and dismisses every man who does not please him.[26]

High mobility of labour in this period is generally reckoned to be to the advantage of workers. On the other hand, it may indicate serious under-employment. Many outback jobs were seasonal in nature, as were the transport and processing jobs associated with rural produce. For example, unskilled workers were employed in sugar-mills for only six months of the year: the milling season. In a number of industries casual work was common. Wharf labourers were often in heavy demand one day and unemployed (and unpaid) the next. Similarly, work could be intermittent for building workers, especially during winter months, while the availability of work for women outworkers in the clothing industry was notoriously erratic.

Fluctuations in a worker's weekly earnings were often severe as a result of such conditions. Uncertainty of employment affected unskilled workers most, and the relative steadiness of employment for skilled workers may have been as important to them as the wage differential they received. Shortage of labour was primarily a rural phenomenon, and one historian suggests that the presence of a large casual labour force in a city like Sydney may be taken as 'an indication of a floating reserve army, functioning on the periphery of the work force for the benefit of the smooth progression of the boom period'.[27] Part of its function undoubtedly was as a source of blacklegs during strikes.

In a number of industries, workers were paid according to the amount of work done rather than the time spent on it. Marx observed that money paid for piece-work was 'the form of wages most in harmony with the capitalist mode of production'. It was 'the most fruitful source of reductions of wages and capitalistic cheating', pitting each worker in a race against others.[28] This was certainly the case in the outwork section of the clothing industry in Australia. Piece-work also prevailed in the building trades (where it was associated with widespread subcontracting) and in printing and coalmining. In 1876 a parliamentary committee in New South Wales reported that in the Sydney region there were several hundred lads aged from eight to fourteen working ten hours a day as 'puggers-up': they carried heavy loads of wet clay for brickmakers in yards where there was no machinery. The brickmakers themselves were paid on a piece-work basis and they individually paid lads (sometimes their own sons) to work for them. There were instances in coalmining, too, of workers exploiting young fellow-workers.

Some trade unions, notably the Amalgamated Society of Engineers, steadfastly refused to have anything to do with piece-work. Their reasons are well illustrated by an incident in 1870 when T. S. Mort in Sydney offered to sell shares in his engineering company to leading hands and foremen. Mort wrote to his son: 'I look upon this arrangement as of vast importance to the success of the concern because it will secure me against strikes, 8 hour system, and enable me to enforce *piece work* which latter is the only way of breaking down wages.' [29]

Nevertheless, some groups of workers, such as compositors organized in Typographical Societies, were content to work for piece-rates. Indeed, compositors on big newspapers were the most highly paid of all craftsmen. 'The piece-work compositor was virtually a sub-contractor who agreed to perform a certain task ... in consideration of payment offered for each unit of work completed'—although the union devised working rules to minimize competition of one worker against another. Thus highly-paid printers secured a measure of freedom from managerial authority, even to the extent of largely determining their own hours of work, one result being that they played no part in the eight-hour-day campaign of the 1850s. The difference between this sort of situation and the more common one in which low-paid workers suffered under the piece-work system was strongly related to the degree of union control.[30]

In relation to social conditions, there is general agreement among historians that the lot of the workforce in Australia during the long boom was less wretched than in other capitalist societies. Standards of consumption and income were higher than in Britain or probably the USA. In the 1880s average life expectancy for men in Australia was forty-seven years and for women fifty-one years, compared with four or five years less in each case in England. T. A. Coghlan, who was government statistician in New South Wales from 1886, summed up the situation: 'It appeared as if a certain standard of life had been established definitely for Australian industrial workers, far above that of Great Britain.' [31] Yet it is easy to exaggerate in making such comparisons. In an incautious moment, N. G. Butlin once wrote about the 1860s in Australia that 'the picture emerges of a nineteenth century paradise of the south-west Pacific'.[32] Henry Lawson, the people's poet who actually lived in the 'paradise', later wrote:

They lie, the men who tell us, for reasons of their own,
That want is here a stranger, and that misery's unknown.

In fact there was widespread poverty which the bourgeoisie took for granted. Some pleasant suburbs developed around cities as the spread of railways and tramways made it possible for ordinary people to live beyond walking distance from the place of work. Yet rents were high and in central districts there were slums where grasping landlords reaped profit from crowding families into filthy, insanitary dwellings. There too the working class suffered higher rates of illness and mortality, and enjoyed poorer access to medical care and educational facilities, than was the case in middle-class suburbs. In the late 1880s John Andrews, a member of the Melbourne Anarchists' Club, described lanes adjacent to Little Bourke Street:

Waste paper and litter of all sorts, putrid kitchen garbage, dead cats and dogs in all stages of decomposition, human excreta in abundance besides the drainage from leaky and overflowing cess-pans, together with forlorn prowling curs as wretched as any human outcasts ... abomination and squalor.[33]

'Marvellous Melbourne', as a visiting English journalist christened it, was more graphically described as 'Marvellous Smelbourne': sewering of the city did not begin until the 1890s. Disease was endemic, and in the 1880s the infant mortality rate in Sydney was higher than in London. In 1900 more than a hundred people died from bubonic plague in Sydney. In mining and construction camps, sanitary facilities were virtually non-existent: there was no profit for contractors in providing them and a navvy's life was considered to be of little value.

Disease is no respecter of class, and this largely accounts for growth in bourgeois interest in improving urban public health services. At the same time, what were termed 'noxious trades' were pushed out to working-class areas such as Alexandria in Sydney, where ample supplies of water were available. These industries were concerned with processing raw materials from the pastoral industry: skinning, tanning, boiling-down works and so on. They produced stinks that were believed to be responsible for ill-health, so that well-to-do people made sure that the processing was kept out of the suburbs in which they themselves lived. Working-class suburbs were the obvious alternative. Later on, medical science showed that the real danger to health came not so much from the stench as from the pollution of waterways by industrial waste, but right up to the 1970s the pungent smells of fertilizer, leather and glue plants assailed the nostrils of visitors travelling to and from Mascot airport, not to mention the working-class inhabitants of this part of Sydney. By that time the residents had had another pollutant dumped upon them: noise from aircraft using the airport built in their locality. As usual, the concern of middle-class and wealthy people for the quality of their own living standards was paramount in determining where noise nuisance would be concentrated.

There was one grain of truth in the notion of Australia as a paradise 159 in the late nineteenth century. Many workers had reasonable prospects of becoming self-employed or employers themselves and thus moving out of the working class. Manufacturing was generally small-scale, and in a number of industries the cost of necessary equipment was low. For instance, a compositor in Melbourne could set himself up in a small printing business in the 1870s for about £50, which he could save out of his wages without great difficulty. The building industry in particular consisted largely of a network of small subcontractors with little capital. There were opportunities for carpenters, bricklayers and other craftsmen to break into the system and become their own masters. Graeme Davison, in his study of Melbourne, notes that, according to the 1891 census, 16 per cent of plasterers, 24 per cent of plumbers and 17 per cent of slaters were employers or self-employed. Even in the clothing industry, there were some opportunities for women, mainly in dressmaking. According to the New South Wales census of 1891, there were about 17 000 people engaged in the clothing industry there. Godfrey Linge estimates that, of these, about 7000 worked in factories, 6000 were employed in tiny workrooms or shops, and 4000 worked on their own account. The exceptional women who succeeded in dressmaking as proprietors or forewomen made good money: £5 per week or more, compared with an average wage of less than £1 per week for dressmakers in workrooms.[34]

Upward social mobility is a recognized feature of the time, with important consequences. In 1854 the Chief Justice of New South Wales, in the process of finding a group of newspaper compositors guilty of conspiracy for going on strike for higher wages, was reported as saying:

No man would be safe if combinations of this kind could be permitted. And the very interest of these classes [workers] themselves required a maintenance of the law in its integrity, for the labourer of today might be an employer of labour tomorrow.[35]

The complaining employer in that case was Henry Parkes, who had arrived in the colony as a bounty immigrant in 1839 and went on to become Premier. His was an outstanding success story in conventional terms. Much less documented is the reverse process, in which a small business failed and its proprietor became an employee. This happened very frequently in the case of shopkeepers, a high proportion of whom lasted only a few years in business, and in the building industry. Indeed, the standard picture of a high degree of upward social mobility is suspect, as is apparent from Shirley Fisher's study of church marriage registers in Sydney in 1870 and 1887. Comparisons of the stated occupations of bride with groom and with their fathers indicate that movements from one social class or category to another were quite limited and that in particular the persons born into the unskilled group found it hard to break out into another category. Most women married men of the same social status as themselves, although there was more scope for women to improve their position through marriage—for example by a domestic servant marrying a white-collar or skilled worker —because of the relative shortage of women in the colony. However, that shortage did not apply to the Sydney metropolitan area.[36]

It seems that whilst there was indeed social mobility, it was just as likely to be downward as upward, as far as the common people were concerned. There is some confirmation of this in a study by Ellen McEwen of the Newcastle coalmining district. In that relatively closed community, sons and daughters of local shopkeepers and the like mostly married 'beneath' themselves. The general conclusion, however, is again one of little change from one generation to another: two-thirds of miners' daughters married miners and 91 per cent married workingmen, while 81 per cent of miners' sons were also miners.[37]

No matter how flawed the belief in upward social mobility, it was a potent force in the minds of most people; so too was another legend, to the effect that workers became owners of their own homes, mainly through building societies. Actually statistics suggest that while about half of all dwellings in Australia were owner-occupied in 1891, the proportion which were owner-occupied in metropolitan areas (where cheap timber structures were less common) was only 30 per cent in the case of Sydney, and 41 per cent in Melbourne. The figures would be lower if workers alone were taken into account. This is not to deny that the proportion of workers who owned their own homes was high by international standards, even though 'owner-occupier' includes many people buying over a lengthy period of years; but there was certainly a strong element of exaggeration in the traditional picture.

Exaggeration arose partly out of the undoubted vigour of building societies in the 1880s, particularly in Melbourne. However, R. F. Jackson's research indicates that these societies should not be characterized as working-class institutions:

neither in their lending activities nor in the raising of their deposits did the societies deal predominantly with people from the working classes. The building societies' funds came overwhelmingly from the rich and the societies lent much more money to commercial borrowers and to the well-to-do than to working-class owner-occupiers.[38]

Investment in building societies was attractive because they paid higher rates of interest on deposits than banks paid. There was also an ideological aspect. Davison notes that interlocking directorates of   161 building societies, temperance associations, social purity leagues and nonconformist churches 'attest an underlying consistency of social ideals'. More directly, the *Building Societies' Gazette* declared in 1886 that a man buying a home through a mortgage 'has a stake in the country, and it is in his interest . . . to avoid and fight shy of all revolutionary and disquieting or factious movements, such as strikes, violent political agitation, or any calculated to hinder its [the country's] advancement'.[39]

Public education is another sphere where reality has been clouded by sweeping generalizations. Undoubtedly, the Victorian Act of 1872 which provided for free, compulsory and secular instruction through a network of primary schools, marked a great advance. South Australia followed suit several years later, although there the schooling was free only to those who could not afford fees of fourpence or sixpence per week. New South Wales also, under its Public Instruction Act of 1880, demanded fees from those deemed able to afford them. More important, children between the ages of six and fourteen in New South Wales were obliged to attend school for only seventy days each half-year. Compulsory school attendance was not introduced in Queensland until 1900, and it is clear that in all the Australian colonies there was much absenteeism from schools as children from poor families were employed as casual labour in workshops or on farms—or joined larrikin groups on inner-city streets.

Despite the serious problems affecting the working class, it is not suggested that the living conditions of most workers deteriorated—on the contrary, they improved, at least until 1890. Furthermore, working-class divisions were not unique to Australia. It is quite likely that barriers in Britain, for example between craftsmen and labourers, were even greater than in Australia. At all times the working class is subject to processes of disintegration as well as unification. A major task of analysis is to note changes in the relative importance of these contradictory tendencies and to trace their effect upon relations with other classes, which are themselves subject to change.

R. H. Tawney—in days when no account was taken of women workers—once remarked that, in the second half of the nineteenth century, the British working man came to realize that 'if he is to attain well-being at all, he must attain it, not by personal advancement, but as the result of a collective effort, the fruits of which he will share with his fellows'. The remark related to a society where large-scale industry had developed and masses of workers would inevitably remain workers all their lives. In Australia, more opportunities were available but the dictum about collective effort is valid nevertheless.[40]

162   It is essential to take account of the problems and divisions con-

cerning the working class in Australia in the nineteenth century. However, this should not obscure the underlying reality of an expanding capitalist society in which the wage relationship was characteristic. The working class grew in numbers and strength. It also grew in consciousness of its own distinct interests as it developed industrial and political organizations.

10

Confrontation:
Trade Unions, The Eight-hour Day,
Managerial Prerogatives and the Maritime Strike

Awareness of common needs and aspirations developed naturally as workers mingled on jobs, drank together in pubs and swapped yarns around campfires. At a time when trade unions were few and weak, protest against unsatisfactory conditions was often individual in form. Adrian Merritt, in a study of the Masters and Servants Act, found that in the second half of the nineteenth century an increasing proportion of court cases—perhaps most of them—were initiated by workers against employers. The class struggle was fought at a primitive level as workers stood up for their rights. Merritt quotes two remarks taken from evidence in Masters and Servants cases: 'Damn your eyes, am I not your master', said Finlay McInnis to James Clark; while Tuckett of Kiama told his employer, 'A man is as good as his master'.[1]

Assertion of human dignity was a crucial aspect of such disputes. Thus J. Johnson, a shepherd, when told by his master that his 'hut must be kept clean', replied that '*must* was no word to be used to any man'. Women, too, could be assertive. Mary Trevellian, at Merriwa in New South Wales in 1867, refused instructions from her employer's wife but said that she (Mary) 'would do anything to oblige anyone if asked in a proper manner'. Sometimes workers went to court protesting that they had been told to do work of a kind not expressly provided for in the employment contract. On the other side, employers continued to use the Act to enforce labour discipline. In one case, an employer forgot to obtain money to pay wages at the end of the week as promised, provoking an employee to say to his wife, 'Damn and bugger it, old woman, pack up and let us go'. They left and were convicted of absconding, thus forfeiting the wages which the employer had failed to provide.[2]

Such cases reveal the quintessence of capitalism: the division between a class which gives orders and a class which is expected to take them. The very title of the Masters and Servants Act starkly embodies the concept. Yet the prospect of struggle between the classes was ever present, as indicated in a centuries-old couplet:

When Adam delved, and Eve span,
Who was then the gentleman?

Individual action by workers—often requiring great courage—merged into impromptu collective action by groups. In Australia, well before the establishment of the Shearers' Union, small gangs of shearers negotiated conditions before starting work at particular woolsheds—or decided to boycott those stations. On one railway construction project in northern New South Wales in 1884, there was a big strike against a threat by employers to cut wages; and, in the absence of any union, the strike was organized by an *ad hoc* committee of the navvies. The strike collapsed soon after one of the navvies was sentenced to imprisonment on charges of preventing a workman from 'working at his lawful occupation' on the railway line. Prosecutions under the Masters and Servants Act were often used to break strikes.

Another form of spontaneous organization by workers was political. At times of depression, unemployed workers held marches and demonstrations in city streets, demanding that government provide relief work. The governments usually responded with denials that they had a duty to provide work but they often took practical action to alleviate the pressure. This process might be described as collective bargaining through riots or the threat of violence from angry mobs. It achieved some results, although the authorities denied (as they still do) that any concessions they made were prompted by fear, however transitory.

In contrast to temporary or evanescent organizations, trade unions developed. The Webbs' classic definition of a trade union is that it is 'a continuous association of wage-earners for the purpose of maintaining or improving the conditions of their working lives'. The definition is too narrow—trade unionism is about solidarity and class, as well as bread—but it has the virtue of emphasizing permanency and stability. Actually, as it turned out, a number of trade unions in Australia were not continuous over long periods of time. Few of the small trade societies survived the gold rushes of the 1850s: their affairs were disrupted by the departure of members to the goldfields and the

165

inability of many small manufacturing plants to withstand a flood of imports. Nevertheless, there was one very significant development in that decade: the first victories were won in what proved to be a ceaseless struggle to reduce the length of the standard working day and week.

The Eight-hour Day

Australian trade unions led the world in winning an eight-hour working day. A major breakthrough came in 1856 in Sydney and Melbourne, where building tradesmen—especially those in Stonemasons' Societies—forcefully agitated for a reduction of hours and secured employers' agreement to it. Circumstances were propitious: the massive increase in population entailed heavy demand for more buildings, enhancing the bargaining power of the unions concerned; construction work was not subject to competition from imports, so that employers were able to pass on increased costs; and many immigrants found the heat of summer days oppressive—which applied also to building industry subcontractors working alongside their employees. In the next few years, while building trades workers in Melbourne fought to maintain their gains, the movement was extended to a number of other bodies, such as engineering workers, and the eight-hour principle also spread to other Victorian towns. Labourers too benefited in so far as their daily hours of work were geared to those of craftsmen.

Workers often won the eight-hour day initially only at the cost of a cut in hourly wage-rates to compensate employers. Such a cost, in terms of lower weekly take-home pay, was more than many workers could afford to accept; so in order to preserve unity, trade union leaders learned to claim proportionate increases in hourly wage-rates at the same time as demanding an eight-hour day. This was done, for instance, in Sydney in 1873–4 when 1200 ironworkers struck successfully for an eight-hour day. At the time, their brother-unionists in the engineering industry in Britain had just won a nine-hour day (54-hour week), and were still a long way from following up with demands for a further reduction.

Victoria was easily the most advanced of the Australian colonies in reducing standard working hours, and from 1874 the Victorian government incorporated the eight-hour principle in its own contracts. This was an important benchmark, for the government entered into major contracts for the building of railway lines, the supply of locomotives and so on. Yet there remained many workers in Victoria, notably shop assistants, who were on their feet for very long hours each day. Actually, while it is convenient to refer to an eight-hour day, it is not strictly correct. Although stonemasons worked a true eight-hour day, other workers in the latter part of the nineteenth century secured a standard working week of forty-eight hours, and it was customary, for example in the engineering and most building trades, to work this in shifts of 8¾ hours per day for five days and the other 4¼ hours on Saturday. This compared with an earlier regimen of, say, ten hours per day except for two hours off on Saturday. The half-day holiday on Saturday was to some extent a by-product of winning the 'eight-hour' day.

The eight-hour struggle was fought in one industry and colony after another, over decades. In the long boom, employers strongly resisted moves which implied reduction in the supply of labour. Workers, for their part, reckoned that although employers often succeeded in cutting wages during an economic downturn, it was not so easy for the boss to lengthen hours again once a reduction in them had been conceded. Thus the scene was set for a large number of industrial disputes. As a preliminary step, the Miners' Association in northern New South Wales in 1874 won a reduction of hours in coal mines from twelve to ten per day. Many trade unions were formed specifically to campaign for an eight-hour day, and in doing so they received support from unions which had already succeeded. The real significance of the eight-hour campaign was that it served as a focus for labour organization and unity: what had been gained by some unions could be gained by others.

Eight hours a day for work, with equal periods implied for sleeping time and leisure, was an excellent slogan and rallying point for struggle. However, it should not be supposed that winning the demand meant an actual reduction in the average working day to the level posited. When economic conditions warranted it, overtime was worked, often excessively. One worker at the Fulton engineering plant in Adelaide in 1888 stated that he had worked for the company

during one fortnight twice as follows: from 6.30 a.m. till 5.00 p.m. next day, and until 10.00 p.m. every other night, one night excepted, I feeling rather knocked up. We worked during that fortnight 83 hours one week and 84 the other, and on several other occasions.[3]

In the case of Fulton's, trade unions were concerned to note that the company, while demanding overtime work from employees, was paying them the bare hourly rates for it. In such circumstances the eight-hour day became rather farcical; and trade unions were generally successful in securing higher rates of pay for overtime, usually at the rate of time and a quarter for the first two hours, and sometimes time and a half for subsequent hours. Once an eight-hour standard day was estab- 167 lished, the overtime rates of pay generally applied to those hours in the day beyond eight, instead of nine or ten as previously. Thus an eight-hour victory could mean a substantial increase in overtime pay, although this was not directly applicable to workers who were paid on a piece-work basis.

The eight-hour day in Australia was won through industrial action, not legislation. However, there were some efforts to regulate the working hours of women and children through Factory Acts. Victoria led the way with the first such Act in 1873. It stipulated a maximum of eight hours per day for females working in factories, but a factory was defined as an establishment employing no fewer than ten people. Besides leaving small workshops unregulated, the government retained discretionary power to exempt specific large factories from the hours restriction if it thought fit. In fact in 1874 the government authorized a 60-hour week for women working in woollen mills in Ballarat and Geelong. This was in line with petitions signed by a number of the workers, to the effect that they were paid by the piece and were unable to take work home from the factories (as outworkers did), so they needed the longer hours.

Although the mill-owners no doubt had a hand in organizing that petition, it is all too likely that the workers needed no urging to sign it: they needed the money. It is an example of the common dilemma of choice in capitalist society between unhealthy conditions on the one side and wages and jobs on the other: with the profit-seeking employer as the catalyst. A recent tragic example, in a more regulated economy, concerns the asbestos mine at Barraba in northern New South Wales, which was closed in 1983 because it was no longer profitable. Over its working life this mine provided appallingly dangerous working conditions: high levels of fibrous dust were harbingers of asbestosis and mesothelioma. The company made little attempt to clean up, and monitoring by Health Department inspectors was extraordinarily feeble and ineffective. Nothing was said in public, which suited Woodreef Mines Ltd. It also accorded with the wishes of asbestos workers, who feared for their jobs in an isolated area where there was little other work available. The trade unions involved, such as the AWU, accepted the conspiracy of silence until the mine closed.

In the earlier situation relating to the Victorian Factory Act of 1873, the problem was not so much that unions were providing no leadership as that they evinced little interest in the working conditions of women. The Act was a dead letter. Trade unions played a more active role in the enactment of the Victorian Factories and Shops Act of 1885, although the influence of 'liberal' manufacturers may have been equally important. Some large Melbourne manufacturers, fearing competition from provincial employers who paid low wages to non-union labour, saw advantage to themselves in action to force such competitors to eliminate abuses in working conditions. The amending Act of 1885 extended the definition of a factory to establishments employing no fewer than six people, as well as virtually eliminating child labour (under the age of thirteen) and creating an inspectorate for factories. It is doubtful whether this made much difference to the working hours of women in the clothing trade, particularly outworkers, but the legislation represented a marked improvement over the situation in neighbouring New South Wales, where no Factory Act was passed until 1896.

Because of the piecemeal approach to shorter working hours, it is difficult to summarize the progress of the eight-hour movement. In New South Wales, it seems that factory hands worked a ten-hour day by the mid-1870s, and bootmaking and clothing factories continued to work their employees from six o'clock in the morning till six o'clock at night in the 1880s. In other occupations an eight-hour day was common by then, but there were still numerous exceptions. Rural labourers worked longer; while butchers worked seventy, and grocers' assistants sixty-six, hours per week. Similarly in Brisbane, although stonemasons won the first victory in 1858, and other men in the building trades worked eight hours a day from the 1860s, one labour leader, William Lane, wrote in 1890: 'This is called an eight-hour country, but how many work 8 hours. Twice as many wage-earners work Ten and numbers [of wage-earners] Twelve right here in Queensland.' [4]

Craft Unions in Manufacturing and Building

There was a remarkably rapid growth of secondary industry in Australia between 1860 and 1890. The rate of growth, in percentage terms, is rather misleading, because of the very low level at the outset. Nevertheless, it is significant that in 1891 about 17 per cent of the Australian workforce was engaged in manufacturing industry and another 14 per cent was in building and construction. The combined figure of 31 per cent was substantially greater than the figure of 24 per cent of the workforce engaged in agriculture and pastoral activity. These statistics reflect the growth of an urban society in Australia—a development which was most marked in Victoria, where about 20 per cent of the workforce was occupied in manufacturing.

Four industries dominated Australian manufacturing: metalworking and engineering; clothing and footwear; production of building materials; and the processing of food, drink and tobacco. In general, manufacturing was not highly sophisticated, and the average number of employees per workshop/factory was less than twenty. Yet there were some anomalous features in this pattern of small-scale development. A remarkable number of segments of manufacturing were dominated by   169 establishments employing more than a hundred people. By 1891 there were ninety-two such factories in Victoria; while in New South Wales, most boots and shoes were made in sixty factories employing an average of forty-seven people, one-fifth of whom were female. A number of engineering works employed hundreds of men each; and locomotives, requiring high levels of skill, were manufactured—with the aid of government subsidies—in all four eastern mainland colonies.

The structure of the printing industry in each colony was fairly typical. It consisted of a handful of big newspapers and government printing offices, employing many workers, while a large number of jobbing firms employed only a few workers each. Much the same was true of firms in the building industry. This, broadly, was the setting for the growth of craft unions, both in manufacturing and building. There was an astonishing variety of crafts—tailoring, baking, butchering, carriage-building, cabinet-making and so on—and many craft societies were established by such workers in the 1870s and 1880s. Often, these unions were small, with memberships of up to one hundred concentrated in one large city. The small-scale nature of most businesses, and the fact that in small firms there was no great economic or social difference between working proprietor and craftsman-employee, made for generally amicable industrial relations—although this did not preclude disputes over hours of work and wages, which erupted into strikes or lockouts from time to time.

In manufacturing industries where large concentrations of capital figured prominently, general working standards were usually set by those big establishments. There, craft unions engaged in crucial struggles, the gains or losses from which were likely to be passed on to workers in small plants. The metalworking and engineering industry was central to this process. It was the fastest growing sector of Australian manufacturing during the long boom, fitters being needed not only in heavy engineering but also for repair work in a very wide range of industries, such as shipbuilding and mining. Fittingly, the iron trades unions were headed by the Amalgamated Society of Engineers (ASE), which established branches in Australia, beginning in Sydney in 1852.

In Britain the ASE was regarded by other craft unions as a model of efficient organization, and its Australian branches were subject to the same rules as those in Britain. The integral link facilitated movement of members from one country to another as well as within a given country. It also meant that branches in need could call upon the resources of a powerful organization. For instance, at the time of the Maritime Strike in 1890, £1600 was sent from Britain to the ASE in Australia, to be used to support unions engaged in the strike. It was an example of international solidarity in action, and such flows of money also went in the reverse direction as circumstances changed.

In Australia as in Britain, the ASE deliberately restricted membership to men who had served an apprenticeship of five to seven years as a fitter, turner, blacksmith, patternmaker or other specified craft. Although such skilled workers were relatively well paid, there was always an element of insecurity in their lives, particularly in relation to unemployment, so the union had a system of benefits, payable weekly to a member when he was unemployed or ill. There was also a superannuation benefit for long-term members who were too old to work, and funeral benefits for members and their wives.

On the face of it, most such benefits could be obtained from friendly societies, without the need to be a trade unionist at all. Friendly societies certainly catered for a large number of people—as early as 1874, 50 000 men in Victoria were members, with 30 000 registered wives—and the members included many skilled workers, as well as miners and, to a lesser degree, labourers. The dinners and rituals of these organizations often had a flavour of working-class ceremony in them, satisfying a desire for fellowship. However, friendly societies also included people from the middle class, and the societies are best regarded as agents of social adjustment, not social change. The state recognized this and encouraged them as institutions of self-help. Moreover, even in provision of benefits, there was an important distinction between friendly societies and trade unions such as the ASE. The former, like insurance companies, functioned on actuarial lines, whereas the ASE had no separate benefit fund balancing income and expenditure. Benefits were paid out of the union's general fund derived from membership subscriptions for all purposes. Indeed, the aim was not simply to help members who were in difficulties. In relation to unemployment benefit, the cardinal aim was to safeguard the position of those members who still had jobs—by making it possible for the unemployed to live without having to accept jobs at very low rates of pay which would undercut other workers in the trade.

In any case, payment of benefits was only one aspect of a craft union's activities. More important was the perennial struggle over wages and hours. Here, appearances are often misleading. Historians have noted the growing acceptance by employers of the craft unions' right to exist, the development of collective bargaining and the infrequency of strikes—at least until the 1880s. These observations are valid but they fail to take account of the general thrust of union policy. Craft unions such as the ASE aimed at restricting the supply of skilled labour in various ways. They tried to limit the number of apprentices to a set proportion of the number of craftsmen; and they generally objected to being in the same workshop as unqualified workers who were using the craftsmen's tools. Craft unions also fixed a standard rate of wages for union members in a given district. If wages paid in a particular workshop fell below the union rate, ASE members 171 walked out of that shop and took jobs elsewhere (or received unemployment benefit from their union). Except where there was a concerted wage-cutting drive by employers, this procedure did not formally constitute a strike—though employers might be forgiven for thinking otherwise!

Consequently there were relatively few big official strikes. Moreover, the incidence of strikes was limited by the inadequacy of funds to support them. Strike pay was not generally available from union funds without a prior vote by members in favour of a special levy. This usually delayed union action, and some union leaders, such as W. G. Spence, regarded the procedure as a useful check to members' inclinations to go on strike. In the period up to 1890, the Amalgamated Miners' Association spent less than £7000 on strike pay, compared with £84 000 paid out in accident and funeral benefits. Nevertheless, strikes were more frequent than these figures suggest; and whilst union leaders often deprecated the strike weapon, it was not discarded. It was held in reserve, for use if necessary.

Craftsmen also used their collective monopoly of skill to enforce old customs, which were in effect restrictive practices designed to make jobs last longer or to spread the work. For example, the ASE acknowledged that overtime work might be necessary in emergencies, but the union opposed *systematic* use of overtime. Other unions in the iron trades, such as the Boilermakers' Society and the Ironmoulders', followed similar restrictive policies, the Boilermakers being noted for exercising strict control over apprenticeship. It was customary for indentured apprentices to be sons of craftsmen—a form of patrimony. On the other hand, formal apprenticeship was virtually limited to the metalworking and engineering trades in Australia. In other trades, whilst fixed periods of training for youths were quite common, there was no proper system of indenturing, binding both employer and apprentice to specified conditions. In general, employers found it cheaper to rely upon immigrant skilled workers than to provide training themselves, and this was particularly true of the building trades.

Building trades unions were a large and distinct group. Some of them had little control over entry to their trade, with the result that skills were diluted and piece-work proliferated. This was the case with carpenters, whose position was weakened by the existence of rival unions. One was the Amalgamated Society of Carpenters and Joiners (ASCJ), which was the one big English-based union, apart from the ASE, with branches in Australia. Its rival, in Sydney and Melbourne, was the Progressive Society of Carpenters and Joiners, which appears to have had a distinctly higher proportion of colonial-born members. Competition between the two unions did not result in greater membership overall: probably fewer than 10 per cent of all carpenters in Melbourne belonged to either union in the 1880s. Alice Coolican estimates that the comparable carpenters' figure for Sydney in 1890 was 9 per cent; and for New South Wales as a whole, it was only 5 per cent.

Other unions in the building trades covered stonemasons, bricklayers, plasterers, plumbers and, at the weakest point, house painters, entry to whose trade could be threatened by virtually anyone with a brush. The Stonemasons' Society was exceptional in the vigour with which it guarded traditional craft customs concerning entry to the trade and opposition to piece-work. The Stonemasons' success was related to their employment in large gangs, particularly on public buildings, which facilitated union organization. It may be remarked that the development of the Builders Labourers Federation (BLF) in the 1960s was related to similar factors. New techniques of high-rise construction required large numbers of workers at each concrete 'pour'. A disruption of operations at this crucial moment is expensive for employers, and the BLF used the new development as a weapon to expand union strength.

In the nineteenth century the fragmented state of the building industry, and the ease of transition from journeyman to subcontractor and back again to journeyman, helps to explain why there were few notable disputes in the industry after the eight-hour victories of the 1850s. Indeed, building trade unions became complacent, tending to wink at breaches of their own rules. These tradesmen were well paid in the boom of the 1880s, and smugness caused them to be slow in responding to changes in employers' practices which entailed greater management freedom and a reduction in craft privileges. Complacency was linked to insularity, as in Sydney in 1886, when a separate Building Trades Council was established. It was formed by unions seceding from the NSW Trades and Labour Council, partly in objection to that body deciding upon a levy in support of coalminers who were on strike. Evidently, for building tradesmen, the concept of solidarity did not extend beyond their own industry.

In one important respect, neither of the two English based-unions, the carpenters' and the engineers', was typical of unions in Australia. Members of the ASCJ and the ASE paid high weekly subscriptions, ranging from one shilling to one shilling and sixpence per week. The high level of these union dues, prescribed in England, was a corollary of an elaborate benefits system particularly designed to combat unemployment. However, it seems that most Australian trade unions, including some in the iron trades such as the boilermakers', charged their members only six or nine pence per week. This was enough to provide some benefits, though not a viable unemployment benefit scheme. Poor cover for unemployment probably reflected the low level of unemployment during the long boom.

High union dues charged by the ASE deterred numbers of prospective members and caused many members to drop out through inability to maintain subscriptions, especially during a depression. Conversely, 173 the fact that other craft unions in Australia were less exclusive in membership than their counterparts in Britain was no doubt a factor in the remarkably high degree of union coverage reached in Australia by 1890, compared with other countries. However, this was not simply a matter of lower contribution rates in Australia. There was also the impact of bushworkers' unions. Further, a number of craft unions in Australia, including the ASE, showed unusual willingness to accommodate semi-skilled workers, either by opening membership to them (as in the case of the Bootmakers' Union) or by assisting them to form unions of their own.

There were exceptions to the general trend. For example, until 1890 the Sydney Wharf Labourers' and Coal-Lumpers' Unions charged an entrance-fee of five guineas to new members. This fee— additional to regular subscriptions—was designed partly to keep out deserters from overseas ships who were attracted by Australian wage-rates, but the effect was to make these unions unduly exclusive. Even so, the general impression is that Australian unions developed markedly in terms of local circumstances: they were not simply replicas of unions in Britain. The differences were not all in favour of the Australian unionists, who lagged behind their brothers in Britain in certain respects. Australian workers showed considerably less interest in factory acts and legislation to legalize the position of trade unions, and much the same applied to school education. Also, there was no Australian development of consumer co-operatives (except in coalmining areas), which was curiously in contrast to the strength of the co-operative movement in Britain. On the other side of the account, Australian unions were generally more flexible and less bureaucratic, which facilitated their expansion during the long boom.

An important question arises as to where real strength lay in the union movement. Australian historians, noting the establishment of a number of unions of unskilled workers, have traditionally regarded this as a development comparable to the upsurge in Britain exemplified by the London dockers' strike of 1889. New unions of this kind had no possibility of achieving their aims through restriction of apprenticeship and the like: their main hope lay through mass action, the force of numbers. Consequently, there is a traditional tendency to ascribe the growth of militancy in Australia in the 1880s to the new unions.

There are serious problems with this approach. Growth in union strength and aggressiveness was actually more marked among skilled than among unskilled workers. The ASE increased its Australian membership three-fold from 800 in 1881 to 2500 ten years later. Many new craft unions were established in that decade. Some new unions were basically for semi-skilled workers, while others were not all that they seemed to be. For example, the Australasian Institute of Marine Engineers, formed in 1881 and sometimes quoted by historians as an example of the 'new unions' because it had a low subscription and no benefits scheme, was in reality a body of skilled seagoing engineers intent upon breaking away from the ASE. Far from being militant, the Institute made a deal with shipowners in 1890 and effectively scuppered the Maritime Strike by keeping ships running.

Bushworkers' unions are generally considered militant at this time, but such action as they engaged in came usually from their skilled component, the shearers. The ambiguous position of unskilled and semi-skilled workers is suggested by the history of railwaymen's unions in Victoria and New South Wales. In the latter colony, the Amalgamated Railway and Tramway Service Association was established in 1886 to cater for all grades of railway workers. Railway management, on behalf of the state, refused to recognize the union on the ground that it might engage in strikes. Despite this the union recruited several thousand members within a few years, but it proved quite deferential in attitude towards the employer. Its members were largely concerned to maintain the unusual regularity and security of their employment. Real union strength on the railways lay with the Locomotive Engine Drivers' Association and, in the workshops, the ASE and other craft unions.

This is not to belittle the efforts of labourers. Some of their organizations, such as Ironworkers' Assistants Unions formed in the 1880s, engaged in strikes; but usually they had little chance of success unless they had support from craft unions in the industry. General labourers' unions came and went. Craftsmen are commonly depicted as sober, conservative citizens, relatively well off and imbued with a sense of superiority. There are considerable elements of truth in this kind of portrayal, and it is said that newspaper compositors, regarded as being among the aristocrats of labour, up to the 1920s 'usually came to work in stand-up collar and tie, and not infrequently in bowler hat and frock coat'.[5] Yet there is another side to the story. For example, the Melbourne Typographical Society in the 1880s campaigned for factory reform in the interests of other workers.

There were considerable variations between craft unions, but what their members had in common, through their acquired skills, was a degree of independence. Self-respect and respectability are generally considered as traits of the middle classes, and their prevalence among craft workers might be regarded as a sign of adoption of middle-class values and style. The appearance is superficial, for respectability had different connotations for craftsmen. They were proud of being manual workers, confident in their craft dignity. The initial eight-hour victory was celebrated each year as Labour Day, an occasion on which workers marched behind the banners of the various unions, demonstrating in ritual form their strength and achievement. They knew from experience that poverty and unemployment were not basically due to

NO PARADISE FOR WORKERS

personal failings. In contrast to labourers, craftsmen were distinguished by their degree of control over jobs and the work process—which was not to the liking of employers. This was evidenced in such matters as union resistance to systematic overtime. Furthermore, works foremen, who chose workers for particular jobs, were commonly members of such unions as the ASE, and they tended to give preference to brother-unionists. Such foremen also helped to enforce union standards.

This is not to imply that craft unionists had a broad vision or that they aimed at destroying the capitalist system. Rather, they had a strong sense of their own worth and they built up some powerful organizations possessing financial reserves. The result was that when a union such as the ASE decided to stand and fight—often in defence of craft prerogatives—the employers faced a protracted battle. Granted that such occasions were fairly rare before the 1880s, it appears that since then the real militancy in Australian trade unionism has come from sections of skilled workers, rather than from the unskilled whose plight has often led radicals to romanticize them. Verve and enthusiasm, and sometimes a dash of anarchy, are useful in industrial disputes, but they are not substitutes for good organization and finance for strike pay.

There are other matters for consideration in this connection, notably the desirability of establishing industry-wide unions embracing both skilled and unskilled. This question was seriously debated in the early twentieth century, but it was not on the union agenda at all in the 1880s, when skilled and unskilled workers' unions developed separately. Some mass unions developed, such as the miners' and the shearers', but they were not industrial unions in the standard sense of that term. For example, craft unions continued to cater for skilled workers in mines. Besides the amalgamation of some unions, various forms of inter-union co-operation were pursued. Thus some federations of associated unions were formed. Intercolonial Trades Union Congresses were held to discuss questions of common interest, including the need for labour legislation; and there was considerable strengthening of the central role of Trades and Labour Councils as co-ordinators of support for affiliated unions involved in industrial disputes. These developments reflected growth of a broader outlook, and beyond that lay a remarkable change in the ethos of the labour movement in the 1880s.

Confrontation

Present-day Australians who went through the 1960s and 1970s with a
176   modicum of political consciousness recall the sweeping nature of new

ideas and movements at that time. The old order seemed threatened by radical changes in the climate of opinion, by challenges to established authority in universities and other institutions, and the amazing spectacle of middle-class people, as well as workers, demonstrating against Australian participation in the Vietnam War. Quite suddenly, questions of morality and politics which interested few people in the 1950s gained new life and meaning for masses. It was not simply an Australian phenomenon. It occurred in many other parts of the world, although this does not mean a mere copying of developments elsewhere. There was a degree of spontaneity, although it is very difficult to account satisfactorily for such swift cultural changes. The reaction from conservatives is much easier to understand: as the Whitlam Labor government discovered in 1975, no social force is so dangerous as a ruling class which feels its position threatened.

On a smaller scale, something like this occurred in Australia (and Britain) in the 1880s. There was a ferment of new ideas, along with an intensification of class conflict. Looking back on this period, George Black, a Labor leader in New South Wales, recalled it as a time of 'great intellectual upheaval among the thoughtful youth of Australia, and even a mental readjustment among those of middle age'.[6] Several strands of thought contributed to the excitement, propagated through *The Bulletin* in particular. There was a flowering of Australian nationalism. Nationalist views were by no means confined to the common people, but people of humble origins generally identified themselves more strongly with Australia than did wealthy people. Moreover, working-class leaders such as William Lane in Queensland injected collectivist ideas into nationalism: the concept of social change in a free democratic Australia for working people. Lane attacked the Old Order as 'that which produces scrofulous kings, and lying priests, and greasy millionaires, and powdered prostitutes, and ferret-faced thieves'. At one extreme, republicanism became a serious subject for debate, especially after the German annexation of New Guinea in 1884. Radicals noted the German antecedents of the British royal family.

Another influential body of ideas came from Henry George, who himself visited Australia in 1889–90 to give lectures. He was generally well received, though with coolness in Melbourne, where protectionist trade union leaders regarded him with some suspicion. The basis for George's influence among ordinary workers may be seen from the manner in which his ideas were paraphased by Lane in his novel, *The Workingman's Paradise*, published in 1892. Lane put the following words into the mouth of one of the characters in the book:

George's is a scheme by which it is proposed to make employers compete so fiercely among one another that the workman will have it all his own way. It

177

works this way. You tax the owner until it doesn't pay him to have unused land. He must either throw it up or get used to it somehow and the demand for labour thus created is to lift wages and put the actual workers in . . . a satisfactory position.[7]

Lane himself, while respecting George, did not endorse his single-tax theory, for he felt that the logical consequence of capitalist competition was monopoly, leading to high prices. For Lane the preferable alternative was co-operation and a socialist society. Socialism indeed provided another significant stream of thought in the 1880s. Some organizations were set up to debate socialist theory but their membership was very small. More lasting was the dissemination of socialist ideas of a broad, idealist kind, visualizing socialism as a rational form of society which would come into being simply as a result of sufficient people being persuaded of its merits. Vague though this was, it accorded with a growing feeling by workers that they were entitled to a greater share in the product of their labour, and that united action through trade unions was the best way to obtain it.

This is not to say that trade unions or their leaders became socialist in outlook. In particular, there was little evidence of socialist influence in Melbourne—partly, perhaps, because of the pervasive febrile excitement of land speculation there at the time. Notions of class warfare were indistinct in all the Australian colonies. However, there were some signs of a growth of class-consciousness, as when a delegate at the Intercolonial Trades Union Congress in 1889 declared that 'it was all bosh to talk about the harmony existing between Capital and Labour'. There were also indications of some change in the attitude of craft unionists towards labourers. For example, another delegate at the same TUC gathering stated that unless unskilled workers were brought into unions they 'would cut the tradesmen's throats whenever a strike occurred'. This sharpened a practical point made the previous year, that 'tradesmen were united as a rule, and unionists were pretty well protected; but what was wanted was the organization of unskilled labour, so that all might be protected.'[8]

Changes in mood among trade unionists may be traced partly to industrial developments affecting many workers. Such factors as erosion of apprenticeship, growing subdivision of labour and dilution of skills, and the appearance in some industries of new grades of semi-skilled operators, roused anxiety and antagonism among craftsmen. This related not so much to introduction of new machinery (which came mainly later, from the 1890s, in industries such as printing and bootmaking) as to general reorganization of productive processes by employers. There were even some notable industrial disputes involving building tradesmen (normally quiescent) in Sydney in the late 1880s, and these disputes were associated with the spread of large-scale developers dominating small subcontractors.

Industrial tension and the influence of new ideas found an outlet in union militancy and efforts to establish more control over jobs. By 1890 a number of unions had won closed shops for their members. They included boilermakers and moulders in Victoria, wharf labourers in Melbourne and other ports, and metal miners at Broken Hill. The ASE could not adopt the policy of the closed shop, for its rules debarred from membership craftsmen with some physical disability or who were over forty years old. Nevertheless, the union established an Auxiliary Association to cater for such men in 1890. The peculiar combination of both militancy and conservatism in the ASE is well illustrated by a letter from W. Campbell, its Melbourne secretary, to an employer about the organization of his workforce:

F. Allen has to go to the drilling-machine, and a boy (apprentice) can, if you like, work the lathe ... Scott must be taken from our trade. You can make a labourer or anything else out of him but he is not to handle the [craftsmen's] tools ... Hoping to receive an answer not later than Thursday, at midday, and that it is to the effect that the agreement is carried out.[9]

Employers naturally resented such aggressiveness on the part of those whom they were accustomed to command. In reaction, employers formed their own organizations. Indeed it was common in the 1880s for employers' associations to be established soon after trade unions had made their presence felt in a particular industry. One of the most powerful employers' groups comprised shipowners, who initially set up an organization in Sydney in 1878, at the time of the strike against Chinese crews employed by the ASN company. Six years later, this body was strengthened to become the Steamship Owners' Association of Australasia (SOA). The temper of these employers may be judged by a private comment by one of them, James Burns, concerning the conference which established the Association:

The Conference is being held with a view to resist the Unions, Seamens Union, Firemens Union, Engineers Union and Wharf Lumpers' Union etc. They are getting very dictatorial certainly ... ASN propose that one third of the shipping of each Co. be laid up unless the seamen allow the 8 hour clause to be cancelled ... Others [owners] propose to raise a few thousand pounds and import Firemen etc. and so glut the market and as Smith terms it smash the Union.[10]

As it happened, no such action was taken by shipowners at the time, but in 1886 wharf labourers in Melbourne struck successfully for an eight-hour day. They were supported by the Seamen's Union, which brought its members out in order to cut off the supply of non-union labour on the wharves. The Seamen said: 'We are compelled to take this course, owing to the struggle having assumed a new phase, viz: 179

Capital *vs* Labour.' It was a fateful phrase, which was echoed by Jesse Gregson, an important representative of capital. Gregson was superintendent of the Australian Agricultural Company, one of the biggest producers of coal in New South Wales. He was hostile towards trade unions and recognized the value of links between related groups of employers, notably colliery owners and shipowners. The basis of the relationship was that steamships were big users and carriers of coal.[11]

Between 1885 and 1890, employers' unions were established in all four of the eastern mainland colonies. The core of these bodies consisted of the SOA, and shipowners were well placed in other respects. For example, J. R. Carey, chairman of the board of the *Daily Telegraph* in 1890, was a wealthy steamship owner, and understandably this Sydney newspaper was hostile to workers in the Maritime Strike. There is evidence to suggest that some coastal shipowners, through fierce competition, were suffering a decline in profits at this time, but firms like Howard Smith of Melbourne needed no such spur to be anti-unionist.

Another body of employers undergoing economic difficulties in the late 1880s consisted of pastoralists. Wool prices tended to decline during the decade while shearing costs rose. No doubt this was a factor in the formation of the Pastoralists' Union of New South Wales in July 1890, yet the gains made by shearers were quite modest. G. Mair, a foundation member of the council of this union, wrote privately that the increase in cost of shearing was 'comparatively unimportant ... The question is whether we shall preserve to ourselves the control of our business, or put ourselves under the rule of our own workmen.'[12] This was the nub of the matter, in the eyes of other employers besides pastoralists: managerial prerogatives were being challenged by the trade union advance. In shipping, for example, unions were campaigning for the employment of more men on each vessel than the employers deemed necessary. The capitalist class felt that it must make a stand at some point, and the formation of the Pastoralists' Union represented the forging of the last link in the employers' chain. Significantly, the first secretary of the union was J. W. Ferguson, a shipowner's representative who was secretary of the NSW Employers' Union by the time of the Maritime Strike; and Jesse Gregson was active in the Pastoralists' Union.

The Maritime Strike

The decisive clash between labour and capital which is rather inaccurately described as the Maritime Strike mainly affected New South Wales, Victoria and South Australia. There were about 120 000 trade unionists in these three colonies at the time, including 50 000 in Victoria and 60 000 in New South Wales. It is often forgotten that in addition there were many ex-unionists: people who had allowed their membership to lapse for various reasons but were not usually lost to the cause. Mostly they were willing to respond to a union call for strike action. Nevertheless, this still left a high proportion of the workforce untouched by unionism—people who were potential scabs.

Essentially, the Maritime Strike was the product of two converging forces: on the one hand the rapid growth of trade unionism, assertive and buoyed by a confident expectation of continued gains; and on the other hand the parallel organization of bodies of employers, dismayed at the trade union advance and intent upon stopping it. Against the closed shop, the employers posed the principle of 'freedom of contract' —their right to employ unionists or non-unionists as they pleased. The implication of this was that employers were free to contract with individual workers as to wages and other conditions, irrespective of trade union standards. In the final analysis, it could be said that the unions were the prime movers in the great strike, for they were the ones seeking a change in the relationship between capital and labour. Yet managerial intransigence was equally responsible: the most powerful sections of the capitalist class were not merely prepared for the fight but were anxious for a showdown.

Events moved swiftly in 1890. In the early part of the year, shearers in Queensland won a closed shop, and W. G. Spence planned to extend this to New South Wales. Before the plan could be put into effect, the Pastoralists' Union was established as a counter. At the same time problems came to a head in the shipping industry. In June the SOA, under pressure, conceded a number of demands put forward by the Sydney Wharf Labourers' Union, including an eight-hour day and a closed shop. Shortly after, the Seamen's Union and several other maritime bodies including the Marine Officers' Association lodged claims for pay increases and other improvements. The shipowners asserted that these claims, if granted, would cost them £200 000 per year, and they decided to fight; they were ready to lay up ships if the unions insisted on their demands. James Burns, chairman of the SOA, told a Royal Commission after the strike was all over: 'We decided eventually to carry on our business clear of these tyrannical labour organisations.' [13]

The Maritime Strike was precipitated by a minor incident. The SOA refused to negotiate with the Marine Officers' Association while it remained affiliated to the Melbourne Trades Hall Council. This refusal was basically a pretext to throw the onus of responsibility for the imminent upheaval upon the unions; yet the refusal was also symbolic of concern about management rights, for the shipowners argued that proper discipline could not be maintained on ships if officers were

181

linked with trade unions representing ships' crews. Be that as it may, marine officers walked off ships in Australian ports in August and were followed by sympathetic seamen and others. Waterside workers, who had already resolved not to handle 'black' wool in the separate shearers' dispute, also stopped work.

Various other bodies of workers became involved. Coalminers decided to refuse to supply coal to ships manned by non-union labour, whereupon the Newcastle Coal Owners' Protective Association locked out all miners. Then, in September 1890, work was suspended at Broken Hill, the mine owners claiming that this was necessary because of the accumulation of ore due to shipping restrictions. As indicated by these kinds of action, the Maritime Strike was on a scale not previously seen in Australia. Gregson, in despatches to the London directors of the Australian Agricultural Company, remarked upon the extent to which 'capitalists and employers of all classes ... seem to be thoroughly convinced that their very existence depends upon their standing together'. On the other side, as Gregson noted: 'It was openly avowed, time after time, that society was to be reorganised, that the labourer was to have the large proportion of the profits and that capital was to be distributed.' [14]

Employers' bodies and trade unions both set up broad intercolonial co-ordinating organizations to guide their members during the strike. Sydney was the storm centre, and the president of the NSW Trades and Labour Council said later that in the early stages of the strike one-third of the efforts of the Sydney Labour Defence Committee were spent in 'stopping two thirds of the different societies from striking or taking part in the strike'. It is generally considered that Melbourne craft unions were less enthusiastic, yet W. Campbell, the forthright local secretary of the ASE, was reported as saying to a meeting of 50 000 people there:

The people possessed the railways, and why should the people not also possess the gasworks and the shipping, and break up those huge monopolies? He hoped the outcome of this struggle would be a great international congress of labour, which would take steps to raise a fund that would enable them to fight capital whenever it tried in any shape or form to tyrannise over labour. [15]

There were some serious incidents as feeling mounted. In Sydney, after the Trolly and Draymen's Union (covering road transport drivers) joined the strike, there was uproar and stone-throwing one day when ten carts loaded with wool were ostentatiously driven by businessmen and pastoralists from railway yards to wharves. The Riot Act was read, mounted troopers charged protesting strikers and a number of them were arrested and imprisoned. Such direct use of state power in support of employers caused many workers to realize that the state was not neutral, particularly at a time of crisis: it was an instrument of class power. On the other hand, there were large numbers of middle-class people who were shocked by reports of violence or threats. They rallied to the bourgeois cause, and about 3000 were enrolled as special constables.

One month after the Maritime Strike had begun, it was apparent that the trade unions were losing. Particularly in Melbourne, there was a considerable pool of unemployed labour which waterside employers used for strikebreaking purposes. Coastal ships sailed with makeshift crews, the critical component of skill being supplied by the Australasian Institute of Marine Engineers—the only union which ratted in the strike. In desperation, the Labour Defence Committee in Sydney then arranged for shearers to be called out on strike, but this was a tactical mistake. One leading pastoralist, A. A. Dangar, wrote gleefully to Gregson, saying 'we shall give these labour fellows a dressing that they won't forget'.[16]

Strike funds dwindled, especially in Sydney. At one stage, the Defence Committee there was providing for 14 000 strikers, and the initial payment of one pound each per week fell to one-quarter of that amount. Facing defeat, unions were prepared to compromise but the employers stalled on requests for negotiations—a piece of procrastination which prompted the Victorian Chief Justice, Higinbotham, to donate £50 to union strike funds. However, in October-November 1890, the strike collapsed. Employers gained the right to employ nonunion labour in a number of spheres where a closed shop had operated previously.

Directly involving 25 000 to 30 000 workers (not counting shearers), the Maritime Strike was the most decisive confrontation between capital and labour in Australia in the nineteenth century. Workers drew some lessons from it. The phrase 'law and order' became suspect, and one union journal declared:

For a blackleg to take a striker's billet is moral robbery even though it may be legally honest . . . And as moral laws should override all laws that are not moral strikers are quite justified in using physical as well as moral strength in preventing men from stealing their billets.[17]

Clearly, the trade union movement seriously over-estimated its strength and was badly beaten. The point was rammed home by employers in industrial disputes in the next few years. Whereas the Maritime Strike was fought basically about management prerogatives, the sequel took the form of cuts in pay and other conditions which weakened unions were unable to resist. Yet the failure of the Maritime Strike may not in itself have been as conclusive as is commonly supposed. For example, while the strike was in progress, wharf labourers

183

at Port Pirie in South Australia secured a reduction in their working day from ten to eight hours; and the Trades and Labour Council in Adelaide expanded the number of its affiliated unions from forty-two in August 1890 to fifty-four in February 1891. In Sydney also, the Trades and Labour Council reached its peak number of affiliated unions in 1891, after the strike.

Particularly significant was a comment made by R. Parkin, secretary of the Australasian Council of the ASE, shortly before the end of the Maritime Strike. Writing from Melbourne to the union's head office in London, Parkin referred to the Australian employers' elation over success 'in their crusade against unskilled labour for so far that is the only class that has been directly affected'. He added that the employers might now turn their aggression against the ASE, 'thinking that as they expect to meet with success in dealing with poor wharf labourers and other unskilled occupations they may as well be in for a pound as a penny'.[18]

What Parkin and other unionists could not foresee was the devastating effect of the economic slump which was just beginning. It was much worse than strike defeats: it was the capitalist system itself wreaking vengeance upon those who questioned its operations, as well as many others who had thought the system wonderful.

11

Depression, the Collapse of Trade Unions and the Formation of the Australian Labor Party

---

*Something irrevocable passed from Australian community life
in the last lean years of the old century. What took place was
like the ending of childhood; the curtains fall on wide-eyed
expectation, the entrance instead of uncertainty, doubt and
mistrust. The second Australian land boom—fifty years after
the first—had collapsed, with calamitous effect ...*[1]

Imbalance in the Economy: Pastoral Debts

The seeds of the terrible depression of the 1890s were sown in the
preceding boom. Reaching a peak in the 1880s, capital investment in
that boom was concentrated upon the pastoral industry, the building of
railways and the construction of cities. One unforeseen result was that
by 1890 serious problems were emerging in the form of distortions in
the structure of the Australian economy; and the lack of balance was
associated with the flood of capital imported from overseas.

A high proportion of long-term investment capital came from Britain. For railway-building, it came from colonial government issues of
bonds on the London Stock Exchange. For private investment in the
pastoral industry and urban building, a group of banks of issue (issuing
their own banknotes) provided the main conduit. In addition, there
were a dozen large pastoral finance companies providing loans for their 185

NO PARADISE FOR WORKERS

clients; and in the urban sector, as the building boom intensified, a considerable number of fringe banking institutions—variously styled as land banks, mortgage companies and building societies—were established. Practically all these organizations were involved in the business of raising capital in Britain and transferring it to Australia, mainly in the form of company debentures and fixed deposits. A typical example in the pastoral field was the Australian Mortgage Land and Finance Company, which was based in London though it operated from Melbourne. In the 1870s and 1880s this company lent more than £2 000 000 to pastoralists—and it paid an annual dividend of 20 per cent to its shareholders thoughout the 1880s. Such mercantile bodies were primarily interested in securing control of the wool clip for sale, but this entailed provision of heavy capital support for graziers. The main commercial banks also became involved in financing wool exports.

Some pastoralists used their borrowed funds, along with profits, to build fine houses and to send sons to Cambridge University. However, most capital expenditure went either into station improvements designed to improve productivity, such as fencing, or into the purchase of strategic portions of stations in order to forestall selectors. As security for loans, squatters mortgaged freehold property and transferred to banks and loan companies the titles to crown leases of the land comprising the bulk of stations. In New South Wales in 1866, 98 per cent of all pastoral leases were held by individuals or partnerships, but twenty-four years later nearly 40 per cent of the leases were formally held by companies. By 1890 almost half of the pastoralists of New South Wales were mortgaged clients of banks or wool brokers. The average amount owed was about £100 000, though in some cases it was as much as £500 000. In practice, stations were generally still held by the same families as before, yet the squatters' equity in their holdings was diminished to a point where they were dangerously dependent upon their financiers.

Nevertheless, graziers before the 1890s felt quite secure in the interlocking of pastoral and mercantile interests. It was widely known that banks were reluctant to play a direct role in the management of pastoral stations, so long as interest payments on loans were forthcoming. In the 1870s and 1880s, banking profits were so high that the banks were able to pay annual dividends of well over 10 per cent to shareholders, besides allowing for additions to bank reserves. Consequently, banks were not inclined to place mortgaged squatters under strict supervision. On the contrary, banks were ready to extend greater loans to them. This raises a question concerning the role of imported British capital. Superficially, it appears that Australian pastoralists and businessmen took the initiative in making investment decisions, borrowing the necessary money and then being responsible for the success or failure of the enterprise. In this view, the part played by British investors was quite passive. The reality was more complex than this, for the availability of capital from Britain depended partly upon conditions outside Australia, and British investors could decide to stop the flow of capital in certain circumstances. Thus there was a subtle interaction between conditions in Britain and in Australia.

In the case of graziers, there was a fatal flaw in the cosy relationship between them and banks, irrespective of whether the particular bank happened to be English-based or colonial. While mortgage loans were understood to be long-term in nature, in the eyes of the law they were repayable on demand. Hence, if a bank or loan company decided to make such a demand, the pastoralist stood to lose his station through foreclosure—except in the unlikely event of his being able to raise the cash immediately to pay off the loan. Many squatters discovered this to their cost in the depression of the 1890s. At the time of the Maritime Strike, graziers stoutly rejected what they saw as a threat of trade union intervention in their business. Yet ironically they appeared to be oblivious of the reality that control of pastoral properties had already passed or was being passed, not to workers but to financiers. Many graziers became salaried managers as a result, leading Brian Fitzpatrick to remark that 'it was the pastoralist who did the work, the financier who got the money'.[2]

Before this, in the 1880s, the fortunes of graziers varied considerably. Their heavy investment in improvements tended to relate to long-term considerations rather than immediate profit, and it was difficult to predict accurately the return from capital outlays, especially in marginal areas where fast-breeding rabbits, overstocking of relatively poor pastures and erosion of land were common. This was mainly true of the drier plains of western New South Wales and Queensland. Extension of grazing into these areas in the 1880s was responsible for much of the increase in wool production, yet it was these semi-arid regions which required relatively heavy capital outlay on water facilities and the like. Furthermore, the NSW government, in need of revenue, increased rents for pastoral leases in 1884. The increases were long overdue but they accentuated the cost–price squeeze which many graziers were feeling.

Actually, graziers were not in dire straits in the 1880s. Many, probably most of them, fared well. There was a downward trend in wool prices from 1875 onwards but it was not steep. Indeed wool prices were fairly stable for a few years from 1886. More important in the long term was the continued growth in the volume of Australian wool exported to the London market, where Australia was the main supplier. Overproduction of wool seems likely to have been a major factor in the precipitate fall in British wool prices from 1891. The weight of wool depressed prices; wool growing was an industry of diminishing returns, indicating a serious imbalance in the Australian economy. The seriousness is implicit in the fact that the wool cheque each year accounted for between 50 and 60 per cent of the total value of Australia's exports.

Excess capacity was also a feature of the building industry by 1890, in the sense that the provision of dwellings had out-run the capacity of people to buy or rent them. The building boom of the 1880s was initially based upon a very real social need. The enormous increase in immigration associated with the gold discoveries of the 1850s had resulted in an unusually large number of births in the early 1860s; and when these children grew up, joined the workforce and established families of their own there was a correspondingly larger number of young couples requiring accommodation. This happened in the 1880s, at the same time as a fresh flood of immigrants arrived in Australia. Thus there was a strong stimulus to the building industry. These were years when the populations of Melbourne and Sydney spread into new suburbs, movements between home and workplace being facilitated by construction of powered tramway systems.

The strength of demand, for buildings such as warehouses and offices as well as homes, sustained the urban land boom for years, although there was a growth in the number of 'spec' builders who gambled on the chance of buyers appearing after construction. It was a risky business, especially as the assets created were long-lived: an investor must expect the return on capital to be spread over a long period. The element of uncertainty was compounded by fluctuations in the incomes of prospective buyers or tenants. The outcome was excess capacity. In New South Wales, while the population grew by 50 per cent between 1881 and 1891, the number of dwellings rose by 68 per cent. In Victoria the contrast was even more marked. This does not mean that every family was adequately housed by the end of the decade. Rather, there was a limit to the number of people who could afford to buy or pay high rents for homes. When that limit was reached, there was a tailing-off in building operations and a fall in rents which made landlords less inclined to invest in new buildings.

In cities such as Melbourne, Sydney and Brisbane, the final stages of the urban land boom were marked by increasing speculation in real estate. Institutions such as land banks and building societies bought blocks of land not so much for productive purposes as with the intention of re-selling quickly at a higher price. For a time this was feasible, and property values were inflated artificially. Graeme Davison detects in Melbourne's boom suburbs

the same close-knit pattern of social and business connections: municipal councils dissolve into railway leagues which reconvene, in turn, as boards of mortgage companies and building societies. Hardly a local council was without a brace of building society directors, a sprinkling of real estate agents and a predominance of local investors.[3]

Pertaining to a more exalted political level of society, there is Michael Cannon's colourful description of the parliament of Victoria, which in the 1880s

became a sort of speculators' club, when the most blatant 'log-rolling' . . . became commonplace. Fantastic sums were borrowed and spent on extending the railway network; and when the rails reached any particular point, it was often found that syndicates of M.P.s and their associates had bought up the land in advance for subdivision and resale.[4]

Other areas of the economy were also affected by speculation. The silver discoveries at Broken Hill sparked the first national boom in mining company shares. Even the Governor of Victoria gambled in silver shares; and on the Melbourne Stock Exchange, BHP shares, nominally valued at £19 each, shot up from £175 to over £400 in the first two months of 1888. Shares in Queensland gold mines were also boosted, often fraudulently, though there was nothing novel about that sort of thing. In 1872, at the time of the Hill End gold discoveries in New South Wales, an anonymous satirist published a bogus prospectus for 'The Gigantic Bamboozle Gold, Tin and Copper Mining Company (Ltd), Vulture's Hill'. The prospectus stated that the company promoters' motives were 'of the highest character and may be expressed . . . Heads I Win—Tails You Lose'. Brokers for the share issue were stated as 'Catchem Quick, Nabbum and Co., the Devil's-Chambers, Bottomless-pit-street'.[5]

Import of Capital and Speculation

The general conclusion to be drawn from this account is that by the late 1880s there was domestic over-expansion of key sectors of the economy, and a decline in the marginal return on investment. The looming problems were not to be remedied by minor adjustments: long-term restructuring was required. Difficulties were internal in nature and they precipitated the depression of the 1890s. Yet they were also reflected in the external economic position of the Australian colonies, which became very serious.

There was a rise in the value of Australian exports in the 1880s, but it was sluggish, particularly by comparison with the growth in imports. The deficit was made up by imports of capital. Australian borrowing overseas was never greater than £8 000 000 in any year before 1881; yet it was higher than £20 000 000 in most of the years between 1882 and 1890. There was no central bank with functions of overseeing or controlling the influx of capital which flooded into Australia. Indeed, about half of the imported capital in the 1880s was raised by the colonial governments themselves, mainly to finance railway building. In the long run this public borrowing provided an infrastructure which aided exports, but in the short term there was little profit from railway-building: it took time for the flow of goods through a new line to reach a satisfactory volume. In the case of metropolitan suburban railway networks, extension of lines had virtually no impact upon exports. The same could be said of the building of urban dwellings, which nevertheless attracted part of the inflow of capital.

In short, most of the imported capital was used in ways which made little contribution to Australian exports. Capital investment was concentrated on a few large sectors of the economy, and only one of these —the pastoral industry—was capable of adding significantly to exports. Yet that one exceptional industry was affected by a long-term decline in the price of its main product, wool. The net result for the balance of payments was that, by 1889, 37 per cent of export income was earmarked simply for payment of interest and dividends on overseas debts, compared with only 20 per cent six years earlier. This process could continue only so long as increasingly large loans were raised overseas.

There are ominous parallels between this situation and the condition of the Australian economy a century later. Of course there are major differences in industrial structure between the two periods. Nevertheless there is a correspondence in terms of the Australian overseas debt, which rose very rapidly in the early 1980s. The cost of servicing that debt reached a level in 1985–6 equal to about one-third of export income, partly as a result of a decline in Australian export prices relative to the prices of imports. The parallel may be extended further. A century ago, the boom terminated in a frenzy of speculation, a welter of buying and selling of existing assets which added nothing to their real value, and much of this was possible due to the inflow of overseas capital, made available to Australian speculators by banks and other institutions. Similarly today, a large part of the funds for the essentially unproductive takeover struggles for big companies comes from overseas sources. This worsens the balance of payments problem and is facilitated by the recent dismantling of financial regulations by government. As part of the deal, governments (both Labor and Liberal) serve the interests of capital by permitting Australian businessmen to evade much taxation on their borrowings and profits. The common people pay more in consequence.

Land Boomers and Bank Crash

The depression of the 1890s was one of the three worst in Australian history. Between 1891 and 1895 a number of major banks crashed, national output fell by about 30 per cent, and employment and incomes dropped disastrously as a result. The first real sign of approaching trouble came in Victoria in 1889, when land speculation ended abruptly. Melbourne land prices dropped and sales fell off. Land and loan companies were then in difficulties. They had based their operations on high prices and a quick turnover at land sales, and because much of their capital was tied up in land which became virtually unsaleable, some mushroom companies failed. Others managed to stave off the day of reckoning by raising fresh capital from unsuspecting investors in Britain.

In itself, the pricking of the bubble of land speculation in Melbourne did not bring about depression. Building societies there continued their operations, though at a reduced level of activity. In the other Australian colonies the boom levelled out, to be succeeded by sluggishness rather than depression for the next two years. Some effects of imbalance in the economy appeared, yet it seemed that the recession might prove to be quite mild. Beneath the surface, however, there was considerable unease. A high proportion of loans from banks were secured by mortgages on landed property, and the fall in land values meant that these loans were perilously insecure. As one Australian merchant noted apprehensively in 1892:

The whole of the banks suddenly find that securities which were supposed to be worth large sums cannot realize ½ and in some case ¼ or even ⅕ of the book values of 3 or 4 years ago. This has engendered a nervous and distrustful feeling ... boards [of bank directors] are all on the 'qui vive' investigating, strengthening and forecasting their financial positions.[6]

By that time, investors in England and Scotland were aware that all was not well with the Australian economy. They were also worried by the failure of the great financial house of Baring Brothers, although that failure followed from investment in the Argentine, not Australia. Uncertainty about the Australian economy was associated with a narrowing of the margin between British and Australian interest rates; and concern became evident in 1891, when several of the Australian colonial governments were unsuccessful in attempts to raise fresh loans on the London money market. This check to the supply of overseas funds meant drastic curtailment of public works programmes. The effect upon the building industry, already suffering from a fall in demand for houses, was seen in a sharp growth of unemployment. There was soon a series of failures of building societies and land and mortgage companies in Melbourne, Sydney and Brisbane. In Melbourne, where there were seventy building societies in 1890, only thirty-eight survived the disaster, and land companies fared even worse. Their cash reserves were drained away as fearful depositors withdrew their money.

In many cases, deposits had been placed in banks and other financial

191

institutions for fixed terms of one, two or three years. These investors were therefore unable to withdraw their capital immediately and this was particularly true of investors living in Britain. Thus although there was a sharp break in the flow of fresh funds to Australia from overseas, there was a time-lag before this was translated into a rush of overseas investors to cut their losses by withdrawing capital. That moment of panic arrived in 1893, being preceded by precipitous falls in the world prices of wool, wheat and silver. Associated with this was the fact that both Britain and the USA experienced economic depression in the early 1890s, though not on such a severe scale or for so long.

For the Australian colonies, dependent upon exports and a continued flow of capital, the consequences were calamitous. Graziers desperately tried to increase the size of the wool clip to compensate for the fall in price, and to some extent they succeeded: there was an increase in exports. As against this, the market price for surplus sheep dropped very sharply as expansion slowed, and graziers' profits were affected accordingly. Pastoral investment slumped. The decline in property values reduced or wiped out the equities of many graziers in their holdings, besides affecting their creditors. Banks, with assets locked up in mortgages on land, came under increasing strain from this quarter, at the same time as they were hit by the collapse of land and building societies to which they had lent money.

Early in 1893 there was a wholesale collapse of banks, as a run on deposits developed strongly. Banks closed their doors in order to preserve their dwindling cash reserves. Out of twenty-two note-issuing banks doing business in Australia, only nine remained open continuously. The others suspended payment, some permanently. The Victorian government declared a week's 'bank holiday' at the height of the crisis. In their turn, bankers pressed clients for repayment of loans, so that there was a cumulative effect. Scandalous instances of fraud came to light as hard-pressed businessmen sought to keep afloat or to conceal their assets from creditors.

In the preceding land boom, one Melbourne banker is reputed to have advised a young man: 'If you ever feel a desire to go wrong, don't prig pretty cash or enter threepenny letters as sixpences. Collar £10,000 and be sure to burn the bally books.' No doubt this was said in jest, yet it was actually done on a large scale by a number of speculators. Indeed, it became unnecessary to burn the books when depression came in Victoria, for the Voluntary Liquidation Act, rushed through parliament in one day in December 1891, provided that no company, including a building society, could be made bankrupt simply on the demand of a creditor who could not be paid; for such a demand to be effective, at least one-third of the creditors of a company must join in, and this was very difficult to organize. The alternative was voluntary liquidation, under which the directors of shaky companies were

192

allowed to wind up their affairs without independent investigation. Cannon comments that this was 'the nearest thing to legalised repudiation passed through an Australian Parliament in the nineteenth century'. Politicians looked after themselves and their friends. James Munro was Premier of Victoria when the Voluntary Liquidation Act was passed. Shortly afterwards his own companies took advantage of the Act, but he did not stay to supervise their voluntary liquidation. As Premier, he appointed himself Victorian Agent-General in London and quickly left the colony. He was by no means the last Australian politician to see the London post as a sinecure.[7]

Another ingenious legal manoeuvre in Victoria allowed bankrupt businessmen to make secret compositions by arrangement with their creditors. Thus in 1892 Benjamin Fink, the most flamboyant of the land-boomers, settled his debts of over one million pounds through a composition under which he paid one halfpenny in the pound. Before this event Fink had the foresight to ensure that much land, together with rich furnishings and antiques in his Melbourne mansion, were in the name of his wife; and when he died in London in 1909, he left an estate worth £250 000. Clearly, creditors did poorly out of compositions by arrangement. Their willingness to enter into them was probably due to fear that any public disclosure of their involvement in speculative concerns would have damaged their own credit and reputation.

A number of prominent Victorian land-boomers used compositions by arrangement to escape their difficulties. A lawyer, Theodore Fink (brother of Benjamin), is believed to have devised the stratagem for clients of his firm. He may be regarded as a precursor of those professional advisers of the late twentieth century who have helped businessmen to evade payment of colossal amounts of tax through 'bottom-of-the-harbour' schemes and the like. Theodore Fink did more than advise: twice in 1892 he compounded with his own creditors. It was done in secret, so that he was able to remain in legal practice, and in 1894 he was elected to the Victorian Parliament. Incidentally, many of the revelations of business fraud which surfaced in the 1890s would probably never have been exposed but for the depression.

Depression: Effects upon Capital

The depression of the 1890s affected all classes. Of course some people were better placed to withstand losses than others. Sir William Clarke, son of 'Big' Clarke, inherited large Victorian properties and a leading position in the Colonial Bank of Australia in 1874. The bank became involved in land speculation, and Clarke lost heavily in the bank crash of 1893. Nevertheless, when he died in 1897, he left an estate worth more than one million pounds. Many squatters were not so well padded, and there were numerous foreclosures on properties in the depression. Although the banks were disinclined to operate pastoral stations directly and there was little prospect of being able to sell a foreclosed station profitably while property values were so low, the general trend in the depression is clear. In 1901, 25 per cent of all the pastoral leases in the Western Division of New South Wales were held *in possession* by banks and pastoral financial companies, quite apart from cases where such institutions held formal title to leases while allowing the indebted grazier to go on working the property. When economic conditions improved early in the twentieth century, most of the foreclosed stations passed into the hands of individual pastoralists; but banks, through inspectors, exerted much closer control than before.

The same feature of strict financial control was evident in the operation of pastoral land-mortgage companies. Most of the largest were in serious difficulties in the depression. For example, Goldsbrough Mort & Co. suspended business in 1893 and had to undergo financial reconstruction. It is interesting to note in this connection that J. M. Niall, who was a leader of the Queensland squatters in the shearing strike of 1891, became Rockhampton manager for Goldsbrough Mort in 1896 and general manager of the company in 1900. No doubt he was gratified by the promotion but his career illustrates the frequent transition from independent grazier to salaried manager. Niall's friend, R. G. Casey (father of a future Governor-General of Australia) was also a Queensland grazier. Casey terminated his involvement in indebted stations in 1893, speculated successfully in mining companies and became a director of Goldsbrough Mort in 1896.[8]

Many other merchants, besides those engaged in the wool trade, were hit by the depression. Thus a prominent Melbourne importing firm, Paterson, Laing & Bruce, was in difficulties. One of the partners, J. M. Bruce (father of a future Prime Minister of Australia), had to move from his comfortable Toorak mansion, although he recovered it later. The failed speculations of Queenslander Robert Philp forced him out of business and into a full-time political career—he later became Premier. In such ways the depression of the 1890s undermined the predominance of mercantile capital.

The position of finance capital was uncertain and contradictory. On the one hand the banks suffered heavily in consequence of the crash of 1893. Most of the banks which failed resumed business after an interval for financial reconstruction, which was mainly at the expense of their customers and shareholders, who had to accept deferment of deposit repayments for a number of years and compulsory conversion of some deposits into bank shares. It took more than a decade for banks to work themselves out of their difficulties, and in the meantime their public voice and influence were subdued. On the other hand, as banks cut loans and pursued very cautious policies, their restrictive influence on business was more marked. In the labour movement they were commonly referred to as 'the money power', and were cursed accordingly.

One important consequence of the depression was that the inflow of capital and labour from overseas practically ceased until well after 1900. For a time the Victorian economy in particular had to be less reliant upon capital from Britain. Many British investors who were unable to withdraw their capital in time in the early 1890s suffered losses. To the extent that the losses were incurred in the private sector in Australia, mainly through banks and in the pastoral industry, those investors could do little more than complain. Their position was no different from that of many Australian investors. Indeed, in the case of the banks which suspended payment in 1893, only about one-third of their liabilities were due to owners of fixed deposits who were resident in Britain. As for the public sector, colonial governments continued to pay interest on overseas loans. There was no suggestion of repudiation of such debts, so that bondholders did well.

Nevertheless, there is some evidence of the British government being particularly concerned to protect the interests of investors based in Britain. In 1891 the Colonial Office sent despatches from London to Australia, regretting the outbreak of strikes and approving their termination. 'Sir Henry Norman, Governor of Queensland, suggested the possibility of using Royal Navy personnel on the Australian station to assist in the suppression of strikes'. At a broader level, one historian comments that the Colonial Office had

a policy of supporting the federation of Australia, which derived support from the desire to protect British investment there. Federation would improve the security but only if concluded on the right terms ... [including] the preservation of the imperial connection with the maintenance of a right, however tenuous, of veto on legislation and the right of appeal to the Privy Council ... The British government retained a more important role in relation to federation than is sometimes conceded, since the legislation had to be British.[9]

Unemployment, Poverty and Pensions

Although capitalists were hit by the reduction of property values in the depression it was the common people who suffered most, as usual. Recourse to legal proceedings for insolvency had no practical meaning for those who had never possessed capital assets. Their lot was unemployment or wage cuts. Apart from that, some skilled workers, as well as middle-class people, either lost personal savings in banks and

195

building societies or found them frozen. Many people also lost their homes, being unable to keep up payments on housing loans. Building societies foreclosed and repossessed, to the extent that for a time they became Melbourne's largest landlords. Concurrently, there was a marked increase in tenancy, and there was some popular resistance to evictions from homes.

Unemployment at the level experienced between 1891 and 1895 was unprecedented. There was no official count of the number of unemployed, but some trade unions kept careful records concerning their own members. Thus it is known that one-sixth of the members of the ASE throughout Australia were jobless. These engineers were skilled workers. Amongst unskilled workers, the level of unemployment was probably much higher; and in Melbourne, which was worst hit, nearly one-third of all workers were unemployed in 1893. Building trade workers were particularly badly affected as their industry collapsed. In Sydney about 50 per cent of the members of the Amalgamated Society of Carpenters and Joiners were unemployed.

Wage-earners who were able to keep jobs experienced wage reductions varying from 10 to 35 per cent. For example, Melbourne tramwaymen suffered cuts amounting to 23 per cent in 1891–4. Such reductions were not as drastic as they might seem, for prices also fell sharply. However, there was also much short-time working which reduced pay packets. Railway workshop employees in New South Wales and Victoria were working only three-quarters of the standard week in 1893.

The governments of several of the colonies established Labour Bureaus in 1892. It seems that the prime function of these organizations was to shift thousands of the unemployed from city to country by providing free rail passes. Particularly at the time of the shearers' strike in 1894, many of the workers drafted to the country in New South Wales were used as strikebreakers. To the limited extent that Labour Bureaus helped to provide urban employment, it was at substandard wages, reinforcing the general trend towards wage reductions. For the rest, the poor and hungry were dependent mainly upon private charity, provided by bodies such as local Ladies Benevolent Societies in Melbourne. As Shurlee Swain has observed:

Ironically the various charitable agencies competed amongst themselves to assist most generously those of noble birth who, through alcoholism or mental illness, had lost their financial resources, while they denied the very poor all but the barest essentials . . . Needy children of respectable birth were placed in orphanages, or, increasingly, allowed to remain at home with their mothers to whom a weekly allowance was paid.[10]

Officialdom was cold as charity to those who were down and out. One unfortunate man who was arrested for vagrancy in Melbourne, when asked by the magistrate how he lived, 'replied "I starves" and was promptly rewarded with twelve months hard labour'.[11] Although this treatment was vicious, it may be noted that there were no official institutions to accommodate invalid or destitute old people. 'The nearest thing the state had to a network of caring institutions were its jails'; and the agitation for introduction of old age pensions in Victoria in the 1890s was 'greatly strengthened by revelations about the practice of committing the old to jail'.[12] New South Wales, in 1900, was the first Australian colony/State to pass legislation for an old age pension scheme. Pensions were payable at the rate of ten shillings per week and in principle the Act was an important social advance, although there were severe limitations upon eligibility, not only in terms of age and income, but also according to criteria of race and moral character: Aborigines and Asians were excluded from benefit, and applicants for pensions had to provide evidence of good character. Victoria adopted a comparable scheme soon after, and the Commonwealth followed suit in 1908.

Trade Unions and the Formation of the ALP

The worst of the depression was over by 1896. Some relief came from rich gold discoveries in Western Australia, which led to a migration westwards of thousands of people from Victoria and South Australia. By 1900 there was a bigger population in Western Australia than in Tasmania, which was generally regarded as having been somnolent in the latter part of the nineteenth century. Incidentally, both these areas at last came into line with the other colonies, in formal democratic terms, by introducing manhood suffrage, in 1893 in the case of Western Australia and 1901 in Tasmania. In the circumstances of the gold discoveries, workers in Western Australia also secured general recognition of the eight-hour day, and fledgling trade unions expanded there.

Nevertheless, in the eastern Australian colonies there was no more than a mild recovery, patchy in its incidence, in the later years of the 1890s. The building industry remained stagnant and economic recovery was retarded by the withdrawal of British capital. There was a strong economic upsurge around 1900, but this did not last long, being blotted out by the worst recorded drought in Australia. The drought, which had begun in 1895 in some areas, was devastating in Queensland and New South Wales. There were only 54 million sheep in Australia by 1903, compared with 104 million in 1891. The number of cattle also dropped heavily. Because of the dominance of pastoralism and agriculture in the Australian economy, the general result was a renewal of depression until 1906. Thus from 1891 there was a fifteen-year period of severe depression or at best very sluggish growth, in which gross national product per head of population was appreciably lower that it had been.

This long spell of adversity profoundly affected the labour movement. Trade unions were largely destroyed in the 1890s. Whereas about 20 per cent of all wage-earners in New South Wales were members of trade unions at the beginning of the decade (a proportion which was probably higher than anywhere else in the world), some two-thirds were lost in the depression. Unemployed workers unable to keep up subscriptions dropped out, there was a scramble for jobs, and weakened unions were in no position to defend wage standards. The position was even worse in Victoria, where nearly all unions of unskilled workers disappeared, as did some craft unions. One of the survivors, the Melbourne Typographical Society, lost £2000 which it had deposited in banks or building companies. At the end of the nineteenth century there was probably a smaller proportion of trade unionists in the workforce in Australia than in Britain.

In these circumstances, a turn towards political action made sense. At the end of the Maritime Strike, the Sydney Defence Committee stated that 'whilst we must go on ever increasing our capacity for fighting as we have fought before, the time has come when Trades-unionists must use the Parliamentary machine that has in the past used them'.[13] The idea of political activity was not new. In the 1880s trade union bodies in Sydney and Melbourne established parliamentary committees whose task was to lobby for political action in connection with legislation which concerned unions. From this, a crucial step forward was the setting up of a labour political party, functioning independently of existing parties. That move was begun in Queensland in 1889 with the establishment of the Australian Labour Federation which, inspired by William Lane, had a socialist objective for a short period of time. New South Wales moved in a similar direction and the union defeat in the Maritime Strike provided the final stimulus. At the end of 1890 the Trades and Labour Council of New South Wales decided to establish Labor Electoral Leagues in electorates; and in the parliamentary elections of 1891 an astonishing degree of success was achieved. Thirty-five Labor candidates were elected to the 141-member Legislative Assembly. They constituted a group which could not be ignored —although its members could be seduced from their allegiance, as they were divided on the important issue of free trade or protection.

Aided by the general adoption of payment of MPs from the public purse, by the abolition or restriction of plural voting, and perhaps by the granting to women of the right to vote (first in South Australia in 1894), Labor parties were also established in other colonies. There was notable success in Queensland, despite the departure of Lane in 1893. With the depression biting deep and the shearers defeated in strike action, Lane and his supporters sailed off to found a 'New Australia' in Paraguay. This utopian venture drained off hundreds of idealistic Australians. Even so, Queensland in 1899 had the distinction of being the first country in the world to have a Labor government. It was an achievement without substance, for the Dawson ministry held office for only one week.

In Victoria the evolution of a Labor party followed a rather different path. The Melbourne Trades Hall Council in 1891 sponsored formation of a Progressive Political League, which became the United Labor Party five years later. This body was much less successful than its counterpart in New South Wales and could hardly be considered as an independent party, since it functioned mainly as a wing of the Liberals. There was a longstanding association in Victoria between manufacturers and trade unions, based upon common support for protective tariffs. The link had ramifications in social reform, although it may be noted that in the political sphere Victoria was last to concede female suffrage, which it did in 1908.

The general character of the various Labor parties is most usefully assessed by considering the organization in New South Wales. Initially the party there had an explicit class standpoint, which may be exemplified by the words of a declaration by the Intercolonial Trades Union Congress of 1891 that 'class questions require class knowledge to state them, and class sympathies to fight for them'.[14] Unskilled workers—represented, for example, by the Balmain Labourers' Union, which later became the Ship Painters and Dockers Union—appear to have been exceptionally enthusiastic in the successful political campaign of 1891; and this probably reflected the fact that the unskilled were particularly hard hit by the defeat of the Maritime Strike and the deepening depression. Labor representatives in parliament continually agitated for improvements in working conditions for people in government service, such as railwaymen. There was also strong pressure to extend direct government employment through use of day labour, instead of letting public works projects out to contract.

Yet the Labor Party in New South Wales was not simply a working-class organization. Its main strength lay in urban areas but it also won a number of rural parliamentary seats; and in order to expand, the party needed support from small farmers as well as bushworkers. At the same time as this became apparent, the leadership position originally held by the Trades and Labour Council was lost. In effect, the Council, weakened by the depression, went out of operation in 1894. For the next six years, its place was taken by a District Council of the Australasian Labor Federation, which had comparatively little standing in Sydney.

Socialism was important in the NSW Labor Party in its early years. It 'explained the sense of separate class identity . . . and it pointed towards a new form of mass activity by the class, a workers' party seeking access to the state'.[15] At a time of working-class mobilization, socialism was the appropriate ideology, and socialists were active and influential in the Labor Party. However, the Australian Workers' Union assumed a dominant position in the party from 1895. The AWU, through its paid organizers, was able to 'deliver' a number of rural parliamentary seats, and several leading Labor MPs, such as W. M. Hughes, W. A. Holman and J. C. Watson, were associated with the union. By 1900 the 'AWU and Labor leaderships had become virtually indistinguishable', and the AWU was 'primarily a political rather than an industrial organisation.'[16] The old Trades Council was revived in 1900 under the name of the Sydney Labor Council, and its constituent urban unions joined the Labor party (reluctantly in the case of some craftsmen) but the party's structure and methods had become settled by then. A moderate parliamentary strategy under the guidance of professional politicians was the order of the day.

One of the first casualties of AWU political dominance was the old trade union aim of introducing a universal eight-hour day through legislation. The AWU, which had connections with small farmers and rural shopkeepers and tradesmen, argued that the eight-hour plank in Labor policy would alienate many rural voters, so the policy was watered down, becoming meaningless. Instead, Labor went after the rural vote with policies of agrarian reform, particularly support for small wheat farmers through programmes of closer settlement. As summed up by one historian, in the early years of the twentieth century

Adelaide and its suburbs, the small farmers, the Tasmanian apple-growers were all won over to Labor. Labour in Britain was the party of the working class; in Australia the party could be persuasively presented as both a 'class' and a 'national' party.[17]

Origins of Compulsory Arbitration

The new Labor political force played a major role in the labour movement's adoption of the notion of compulsory arbitration for the settlement of industrial disputes. This is a complex matter, requiring distinctions to be drawn between voluntary and compulsory arbitration, and between state and private schemes. In the 1880s Australian trade unions favoured the establishment of private, voluntary boards or committees of conciliation and arbitration, representing employers and employees. With varying success, a number of such bodies were set up, for example in bootmaking in Victoria. These schemes were dependent upon both sides agreeing about their usefulness. Trade unions were generally divided as to whether the state should be brought into the process, and most unionists were opposed to any suggestion of compulsory arbitration. Collective bargaining was the preferred method.

Attitudes changed in the 1890s, when unions were crippled by strike defeats and depression. A number of trade unions now felt that they might gain more (or rather, lose less) through state intervention in industrial disputes. Employers, on the other hand, were confident of their industrial strength and saw no point in bringing the state into the picture. In between were middle-class elements of the population who were worried or appalled by the polarization of society revealed by the Maritime Strike. Those who were concerned for the future considered that sustained efforts should be made to moderate or limit class strife and that the state should play a role in this. At the end of 1890 C. C. Kingston, a leading Liberal lawyer-politician in South Australia, introduced a bill there to provide for compulsory arbitration. The bill failed to pass; and indeed, in the various Australian colonies in the 1890s, parliamentary consideration of machinery to deal with industrial disputes was largely confined to proposals for voluntary conciliation. These proved futile, as most employers were more interested in smashing unions than in negotiating with them. Broken Hill mine-owners made this very clear in 1892.

Despondently, more and more unions were converted to the view that a compulsory form of arbitration was desirable. The Labor Party in New South Wales, after steadily moving towards compulsory arbitration, adopted it as a platform policy in 1899, thus lining up with Liberal reformers in parliament. Labor leaders such as Holman expatiated on the substitution of 'the methods of reason, arbitration, commonsense, and judgement for the methods of brute force'.[18] In effect, Labor politicians advocated compulsory state arbitration in absolute terms, as a piece of social machinery which was desirable in principle, irrespective of the circumstances. This attitude ignored class interests, which varied from time to time. Compulsory arbitration was acceptable to unions in the 1890s because they were weak. In practice, the advent of compulsory arbitration at the beginning of the twentieth century made a very favourable impression upon trade unionists, yet there were occasions later when many of them recognized the disadvantages of the system: when unions were strong, they could achieve more by unrestricted industrial action.

In a similar fashion, changes in circumstances led employers and their parliamentary representatives to modify their standpoint. Initial hopes of wiping out trade unionism were dashed and in the early years of the new century more and more employers saw benefits for themselves from compulsory arbitration and were willing at least to give it a trial. It is worth noting the context of the first effective legislative   201 enactment of compulsory arbitration in Australia. Unexpectedly, that occurred in 1900 in Western Australia, which was far from being an industrially developed region. However, the legislation flowed from a major strike by lumpers (wharf labourers) in Fremantle the previous year. Shipping companies made a dictatorial attempt to reduce lumpers' wages and to worsen their working conditions, and the employers underestimated the strength of resistance to this. There were some violent incidents and the strike went on for five weeks before being settled by a private citizens' committee which arbitrated between the two sides. Public opinion was a factor in a colony which was heavily dependent upon shipping for trade, and the government of Western Australia was sufficiently impressed to put a compulsory Conciliation and Arbitration Act on the statute book—though in practice the Act had little effect for a couple of years or more.

In 1901 the New South Wales parliament took similar action, using New Zealand legislation as a model. The immediate background to this NSW Industrial Arbitration Act was a short-lived economic upturn, which led to a revival of trade union strength. The subsequent development of Australian arbitration, through courts and wages boards, will be considered more closely in later chapters, but one general point may be made here. Once established, the system had a logic and momentum of its own, which made it very difficult for unions to stay outside it, even if they wished to do so. Their members might be poached by unions operating within the system, as the Amalgamated Society of Engineers realized in 1903, with reference to the Arbitration Act of Western Australia. In that State there were many engineers scattered in such establishments as timber mills, and the union noted that

a factor that the ASE have to practically compete against is the composite Unions, who embrace all and sundry, and by their permanent officers travelling the various districts are enabled to induce mechanics to join their ranks . . . These unions have industrial agreements or awards of the Arbitration Court which are a foundation that their members can work upon.

Even so, Tom Mann, labour leader and one-time organizer for the ASE in Australia, wrote a little later that 'whatever may be said by Arbitration Courts, the only rightful reward to the workers is the full produce of their labours', and 'Act or no Act, the standard won't be high unless there is a powerful organisation'.[19]

12

Restructuring, Federation, New Protection and Arbitration

No social order ever perishes before all the productive forces for which there is room in it have developed; and new, higher relations of production never appear before the material conditions of their existence have matured in the womb of the old society itself. Therefore mankind always sets itself only such tasks as it can solve; since ... it will always be found that the task itself arises only when the material conditions for its solution already exist or are at least in the process of formation.[1]

There were two short-term responses to the balance of payments problem which erupted in the depression of the 1890s. Investors in Britain cut their loans to Australia; and Australian imports of goods were reduced drastically, as a result of cuts in living standards associated with heavy unemployment and reductions in income. This was the classic brutal capitalist way of dealing with a depression.

Over a longer period, extending up to the outbreak of the First World War, there was a substantial restructuring of the Australian economy to cope with the crisis of the 1890s, particularly in ways which required little capital investment. On the land there was diversification of production from wool to meat and wheat. There was also a marked growth in manufacturing. These changes affected class structure: big graziers were less dominant; thousands of small farmers established themselves, especially in New South Wales and Western

Australia; and the industrial working class developed strongly. One important consequence was a swing towards populist ideas. Populism was a movement of 'small men', especially farmers. It is no accident that populism grew in Australia as well as in the USA: these were countries where, in contrast to older societies, land could still be obtained by small producers. In the USA, populism gradually declined after 1904, whereas in Australia a stronger labour movement, with its own political party, absorbed populist ideas. However, this did not deter Australian rural interests later from forming a third party, the Country Party.

Restructuring the Economy

In the main, economic adjustment following the depression of the 1890s was in the form of diversification of agricultural production. Graziers reacted to the decline in profitability of wool by shifting attention to meat production, especially in Queensland. The technical problem of refrigeration had been solved in the 1880s, but it required the spur of depression in the 1890s to induce large-scale export of refrigerated carcasses from Australia. The same applied to a growth of exports of Victorian butter and Tasmanian fruit. Steamships and refrigeration opened up big markets in industrial Britain.

More important in the long run was expansion of the wheat industry. Wheat did not drop as steeply in price as wool in the 1890s, and the amount of land under wheat in New South Wales trebled in the decade. A large part of the increase occurred in the Riverina, an area previously noted for vast pastoral stations. One interesting development here was the growth of share-cropping, a system in which a tenant-farmer provided labour, machinery and draught animals to cultivate cleared land leased to him by a landowner who also provided fencing and seed. The proceeds of the crop were shared equally. It was a method which gave opportunities to small producers who were unable to afford the full cost of establishing a farm. By the same token, such farmers were at a disadvantage in bargaining with landowners, who minimized their own risks.

After 1900 new wheat varieties and the application of fertilizer greatly aided Australian wheat production and exports. In Western Australia, growth was also related to the construction of light railways which opened up the wheat belt, so that output in that State rose from 2.5 million bushels in 1908 to 13 million in 1913. By that time, wool prices had risen and the wool industry recovered. Indeed, after the drought period around 1900, wool regained its position as the leading export commodity, but the economy was no longer so heavily dependent upon it. There was a marked trend towards more mixed farming and a growth in small holdings. Beginning in the 1890s, governments assisted this process through Closer Settlement Acts, under which a number of large freehold estates were bought by the state for sub-division and resale to small farmers. Compulsory purchase provisions were introduced in 1904 by New South Wales and Victoria, although this did not prevent the cost to government being heavy. The logical absurdity of this policy in relation to land originally granted or sold cheaply by governments was ignored in the process of establishing thousands of new settlers on the land.

These changes in agriculture had significant consequences for class structure. On the one hand, graziers (and their mercantile allies) were not so dominant as before. John Merritt comments: 'By 1911 the wool giants had died, left the industry or were operating on a much smaller scale'.[2] Yet Australia was still the world's greatest producer of wool. Banks, in their loan policies, continued to prefer graziers. Moreover, many pastoralists became involved in wheat growing. Rentier land-owners who linked up with share-farmers benefited from the success of wheat exports. In New South Wales the proportion of the total wheat area worked on the share system rose from 17 per cent in 1904 to 28 per cent ten years later.

In the 1890s there was an interesting legislative indication of the continuing influence of pastoral interests. As wool and other prices fell, and more animals were slaughtered because of depression and drought, there was increased emphasis upon production of pastoral by-products such as leather, bones, glue, hair and tallow. There were export markets for these commodities, and production in New South Wales became increasingly centralized in suburban areas of Sydney. Some municipal councils resisted the spread of these 'noxious trades', and in 1894 the NSW parliament passed a Noxious Trades and Cattle Slaughtering Act, providing for certain controls over such industries. However, the first step in control was the gazetting of industries under the Act; and as few were gazetted initially, the Act might be regarded as being aimed at protecting manufacturers. Yet more important were the interests of the pastoral export sector. As Shirley Fisher remarks: 'The exporters' need to produce in a low cost situation, unfettered by government controls, was deemed more important than was the pres-ervation of Sydney's environment and the health of Sydney's popula-tion'. Rural interests were as unconcerned about urban pollution as they had been in stripping the land of its forest cover and fertility.[3]

Nevertheless, the strength of the old grazing element was modified by the development of other class forces. In particular, there was a big increase in the number of farmers. They were aided by the state in a variety of ways, notably by provision of easier credit facilities through State Agricultural Banks. An important motive for this was the stimu-lation of primary production and exports as part of the restructuring of   205 the economy. In addition, there was a strategic social aspect to agricultural policy: the labour struggles of the 1890s indicated a sharp polarization of society, which could be moderated by building up a bloc of yeoman farmers. Small farmers, mostly employing only the labour of their own families, could be expected to stabilize the class structure by reinforcing the middle classes. Thomas Bent, a conservative politician and land speculator, made this point to members of the Victorian Legislative Council in 1903:

Is not the selector . . . as conservative as any man in the community? I have known a man carry his 'bluey', and twelve months afterwards I have known the same man so conservative that he would not let you tread on the bit of land he had got in the meantime.[4]

On the whole, the expectation that farmers would constitute a solid conservative element in Australian society was realized, though not in such a straightforward way as Bent supposed. There were still differences between grain producers and graziers, and between large and small farmers. Farming remained a hard life, subject to exploitation by moneylenders and merchants. A South Australian Royal Commission in 1908 found that nine Adelaide grain merchants and flour-millers had an 'honourable understanding' to regulate prices; and a Victorian Commission of 1913–14 came to the same conclusion about a group of Melbourne traders.

Development of small farming gave a strong boost to populist ideas, which had antecedents in nineteenth-century Australia. Populist ideology was based on the small producer's dream of achieving independence and security as a farmer, miner, shopkeeper or small manufacturer. The emphasis was upon the individual and 'the people', with barriers to progress being envisaged as parasitic ruling elites rather than a specific capitalist class and state. At the same time, populists were suspicious of the extension of capitalist social relations, especially in the shape of big business or monopoly.

Such ideas flourished among small farmers. The labour movement was also receptive. Thus the Shearers' Union in New South Wales joined in a campaign for closer settlement in the 1890s, seeking fulfilment of a vision of a yeoman class, and it is likely that many sharefarmers, tenants and leaseholders were sympathetic towards the Australian Labor Party. The party supported agrarian reform and introduced Commonwealth land taxation in 1910. The tax was ostensibly designed to break up large estates, although its practical effect in this respect was very limited.

The effect of populism on the labour movement was much broader than this. Ideological assumptions which blurred class distinctions and portrayed the state machine as neutral had a profound impact in such areas as nationalism and defence, White Australia and arbitration. Moreover, although the depression of the 1890s restricted upward social mobility, Australian capitalism in the early twentieth century was expansive enough to give many workers access to the ranks of the small business class. This was most noticeable in industry, but even on the land there were some workers who found opportunities. Thus in 1910 the Broken Hill branch of the Amalgamated Society of Engineers bade farewell to its secretary, who was going farming 'to better his position in life', as he put it.[5] Australian capitalism was far from having exhausted its possibilities for growth and this was reflected in the relative weakness of socialism in the labour movement. There was support for state intervention in society, and there was a degree of trade union militancy, but these were not synonymous with the adoption of socialist views.

Manufacturing and Protection

Apart from the restructuring of Australian agriculture, the main growth sector of this period was manufacturing. This should not be exaggerated, for Australia could not be described as an industrial society before World War II. Nevertheless, the real beginnings of movement towards that position may be seen from the 1890s. Actually, statistics relating to that decade suggest that manufacturing contributed little to recovery from depression. There was no increase in the proportion of the total workforce which was engaged in manufacturing. However, these figures are deceptive. A big drop in production and employment in the building materials industry, due to the slump in building, masked a growth of other kinds of manufacturing. Employers gained from cuts in real wages, and a trend towards social and economic equality for women was slowed down. As Desley Deacon notes, such benefits as the winning of equal pay by female public servants in New South Wales in 1895 were eroded by the establishment or intensification of separate labour markets for men and women. Also in New South Wales, the Government Statistician noted that very low pay for women in the depression was 'influenced by the competition of other women, chiefly wives, who are not solely dependent upon their own earnings for support, and who, therefore, are in a position to undersell their less fortunately situated sisters'.[6]

This quotation should perhaps be treated with caution, since its author felt that it was undesirable on social grounds for women, especially married women, to go out to work. Nevertheless, the figures for Melbourne, the most important city for female employment, show that the proportion of all women of working age who were in the paid workforce rose from about 37 per cent in 1891 to 41 per cent in 1901.   207

Of these, about 10 per cent had professional jobs such as teaching and were relatively well off. The others were poorly paid, though more jobs were offered to them. In Sydney there was a growth of light manufacturing industry—for example, jam, pickle and sauce factories—and there was an influx of young women from rural areas. The underlying reality surfaced in an incident in 1899, when A. Hirschman, proprietor of a cigar factory in Sydney, told a trade union deputation that he was willing to recognize the relevant union, on condition that none of his female (and underpaid) employees were allowed to join it. When this proposal appeared to be acceptable to the male unionists, a letter from 'Jemima Jorkins' was published in *The Worker* newspaper, saying that the members of the deputation

made a big mistake in agreein' with the employer not to countenance the formation o' a Union among his female operatives. It's time they knew that the men's battle is the wimmin's, an' that if the wimmin 'as ter work fer next to nothin' they'll take the men's billets . . . It ain't right ter slight the female sex; it can't be did to eny great extent without recoilin' on the offender's 'ead.[7]

Whoever Jemima Jorkins may have been, these percipient remarks went unheeded. In 1899 there were 544 males and 197 females employed in tobacco, cigar and cigarette factories in New South Wales. In 1913 the figures were 692 males and 805 females. Women's wages were about half those of male workers. In the NSW bootmaking industry there was a parallel trend, though with less displacement of male labour. Thirty-five per cent of the workforce of 4475 people in this industry in 1910 were female, compared with 19 per cent of a much smaller workforce in 1891. By the later date, the Australian Bootmakers' Employees' Union, though overwhelmingly male, included some females, and in most States it was actively organizing women from 1911.

Besides the question of labour costs, another big issue affecting the growth of manufacturing in the nineteenth century and later was protection. This was a much more complex matter than might be supposed from the common designation of Victoria as a protectionist colony as against New South Wales which favoured free trade. Certainly, Victoria from the 1860s introduced higher import duties which were avowedly protectionist for the commodities affected—usually consumer items, not capital goods. On the other hand, it is difficult to ascertain whether particular changes in the Victorian tariff resulted from protectionist rather than revenue motives. In the late nineteenth century, Victoria was much more dependent than New South Wales upon tariff revenue. The latter colony had a great revenue from land sales, and the erection of tariff barriers raising the prices of imported goods was not to the advantage of graziers and merchants except perhaps as an alternative to income taxation. There is little evidence of intention to protect particular industries through tariffs in New South Wales.

In terms of results, Victorians pointed to greater development of factories and manufacturing employment, especially clothing, in their colony, claiming that it was due to higher protection. Also, Victorian farmers sought and obtained protection for their produce. However, these phenomena were not necessarily matters of cause and effect. Victoria's relatively small land area and large labour force might be expected to produce an early turn towards both manufacturing and a more intensive form of agriculture. The latter encouraged considerable growth of agricultural machinery manufacturing in Victoria and South Australia, though not in New South Wales. Moreover, Geoffrey Serle argues that, until the 1890s, Victorian protective tariffs were low compared to those of the United States, Canada and many other colonies. He therefore describes 'protectionist Victoria' as a 'myth'.[8]

On another plane, G. J. R. Linge claims that historians have traditionally 'grossly exaggerated' the beneficial influence of the Victorian tariff on industrial development, at least in relation to the 1880s, while simultaneously they underestimated such factors as population increase and government contracts, especially for the metal trades. This raises the important point that protection or encouragement could take forms other than the obvious one of import tariffs. New South Wales, like Victoria, gave subsidies to local engineering firms by placing contracts with them for the manufacture of locomotives at prices higher than those tendered by overseas firms. The price preference was perhaps as much as 16 per cent in New South Wales and 22 per cent in Victoria. More generally, colonial governments allowed a margin of 10 per cent on tenders submitted by local manufacturers of a variety of goods. This hidden form of protection extended into the twentieth century and indeed still functions today.[9]

Federation

Federation of the six Australian colonies came into force in January 1901. There were many contributory factors, including nationalist sentiment and a desire for a unified approach on defence and foreign policy (a concern stimulated in the 1880s by the German occupation of New Guinea), as well as a need for national policy in such areas as immigration, postal services and banking. Those bankers and merchants who did business in more than one of the colonies generally favoured federation as a means of facilitating trade and payments. Trade was a crucial issue in the move towards federation and it was often crudely exploited, as in the case of a Tasmanian federalist who said:

Gentlemen, if you vote for the Bill you will found a great and glorious nation under the bright Southern Cross, and meat will be cheaper; and you will live to see the Australian race dominate the Southern seas, and you will have a market for both potatoes and apples . . .[10]

Federation meant the creation of a common market within Australia, free from intercolonial tariff barriers. Previously, for example, Queensland sugar sent to other Australian colonies had been subject to import duties in the same way as imports from overseas. The removal of such internal obstructions to trade offered the prospect of an extension of markets and more support for manufacturers—though not all of them. Not surprisingly, well established Victorian manufacturers were foremost in pressing for federation, which entailed a common Australian tariff against the rest of the world, in conjunction with a free internal market. At the same time, manufacturers in smaller colonies such as South Australia tended to oppose the federation proposal: their industries had grown up under protective tariffs and they did not feel confident about competition with Victorians in a free market. On the other hand, the efficient South Australian wheat farmers, reckoning that they could beat any competition in their local markets, were free traders favouring federation.

There were numerous other cross-currents and conflicts of interest. Those merchants whose interests lay mainly in overseas trade tended to oppose federation. Another complication was that certain regions in Australia overlapped the borders of two or more colonies. One such region was the Riverina, where trade was subject to attempts by rival Sydney and Melbourne interests to influence its direction through tariffs and differential railway rates. Of course some regional interests benefited from such distortion, but in general the Riverina viewed federation as a means of obviating uncertainty and allowing trade to flow in natural channels. Sugar planters in northern Queensland, employing black labour, feared federation because of the White Australia policy associated with it; whereas miners in Queensland favoured federation for the same reason. Indeed miners throughout Australia generally supported federation. They often migrated across colonial borders, their trade union was a federated body and they were little concerned with petty colonial rivalries. Goldminers in Western Australia—many of them from colonies in the east—looked upon federation as a means of undermining the conservative government of the colony.

Given the diversity and cupidity of capitalist interests, it is quite remarkable that federation was adopted in the 1890s. The depression

210

may have provided impetus, and federation was undoubtedly to the advantage of the capitalist class as a whole. Even so, certain conditions and understandings were the basis for the emergence of the Commonwealth of Australia. In particular, the major rivalry between Victoria and New South Wales was the subject of a compromise. This issue involved both trade and revenue, which were entwined. For instance, a tariff which was nominally designed to produce government revenue might prove to be protectionist in practice; and free-trade New South Wales, with its large land revenue, feared that a federal government would impose substantial increases in taxation through the tariff, which would be disproportionately heavy for New South Wales compared with other colonies which had been largely dependent upon tariffs for revenue. The solution agreed upon was that, for the first ten years after federation, three-quarters of Commonwealth revenue from customs and excise would be passed on to the States, and this revenue would be distributed among them in proportion to the amount raised in each State. Decision on the related question of a protectionist tariff was deferred on the understanding that the first Commonwealth government would provide protection for existing industries of some size.

Another important step towards national unity was agreement that it should take the form of a federation of the six colonies. Theoretically, full integration along the lines of government in Britain was an alternative, but it was not feasible politically. The colonies had developed as separate entities and there were many politicians and businessmen who had no intention of giving up their local power bases. Thus the model of the USA was broadly adopted: a federation which preserved for the colonies/States their existing control over such matters as land settlement, education, health, justice and police. The process of submitting the federal proposal to popular votes for approval was important in boosting public interest, but the only question put in the referenda of the 1890s concerned federation. The people were asked to vote 'yes' or 'no' on that and not on any other form of national government.

This limitation of democratic choice prompts speculation as to what Henry Parkes had in mind in 1891 when he first proposed the name 'Commonwealth of Australia' for the new political entity. 'Commonwealth' was an honourable term of some antiquity, used, for example, in the naming of England's colony of Massachusetts in the seventeenth century. Parkes was not a republican but he was an admirer of the men of the American Revolution who fought for the independence of the USA in the eighteenth century. Moreover, 'the common weal' had a warm Anglo-Saxon ring to it, calculated to appeal to nationalist sentiment. Incidentally, the *Macquarie Dictionary* (1981) records that the definition of 'commonwealth' as 'the public welfare' is obsolete. Perhaps Parkes was being more subtle than is usually thought.

Hobson's choice applied to the particular structure of federal institutions as well as the fact of federation. The framework was devised by men of property: merchants, lawyers and pastoralists, plus a token representative of the working class in the form of a Victorian craft unionist. Inevitably, the constitution which they drew up embodied safeguards against radical change. Federal parliament was to consist of two chambers, one of which, the Senate, was endowed with significant blocking powers in relation to money and other bills. The Senate was a conservative watchdog comprising equal numbers of representatives from each State. Thus a small and backward State like Tasmania was given as much power in the Senate as Victoria or New South Wales, despite the great disparity in population. The structure was loaded particularly against New South Wales, viewed by conservatives as a State where the labour movement was strongest. The nationalism of the federal movement was essentially conservative.

Many labour people, whilst favouring national unity, looked askance at the democratic credentials of promoters of the federation project as drafted. On 7 March 1891, the *Workman* put the question: 'What is there in this federation of the colonies . . . that is likely to benefit the toilers of Australia?' Ben Tillett, the British dockers' union leader, when he visited Australian in 1898, found many who agreed with his warning about the draft constitution:

If there is to be one destiny, there must be unity . . . there must be democratic administration . . . we must have sovereign authority. But the only sovereign power, the only sovereign authority that a free people will accept, is the sovereignty of the people themselves . . . Guard well your liberty; remember the fightings, the imprisonment, the police, the bludgeonings of the past . . . and beware lest you give these dearly won liberties to those who will be the parasites of the future, robbing you of your political, economical and social birthrights . . .[11]

Certain other aspects of the Commonwealth constitution reflected conservative dominance. First, there was the institution of a High Court, which was given the role of interpreting the constitution—and if the precedent of the US Supreme Court was anything to go by, there would be no radical interpretation. Second, the mechanism for formal amendment of the constitution through the process of referendum was so heavily weighted against a simple majority of votes that few of the many proposals submitted to the people since then have been adopted.

Finally in connection with federation, there is the question of

Australia's position in the British Empire. It was clearly that of a colony: the Commonwealth of Australia came into being following the passing of an Act by the Westminster parliament, and that imperial institution had the power to amend the Act later if it thought fit. While the constitutional debate was going on in Australia in the 1890s, the British government raised no fundamental objection to federation and indeed welcomed it in some respects. However, the Colonial Secretary, Joseph Chamberlain, was intent upon protecting imperial rights and, in 1897, he secretly briefed George Reid, Premier of New South Wales, to procure amendment of certain draft federation proposals. Two points were particularly significant. One was Chamberlain's objection to a draft proposal (linked with the creation of a High Court) to place severe limits on rights of appeal from Australian courts to the Privy Council in London. In Chamberlain's view, continuation of the right of appeal was a necessary protection for investors of British capital in Australia. The other point concerned the prerogatives of the Queen and her representative, the Governor-General. Chamberlain was suspicious about a draft proposal that the Governor-General should exercise his powers only on the advice of the Executive Council (in effect, the federal government).

Through Reid's advocacy, the Colonial Office obtained basic satisfaction on both of these matters in the final draft of the constitution. The possibility of a wide range of appeals to the Privy Council was left open, and the Governor-General was formally empowered to act with or without the advice of the Executive Council. This was a continuation of the power previously vested in the governors of the individual Australian colonies, although the convention was that action in virtually all cases would follow the advice of the government. 'Reserve powers' seemed to have no real meaning—until Sir John Kerr in 1975 peremptorily dismissed the Whitlam Labor government, despite its commanding majority in parliament. In doing so, Kerr provided powerful grounds for the abolition of the office of Governor-General and that of the monarchy which he professed to serve. Both institutions were revealed as potent conservative weapons, besides being tawdry relics of an imperialist past.

Sol Encel sums up on the wretched history of the Australian constitution in the twentieth century:

By stimulating parochialism, it places a premium on the value of putting local interests before national interests. By frustrating the development of policies at the national level, and by giving the conservative parties a virtual mortgage on the national government . . . it damages democracy and leaves the country without any real national plans for the future. The conservatism engendered by the constitution serves, in many ways, to perpetuate a colonial frame of

213

mind after the colonial relationship has disappeared ... Real independence requires, among other things, the radical transformation of a constitution that belongs to the colonial era.[12]

Protection and Arbitration

Well before Federation, there was a considerable degree of economic integration between the Australian colonies. Capital and labour flowed freely across political borders. Federation promised a bigger domestic market, but distance and the cost of transport were still important barriers to trade so that probably most manufacturers remained dependent upon a single State market for some years after Federation. Even the political barriers were slow to come down: in 1905 there still existed some differential rail freight rates designed to divert trade from one State to another. Yet more important as a constraint upon manufacturing was the smallness of the Australian market. A population of 3.8 million in 1901 was not a good base on which to build large-scale manufacturing. Overall, economic development waited upon a strong upturn in the trade cycle, which did not come until 1907. In the interim, there were important developments concerning protection and wage-fixing by official tribunals.

A link between these two areas of policy-making emerged first in Victoria. In 1896 the Victorian Factories and Shops Act was amended in response to popular agitation, led by middle-class reformers, against 'sweating' in certain industries. The government aimed at strengthening the Act's provisions relating to factory conditions and the employment of women and children. Beyond this, the amending Act introduced a novel feature: the establishment of wages boards with power to fix minimum wages and some conditions of work in six specified trades or industries. These sweated trades, notably clothing, were those in which female workers figured prominently. It was acknowledged that low wages and piece-work rates of pay were bound up with the question of sweating and outwork.

The idea of a minimum wage was not entirely new. Labour representatives claimed it for government employees and in 1895 the principle was applied to workers employed by contractors to the Victorian government. Attempts to curb sweating of female workers were of older origin. What was really new about the amendment of the Factories Act in 1896 was the inclusion of male workers as well as female in the coverage of wages boards. The initial proposal was simply to set up wages boards for female workers in the clothing trades. The extension to male workers was adopted by the Victorian parliament with surprisingly little opposition, partly because the experiment of wages boards was to be confined to a few urban trades—country MPs were placated by the exclusion of butter factories and agriculture. More important, however, was involvement of the issue of protectionism in the debate about wages boards. Some Victorian advocates of free trade were asserting that sweating flourished under the cover of protective tariffs; and, in rebuttal, the Protectionist Association expressed its support for the principle of a minimum wage.

In the context of a quickening debate on protection and federation, manufacturers in Victoria were anxious to maintain their old alliance with trade unions over protection; and the Protectionist Association, in coming out in support of a minimum wage, was one step ahead of labour representatives in parliament. A perverse element in the debate in 1896 was that some free traders in the Victorian parliament probably voted for the minimum wage proposal in the hope that its introduction in protected industries would rebound upon the employers affected, causing them to reconsider their support for protection. For a variety of reasons, then, the legislation was passed and six wages boards were set up. They were composed of equal numbers of representatives of employers and workers, together with chairmen who were supposed to be impartial. In each of the industries, the representatives were elected respectively by employers and employees, except that in the furniture industry the board was nominated by the government in order to keep Chinese out. There is further evidence of racial discrimination in the fact that the Act, for purposes of government regulation of working conditions other than wages, defined a factory as a place in which four or more persons worked, except that the minimum number stipulated was only one where Chinese people were involved.

The record of Victorian wages boards in the first few years was patchy. On the whole, they raised wages in the sweated industries concerned. This was true of both male and female workers, yet at the same time the low-wage status of women was institutionalized. For example, the clothing trade board, in its first wage determination, fixed a minimum wage equivalent to forty-five shillings a week for men and twenty shillings for women. In other words, the women's minimum was 44 per cent of that of men in the trade. Subsequently, this board 'awarded equal pay in select areas, such as for seam pressers in 1901, in which there was job competition, or a threat of it, between the sexes . . . Equal pay for pressers effectively ensured that this remained a male occupation'.[13]

Originally the wages boards, regarded as experimental, were scheduled to operate for only three years. However, in 1900 the boards continued to exist and the system was extended by providing that a wages board could be set up for any industry by a resolution of either house of the Victorian parliament. The rationale was still the presence of sweating. Indeed, in the depressed conditions of the 1890s, inordinate exploitation had spread well beyond the industries where it was

215

notorious. In 1899 there were friendly discussions between the Melbourne Trades Hall Council and the Chamber of Manufactures concerning sweating, and it is evident that a number of manufacturers favoured wage regulation as a means of protecting themselves from being undercut by unscrupulous rivals.

As in 1896, so in the legislation of 1900, the tariff issue was a factor, particularly from the viewpoint of manufacturers who were looking to the future of tariff protection under federation and did not wish to alienate trade unionists. Of course, there were many other employers, particularly in commerce, pastoralism and mining, who were opposed or indifferent to protectionism and were accordingly less restrained in opposing wage regulation. The Victorian Chamber of Manufactures itself, through its president, F. T. Derham, was inclined to oppose the extension of the wages board system. Derham was still managing director of the big biscuit firm of Swallow and Ariell, despite the fact that in 1892 his career as a land-boomer had collapsed with him owing about £500 000 and making a secret composition of one penny in the pound with his creditors. He was also a prominent Victorian politician who later became a paymaster of the protectionists in Commonwealth politics. Yet it is doubtful whether Derham's conservatism about wages boards was really representative of manufacturers, and the Chamber did not express outright opposition to the scheme in 1900.

In both Victoria and New South Wales at this time, the bourgeoisie was in some disarray in the political arena. The powerful employers' unions formed in the 1880s had become defunct: employers felt less need for them after trade union strength declined sharply. A degree of disunity among employers, evident as between Chambers of Commerce and of Manufactures, left initiative in the hands of middle-class politicians, particularly lawyers, and facilitated the spread of wage regulation. By the end of 1900, twenty-one new wages boards had been created in Victoria and another eleven came into existence in the next year or two. They covered about half of all factory workers in the State and by no means all of these were in sweated trades. Indeed, it is noteworthy that before 1907 most of the boards were concerned primarily with skilled or semi-skilled workers in the industries over which they had jurisdiction. Incidentally, the system had a bearing upon the introduction of old age pensions in Victoria, for a standard criticism of minimum wages voiced by employers was that old or infirm workers were likely to be sacked. The solution seemed to lie in providing pensions for such people.

Developments in Victoria were noted in other colonies/States. South Australia adopted wages boards in 1900. In New South Wales the labour movement considered the Victorian system alongside an alternative: an arbitration court with powers of compulsion. Trade unions reckoned that the latter model was preferable, partly because it was more comprehensive in coverage. An arbitration court could deal with disputes in any industry, and the device of a 'common rule' made it possible to extend minimum standards in a particular case to all employees in that industry. Even more important from a union viewpoint was the formal recognition accorded to representatives of trade unions in arbitration courts. In contrast, workers' representatives elected to wages boards were not necessarily trade unionists. In Adelaide the Amalgamated Society of Engineers, after experiencing the system, criticized wages boards for being sectional and local. The boards were also

distinctly handymen's protection boards, which do not recognise unions, but give non-unionists as much opportunity of becoming members of the board as unionists ... Wages Boards do not abolish sweating; they only change the locality of the sweat-shop [to escape the jurisdiction of the city-centred board].[14]

Non-union workers elected to wages boards were more susceptible to pressure from employers. In the first place, such workers could easily be sacked. This sort of victimization was not a remote possibility, as Cannon points out. 'Of five workers who became members of the [Victorian] jam industry wages board and voted in 1900 to increase adult wages from 30s to 35s a week, four immediately lost their jobs'. Moreover, since wages boards took decisions by majority vote, the balance of power on a board could be decisively altered by one or two worker-members betraying their mates, and this was more likely to happen in the absence of trade union representation.[15]

Introduction of the kind of arbitration court envisaged by labour leaders in New South Wales depended upon securing enough votes in a parliament where the Labor Party was in a minority. A crucial factor in this situation was realization, by far-sighted representatives of the bourgeoisie, of the need to moderate the polarization of classes which had become so apparent in the early 1890s. Giving formal recognition to trade unions under moderate leadership would enmesh those bodies in the machinery of state. This was the approach of the NSW Attorney-General, B. R. Wise, when he piloted an Industrial Arbitration Bill through parliament in 1901.

The reaction of manufacturers to this proposal for compulsory arbitration is not clear. There were discussions in Sydney in 1899 between trade union representatives and the National Protection Union, in which it seems that a bargain was struck: union support for protection in return for support by protectionists for wage regulation. On the other hand, the NSW Chamber of Manufactures objected to the minimum wage concept in Wise's Bill, as did other employers' 217 organizations. Even so, the Chamber was indecisive and did not oppose the Bill outright. Some manufacturers certainly linked the legislation with protection. W. Sandford, proprietor of the Eskbank ironworks at Lithgow, pointed out that employers, in order to gain a protective tariff, 'would have to depend on the votes of the men they employed'.[16] Thus he acknowledged that politically the power of manufacturers depended not so much on their economic and social position (as yet they were not highly regarded in society) as on their ability to influence the votes of ordinary people.

The NSW Act of 1901 provided for an arbitration court consisting of a judge and two assessors, the latter being elected by representatives of trade unions in one case and employers' associations in the other. The court was empowered to fix a minimum wage and to make awards to settle industrial disputes. Awards were to have binding legal force, strikes and lock-outs being prohibited while a dispute was under consideration by the court. Initially, the Act was to operate for a trial period of seven years, a limitation which may have mollified some of its opponents.

The Commonwealth Conciliation and Arbitration Act of 1904 broadly followed the pattern of the NSW Act, with unions being encouraged to register with the Commonwealth court. The main difference was that the jurisdiction of the federal court was limited to interstate industrial disputes. Shearers and seamen on coastal ships were the main bodies of workers envisaged. Although most employers still opposed wage regulation as 'class legislation'—implying that of course legislation inspired by themselves was not of such a character—other employers modified their stance. A shipping magnate and protectionist, Sir Malcolm McEacharn, indicated the latter trend. Speaking in federal parliament on the Commonwealth Arbitration Bill, he said:

There was a time when I was utterly opposed, not only to unionism, but to conciliation and arbitration in any form . . . The unionism to which I had been accustomed during the great strikes . . . was of a more arrogant and 'stand-and-deliver' type than the unionism of to-day. I hope that the newer unionism . . . which has enabled those of us who are employers to meet our men with pleasure and discuss matters in a conciliatory spirit, may continue.[17]

New Protection

The first Commonwealth tariff, adopted in 1901–2, was weighted in favour of important Victorian industries. Nevertheless, it did not constitute a victory for protectionists. For example, it included an import duty of 12.5 per cent on most items of agricultural machinery and implements, whereas before Federation the corresponding duty was

15–25 per cent in South Australia and Victoria, and nil in New South Wales. In relation to all imports, natural protection due to the cost of transport from overseas amounted to about 10 per cent, but this was not a new factor.

The fight over protection entered a new, decisive phase in 1905, when the Commonwealth government appointed a Royal Commission to consider customs and excise tariffs. The agricultural machinery industry was the key case investigated by the Commission, for this industry epitomized the problems. On the one hand its customers were farmers, who objected to the prospect of paying higher prices as a result of increased protection for Australian manufacturers. On the other hand agricultural machinery making was an industry of some importance, employing 1600 workers in Victoria and 700 in South Australia; and these manufacturers, led by H. V. McKay of the Sunshine Harvester works, claimed that they needed greater protection in order to survive against overseas competitors in the Australian market.

The origins of these complaints are interesting. In 1904 the leading Australian manufacturers in the industry entered into an agreement among themselves, and with the US International Harvester Co. and the Canadian Massey Harris company, to fix prices for harvesters and other equipment in Australia. This resulted in some increase in prices but the cartel was broken by the withdrawal of a South Australian firm. The Australian manufacturers then rounded on the Americans and demanded higher protection against them. McKay and others, in presenting evidence to the Royal Commission, spoke as though they had read socialist textbooks: they criticized American combines and trusts, describing the International Harvester Co. as an 'octopus' squeezing out Australian producers. They even shed crocodile tears over the fate of American workers who laboured like slaves and were thrown on the scrapheap after the age of thirty-six, whereas Australians, they said, worked like men for forty-eight hours a week and were treated fairly (shades of the depression of the nineties!). Rhetoric aside, McKay's case was not strengthened by refusal to divulge figures of his production costs and profits.

The upshot was that the Royal Commission was evenly divided in its report in 1906. Four of the eight members advised against any increase in protective duties, while the other members recommended doubling the duty on most items of agricultural machinery. The protectionist commissioners added two stipulations concerning the proposed additional duties: that prices of farm machinery must not be increased as a result; and that the Australian manufacturers must pay their employees 'a fair and reasonable rate of wages'. In effect, the protectionists outmanoeuvred free traders by offering a sop to farmers (who were probably not impressed by it) and, more important, by making 219 a bid for the support of labour. Alfred Deakin, as Prime Minister, adopted the policy advocated by the protectionist section of the Royal Commission. As stated in an official Explanatory Memorandum:

The 'old' Protection contented itself with making good wages possible. The 'new' Protection seeks to make them actual. It aims at according to the manufacturer that degree of exemption from unfair outside competition which will enable him to pay fair and reasonable wages . . . Having put the manufacturer in a position to pay good wages, it goes on to assure the public that he does pay them.[18]

The principle of 'new' protection was embodied in Commonwealth legislation in 1906. A Customs Tariff Act declared much higher rates of duty on imported agricultural machinery; while an Excise Tariff Act imposed countervailing duties on agricultural machinery made in Australia, with the proviso that manufacturers could secure exemption from these duties if they were certified as paying fair and reasonable wages to employees. The Excise Act thus linked protection for manufacturers with a better deal for workers. This was all very well, but the realities of capitalism meant that employers and workers were unlikely to agree on whether given wages were 'good' or 'fair and reasonable'. The following year it became the responsibility of Justice H. B. Higgins, as president of the Commonwealth Arbitration Court, to inquire into a test case concerning McKay, the proprietor of the Sunshine Harvester works in Victoria.

McKay was both strongly protectionist and anti-unionist. The small Agricultural Implement Makers' Society was virtually kept out of McKay's works and he was known to be hostile to any form of wage regulation, including wages boards. 'Laborites, including Tom Mann, branded him a free trader in humans'. As against McKay's attitude, Higgins (unlike most judges) was deeply humanitarian, with a compassionate concern for the poor. In the court hearing of the Harvester case, reference by unionists to McKay's insistence upon 'freedom of contract' brought an interjection from Higgins: 'Like the freedom of contract between the wolf and the lamb'.[19]

In the Harvester case, Higgins concluded that a fair and reasonable wage for an unskilled (male) labourer would be seven shillings per day. As McKay's labourers were currently being paid only six shillings a day, Higgins refused to grant a certificate of exemption under the Excise Tariff Act. Leaving aside the broader significance of this judgement concerning a living wage, the relevance to new protection may be noted briefly here. McKay went to the High Court, claiming that the Excise Tariff Act was not really a taxation measure: rather, it was designed to regulate conditions of employment, a sphere which was outside the direct legislative power of the Commonwealth. The High

Court agreed and it declared the Act unconstitutional in 1908. This marked a clear break in the link between protection and better wages which had been dubbed 'new protection'.

Workers might well have regarded themselves as victims of a confidence trick, based essentially upon the High Court's reliably conservative, legalistic outlook. Manufacturers certainly did well out of the fiasco of new protection. Shortly before the High Court decision, the Commonwealth parliament adopted a new Customs Tariff Act which raised import duties on a large number of commodities. Though still only moderately protectionist, this Lyne tariff represented a clear victory for protectionist forces. Thenceforth, employers were under less pressure to secure labour support for protection. Indeed, the NSW Chamber of Manufactures in 1908 applauded the High Court decision, adding that 'the interests of both employers and employees will be amply safeguarded under the provisions of the Industrial Disputes Act of this State'.[20]

The employers' victory was underlined by events in the Victorian agricultural machinery industry. Because the federal arbitration court seemed relatively sympathetic towards workers, the Harvester judgement 'made McKay an instant convert to the Victorian wages board system'.[21] The Agricultural Implement Makers' Union, unable to obtain access to the federal court, had to rest its hopes upon a local wages board—which set down a scale of wages lower than the federal Harvester standard. In 1909 a federal Royal Commission found that the cost of making a Sunshine harvester was £45, compared with £35 for an imported Deering (International Harvester) machine; yet each sold for over £78. McKay's profits mounted.

In 1911 the Agricultural Implement Makers' Union embarked on a long strike aimed at establishing a union shop and bringing the industry under a federal award. McKay's response was to instigate the establishment by the Victorian Employers' Federation of a Free Labourers Association. This was the standard euphemism for a bunch of scabs. The strike ended disastrously for the union, which virtually collapsed. The industry did not come under a federal award until 1925—three years after McKay had died, leaving an estate of £1.45 million. If 'Commonwealth' ever implied equality and wealth held in common, the reality was far removed. Ironically, in view of the events leading up to the crucial Royal Commission of 1905, McKay's family firm was merged with the Australian interests of the Canadian Massey Harris company in 1930.

Incidentally, it is a reflection upon the intellectual calibre of the Australian hard-line employers who established the H. R. Nicholls Society in 1986 that they adopted as patron saint an obscure Tasmanian newspaper editor who had been involved in an arbitration court case of no particular significance. It would have been much more   221 meaningful for the society to have adopted the name of McKay. He was a real union-buster, of a kind which members of the society wish to emulate. Moreover, McKay was an effective myth-maker, not least in his claim to have invented the combine harvester, an honour which rightly belonged to another Victorian, James Morrow. There were others like McKay in Australian history, but today's extreme reactionaries have little knowledge of their own forerunners. Businessmen's reading appears to be more or less limited to Stock Exchange reports and the autobiographies of recent conservative politicians like R. G. Menzies—plus selected arbitration reports in the case of the industrial lawyers associated with employers.

Finally in relation to the concept of new protection, it may be noted that, although the High Court negated its legal enforcement in 1908, the idea retained some validity. Indeed, the formal concept itself was later applied to one industry, sugar. From 1902 the Commonwealth imposed a substantial excise duty on manufactured sugar, subject to a rebate or subsidy being paid to those producers of cane-sugar who employed only white labour. The purpose was to induce Queensland planters and farmers to switch from black to white labour. Then, in 1910, 'new protection' was grafted on to the excise-bounty system: an amending Act provided that the bounty might be withheld if rates of pay and conditions of work were found to be below standard. This provision was probably just as unconstitutional as that which had been struck down in relation to the Harvester case, but the sugar interests did not mount a legal challenge, perhaps because they feared that this would imperil payment of the bounty or because the Act was not effectively enforced in respect of wages. In any event, a few years later the sugar industry in Queensland came under state arbitral regulation and the excise-bounty system was dropped.

As for the general idea of new protection, most workers did not consider that employers had deliberately deceived them in the situation leading up to the High Court decision of 1908. Wage-fixing tribunals continued to function, with a growing number of employers favouring their operations; and from time to time tactical alliances were formed between manufacturers and trade unions, with the latter supporting higher protection to underpin better wages or, more important, to provide job security. These alliances were generally one-sided, employers having most to gain from them.

However, the alliances were not a 'zero sum game', where what one party gained, the other lost. *Both* parties could gain, at the expense of a third party, exporters, mainly at that time farmers and graziers. Thus, tariff protection allowed higher prices for local manufactured goods. Out of these higher prices workers could be paid higher wages, and manufacturers could receive profits, adequate or (depending on the height of the tariff) more than adequate to enable them to survive. In other words, in an economy exporting primary produce the price of which is set by the world market, protection of manufacturing industry re-distributes the national income away from the exporters, towards capitalists and workers in manufacturing industry.

This may be regarded as the 'Ricardo effect in reverse', for in early nineteenth-century England, the political economist David Ricardo argued against the protection of *agriculture* through the Corn Laws, which in effect were a tariff on the import of grain. This he said caused higher food prices, which increased the rents the landlord could charge, hence redistributing the national income in their favour, which increments they spent on high living and did not invest in productive investment. The manufacturers as a result made less profit, because they had to pay workers higher money wages to compensate for the high cost of food. Consequently they were at a disadvantage competing with industrialists in other countries, where grain imports were not protected, and they made insufficient profits to invest in new capital equipment.

In Ricardo's time this amounted to a straight-out class struggle between landlords and industrialists, because workers received little more than subsistence wages, whether in manufacturing or on the land. Trade unions were in their infancy in both sectors. In the Australian case a hundred years later, trade unions had become strong enough to raise wages well above the subsistence level, and by forming a coalition or class alliance with manufacturers, they were able to appropriate to themselves a part of the national income formerly accruing to the exporters of primary produce. Similarly with the industrial capitalists: in the contest between free trade and protection, the economic stakes were high, crucially affecting the distribution of the total income.

There is another important twist to the argument. Manufacturing for the home market implies that workers have adequate incomes to buy the products, whereas exporters by definition sell their products abroad and low wages at home keep their costs low and competitive. Hence there is a suggestion that the rise of large-scale manufacturing for domestic markets produced the conditions for a coalition between organized workers and such manufacturers against foreign traders, merchants, and finance capital, in the early part of this century.[22] It is arguable that such a coalition occurred then in Australia, expressed through the 'new protection' and arbitration, laying the foundations for industrialization through two world wars and the Great Depression, only to break down in the late 1960s and 1970s when it had run its course and no longer suited the interests of a restructured global capitalism.

13

Capital and Labour: Monopoly and Wealth, the Basic Wage and Militancy

I can perceive nothing but a certain conspiracy of rich men, procuring their own commodities under the name and title of the Commonwealth. They invent and devise all means ... first how to keep [what] they have unjustly gathered together; and next how to hire and abuse the work and labour of the poor for as little money as may be, and oppress them as much as they please.[1]

Boom

The long phase of depression or stagnation in the Australian economy came to an end in 1906. It was followed by a period of strong economic growth which developed into a boom between 1909 and 1913, when the rate of economic growth was comparable to that of the 1880s. By 1909 average real income per head exceeded the peak reached in the 1880s and continued to rise, although the benefits were not evenly spread.

The initial stage of expansion after the long depression occurred while British capital was still being withdrawn from Australia. Increases in export income from such products as wheat, meat and butter made it possible to repay a substantial proportion of debts owed to British investors. The corollary was a slow maturing of the capital market in Australia itself, as stock exchanges began to cater for more

224

than a narrow range of mining, banking and mercantile companies. More funds were raised through exchanges and there was a rapid growth of Australian companies in the decade prior to the First World War. Improvement in Australia's creditworthiness in the London money market, added to boom conditions, led to a resumption of large-scale export of British capital and labour to Australia, particularly between 1911 and 1914. In those four years, 234 000 immigrants arrived in Australia, compared with only 100 000 in the twenty years from 1891. Approximately half of the immigrants from Britain in the boom years received some State assistance to make the voyage. In effect, this was a government contribution towards employers' labour problems. As for the capital imported into Australia at this time, it was mainly on public account, used by governments primarily in a renewed burst of railway building.

There was rapid agricultural advance. Between 1901 and 1914 the area under wheat almost doubled and the yield rose more than proportionately. Agricultural expansion provided a stimulus to manufacturing in various ways. For example, whereas a high proportion of the income of pastoralists tended to be spent on imports, the producers of wheat, dairy products and sugar spent proportionately more on Australian-made products. Thus employment in the agricultural machinery industry rose to about 5000 in 1911. Other factors such as protection and a larger market—total population rose to nearly five million in 1914—also played a part in manufacturing growth. The share of manufacturing in national output rose from about 11 per cent in 1905 to 14 per cent in 1913.

There was a comparable increase in the proportion of the total workforce engaged in manufacturing. It rose to about 19 per cent in 1911. In terms of employment, the largest manufacturing industry was clothing and textiles, a sector characterized by a low level of investment in plant and equipment. The corollary was low wages, paid to a predominantly female workforce. About 70 per cent of all of the women engaged in manufacturing were in clothing and textiles. To some extent, the industry overlapped with the retail trades, as some large department stores, such as David Jones and Grace Bros in Sydney, operated clothing factories of their own. Besides a multitude of small shops, in 1911 there were in Sydney eight retail firms employing over 10 000 workers between them. The degree of exploitation of female labour—that is, the employers' appropriation of surplus value —is suggested by the evidence of a dressmaker to a Royal Commission in New South Wales: 'that is how I came to leave Grace Bros. They gave me blouses to make. They were getting 9s. or 10s. in the shop for them, and from my book I saw I was only getting 9d.'[2]

There was a similar type of structure, though with substantially   225 larger capital investment and a male workforce, in Australian metalworking and machinery, which was the fastest-growing industry in the early twentieth century. On the one hand there were many backyard workshops, some of which were run by erstwhile trade unionists. S. Hampson, representing the ASE in Melbourne, remarked in 1914:

Several of our members are the proprietors of these places, whose enterprising love of their trade has lured them into business on their own account, but few weather five years. Engineering manufacture is not the business for small capital.[3]

Hampson was right. There were a number of large engineering plants and foundries and it is easy to overlook the point that when the Broken Hill Proprietary Co. (BHP) resolved to enter into production of pig iron and steel in New South Wales, in 1912, the decision was taken in the knowledge that a substantial market for these products already existed in the secondary metal-manufacturing industries. Until then those industries had imported primary iron and steel from Britain. BHP was an early example of a significant flow of investment capital from base-metal mining to associated manufacturing plants, a process which developed strongly from the time of the First World War.

Capital Accumulation and Monopoly

The economic boom in the decade preceding the First World War presented opportunities to both employers and workers. To employers it offered profits and heavy capital accumulation, while to workers it held out the prospect of better wages and conditions. Each side stood to gain more to the extent that it could squeeze, scare or cajole the other class. There were serious struggles between labour and capital, intersected by divisions between sections of the bourgeoisie. In between were farmers, whose incomes rose through a run of good seasons and prices but were still quite small. It is conceivable that most farmers felt the benefit not so much through increased profits as from a capital increment resulting from a steady rise in land values.

Considering first the employers' position, there is no doubt that profits were high and this was reflected in share prices and dividends. Goldsbrough Mort's shares, 'quoted at 3s.3d. early in 1904, were at 31s.6d. by early 1906, 63s. by early 1910'.[4] The rate of return on the capital of Burns, Philp & Co. Ltd varied between 10.6 and 14.4 per cent per annum between 1907 and 1913 (apart from a drop in 1908), compared with 7.4 to 9.8 per cent in the previous four years. No wonder that James Burns, the company chairman, exulted in 1912, when the net profit of £104 000 was twice what it had been three years earlier: 'It is wonderful how the funds come in, and a special Providence seems to watch over the Co.'[5] It is also indicative of the growth of manufacturing in Australia that Burns Philp, in selling groceries in South Pacific markets, was using an increasing proportion manufactured in Australia instead of in England.

Many other Australian companies expanded their capital rapidly. In 1913, when there were some 12 000 manufacturing establishments employing up to twenty people each, there were also 580 establishments which employed more than one hundred. These very large concerns employed 41 per cent of the workforce engaged in manufacturing, indicating a high level of concentration which has remained characteristic of Australian industry.

Particularly from 1907, profits were enlarged by restrictive trade practices, which became increasingly common and contributed to the trend of rising prices. At one end of the scale were price-fixing agreements between manufacturers, such as those making jam, biscuits and dried fruit. Then there were large-scale rings, cartels or monopolies in certain industries, notably sugar-refining, meat-export, and coal and shipping, often in association with attempts to restrict production. Import-merchants, while objecting to tariff protection for manufacturers, often organized rings of their own designed to keep up the prices of imported goods. Shipowners, who stoutly defended the principle of free trade and opposed government regulation, were by no means averse either to self-regulation or to official regulation so long as it was in the interests of their own particular trade. In pursuit of capitalist profit, truth and consistency are always at a discount.

Foreign combines figured prominently in the marketing of some commodities in Australia. Thus the tobacco trade by 1906 was controlled by a world-wide British-American combine or trust, which both imported tobacco and tied up distribution facilities for it. The result was that prices paid by Australian consumers rose, Australian tobacco farmers suffered as a lower proportion of their leaf was bought by the combine for processing, and retailers' margins were squeezed. The *Australian Tobacco Journal and Hairdressers' Record* criticized the combine in mid-1909 and ceased publication at the end of that year. Before this, *The Bulletin* in Sydney also spoke out against the trust, but its condemnations died away as it carried 'full-page advertisements extolling the virtues of certain well-known brands of tobacco, cigars and cigarettes'.[6]

Adverse comment on foreign trusts in the tobacco and agricultural machinery industries led to the first Commonwealth attempt to regulate monopolies. This was supported by the Australian Labor Party, which resolved in 1905 to include in its objectives 'the securing of the full results of their industry to all producers by the collective 227 ownership of monopolies'. Yet it was a non-Labor federal government which was responsible for the Australian Industries Preservation Act of 1906. In prohibiting certain kinds of combination or monopoly, this Act did not differentiate between domestic and overseas firms operating in the Australian market. However, the prime target was seen as monopolists from overseas and the legislation was aimed at protecting the interests of the national bourgeoisie. The Act was meant to accompany a national tariff and was 'an expression of this dominant protectionist philosophy rather than of any serious concern to strike at the anti-competitive practices of rings and trusts in Australia . . . The Act was designed to regulate the affairs of business in the interests of certain sections of business'.[7]

Nevertheless, the ALP took to heart the Act's formal prohibition of combinations which were designed 'to restrain trade or commerce to the detriment of the public' or 'to injure or destroy by means of unfair competition any Australian industry'. In 1910 a federal Labor government initiated prosecution of certain interstate shipping firms. There was a long history of restrictive trade practices in both shipping and coal, and such arrangements were given a more stable basis from 1906 by an agreement entered into by shipping companies such as Howard Smith and Adelaide Steamship on the one hand and a group of Newcastle colliery proprietors (the 'Vend') on the other. In effect, the colliery owners bound themselves not to supply coal for interstate trade except through the shipping companies in the agreement, and these in turn would not buy or carry any coal other than from the signatory coal owners. Thus competition was excluded and prices and output could be fixed. Precise details are not known because there was 'a wholesale burning of documents' when federal prosecution seemed likely. 'Trip after trip between the shipping offices and the ships lying in port was made by senior personnel who struggled down greasy ladders clutching bundles of documents which they personally consigned to the devouring flames'.[8]

It is significant that this combination, by raising the price of coal, was detrimental not only to ordinary consumers but also to sections of the bourgeoisie such as Melbourne manufacturers who needed fuel for their factories. The shipowners' use of deferred rebates—discounts payable only to customers who had dealt exclusively with them during the previous year—was a potent means of enforcing customer 'loyalty'. It may be added that similar methods were adopted by another, more powerful, shipping conference which charged high freight rates on goods transported between Australia and Europe. This particular conference, comprising big companies such as P. & O., was subject to relatively little criticism in the period before the First World War. Further evidence of the continuing influence of capital based in Britain is seen in the fact that the new Australian tariff of 1908 provided, for the first time, preferential rates of duty in favour of imports of British goods as against those from foreign countries. Commonwealth prosecution of the Australian coal–shipping combine ended in failure in 1912. Initial convictions and fines imposed upon the companies were overturned on appeal to the Full High Court, whose verdict was subsequently endorsed by the Privy Council in England. The appeal judges considered that regulation was preferable to 'unlimited and ruinous competition'; and more specifically the judges held that, while the combine had undoubtedly raised the price of coal to the detriment of consumers, there was no evidence that the raising of prices was brought about intentionally 'to the detriment of the public'. The judges' economic reasoning was naive: who did they imagine would pay the higher prices and for whose benefit? It is unlikely that the judges knew what Adam Smith had written in his celebrated *Wealth of Nations* in 1776: 'People of the same trade seldom meet together but the conversation ends in a conspiracy against the public or in some diversion to raise prices'. Yet even if the judges had been aware of this practical approach, it is doubtful whether they would have determined differently. The Australian Act was modelled on the United States Sherman ('trust-busting') Act, and in 1911 the US Supreme Court construed the statute as applying only to trade restraints and monopolies which were 'unreasonable'.

After losing the Coal Vend case, the Fisher Labor government made no further attempt to implement the Australian Industries Preservation Act. Instead, the government sought amendment of the constitution so as to allow the Commonwealth to nationalize combines. However, referenda to this effect were lost in 1911 and 1913, though only by a narrow margin. Rather oddly, half a century passed before there was another anti-monopoly case in Australia. This was despite the fact that the Australian Industries Preservation Act remained on the statute book. The Coal Vend case turned on so-called questions of fact, not law, so that the verdict did not really dispute Commonwealth powers to act against detrimental monopolies. No doubt the Act was allowed to remain dormant partly because governments had little or no wish to curb restrictive trade practices, which benefited many businessmen. The sort of people who stood to gain most from the Act (mainly small businessmen) could not afford to fight a case all the way to the Privy Council, as shipping companies had done.

There was a change in official attitude in 1964–5, when several prosecutions were launched under the old Act. In one of these cases, two wine wholesalers were fined by the High Court for having imposed sanctions on a Canberra retailer who had bought supplies from a price-cutting wholesaler. Suddenly it appeared that the Industries Preservation Act had teeth after all. However, the Act was then repealed to make way for the Trade Practices Act of 1965, which proved largely ineffective for its first six years. In any case, it was not possible to use it to break up monopolies such as those in steel and sugar, and shipping conferences were exempted from control.

The Bourgeois State

Faced with a growing threat from labour from 1907, employers moved to strengthen their organizations. The luxury of having two bourgeois political parties, divided from each other on the issue of protection, could no longer be afforded. In 1909 the two groups in the Commonwealth parliament were fused to establish a single anti-labour party, styled Liberal. Rather surprisingly, although this move was in the long-term interests of the bourgeoisie, the immediate effect was a contribution to the federal Labor election victory of 1910 through a deepening of class-consciousness. Herbert Brookes, a leading Victorian businessman and politician, noted this: 'The union of Liberals created officially and permanently the Gulf between the two parties and so rallied all laborers, wage earners etc. to their class in the absence of better and more sane promises from Liberals.' [9]

Labor electoral success produced no basic change in the orientation of the bourgeois state. When one section or other of the capitalist class was in difficulties, the state came to its aid. For example, coastal shipping companies were under pressure from two sides: competition from overseas-based ships trading around the Australian coast; and demands from Australian maritime unions for better wages and conditions. In 1912 the Navigation Act was passed, aimed at reserving the coastal trade for vessels registered in Australia. Ironically, this concession, which was coupled with relatively good conditions for Australian seamen, coincided with the failure of prosecution of the coal–shipping combine. However, the Act did not come into force until after the First World War.

Just as there were significant divisions in the working class, so too there were important differences between sections of the bourgeoisie. Differences over such issues as monopoly and protection have already been noted. These gave rise to organizational problems in employers' ranks, despite a general move towards unity. In 1904 representatives from recently formed Employers' Federations of Victoria, NSW, Queensland and South Australia decided to establish a Central Council of Employers of Australia; and it was this Council which financed the successful challenge to the Harvester decision in the High Court in 1908. Nevertheless, differences over protection led Chambers of Manufactures to distance themselves from Employers' Federations in New South Wales and Victoria. By 1908 the Associated Chambers of

Manufactures of Australia was functioning as a separate national body.

Whatever their sectional differences, employers were as one in aiming to keep wages and working conditions down as much as possible. This still left room for divergencies concerning methods, especially attitudes towards arbitration. Some employers remained completely opposed to trade unionism. For example in 1903, when John Brown, a big colliery owner in New South Wales, introduced new coal-cutting machinery manned by American technicians and 'free' labour, he told the manager of the mine to 'break up the union and work the mine with non-union men'. The manager was evidently better acquainted with the temper of the miners, for he replied to his boss: 'The man (nor the time) has not yet arrived who can break up the Miners' Union and defy the laws of the country. If the above is what you expected from me I do not wonder at your disappointment.' [10]

On the other hand, most employers displayed considerable flexibility in meeting the challenge from a labour movement in the context of economic boom. In the early years of the twentieth century, Australia acquired an international reputation as a 'social laboratory', a country of advanced social legislation and experiment. The reputation was largely undeserved, for it assumed that increasing activity by the state was directed towards benefiting workers and the poor. Actually, much state intervention was primarily in the interests of the wealthier classes in Australia, for example in the protection of manufacturing, regulation of monopolies, and encouragement of rural settlement and marketing. In addition, the Commonwealth provided bounties on production for certain industries.

The working class gained some indirect benefit from these measures, as well as from restrictions upon immigration (including the entry of indentured labour). Direct benefits in the form of social welfare were much more limited. True, old age pensions were instituted, as they were also by a Liberal government in Britain at the same time. The only other important Australian initiative in the social welfare sphere was the Maternity Allowances Act of 1912, which provided a benefit payable to any woman on the birth of a child. Apart from these measures, and the development of the arbitration system, talk of Australia as a social laboratory was so much hot air. What it really signified was the incorporation of a large proportion of the labour movement within the state apparatus. If labour strivings were to be contained, the bourgeoisie had to treat the movement with some respect, at least to the extent of offering recognition to a number of labour representatives willing to be co-opted.

Australia was not unique in this respect. In Britain, Sidney and Beatrice Webb noted in 1920 that trade unionism had become recognized by government as 'part of the social machinery of the State'.[11] The Webbs attributed this mainly to the exigencies of the First World War, but it can be traced back to the work of Liberal governments and leaders such as Lloyd George between 1906 and 1911. Similarly in Australia, employers and their parliamentary allies, notably lawyers, displayed much ingenuity in accommodating labour aspirations. There was a new emphasis on justice rather than philanthropy, and Stuart Macintyre remarks that 'turn-of-century liberals brought social justice to the forefront of Australian politics because they considered it vital to national cohesion and purpose'.[12]

Although Australian social welfare measures at this time were not impressive, the form which they took had long-term significance. In other countries such as Britain and Germany, age pensions and other provisions developed on the basis of universal coverage of the population through compulsory social insurance schemes. In Australia, on the other hand, the aim was to provide 'only a welfare safety-net for those outside the labour market'. Thus benefits in Australia were noncontributory but were subject to a means test; and this remained the case until well after World War II.[13]

A Living Wage

Reality was often in conflict with theory and ideals in the arena of judicial wage-fixing. Compulsory arbitration was the aspect of Australian experimentation which attracted most attention, both nationally and internationally. To some extent the attention was misplaced, for there was no sudden or wholesale replacement of the old methods of collective bargaining and strikes. Indeed strikes remained legal under the Victorian wages board system and in many respects these boards simply provided a formal structure for collective bargaining— with the difference that a board's decision on wages had the force of law. In any case, boards and arbitration courts alike could fix only minimum rates of pay, which left scope for a great deal of collective bargaining outside these institutions. If agreement could be reached directly, the two parties could ask an arbitration court (in cases where a court had jurisdiction) to register the agreement formally, which gave it the same effect as a court award. Often, however, individual employers simply agreed to pay over-award wages which were not officially recognized but were absolutely legal. These features of the arbitration system still persist.

Less humdrum matters caught the public eye. In particular, there was the question of a living wage: a basic minimum for an adult male worker. Arbitration courts were given no guidelines concerning the determination of an appropriate minimum wage in any industry. Inevitably, employers in a dispute claimed that they were unable to pay

more and that higher wages would result in unemployment. Wage-fixing tribunals tended to accept such arguments, and in practice the 'capacity to pay' principle meant that the minimum wages prescribed were little different from existing wages as determined by the forces of supply and demand in the labour market, modified by union pressure. True, in 1905 the president of the NSW Arbitration Court, C. G. Heydon, enunciated the doctrine that every worker should 'receive enough to enable him to lead a human life, to marry and bring up a family . . . [in] some small degree of comfort'. Yet Judge Heydon paid no more than lip service to this ideal; and when he suggested that if men were unable to earn full wage rates they must take what was offered to them, he was attacked by the *Worker*, which described him as a 'capitalist second-class lawyer . . . This strangely-favoured mediocrity who never earned half of his present income when hustling among his brother sharks for a living at the bar'.[14]

It is a sorry reflection upon the decline in freedom of expression since then that nowadays nobody, apart from politicians in parliament and judges in court, would dare publish such a robust statement for fear of prosecution for defamation or contempt of court. Further, if the phrase quoted above seems scurrilously personal, it may be read along-side a statement by E. W. Riley, the employees' representative on the Arbitration Court in 1906. Riley accused the judiciary generally of class bias, saying:

One of the greatest bulwarks of conservatism and capitalism today lies in the fact that the judges are drawn from the most conservative members of a conservative class, and can always be relied upon to lean against the liberal interpretation of democratic measures.[15]

The work of Justice Higgins in the Commonwealth Arbitration Court was highly significant in relation to the concept of a living wage. In the Harvester case in 1907, when Higgins had to decide what were 'fair and reasonable' wages for McKay's agricultural machinery employees, he adopted as his criterion for judgement, 'the normal needs of the average employee, regarded as a human being living in a civilized community'. This was to be used to calculate a minimum wage for unskilled workers, to which would be added margins for skilled and semi-skilled workers. Incidentally, there is a striking similarity between this procedure and Marx's analysis of wages in capitalist society, as outlined in chapter 9 above—although Higgins was certainly not a Marxist.

In the Harvester case, Higgins decided that a fair wage for an unskilled labourer was seven shillings per day (forty-two shillings a week), with a margin of three shillings a day for a skilled worker. The crucial aspect of this judgement was that it was based on the 'needs' principle—what an employee with a wife and 'about three children'   233 needed to live on. Although the precise figure of seven shillings was dubious from a statistical viewpoint, the 'needs' principle provided a firm foundation for the future. The alternative—letting an employer's supposed capacity to pay be paramount—meant that in the hands of wage-fixing authorities such as Heydon a minimum wage was ill-defined and fluctuating.

Higgins's judgement in the Harvester case was nullified by the High Court in the following year. However, Higgins re-asserted the 'needs' principle in subsequent arbitration cases, and he could not be challenged constitutionally on this point, for he related the establishment of a fair wage directly to his court's function of settling disputes. Thus the Harvester standard became general in the federal arbitration court in course of time. In 1911 Higgins for the first time referred to it as the 'basic wage'.

The practical importance of the Harvester decision in raising wages was much slighter than claimed by Higgins in his apologia, *A New Province for Law and Order*. Certainly seven shillings a day was a generous wage for an unskilled worker in 1907; it was more than most of them received at the time. Unfortunately that continued to be the case for some years. For one thing, trade unions found it difficult to secure access to the Commonwealth Arbitration Court. Workers in the boot and shoe industry in New South Wales and Victoria gained a federal award in 1910 by creating an interstate industrial dispute, but manufacturing workers generally had to rely on state tribunals. Moreover, Higgins was very cautious about raising money wages for the purpose of maintaining the real value of his Harvester standard. Retail prices in Australia rose by about 27 per cent between 1907 and 1914, yet Higgins continued to award seven shillings a day for labourers until 1913, when price adjustments were belatedly introduced.

Leaving aside its limited practical importance, the Harvester judgement had symbolic significance because seven shillings a day was a wage earned by many labourers in the boom years of the 1880s. In the depression of the following decade, labourers' wages fell to five or six shillings a day, and trade union policy aimed at regaining the earlier figure as the depression lifted. Nevertheless, success was not easily achieved through state wage-fixing tribunals, which appear to have been little influenced by the Harvester standard at first. In Victoria, the chairman of the Agricultural Implement Industry Board in 1908 stated that 'he would pay no regard to the decision of Mr Justice Higgins . . . as he [the chairman] had been connected with industrial works all his life he was more competent . . . to come to a proper determination'.[16]

Perhaps this explains why trade unions at the time (unlike historians later) showed little interest in the Harvester judgement. This was particularly true of skilled workers, such as members of the ASE. In awarding a margin of three shillings a day for engineering craftsmen such as fitters, Higgins believed that he was merely applying the current ratio of pay for skill. He was unaware that the men described as fitters and blacksmiths in the agricultural implement industry were workers who were not fully skilled. They generally received wages of one shilling per day less than the ASE's minimum rate and consequently very few of them were members of that trade union. The upshot of the Harvester case was that arbitration courts tended to regard the engineer's proper margin for skill as being about three shillings per day (in terms of 1907 prices), instead of four shillings as might well have been the case if Higgins's judgement had dealt with an industry in which ASE members worked.

Over a longer period, the Harvester wage standard acquired greater significance in terms of the 'needs' principle which it embodied. In the short run, however, the main effect of the judgement was to cause employers to look with much more favour upon State wage-fixing tribunals. This was in marked contrast to the previous attitude of employers. In Victoria, after the initial rapid spread of wages boards around 1900, employers' representatives were successful for several years in restricting both the expansion of the system and the powers of wages boards. In particular, as a mechanism for disciplining any board chairman who might be inclined to be generous towards workers, a Court of Industrial Appeals was established in 1904. Between then and 1915, the court considered a total of seventeen appeals, and in fourteen of these cases the court reduced the wages and/or lengthened the hours of work prescribed by the particular wages boards.

Similarly in New South Wales, parliamentary and court action by employers severely limited the effectiveness of the arbitration court which began to operate in 1902. A decision by the High Court in 1904 barred the NSW Arbitration Court from making an industrial agreement a common rule. More generally, congestion and delays in the NSW court became so chronic that in 1907 its president, Heydon, lamented that 'the Act has been riddled, shelled, broken fore and aft, and reduced to a sinking hulk'.[17]

Then came the Harvester judgement. The employers' general response was to adopt a two-pronged strategy: first, that judicial wage-fixing processes must be accepted as being in their interests in the existing circumstances; and second, that as far as possible the federal arbitration court should be bypassed or restricted in function because its president, Higgins, was regarded as hostile to employers. In other words, he was not a reliable representative of his class. The crucial factor in the situation was the economic boom, which was expected to improve the bargaining power of trade unions. One abiding feature of judicial arbitral procedures is that they entail considerable delay by comparison with collective bargaining. Such delay is usually to the 235 advantage of employers at times of economic prosperity, when work-ers are demanding wage increases. Alfred Deakin probably had this in mind when he envisaged an arbitration court functioning as an engineer, 'interfering, by carrying around an oil-can, from which drops the necessary conciliation to cool any heated bearings'.[18] More to the point, if trade unions press their advantage by resorting to strikes, arbitration tribunals have power to restrain or coerce them.

There was a rapid extension of the wages board system in Victoria after 1907, and Tasmania adopted the system a few years later. In New South Wales the arbitration court or commission was retained, but a network of wages boards was grafted to it from 1908. South Australia also adopted a hybrid system in 1912; while Queensland, after trying wages boards, opted for compulsory arbitration. In prac-tice, the distinction between State arbitration courts and wages board systems diminished. It was more important from the employers' viewpoint to hamstring the federal arbitration court and in this aim they had a considerable measure of success up to 1913.

There were five High Court judges in this period. Three of them— Griffith, Barton and O'Connor—were end-products of conservative political establishments of the colonial era, supporting the doctrine of States' rights. Higgins and Isaacs, who were both appointed to the High Court in 1906, were more centralist or democratic in attitude, but they were in a permanent minority, particularly in relation to questions of the constitutional powers of the Commonwealth Arbitra-tion Court. In the loaded numbers game, it was of little avail to Higgins to be himself a member of the High Court when it considered legal challenges to the jurisdiction of the arbitration court presided over by him. Time and again, employers' organizations won cases of this nature in the High Court. Notably, the Court decided in 1910 that the federal arbitration court could not make an award a common rule, binding on persons who were in the industry concerned though not directly parties to the industrial dispute. A few years later there was another ruling that a dispute could not exist between a union and an employer whose employees were satisfied with their conditions. The practical effect was that union organizers throughout Australia, besides citing as many employers as possible in a case, had to collect signatures of a majority of the workers in each establishment. Delays and frustration were interminable.

Wages and Unions

What did workers gain from arbitration? The answer is not simple, and it is useful first to take another look at changes in the composition of the working class. Broadly speaking, the general pattern of Australian economic development up to 1890 was in the direction of building an infrastructure for industrial society, the emphasis being upon heavy investment in public works, construction, mining and pastoral industry. Unskilled labour was in demand and was well paid compared with other countries. In the following two decades or so, structural changes in the economy included a drastic reduction of mining, a growth of manufacturing and service industries and (until after 1908) a slump in construction. These factors meant that unskilled labour was at a discount. Certainly until about 1907, reduced job opportunities for labourers resulted in their suffering disproportionately: the wage margin for skill grew larger than before.

Even after the upturn in the economy beginning in 1907, labourers were still relatively poorly situated in the labour market. In 1911, when the general level of unemployment in Australia was about 4 per cent, it was only 1 per cent for engineering tradesmen. In these circumstances, unions of skilled workers resorted to courts and tribunals primarily in order to secure official recognition of the unions' own standard rates of pay. These rates were subject to change due to the tightness of the labour market and pressure from unions. Merritt remarks that 'with few exceptions, unions received from the courts only what they had previously won in the market place'.[19] Also outside courts, skilled workers' unions utilized labour shortage to obtain over-award rates of pay. Unskilled workers were not in a position to do this.

Craftsmen did not have things all their own way. The installation of labour-saving machinery was one response by employers and there were some significant changes in technology. Concurrently, there was a growth in the number of semi-skilled operatives in process work such as machining. In 1914 S. Hampson, the Victorian organizer of the ASE, referred to the menace of the handyman 'growing on account of the simplifications of manufacturing processes'.[20] Employers encouraged 'improvers' as a form of cheap labour, and there are indications that such ambitious workers, along with foremen and white-collar workers, played a significant role in the Australian Independent Workers Federation, an anti-union body promoted by employers' federations from 1911 for use as a strikebreaking force.

Another reflection of the growing complexity of working-class structure represented by the emergence of the semi-skilled element is that these workers received margins over the labourers' rate of pay. The shift from the lowest paid occupations to higher paid positions contributed to an increase in average wages. There was an improvement in actual real wages, as distinct from award wages, in the period up to 1913.

There remains a problem concerning the position of labourers. From 1910, State wage-fixing tribunals generally awarded wages of seven shillings a day to labourers, but by then the real value of this amount had already been reduced by a rise in prices. It seems that in 1914 the basic wage, at both State and Commonwealth levels, was still lower in real terms than it had been when Higgins determined the Harvester figure in 1907. This is not to say that wages had actually fallen in the intervening period, for the original Harvester decision applied only to a small number of workers. The arbitration battle was really over extension of the basic wage to other members of the work-force. In this context, the term 'labourer' is misleading, even if it is restricted to males, for arbitration awards prescribed rates of pay for many adult males, such as carters and storemen, which were lower than the rates for full or able-bodied labourers. Gradually after 1907 the sub-labourers were lifted up to the labourers' wage level, but the process had not gone far by 1914.

This leaves out of account a much larger category of workers who were paid less than the standard labourer's rate, that is, most female workers. This was true for both domestic service, which was still the largest category of women's paid work, and manufacturing and distri-butive industries. Actually wages for females probably rose faster than for males in the boom from 1911, but the women's starting point in this comparison was very low. Higgins in the federal arbitration court was characteristic of men of his time in assuming, without investigation, that the great majority of women workers had no dependants and should therefore be paid less than men, who were regarded as bread-winners for families. Edna Ryan notes that in a shop assistants' case in the NSW arbitration court in 1906, the union advocate, a man named G. S. Beeby, recalled another case in which he had contended that 'a woman was worth at least two-thirds [of a man]'. Ryan adds that this would have been an advance on the usual half or less of the male rate, although she questions Beeby's goal:

Whether his motive in increasing women's status and pay was to price them out of the industry, or whether he had suggested the improvement at the instigation of the women urging him to seek equal pay, we do not know.[21]

The general conclusion is that workers gained little from arbitra-tion, except perhaps for some standardization of rates of pay and working conditions such as the eight-hour day. Since arbitration pro-cesses covered about 80 per cent of all Australian trade unionists by 1914, the corollary of this conclusion is that on the whole the perfor-mance of trade unions in advancing the interests of their members was poor, especially given the favourable economic circumstances. On the face of it this is surprising, for there was a strong resurgence of trade unionism. The total number of unionists in Australia rose from less than 100 000 in 1901 to 365 000 in 1911 and more than half a million in 1914. This was perhaps a higher proportion of wage and salary workers than in any other country.

It was generally believed that this growth was due to the arbitration system, which undoubtedly stimulated the formation of unions for the purpose of obtaining awards. The reality was more complex, as suggested by a comparison with other countries where there was no compulsory arbitration system. This was a period marked by working-class mobilization. For example, trade union membership in Britain jumped from 2.5 million in 1910 to 4 million in 1914, and this was connected with big industrial disputes.

In Australia, part of the growth in union membership came from old, well-established bodies such as the Amalgamated Society of Engineers, which quadrupled its membership between 1907 and 1914, reaching a total of nearly 12 000 in the latter year. To some extent this was associated with arbitration processes, but compulsory arbitration was mainly of use to unions which had little industrial strength. The growth rate of new unions was most marked. Some of these asserted themselves vigorously, but arbitration also led to the setting up of a large number of small unions, all seeking industrial awards and having very little power to back their claims. By 1914 there were over 400 separate trade unions in Australia; and dependence upon arbitration, with its heavy legal costs, kept most of them poor. The fragmentation of unions was not to the advantage of the labour movement as a whole, and a legacy of arbitration is the continued existence of many feeble unions, bolstered by barriers to amalgamation posed by the arbitration system as well as demarcation disputes.

In both new and old unions, many workers became dissatisfied with progress under arbitration legislation. Many agreed with Tom Mann's conclusion: 'As a result of the working of these Acts, the unions grew in membership, but lost fighting efficiency'.[22] Mann was a socialist. From 1902 to 1905 he acted as organizer for the Victorian Labor Party but he then decided that there was no hope of transforming that party into a socialist body. Instead, he devoted his energies to trade union work, advocating reorganization on the basis of distinct industries rather than crafts. This was calculated to minimize sectional rivalries and to promote united action, particularly through strikes.

Such ideas were widely discussed by unionists, particularly in New South Wales in 1908-9, when an anti-union State government brought in a 'Coercion' Act which provided an increased penalty of twelve months' gaol for anyone instigating or aiding an illegal strike or lockout. Despite some serious moves towards closer unionism in the form of federation of kindred bodies, conservatism among craft unionists was strong enough to defeat proposals for radical reorganization. 239

Nevertheless, even the craft unions felt some effects. In 1911 D. P. Earsman who, like Mann, was a socialist and a member of the ASE, wrote to the union's Australian journal:

I hear some say 'We don't want any labourers amongst us. We have enough to do to battle for ourselves'. Wouldn't it be better if we were fighting for all instead of only a few? Our fight is the same whether we be mechanics or labourers . . . nothing short of industrial unionism will be of any use.[23]

The IWW and Militancy

While socialists had appreciable influence in the labour movement, they themselves were subject to influence from another quarter: the Industrial Workers of the World (IWW), an organization established in the USA in 1905. In that country it appealed mainly to unskilled, seasonal and immigrant workers, who were virtually ignored by the craft unions comprised in the conservative American Federation of Labor. The IWW was uncompromisingly revolutionary, declaring in the preamble to its foundation statement:

The working class and the employing class have nothing in common . . . Between these two classes a struggle must go on until the toilers come together on the political, as well as on the industrial field, and take and hold that which they produce by their labour through an economic organization of the working class without affiliation with any political party.

This was the language of class struggle, and IWW views on the desirability of organizing all workers into one big union were in line with the experience of socialists and militant trade unionists in Australia. Accordingly, IWW ideas were taken up and propagated, particularly in Sydney and among isolated bodies of workers in mines and in the bush. There were divergencies of opinion, for many if not most Australian socialists were not revolutionary in outlook or practice. Furthermore, the later adoption by the American IWW of a syndicalist standpoint, that political action was useless and all efforts must be concentrated on the industrial sphere, was less relevant to circumstances in Australia, where labour parties had a fair prospect of gaining office through elections.

The IWW in Australia was actually a rather amorphous body, relying upon spontaneous action. At its peak it probably had no more than 2000 members and few of them were union leaders. However, its members were very energetic and enthusiastic and their propaganda was simple and direct. It was also witty, as in a catchy ditty (sung to the tune of Yankee Doodle) which embodied scorn for compulsory arbitration and for Labor politicians, who were parodied as saying:

I know the Arbitration Act
As a sailor knows his 'riggins'
So if you want a *small* advance,
I'll talk to Justice 'Iggins.

So bump me into parliament,
Bounce me any way,
Bang me into parliament,
On next election day.

Understandably, orthodox Labor and trade union leaders like Spence and W. M. Hughes were strongly hostile towards the IWW, as were employers. The IWW was undoubtedly the most colourful organization in Australian labour history, cheerfully ridiculing the conventions of established society and religion. For example, at an open-air meeting in Melbourne, when Donald Grant was asked whether the IWW would compensate the King in the event of his being deposed, he replied: 'Yes . . . with a pick and shovel and a suit of dungarees'. Similarly, clergymen were satirized in IWW songs about 'sky pilots' offering 'pie in the sky when you die'. Defiant talk was matched by direct action. In 1914, when authorities in Sydney and Port Pirie tried to limit freedom of speech at open-air meetings, IWW men deliberately courted arrest. Their aim was to make a nuisance of themselves by packing the gaols. As one of their leaders put it: 'We wouldn't pay fines on principle; we always took it out in the nick'. This tactic had some success.[24]

Partly through the influence of socialists and the IWW, a fresh tide of militancy began to rise in Australia in 1907. Its initial manifestation was among coalminers in northern New South Wales and metalminers at Broken Hill. In the latter region, the Amalgamated Miners' Association re-established itself a decade after the defeat suffered in 1892, and the city became known as a labour stronghold. The AMA secured wage increases of about 15 per cent in 1906, but BHP and other mining companies later insisted upon reverting to the pre-1906 wage levels. The miners refused to accept this and were locked out for a period of twenty weeks in 1909. It was a bitter fight, in which militant union pickets erected mock graves, each with a headstone bearing the supposed obituary of a scab, around the companies' land. The result of the struggle was not clear-cut. BHP had to give in on its proposed wage-reduction, but the company (most of whose shares were held by investors in Britain at this time) did not re-open its mine for another two years and it victimized some leading unionists. On the other hand, in contrast to 1892, the unions at Broken Hill lived to fight another day.

The most interesting instance of militancy occurred in 1912, when there was a general strike in Brisbane. Queensland was a conservative State. Despite this, a strong radical union movement developed among miners, meat workers and sugar workers in the north. There was some reflection of this union growth in Brisbane, despite the fact that many employers were strongly anti-unionist. In particular, the manager of the English-owned Brisbane Tramway Company was an arrogant American who refused to allow employees to join any union. A number of them defied the ban and then attached the badge of the Australian Tramway Employees' Association to their watch chains. The company manager gave the offenders the choice of no badge or no work—which meant a lock-out, as most chose the right to wear the union badge. Following this, forty-three trade unions in Brisbane resolved that the company's action constituted 'an attack on the principles of unionism'. They embarked on a general strike in support of the tramway-men.[25]

The strike, involving about 20 000 trade unionists in Brisbane and thousands of others outside the city, was an impressive display of solidarity. For a time in February 1912, Brisbane was practically at a standstill. A combined unions' strike committee issued a limited number of permits to butchers, bakers and other food purveyors to enable them to carry on their business—provided that they employed only unionists. Such evidence of the establishment of a rival to the official State authority infuriated the Queensland government, which fully supported the tramway company. Extra police were drafted into Brisbane, 3000 special constables were enrolled, and a large procession of workers was brutally broken up by a police baton charge. The British government was requested by State authorities to send a warship to stand off the coast of Queensland, ready to help put down the strikers if necessary.

After five weeks the general strike collapsed. Union funds were limited and although some financial support came from unions in New South Wales, W. M. Hughes persuaded Sydney wharf labourers not to join in the strike. In Queensland itself, it was evident that the unions had underestimated the strength of the ruling and middle classes. A general strike, particularly one more or less confined to a single city, could not succeed if the government held firm. In the Commonwealth Arbitration Court, Higgins declared that the tramway dispute was a lock-out and he issued an order restraining the Brisbane Tramway Company from dismissing employees for wearing a union badge, but this was quite ineffective as the court had no power to reinstate those who had been dismissed. In fact, the Tramway Employees' Association in Brisbane was smashed in the dispute, while a company union, subsidized by the management, remained in existence.

The unions were beaten, but the outcome of the general strike was not a crushing defeat for the labour movement. Militancy remained a significant force, both in Queensland and other States. While the Brisbane strike was on, metalworkers on the railways in Western Australia were also on strike—or rather, as a union organizer said ironically, 'it would have been termed a "strike" a few years ago, but in these enlightened days we do things in a different way'.[26] Unions in Western Australia had devised a way around their State's ban on strikes by holding a 'conference' of workers involved in a dispute, the conference being adjourned from day to day indefinitely until the dispute was settled.

There were reflections of militancy, and of the employers' consciousness of need to soften it, in subtle changes in the climate of ideas. While the struggle to win the Harvester standard of wages met with varying success, there was growing public acceptance of the idea that workers were entitled to 'fair' wages, not merely what employers were willing to offer. The point may be illustrated by reference to a strike by sugar workers in Queensland in 1911. Mill workers, supported by the Amalgamated Workers' Association, gained considerable improvements in pay and conditions, although these were not passed on to employees of CSR in northern New South Wales, where the company monopolized mill employment. A year later a Commonwealth Royal Commission on the Sugar Industry found that, whilst cane cutters could earn good wages, in other sections of the industry wages 'were below, and, in the case of the Colonial Sugar Refining Company's New South Wales Mills, distressingly below, the standard of a reasonable living wage'. E. W. Knox, the company's general manager, was questioned about this when he gave evidence to the Royal Commission, and the exchange indicates both the spread of the concept of a fair wage and Knox's own stiff refusal to acknowledge it:

Question. [In your] statement, speaking of labour conditions existing in July, 1911, prior to the strike, you say, 'There cannot be the least doubt they were fair, because there was not any difficulty in securing men to run the mill'. The standard of fairness is supply and demand, of course? *Answer.*—Yes.

Question. A good old 'Liberal' standard, but not generally accepted in Australia? *Answer.*—How do you mean?

Question. There are a good many people in Australia who think that a fair wage cannot be defined simply in terms of supply and demand. Of course, what you say in this statement amounts to the fact that it can be? *Answer.*—I could say something on that point, but it would not be evidence.[27]

Capital and Labour Revisited

Although the growth of militancy and class-consciousness in the years preceding the Great War was striking, it should not be exaggerated. In the labour movement, conservatives remained in control, industrially and politically. Even so, the bourgeoisie was worried. Capitalists were alarmed by the election of Labor governments in the Commonwealth and New South Wales in 1910. Actually these governments proved far from revolutionary, but employers remained suspicious. The IWW appeared a threatening bogey. The strength of employers' feelings comes out in a private letter written by James Burns, chairman of Burns Philp & Co., in 1911:

Surely we will have some cessation from strikes, arbitration court awards and other disturbing labor elements, a continuance must demoralize all concerned both employers and employees . . .
    The Clerks union [being formed] is another scheme which will prove a terrible curse to our own and other large companies, the chief trouble being that if we and our employees cannot work sympathetically then all pleasure of conducting or serving in a business disappears, and they are controlled by the Trades Hall and subscribe to that cancerous institution instead of joining our family circle so to speak.[28]

Burns was both genuine in his concern and typical of Australian businessmen of the time. There was an extraordinary incongruity between such agonizing over trade union assertiveness and the fact that company profits were very high. A parallel may be drawn with the period of the Whitlam federal Labor government sixty years later. That government was intent upon effecting some overdue reforms, without in any way aiming to undermine capitalist society. Yet the bourgeoisie felt and acted as if the end of their world was near. No stratagems were too shady for use in quickly removing the government—and the conspirators were those accustomed to prate about the value of constitutional government.

In the years leading up to the outbreak of the Great War in 1914, there was no real prospect of revolution in Australia. However, the extent of poverty and inequality provided some basis for bourgeois fear. At Broken Hill a working miner in 1909 could expect an income of about £112 in wages in the year, if there were no strikes or lock-outs. In contrast, G. D. Delprat, the general manager of BHP, received—in addition to his £5000 salary—at least £600 in bonus and travelling expenses for his part in defeating the Broken Hill workers that year. Also in 1909, the Sydney department store merchant, Samuel Hordern, died leaving an estate valued at £3 million. Female shop assistants were lucky if they received one pound per week in pay.

There was a war census of wealth in Australia in 1915, which showed that the distribution of wealth was much more unequal than income. The top 1 per cent of male income earners received nearly 15 per cent of total net income, while the top 10 per cent received 40 per cent of the total. For property ownership, the census indicated that half of 1 per cent of adult males owned between them 30 per cent of total wealth, while 5 per cent of the population owned 66 per cent of the wealth. At the other end of the scale, the vast majority, 80 to 90 per cent of individuals, owned little or nothing more than their clothes and a few sticks of furniture. The proportion of women with appreciable assets was even smaller than that of men.

The statistical exercise which revealed this startling disparity in wealth in 'the workingman's paradise' was not repeated in later years. No government, however impartial its census office may be, wishes to lay itself open to embarrassment of this nature. The stark truth about levels of income and wealth is likely to incite disaffection among the common people: the old distinction between 'them' and 'us' is still valid in a class society.

14

Imperialism and Australia's First Multinational: Cheap Labour, Racism and CSR

Australian Imperialism

In the century preceding the First World War, capital recognized no national boundaries, particularly in its quest for cheap labour. Millions of Chinese and Indians were transported as indentured labourers to work in plantations and mines in areas such as the Caribbean, East Africa, Mauritius, Malaya and Fiji. Sugar was the main plantation crop. This meant that producers of sugar in Australia, to the extent that they competed with other areas in the international market or in Australia itself (though this was affected by import duties), were impelled to obtain a supply of cheap labour. That supply was found among the Melanesian inhabitants of islands in the South Pacific, notably the Solomons and the New Hebrides. These people were known as Kanakas, a term which may have been used in a derogatory fashion at the time but nowadays is used with pride to distinguish the indigenous inhabitants (Kanaks) of New Caledonia from their French rulers.

The tapping of supplies of cheap labour in the islands of the southwest Pacific was also associated with an expansion of overseas trade and the development of shipping links. Concurrently there was a growth of monopoly in this sphere. Australian mercantile interests were active overseas from the 1880s, their main focus being on buying copra in exchange for manufactured goods, the copra or coconut oil being then sold on the international market as a raw material for making soap and margarine. The leading Australian firm in this sphere was Burns Philp & Co., which also became a shipowner. In the process, Burns Philp faced competition from powerful German and French shipping lines, which were subsidized by their national governments. Burns Philp in turn secured support, disguised as mail subsidies, from Australian governments.

Thus a close connection was established between the state and a forceful body of mercantile interests involved in the export of capital in search of more profit. Political and strategic considerations also impelled Australian governments—already regulating the Kanaka labour trade—to take a greater interest in the region. This was formalized in one area in 1904, when Britain transferred control of Papua to Australia. There were other areas, such as Fiji and the Solomons, where colonial control remained in the hands of Britain; while some places such as New Caledonia (French), New Guinea and Samoa (German) and Java (Dutch) were controlled by other imperial powers. However, the presence of a foreign administration was not necessarily an effective barrier to penetration by Australian capital.

The first appreciable export of Australian capital, in the 1880s, was limited by the existence of good alternative investment opportunities in Australia itself. Consequently, apart from investment in Fijian sugar production, the process was one of small though significant beginnings in trading ventures. The picture changed sharply during the boom period between 1909 and 1914, when rapid capital accumulation in Australia was reflected in the first substantial wave of capital export to the South Pacific. This capital went into the development of coconut and rubber plantations as well as trade, and the Bank of New South Wales opened its first Papuan branch in Port Moresby in 1910. Among those who formed rubber companies for Papua was Theodore Fink, who had been prominent in the Melbourne land boom in the 1880s. Also about 1910, there was considerable Australian investment in tin-mining in Malaya and Siam. Stuart Rosewarne estimates that 'Australian capital represented almost one-third of the total foreign capital invested in the Eastern tin-mining industry' at this time.[1]

Australia remained basically a junior partner in British imperialism. Yet there was a latent tension in relations between the two countries: their interests were not identical. For example, Burns Philp lacked the kind of personal, top level contacts with government at the heart of the British Empire which were very useful to big English companies such as Lever Brothers. The latter, through its subsidiary, Lever's Pacific Plantations Ltd, in 1906 acquired control of some 200 000 acres of land in the Solomons on 999-year leases. This was achieved through influence at the Colonial Office, whereas Burns Philp was able to secure land for plantations in the Solomons on much less advantageous (though still cheap) terms.

Nevertheless, the political power of colonial administrations was not always as strong as it seemed. This point is illustrated by an incident in 1910, when Burns Philp was approached by Wing Sang, a Chinese banana importer in Sydney. Wing Sang offered to lease land from Burns Philp in the Solomons and to send Chinese to grow bananas on it—which would provide more freight for the Australian company's steamships. W. H. Lucas, a senior executive of Burns Philp, assessed this offer carefully in a memorandum. He noted, for example:

If we could confine them [Chinese] to a small Banana-growing area, it might be a good threat to hold over the other small traders, that we could put Chinamen out in opposition to them, but, again, we have to consider the opprobrium which would attach to us whilst the present White Australia craze is on, and the possibility of our losing mail contracts etc., far outweighing in value the doubtful advantage in the Solomons.

This reference to 'the present White Australia craze' serves as a useful reminder of the fact that some sections of the Australian bourgeoisie, particularly those with leanings towards free trade, did not support the White Australia policy, because it interfered with their access to cheap labour. However, a more telling point, concerning limitations upon the formal power possessed by British government officials in colonies, arises from another passage in the Lucas memorandum:

If we [Burns Philp] want them there [Chinese in the Solomons] we can introduce them without difficulty; if we do not want them we can easily arrange for them to be restricted. There is power under the Pacific Orders-in-Council to issue prohibitions, and we could move the Resident Commissioner or High Commissioner privately to block it, or we could get the men and have them established before the authorities woke up to the position.[2]

Burns Philp's influence was stronger and more intimate in relation to Australian governments. There was mutual benefit. The company secured shipping subsidies and other forms of aid; while the government relied heavily upon Burns Philp, which had branches throughout the South Pacific, for political and economic intelligence. The Commonwealth, operating under the convention that Whitehall was responsible for imperial foreign policy, had virtually no diplomatic representatives of its own overseas and only a rudimentary External Affairs Department in Australia. Despite efforts by some senior public servants to maintain a degree of independence from commercial influence, Australian foreign policy was generally designed to advance the interests of Australian capital.

Yet there was one sphere in which those Australians who were engaged in trade and investment overseas failed to obtain much support from the federal government. This was in connection with the White Australia policy and protection. Not only was official action taken to exclude black labour from the Queensland sugar industry but it was accepted as a corollary that producers of various commodities in Australia should be equally protected against imports derived from the same kind of cheap black labour overseas. Thus a tariff was placed upon imports of maize from the New Hebrides, despite the tariff being detrimental to the interests of Australian-owned (or financed) plantations there. Reconciliation of competing capitalist interests was difficult, although the problem did not apply to the copra trade, for copra was not produced in Australia.

Although the White Australia policy was regarded as sacrosanct, one Australian industry was exempted from it; this was pearlshelling in Western Australia and Queensland. Pearlshell was sold on an international market for use in button-making, and dependence upon exports meant that the industry was not susceptible to the sort of manipulation through import tariffs and exclusions which was used to eliminate black labour in the sugar industry. Indeed it was apparent that if pearlshelling were to survive in Australia, it would be on the basis of continued employment of cheap labour, particularly in diving. The best deep water divers were found to be Japanese, brought in as indentured workers, although Aborigines and Papuans were also employed.

In the depression of the 1890s, Australian owners of pearling fleets induced the Queensland government to discriminate effectively against Japanese capitalists operating boats in Queensland waters. At the same time Australian fleet owners wished to retain Japanese workers, and this object was gained. From the establishment of the Commonwealth, Asians were permitted to enter Australia to work in pearlshelling under certain conditions, and this permit system still operates today.

Actually, in the first decade or so of the twentieth century, supporters of the White Australia policy (mainly Labor) made several attempts to have the Japanese divers excluded in favour of whites, but to no avail. One old operator in the Queensland industry remarked in 1908 that 'there is as much chance of the pearl shell industry being worked by white labour as there is of the Queensland Parliament being run by a black man'. It was not simply a matter of Japanese divers being cheaper labour than white divers. There was a terribly high death rate in the industry, so that it was virtually impossible to recruit white 249 divers. Racist views reinforced the conclusion that Japanese divers must be retained. As a Customs official at Thursday Island told a Commonwealth Royal Commission set up in 1913: 'I should not like to see white men entering an industry in connection with which the death-rate is so frightfully high ... Such a high death-rate as that to which I have referred as relating to coloured divers would be cruel in the case of white men'.[3]

Sugar and Cheap Labour

Australian production of cane sugar began in Queensland in the 1860s and developed extensively, using black labour from the islands. Some Aborigines and Chinese were also employed, and racial stereotypes became fixed in the thoughts of white Queenslanders. 'Aborigines, Melanesians and Chinese were, by virtue of the characteristics generally ascribed to them by Europeans, either regarded as fit only to perform certain menial roles and specialist functions, like wood-chopping and buck-jumping, thrashing cane or growing vegetables—or defined residually, and seen to be fit for no worthwhile role at all.'[4] However, the number of Aborigines and Chinese in the sugar industry was small compared with the Kanakas. The latter were regarded by their white masters as preferable, being not only cheap to procure but relatively docile and tractable as a labour force. Kanakas were isolated strangers in a foreign land. There was little prospect of escape from a plantation, especially as Queensland legislation from 1880 confined employment of indentured Melanesians to the sugar industry. Further legislation in 1884 restricted all Melanesians to unskilled jobs in the sugar industry.

Between 1863 and 1904 about 65 000 Kanakas were brought into Australia, although the number in the country at any given time was probably no more than 11 000. While some stayed on after their first three years in Queensland, many went back to their island homes. Many others died in exile: the official death rate for Melanesians in the colony in the early 1880s was four times higher than for Europeans. Indentured Kanakas were generally poorly fed and housed, often ill-treated by their masters and highly vulnerable to diseases such as tuberculosis. Low status was accentuated by social segregation—a form of apartheid. At one time there were separate railway carriages for Europeans and others in northern Queensland.

An important rationale for the employment of black labour was the belief that white workers could not labour effectively in tropical cane fields. This idea was later disproved in practice, and in any case it was mainly a reflection of the refusal of white workers to accept jobs at such low pay and poor conditions as were imposed upon blacks. Not only did white workers stay out of the cane fields in these circumstances: with some political and trade union backing, they supported the exclusion of Kanakas from other industries, where they might be used to reduce wages. The Kanakas themselves had no political influence in Queensland, although they were not always such docile workers as sugar planters expected. 'Go slow' tactics could be used by blacks as well as whites. On the other hand, some planters, realizing that coercion through hard-driving overseers was not always effective, found that religion was a useful adjunct to labour discipline. H. T. Easterby, in his history of the *Queensland Sugar Industry* (1931), told how

One very pious planter used to conduct a mission to his kanaka employees, and in his sermons combined moral precepts with an eye to the main chance. For instance, in inculcating the necessity of obedience to masters and of walking in the straight and narrow way, he would impress upon them that while working in the cane they should not be idle in the big cane because they were hidden. 'Remember, boys', he would earnestly say, 'God can see you in the big cane just as well as he can see you in the little cane; therefore, work hard, wherever you may be.'

Indentured Melanesians in Queensland were supplied with food rations and primitive accommodation. Their employers were also required by law to pay a minimum wage of £6 per annum, which tended to be the actual amount paid. It did not differ greatly from the sum paid to white convicts in Australia earlier in the nineteenth century, and restrictions upon freedom constituted other parallels between the two kinds of labour force. Like convicts, Kanakas were not slaves but were bound for periods of years. In the case of a Kanaka, the period was a three-year indenture, and breach of the terms of the indenture could result in imprisonment. The services of Kanakas could be transferred from one employer to another through sale of the indenture, regardless of the wishes of the employee.

The first stage of the process was recruitment of blacks in the islands through British trading vessels. This labour trade was run by merchants and adventurers rather than by the Queensland planters themselves. The latter bought the indentures for lump sums after the islanders had been shipped to Queensland ports. Generally the sailing vessels used were old and unseaworthy, and the islanders were packed in like cattle. In 1868 the Queensland parliament passed a Polynesian Labourers Act to regulate the trade. Among other things this made employers of indentured workers responsible for returning them to their islands at the termination of a contract. In effect, the cost of this was embodied in the price paid by planters for indentures. Later, Acts were passed by the imperial parliament, empowering the British Navy to police the island labour trade, not only to Queensland but to areas such as Fiji.

The effectiveness of such regulation in curbing abuses is doubtful. 251

Periodically there were reports of murders or kidnapping in the islands—'blackbirding', as it was euphemistically termed—especially at times of rapid growth in the Queensland sugar industry, as in the early 1880s. The use of direct and illegal force was perhaps not as extensive as appeared: downright fraud and chicanery were more important. The concept of a contract freely negotiated between two parties was mocked by the process of indenturing for labour services. Not only were the signatory parties very unequal in bargaining power but the indenture was a formal legal document written in English, which the Kanaka could not understand. He was supposed to have it explained to him verbally, after which he 'signed' the document—that is to say, he put a cross on it (this being witnessed by a white). Undoubtedly thousands of Kanakas acted with very little knowledge of what they were committing themselves to, or for how long. Yet, short of incontrovertible evidence of misrepresentation, Kanakas were held to the terms of indentures through the sanctity of contract in capitalist law.

In the latter part of the 1880s the cane sugar industry in Queensland and northern New South Wales was severely depressed owing to a dramatic fall in the price of sugar on international markets. This resulted from a big increase in beet sugar manufacturing, subsidized by governments in Europe. The depression badly affected a number of planters in Queensland and prompted a reconstruction of the industry.

In considering this, it is useful to bear in mind the three distinct stages in production of sugar. First, there is the growing and harvesting of cane on farms or plantations. Second, the cane is crushed in mills to produce raw sugar. Lastly, the raw sugar is transported to a refinery and processed for consumers.

By about 1880 plantations with large Melanesian workforces dominated sugar production in Queensland, especially in the north. Generally, each plantation had its own mill, so that planters integrated the first two stages of production. Nevertheless, these mills were small and inefficient. Productivity on plantations was low, investment in expensive machinery being inhibited by the availability of cheap labour. On the other hand, the Colonial Sugar Refining Company (CSR) was exceptional in a number of ways. It began at the last stage of the business in 1855, using imported sugar as the raw material for a refinery in Sydney. Then, in the 1870s and 1880s, CSR extended its operations by establishing plantations and mills of its own in northern New South Wales and Queensland. The CSR mills were large and well equipped.

In the last decades of the nineteenth century Australian sugar planters were squeezed from two sides: by the fall in international sugar prices and by a sharp rise in the cost of labour. The latter resulted from two factors in particular. In the first place, the cost of recruiting Kanaka labour rose as labour was drained from the islands closest to Australia and vessels had to go farther afield. Higher costs, along with the recruiters' profits, were reflected in the lump sums of so much per head paid by planters (including CSR) to the labour agents. Secondly, planters had to pay higher wages to Melanesian workers. This applied not so much to indentured labourers as to those, known as 'time-expired' workers, who chose to remain in Queensland at the end of the period of indenture. They were free to change employers and to bargain over wages, so that they were substantially better off than were fresh recruits from the islands. The effect of this upon labour costs was accentuated by a marked growth in the proportion of time-expired workers in the black labour force. Further, there were some efforts by Melanesian time-expired workers to form unions of their own. 'Attempts by Melanesians to raise their wages were so successful that by 1895 the Queensland planters were clamouring for legislative restriction of the Melanesians' freedom to bargain with employers.' [5]

This is not to suggest that black labour was no longer cheap compared with white labour. Rather, the margin between the two narrowed, and this reinforced pressure to restructure the depressed sugar industry. Over a period of time, plantations were replaced by small cane farms served by central mills. The decisive move towards this transformation occurred in the 1890s, when the Queensland government provided loan funds for the establishment of a number of large sugar mills which were intended to be co-operatively owned by cane farmers. Productivity increased as these central mills took over the role of many old plantation mills, and small farmers in these areas were no longer dependent upon planters who had previously crushed cane for neighbouring farmers as well as themselves. However, there were other areas where proprietary mills remained dominant, this being particularly the case with CSR's large plants.

Many planters decided that the most profitable course to adopt was to cut up their land into small farms to be rented out, or sold on easy terms of payment, to white farmers. In effect, this policy represented an offset to the growing cost of black labour by reducing the cost of white labour in the sugar industry. Many prospective farm operators, given the opportunity to become independent, were willing to work harder. They relied heavily upon their own labour and that of their families. Moreover, the structural change meant that the risks of sugar production were borne primarily by farmers—a technique used by transnational agribusiness today. CSR led the way in disposing of its plantations, concentrating upon milling and refining operations. The company established refineries in several Australian cities besides Sydney.

The great depression of the 1890s also increased the supply of white labour by impelling more workers to enter the sugar industry in search of jobs. Generally they sought relatively skilled work in mills, but there was a growing tendency for whites to compete with blacks for employment. Although the increasing number of small cane farmers resented having to contend on the market with sugar grown by black plantation labour, the small farmers were not loath to employ Melanesians themselves, usually at harvest time. In these circumstances, there was an upsurge of hostility towards Melanesians on the part of white workers and their trade unions in Queensland. The objection was racially based, with whites refusing to recognize Melanesians as fellow workers; and as the new Labor Party developed in Queensland there was an increasing likelihood that the supply of Kanaka labour would be cut off by political action.

Economics and politics were entwined. The Kanaka labour trade had been designed to supply cheap labour for plantations, yet the restructuring of the sugar industry meant replacement of plantations by small farms. 'When plantations passed, so did the need for the large scale importation of field labour' in Queensland.[6] At the political level, racist feelings against Melanesians were widespread among middle-class people as well as workers. Racism was identified with nationalism and cheap labour. In the referendum on Australian federation in 1899, the 'Yes' vote in Queensland predominated mainly in the northern districts, where black labour was concentrated and White Australia was an important issue. A sequel to federation was Commonwealth legislation, the Pacific Island Labourers Act of 1901, passed in the face of opposition from the Queensland government, sugar planters and allied merchants. The Act provided that no islander was to be allowed to enter Australia after 1904 and that any Melanesians still in Australia after 1906 were to be deported.

It may be observed that while the Immigration Restriction Act of 1901 implemented the White Australia policy by use of a dictation test in any language to bar entry to non-Europeans (and other 'undesirables'), the parallel Pacific Island Labourers Act went further by providing for the actual expulsion of many blacks living and working in Australia. The Act was later amended to exempt certain islanders, such as those who had lived in Australia continuously for twenty years, yet in 1906–7 more than 4000 Kanakas were summarily deported from Queensland to the Solomons and New Hebrides. It was a shameful episode in Australian history, in keeping with the 1905 adoption by the Federal ALP of a prime party objective expressed as 'The cultivation of an Australian sentiment based on the maintenance of racial purity and the development in Australia of an enlightened and self-reliant community'. This was an Australian forerunner of the unscientific mythology which was later a bastion of fascist ideology.

254   Following Federation the Commonwealth imposed a high protective

tariff on imports of sugar. This was partly a matter of continuing the previous colonial tariffs on sugar, in New South Wales as well as Queensland. Indeed in northern New South Wales, where CSR mills dominated the sugar industry, commercial agreements between the company and sugar growers in the 1890s provided for substantial lowering of the price to be paid for cane by the company in the event of import duty on sugar being reduced. Naturally, sugar farmers supported Federation only on the understanding that protection would be maintained. E. W. Knox of CSR appears to have opposed Federation.

A high federal protective duty on sugar imports also represented compensation to planters for the impending loss of their black labour supply. At the same time, in order to speed up the substitution of white labour for black in the sugar industry, the Commonwealth introduced an excise tax combined with a rebate for those sugar producers who employed only white labour. Sugar production rose and there was a very marked increase in the number of cane farmers in Queensland (compared with 230 in 1888, there were about 3300 of them in 1905) yet only about one-third of the total amount of sugar was produced exclusively by white labour in 1905. The remainder came from plantations and farms employing black labour, especially in northern Queensland. The subsequent effect of the deportation of Kanakas is evident in the fact that 88 per cent of the sugar crop was produced exclusively by white labour in 1908. Incidentally, it seems that some planters made effective use of exemption provisions in the deportation legislation. About 1000 islanders remained in Australia after 1907, and their descendants still constitute a significant proportion of the population of the sugar town of Mackay. However, the use of Melanesian and Asian labour in the sugar industry was prohibited by the Queensland government from 1913. At that date only two plantations survived as cultivation-cum-milling estates.

The phasing out of black labour in sugar was facilitated—indeed, made possible—by an increase in the supply of white labour. This was related to a decline in the mining industry in Queensland in the first decade or so of the twentieth century, resulting in a redeployment of acclimatized white workers to the sugar industry. At the same time there were substantial numbers of immigrants, many of whom were absorbed by the sugar industry. It is ironic that to some extent the old indentured black labour was replaced by new indentured white labour. Between 1906 and 1919 more than one thousand indentured labourers arrived from Britain to work in the Queensland sugar industry, their entry being made under the terms of a federal Contract Immigrants Act of 1905, which permitted such immigration if approved by the relevant Minister.

In addition, Italian immigrants appeared from the 1890s in substantial numbers. They were not from the poorest areas. Mainly   255 they came from northern Italy—a region of small peasant farming rather than a landless proletariat. These Italians were favoured by CSR, which saw them as being imbued with appropriate petty bourgeois ambition to become cane farmers in Queensland. Further, CSR regarded Italian workers as potential strikebreakers among cane cutters. In 1911 the company's general manager wrote to the manager of one of the Queensland mills, broaching the possibility of offering to pay part of the costs of passage to Australia for several hundred Italian farm immigrants:

This is a matter in which we think assistance might well be given by us, for a large proportion of Italians on your River . . . *were undoubtedly the stumbling block with the Unions* in preventing them from enforcing their demands on the farmers . . . It is however *not* desirable that our active assistance in this matter should become known.[7]

CSR's view of these immigrants may be contrasted with an opinion about British immigrants with a different social background, expressed by an adviser to the company. On 6 July 1909 E. P. Simpson, partner in the prominent Sydney law firm of Minter, Simpson & Co., wrote to Knox suggesting that CSR should not make a further financial contribution to the British Immigration League of Australia, because the people being assisted to emigrate to New South Wales appeared to be radicalized labourers, not farmers. As Simpson put it: 'Nearly all these immigrants—there is hardly an exception—who are being brought here are swelling the ranks of the Labour Party and consequently increasing the voting power of the socialistic element in the community.'[8]

Although Simpson may not have been representative of employers' views concerning the immediacy of need for immigrants, he was worried by the thought that British immigrants came from a society where the common people were accustomed to working-class political and industrial activity. Actually, in that sense they were well attuned to Australian circumstances. Simpson's letter shows that the historically pro-British sentiments of the Australian bourgeoisie should not be taken for granted when class issues are raised. Nowadays objections from this quarter are levelled at militant shop stewards among immigrants from Britain—together with communists among Italian immigrants.

CSR: 'The Octopus'

Whereas Burns, Philp & Co., in its drive across the Pacific, may be regarded as the cutting edge of Australian imperialism, CSR wore the unacceptable face of greed and oppression. CSR moved into sugar production in Fiji in the 1880s, at the same time as it expanded in Queensland. The two moves were related, as E. W. Knox, the company's general manager (and son of its founder) anticipated that Fijian sugar would compete with Australian sugar unless CSR were in a position of control. CSR therefore built several large mills in Fiji, most of the raw sugar product being exported to a refinery which CSR established in New Zealand in 1884.

CSR also acquired large areas of plantation land in Fiji, and the company was directly engaged in cane sugar production as well as milling. It soon became apparent that indigenous Fijians, having access to land of their own for subsistence farming, were very reluctant to work as labourers on plantations. Consequently, indentured labourers from India were imported to work for CSR and other planters. The indentured Indians worked for one shilling per day in pay, earned under harsh conditions. In the Colonial Office in London in 1897, it was noted on an official report from Fiji: 'The mortality is ghastly. The Queensland Kanaka mortality is not a patch on it. 5.28% or one in 19, cannot go on.' Penal labour laws, for such offences as 'unlawful absence', were applied severely in Fiji, some 20 per cent of the indentured Indian labourers being convicted each year. No wonder they called their life on the plantations 'narak', meaning 'hell'.[9]

In the 1890s CSR in Fiji moved towards a policy similar to that adopted in Queensland: it leased out parts of its estates to cane producers. At first these were mainly white planters, a number of whom were former CSR plantation overseers, but increasingly after 1900 plots of land were made available to small Indian farmers. These were former indentured labourers. About 60 per cent of all the Indians stayed in Fiji after their five-year period of indenture. Most remained labourers, but some settled on the land as smallholders. CSR provided financial credit for Indian cane farmers, one effect of which was to give the company more control over production. In the main, however, such control—particularly the power to determine the price paid to farmers for their cane—arose from CSR's dominance of milling. By 1903 four of the six sugar mills in Fiji were owned by CSR, and one of the other two was dependent upon the company. Michael Moynagh comments: 'The sugar from C.S.R.'s four mills alone was worth well over half the colony's total exports and re-exports . . . C.S.R. had not only become dominant in the Fiji sugar industry: it had attained a commanding position in the economy as a whole.'[10]

CSR's mills and chemical processes were technically advanced. The value of the company's assets in Fiji alone was estimated at about £1.3 million in 1903 and £2.3 million in 1911. In formal terms, these figures represent export of capital from Australia but in practice they signify largely the re-investment of profits made from operations in Fiji. Those profits were gouged out of the labour of indentured Indians. E. W. Knox in effect acknowledged this in a letter which he wrote from

Sydney on 16 April 1902 to the Colonial Secretary in London. The occasion was a continuing agitation by the government of New Zealand for a federation between that country and Fiji. Knox opposed this, arguing that 'the prosperity of Fiji depends almost entirely on the success of the sugar industry, and such success is impossible without an adequate supply of labourers from India'. If Fiji were to be federated with, or absorbed by, New Zealand, Knox believed that public opinion in the latter country—comparable with White Australia sentiment— would succeed in stopping the flow of Indians to Fiji.

It may be added that Knox's lobbying on this issue was done quietly, publicity being avoided for fear of possible adverse effects upon CSR capital investment in its refinery in New Zealand. In the event, Fiji remained a separate British colony, and Indian indentured labourers arrived in increasing numbers. In the first decade of the twentieth century, the inflow was at an average rate of nearly 2300 per annum; and the net result was that in 1911 there were about 40 000 Indians in Fiji, compared with 87 000 Fijians. The colony assumed greater importance in CSR operations, being responsible for 44 per cent of the company's total output of raw sugar in 1910, compared with 26 per cent in 1890 and 35 per cent in 1900.

CSR's operations in Fiji, New Zealand and Australia were not treated separately in the company's published financial accounts. Knox claimed that CSR profits in Fiji were very modest as a return upon capital employed there, but he had good political reasons for understating the return. Further, it is clear that CSR engaged in transfer pricing, charging its Australian and New Zealand refineries an abnormally low price for raw sugar. The result was to lower the profit from milling in Fiji while correspondingly increasing the refinery profit.

CSR shareholders certainly had no reason for complaint about the overall level of profits. From 1892 (despite the general depression about that time), CSR paid a regular dividend of 10 per cent every year, increased to 12½ per cent between 1912 and 1915. Moreover, the dividend was paid on a growing amount of share capital, amounting to £3.25 million in 1914. Much of the increase in capital was due to transfers from reserves rather than the subscription of fresh capital. Large profits generated public criticism, and there was an interesting exchange of letters on this subject between R. Gemmell Smith, CSR manager in Fiji, and E. W. Knox. In a letter dated 21 October 1902, Smith described himself as 'the oldest Manager you have out of Sydney and a shareholder with my all in the Company'. He went on:

A monopoly such as ours, if it wishes to avoid abuse from outsiders must do something more than pay bare wages, our keenness (called meanness by outsiders) to save money in every possible way with the sole object of paying large dividends will always be the cause of the C.S.R. being hated. Now why not pay a smaller dividend for a time? (the large shareholders are all rich men) say 7½% and let the other 2½% if earned go towards the payment of a bonus to Officers and Men, erect schools, pay for teachers at all our mills . . . then when letters came to Managers to cut down expenses their hands would be strengthened when they appealed to the officers and wage earners for economy and they would not hear the Company so often called 'mean' or a 'bloated monopoly'.

In so far as Smith was referring to CSR employees in Fiji, he probably meant only the 200 Europeans, not the 4500 Indians directly employed by CSR. The response from Knox, on 3 November 1902, was a classic piece of capitalist logic-chopping. He told Smith that an increase in wages would be unjustified: 'we are giving full market value for the service rendered'. Further, Knox saw nothing wrong with the dividend of 10 per cent, and the 900 shareholders included many women or trustees for women and children, as well as professional men and others. It would be a 'grave breach of trust' to divert part of the profits to the purposes suggested by Smith. Clearly, wrote Knox, 'any business undertaking must be run on business and not on philanthropic principles'. Incidentally, the same principle concerning a company's duty to make as much profit as possible for its shareholders is nowadays frequently claimed to be an overriding obligation for those who control the investment of employees' superannuation funds: they should not allow themselves to be influenced by considerations of morality such as a given company's anti-union stance (as in the case of Peko-Wallsend) or its support for apartheid in South Africa. On this line of thought, profit is the only relevant consideration in investment decisions.

Cane farmers as well as workers reviled CSR as 'the octopus'. Actually public criticism from farmers tended to be subdued as they were fearful of the company's economic power. Many Queensland farmers and storekeepers were in debt to CSR, often for cash advances with which to pay wages, the security for such loans being commonly liens over farmers' crops. The lender had the right to seize the crop if the debt were not paid. Moreover, farmers and workers were not united. Cane farmers were small, with holdings averaging forty acres each; and in terms of income and dependence upon others, there was little difference between small farmers and cane cutters. Yet while the average cane farmer may be counted among the common people in such respects, he was often an employer on a small scale. In the sugar workers' strike of 1911, most farmers sided with CSR in opposing wage increases for field hands, although the point was made that farmers could not afford to pay higher wages because they were themselves being screwed by CSR and its allies.

By 1908 farmers had established canegrowers' unions of their own,   259 advocating a fairer deal in the industry; and this agitation, coupled with widespread public criticism of CSR as a monopoly, led to the appointment of a federal Royal Commission in 1911. Just before this, an incident occurred which provides an insight into relations between big business and a free press. A Sydney newspaper, *The Sun*, published an article attacking CSR as 'a monopoly that does not hesitate to wring the last penny out of the people of Australia' through increases in the price of refined sugar. Knox was incensed, not merely by the contents of the article but by the fact that E. P. Simpson was a director of this newspaper—and Minter, Simpson and Co. handled CSR's legal affairs. It may be added that Simpson also played an important, if shadowy, role in politics. He acted as a sort of bagman for conservative politicians such as R. Philp in Queensland. Thus in 1906 Simpson paid out a total amount of £3000 (evidently from business sources such as CSR) to groups in Brisbane and Adelaide for use in 'the Anti-Socialistic campaign'.

In response to a complaint from Knox about *The Sun* article, Simpson explained, in a letter dated 6 September 1911, that he and other directors of the newspaper had not seen the article before publication and that unfortunately 'the Editors and Sub-Editors of nearly all the leading Journals in Australia have marked Socialistic tendencies'. The incident would not recur: Simpson had arranged, with reference to the sugar question, that 'no original matter shall appear in the paper on this subject unless it has first been brought before the Directors in which case I shall have the opportunity of either approving of the article or resigning if it appears'. Five days later, Knox on behalf of the CSR board of directors stated firmly that, if there were to be another such attack on CSR in *The Sun*, 'we can only assume that it will signify your wish to be relieved of the charge of our legal business which has been in the hands of your firm for between fifty and sixty years'.

Silencing a newspaper was one thing. Dealing with a Royal Commission which was determined to probe the sugar situation was more difficult. In its report in 1912, the Commission analysed relationships between various groups in the industry in Australia. Farmers sold their cane to mills, of which there were about forty manufacturing raw sugar. Most were proprietary mills, and CSR's plants milled one-third of the total output of raw sugar. Each mill determined the price to be paid for cane in its own area and there was virtually no competition between them. Superficially, those farmers who sold cane to the central mills which had been set up with state financial aid were in a relatively good position. However, these central mills were not true growers' co-operatives. Some shareholders were not canegrowers, and a large proportion of canegrowers were not shareholders. The latter group was often discriminated against in the price paid for cane: sometimes it was an abnormally low price, with shareholder-growers taking their profits mainly from the milling side.

Relations between millers and refiners were not subject to such thorny problems. CSR figured prominently in both categories. The company did not enjoy an absolute monopoly of refining, as there was a nominal rival, the Millaquin Sugar Refining Co. at Bundaberg. The utter insignificance of this competition became apparent when J. Johnston, general manager of the Millaquin Co., gave evidence to the Royal Commission. The evidence is reproduced here as an illuminating, not to say hilarious, example of price leadership in Australian industry.

Question. While on the subject of your relations with the Colonial Sugar Refining Company, it was brought under the notice of my colleagues in Sydney that there was concerted action between the two companies as to the price at which you sell your sugar. If the Colonial Sugar Refining Company advertise a rise in the price, Millaquin, in the same paper, and immediately underneath, advertise a rise, and similarly with a fall in price. What is the history of that? *Answer.—* The history of that is that some twenty years ago, when I was managing the Sydney agency of the Millaquin-Yengarie Sugar Company, I found that the Colonial Sugar Refining Company's sugar [price] would rise and fall, and I would know nothing about it until the next day. The result was that the papers got into the country with no advertisement about any change in our prices, and it interfered, to some extent, with my business. One man, Mr. Copland, of Wagga, came in, and I said—'Do you want any sugar?'. He said, 'No. I ordered 10 tons from the Colonial Sugar Refining Company yesterday. You know their sugar is down £1.' I said, 'I know they are down £1, but we are down £1, too.' He said, 'Why don't you advertise it? You never let me know you were down £1.'

The consequence was that I telephoned to the Sydney Daily Telegraph and the Sydney Morning Herald, and arranged with them that, even if was 12 o'clock at night, whenever the Colonial Sugar Refining Company put in an advertisement, they were to ring me up, and I would instruct them. It got a little monotonous having to answer the telephone at all hours of the night. I went to the theatre one night, and when I got home the girl said that the telephone bell had been going nearly all the evening, and that some one at the Daily Telegraph wanted to speak to me. I got on to the Daily Telegraph Office, and found that the Colonial Sugar Refining Company had gone down £1. As a result, I went to the newspaper offices the next day, and gave them written instructions that there was my advertisement, not once a week or twice a week, but if the Colonial Sugar Refining Company raised the price of their sugar, I followed suit, and, if the Colonial Sugar Refining Company lowered their price, I followed suit, and they were to put my advertisement right underneath the company's advertisement, so that my customers would know that I was either up or down.

That is the history of the whole business—which, I may tell you, puzzled the Colonial Sugar Refining Company's people for years. In fact, Mr. De Loitte came into my office one day, and said, 'Well, Johnston, tell me how you do it. I went to the theatre last night, and did not give them that advertisement until I came back from the theatre. I thought I was going to euchre you.'

Question. Of course, the reason for the whole thing is that you cannot compete with the Colonial Sugar Refining Company, and are bound to follow them up or down—they are too strong to fight? *Answer.*—I am always fighting them.

Question. You are not fighting them by means of lower prices. You are fighting them by pushing sugar at prices which are regulated by theirs? *Answer.*—You will see by the profits of refining that I cannot afford to fight them very much.[11]

Because of its monopolistic position, CSR was able to determine both the price of refined sugar to be charged to Australian consumers, and the price of raw sugar. The company's price-fixing policy was subject to only two constraints. One, as the Royal Commission put it, was that the price to be paid to millers for raw sugar must be sufficiently high to avoid squeezing producers of the raw material out of existence. The other constraint was that CSR's price for sugar must not be so high as to encourage large importations of sugar. This second point needs to be considered in relation to the high Australian import duty of £6 per ton on cane sugar. CSR took advantage of this. Actually, some sugar was imported into Australia each year, but not in competition with CSR. Australian production of sugar was insufficient to meet total demand, so that some imports were needed to make up the shortfall. CSR itself was involved in importing.[12]

Summing up, the Commission stated that there was a 'virtual abeyance of competition in the sugar industry'. Drily phrased, the situation was described as follows:

The refiners dictate prices to the millers; the millers dictate prices to the growers. Such dictation is not necessarily inconsistent with a reasonable distribution of profits, presuming the refiners and millers exercise the power, which they possess, subject to the injunction to love one's neighbour as oneself. A priori, an expectation that such an injunction would be observed in the conduct of business concerns would imply a more sanguine view of human nature than can be claimed by Your Commissioners.[13]

As a remedy for this situation, the Commission—after rejecting the idea of nationalizing sugar refining—recommended that there should be public control of the prices of sugar cane and raw sugar. In particular, the price to be paid for cane should be set for each mill area by boards comprising farmers and millers, with independent chairmen. In effect, the function of these boards would be to secure fair prices for growers in much the same way as arbitration tribunals were supposed to fix fair wages for workers. In the following few years, this new system was put into effect by the Commonwealth and Queensland governments, while wages boards were set up to cover sugar workers.

CSR objected to the Commission's recommendations. Claiming to be a free trader, Knox argued that CSR was not a monopoly: it had to face competition from imported sugar and it could do so effectively, no matter how much the import duty might be reduced. It was an argument which might have been valid half a century earlier, before CSR entered the milling sector, but in 1912 the effect of abolishing the sugar import duty would have been to wipe out most of the Australian industry, with disastrous effects upon CSR's heavy investment in mills. For the purpose of argument, Knox chose to ignore this, knowing full well that there was no possibility of the import duty being abolished.

However, Knox had a valid point with reference to the Commission's main rationale. Although the Commission was largely concerned with the economics of sugar, its basic standpoint was strategic, related to national defence, as stated in its report:

The problem of the Sugar Industry to-day is not, save in subordinate respects, a problem of industry, of wealth, or of production; it is primarily and essentially a problem of settlement and defence . . . The Commonwealth to-day is brought face to face with one of the gravest problems . . . the settlement of tropical and semi-tropical areas by a white population . . . If the ideal of a White Australia is to become an enduring actuality, some means must be discovered of establishing industries within the tropical regions. So long as these regions are unoccupied, they are an invitation to invasion . . . it follows that the supreme justification for the protection of the Sugar Industry is the part that the industry has contributed, and will, as we hope, continue to contribute to the problems of the settlement and defence of the northern portion of the Australian continent . . . Relatively to it, all other issues are of minor importance.[14]

This extraordinary statement was a reflection of the peculiar Australian obsession with the fear of invasion from Asia. The context was nationalism, racism, White Australia and the expulsion of Kanakas; and the fear became more acute after the Japanese defeated the Russians in a war in 1905. Four years later, compulsory military training of youths was introduced in Australia, and in 1910 this was extended by a federal Labor government to cover all males between the ages of 12 and 25. However, to place the whole sugar industry within this framework of thought was quite remarkable. Such solicitousness redounded to the advantage of CSR, but E. W. Knox himself saw things differently at the time. He denied claims by the chairman of the Royal Commission that the imposition of a federal import duty on sugar in 1901 was related to a desire to protect north Queensland from possible invasion. Knox declared:

So far as we know, no such argument was put forward at that time, for even people who have no knowledge of war are aware that an invading force can find a foothold and means of subsistence in an agricultural district, while it could not live for a week in the wild country of the Queensland coast line without drawing supplies from its base.[15]

Perhaps Knox developed a more patriotic approach to such matters after the outbreak of the First World War. In 1915 Knox and Prime Minister W. M. Hughes agreed upon the principles of an agreement under which CSR, for a negotiated fee, was to refine and distribute sugar in Australia on behalf of the government. The Commonwealth imposed an embargo on imports of sugar, and this prohibition has remained in force ever since. It is never mentioned by Australian politicians today when they criticize the existence of barriers to trade in agricultural products erected by the USA and the European Economic Community. Protection of sugar is a sacred cow in Australia — and CSR was the first strong home-grown industrial monopoly.

There is an interesting tailpiece to the story of the Royal Commission of 1912. In an effort to unveil CSR's profits, the Commission demanded certain information on production and finance. The company refused to comply, on the grounds that its internal accounts were not such as to allow it to distinguish its operations in Australia from those in Fiji and other countries, and that matters concerning the company's internal management and its activities outside Australia were not subject to Commonwealth jurisdiction. After Knox and other CSR representatives declined to appear at later meetings of the Commission to give evidence, a test case of prosecution for contempt of court was brought against one of the CSR directors, Sir Normand MacLaurin. He was found guilty and fined but this judgement was subsequently overruled by proceedings in the High Court and the Privy Council. The latter body fully vindicated CSR in its refusal to supply information to the Royal Commission.

In this confrontation, CSR feared that disclosure of its inner workings would adversely affect its profitability and standing in relation to both the general public and rival businessmen. Yet in the eyes of men like Knox there was also an important principle at stake: should the capitalist state be allowed to meddle in the affairs of a reputable capitalist company? Knox told the Royal Commission at one stage: 'What the Company most wants is to be left alone, so long as its actions are in conformity with the law.' Of course this begged the question of what the law was in particular instances. Most Australians probably reckoned that CSR was breaking the law embodied in the Royal Commissions Act, and so did Judges Higgins and Isaacs on the High Court of Australia. Chief Justice Griffith and Judge Barton thought otherwise and so did the Privy Council in London.

Capitalism and the Professions

Developments in this Royal Commission illustrated the inter-connections between business, the universities and the professions and showed the beginnings of the subservience of the professions to commercial interests so accurately forecast by Marx: 'The bourgeoisie has stripped of its halo every occupation hitherto honoured and looked up to with reverent awe. It has converted the physician, the lawyer, the priest, the poet, the man of science, into its paid wage labourers.' [16]

Finding loopholes in law at this high level was a costly business. There was large remuneration for lawyers who specialized in company matters, and some of these men were assimilated into higher levels of the bourgeoisie. There was E. P. Simpson, for one. Another was Adrian Knox, brother of E. W. Knox. As a leading barrister, Adrian Knox was briefed by Simpson to advise on certain points relating to the Royal Commission; and in 1919 Adrian Knox was appointed Chief Justice of the High Court, succeeding Griffith.

Sir Normand MacLaurin was a prominent doctor as well as being a director of CSR and other large companies such as the Bank of New South Wales. In addition, he was both a member of the upper house of the New South Wales parliament, and Chancellor of the University of Sydney. E. W. Knox was a Fellow of the Senate of that university.

Another colleague of MacLaurin's at this time was Sir Charles Mackellar, a medical man who was prominent in NSW public administration, including child welfare. Like MacLaurin, Mackellar was a director of CSR and other companies, though he was not on the university Senate. MacLaurin arrived in Australia in 1868 as a navy surgeon; he died in 1914, leaving an estate valued at nearly £70 000. There were often close social connections between such men. Mackellar married a daughter of Thomas Buckland, a businessman who was a director of both the Bank of New South Wales and CSR. Club membership cemented such relationships. Extraordinarily, three successive generations of the Knox family were presidents of the Union Club in Sydney at various dates between 1882 and the 1940s; and the same three generations sat on the boards of CSR, the United Insurance Co. and the Commercial Banking Company of Sydney.

In conclusion, a tentative observation concerning the nature of Australian capitalism in this formative period may be permitted. As is still the case, there were several categories of capitalist. One group consisted of swindlers and charlatans, who were particularly noticeable in the 1880s. Another group comprised a large number of relatively honest small businessmen, some flourishing, others floundering. Then there were clusters of big businessmen of the likes of E. W. Knox. This last category had no affinity with the common people, though acknowledging them as loyal servants on occasion. Yet for all the ruthless, hard-driving character of these men—which may be attributed to the dynamics of capitalism itself—it may be said that they played a constructive role in rapid economic growth in these early generations. CSR's efficiency was the reason given by the Royal Commission for rejecting the idea of nationalizing sugar refining.

In the highly unlikely event of such businessmen ever having read the *Manifesto of the Communist Party*, they would have found that Marx and Engels freely acknowledged the progressive role of capitalism:

> The bourgeoisie, historically, has played a most revolutionary part ... It has accomplished wonders far surpassing Egyptian pyramids, Roman aqueducts, and Gothic cathedrals ... The need of a constantly expanding market for its products chases the bourgeoisie over the whole surface of the globe ... The bourgeoisie, during its rule of scarce one hundred years, has created more massive and more colossal productive forces than have all preceding generations together.[17]

It may be noted further that in the period before the First World War, capitalists like MacLaurin and Mackellar made an intellectual contribution to Australian society. They showed signs of public-spirited endeavour through their activity on the boards of public institutions. To what extent could this be said of many of the big businessmen in the late 1980s? The stars among them are company raiders and takeover operators, interested only in quick financial killings. These 'paper entrepreneurs' create nothing and make no useful contribution to society.

Although it is easy to exaggerate changes of this kind, there were undoubtedly important modifications in the nature of capitalism later in the twentieth century. There were also major changes in the composition and condition of the common people, especially the working class. These are the subject of consideration in the second volume of this work.

Notes

Introduction

[1] See E. L. Wheelwright, 'Marxist Analysis of Capitalism in Australia: Past, Present and Future', in Edwin Dowdy (ed.), *Marxist Policies To-day in Socialist and Capitalist Countries*, UQP, Brisbane, 1986.

[2] P. J. Proudhon, *Qu'est ce que la propriété?*, 1840, and Pierre le Pesant, Sieur de Boisguillebert, *Dissertation sur la nature des richesses, de l'argent et des tributs*, Guillaumin edition, 1843; both cited in Joseph A. Schumpeter, *History of Economic Analysis*, Allen & Unwin, London, 1954, pp. 458, 215–16.

[3] Henry Reynolds, *Frontier*, Allen & Unwin, Sydney, 1987, pp. 19–31, 83–104. See also his *The Other Side of the Frontier: Aboriginal Resistance to the European Invasion of Australia*, Penguin, Melbourne, 1982, which documents in detail the Aboriginal reaction to the invaders: 'The costs of colonisation were much higher than traditional historical accounts have suggested' (p. 2).

[4] The term 'squatter' is peculiarly Australian, originally meaning: 'a person who had "squatted" on unoccupied land for pastoral purposes without official sanction ... Slowly the term took on a class meaning, carrying a capitalistic suggestion and social prestige', *The Australian Encyclopaedia*, vol. 9, Grolier Society, Sydney, 1983, p. 166.

[5] See his 'Essay on Colonial Architecture' [1835] cited in Morton Herman, *The Early Australian Architects and Their Work*, Angus & Robertson, Sydney, 1954, p. 85.

6 Robert Hughes, *The Fatal Shore*, Collins-Harvill, New York, 1987, p. xiv.

7 Patrick O'Farrell notes that 'most of the Irish came from a pre-industrial—pre-modern—rural society, where both tradition and religion remained very strong, as did a peculiarly intense sense of kinship and family life . . . Few were natural radicals. They protested not so much against the system, but against their exclusion from its benefits. Give them a modest share of prosperity and the conservatism of a peasant and religious people asserts itself.', *The Irish in Australia*, University of New South Wales Press, Sydney, 1987, p. 16.

8 Hughes, *The Fatal Shore*, p. xiv. Konni Zilliacus, the British Labour MP, suggested to one of the authors in 1966, that when attempting to compare industrial development under capitalist and communist systems, the original basic capitalist unit taken should be the British Empire, not just Britain. In which case not only should slave labour in plantations and near-slave labour in gold and silver mines be taken into account, but also convict labour in Australia, which could be regarded as Britain's Siberia. On the other hand, David Neal thinks that 'the link Hughes draws between the Gulag and transportation is strained; exterminations in the Nazi concentration camps were undoubtedly worse'. See his review of *The Fatal Shore* in *Australian Society*, March 1987, p. 42.

9 Hughes, *The Fatal Shore*, p. 195.

10 Ibid., pp. 594–6.

11 Jack Mundey, 'A Wider Vision for Trade Unions', in Greg Crough, Ted Wheelwright and Ted Wilshire (eds), *Australia and World Capitalism*, Penguin, Melbourne, 1980.

12 Colleen Ryan, 'Bankruptcy Scam Uncovered: How to Go Broke without Going Bust', *Sydney Morning Herald*, 3 February 1987, p. 17.

13 Warwick Armstrong and John Bradbury, 'Industrialisation and Class Structure in Australia, Canada and Argentina, 1870–1980', in E. L. Wheelwright and Ken Buckley (eds), *Essays in the Political Economy of Australian Capitalism*, vol. 5, ANZ Book Co., Sydney, 1983.

14 J. Fogarty, *Desarrollo Economico*, Vol. 17, No. 65, April-June 1977, p. 140, cited in Ricardo E. Gerardi, *Australia, Argentina and World Capitalism: A Comparative Analysis, 1830–1945*, Occasional Paper No. 8, Transnational Corporations Research Project, University of Sydney, 1985, p. 9.

15 Speech at the anniversary of the *People's Paper*, April 1985, cited in Francis D. Klingender, *Art and the Industrial Revolution*, Carrington, London, 1947, pp. 131–2.

16 Karl Marx, *Capital*, vol. III, ch. XV, International Publishers Co., New York, 1967, p. 254.

17 Patrick Ford, *Cardinal Moran and the ALP*, MUP, Melbourne, 1966, p. 81.

18 Francis G. Castles, *The Working Class and Welfare*, Allen & Unwin, Sydney, 1985, ch. 2.

19 Karl Marx, *A Contribution to the Critique of Political Economy*, Progress Publishers, Moscow, 1970, p. 21.

20 'By 1903 Rev. J. A. Knowles was claiming for the Irish the lion's share of credit for Federation, arguing that the frustration and denial imposed by Irish circumstances produced unparalleled bursts of energy and commitment in Australia', Patrick O'Farrell, *The Irish in Australia*, p. 249.

21 Karl Marx, *Capital*, Allen & Unwin edition, London, 1946, vol. I, p. 640.

22 The nature and extent of these arrangements were outlined in the first book on the subject by H. L. Wilkinson, *The Trust Movement in Australia*, Critchley, Melbourne, 1914.

23 Douglas Niven, 'A Case Study of Unilever Australia (Holdings) Pty Ltd', *Australian Studies of Transnational Corporations: Collected Student Papers*, Transnational Corporations Research Project, University of Sydney, 1981.

Chapter 1

1 James Cook in 1770: J. C. Beaglehole (ed.), *The Journals of Captain James Cook: The Voyage of the Endeavour, 1768-1771*, CUP, Cambridge, 1955, p. 399.

2 Diane Bell, *Daughters of the Dreaming*, McPhee Gribble/Allen & Unwin, Melbourne, 1983, p. 226.

3 N. G. Butlin, *Our Original Aggression: Aboriginal Populations of Southeastern Australia, 1788-1850*, Allen & Unwin, Sydney, 1983; interview with Peter White, University of Sydney *News*, 19, 2, February 1987.

4 C. D. Rowley, *The Destruction of Aboriginal Society*, ANUP, Canberra, 1970, p. 28.

5 Karl Marx, *Capital*, Allen & Unwin edition, London, 1946, vol. I, p. 775.

6 P. M. C. Hasluck, *Black Australians: A Survey of Native Policy in Western Australia, 1829-1897*, MUP, Melbourne, 1942, p. 203.

7 C. D. Rowley, *The Remote Aborigines*, Penguin, Melbourne, 1972, p. 253.

8 C. D. Rowley, *Outcasts in White Australia*, Penguin, Melbourne, 1972, p. 112.

9 Karl Marx, *Capital*, Allen & Unwin edition, London, 1946, vol. I, pp. 738-9.

Chapter 2

1 The sub-heading of this chapter is taken from N. G. Butlin, *Trends in Australian Income Distribution: A First Glance*, Working Paper No. 17, Department of Economic History, ANU, Canberra, September 1983, p. 26.

2 Karl Marx, *Capital*, Allen and Unwin edition, London, vol. I, pp. 736–7. The text quoted here was originally edited by F. Engels in 1889. In this translation from the German, the term 'primitive accumulation' was used. However, Eden and Cedar Paul, in a later translation of the book, preferred the words 'primary accumulation'.

3 Ibid., p. 786.

4 Ibid., p. 737.

5 S. M. Onslow (ed.), *Some Early Records of the Macarthurs of Camden*, Rigby, Sydney, 1973 reprint, p. 2.

6 D. R. Hainsworth, *Builders and Adventurers*, Cassell, Melbourne, 1968, pp. 7, 12–13.

7 S.M. Onslow, *Some Early Records of the Macarthurs of Camden*, p. 51.

8 D. R. Hainsworth, *The Sydney Traders*, Cassell, Melbourne, 1971, pp. 5, 27.

9 M. J. E. Steven, 'Enterprise', in G. J. Abbott and N. B. Nairn (eds), *Economic Growth of Australia, 1788–1821*, MUP, Melbourne, 1969, p. 122.

10 Waterhouse to Banks, 24 October 1795 (Banks Papers, A782, Mitchell Library, Sydney).

11 D. O. G. Shann, *Economic History of Australia*, CUP, Cambridge, 1930, p. 12.

12 Colonial Office Records, 201/123, Documents D, 61, 616, Public Records Office, London.

13 D. R. Hainsworth, *The Sydney Traders*, p. 101. Emphasis in the original.

Chapter 3

1 From Mary Gilmore's poem 'Old Botany Bay', quoted in Stephen Murray-Smith, *Dictionary of Australian Quotations*, Heinemann, Melbourne, 1984, p. 93.

2 L. L. Robson, *The Convict Settlers of Australia*, MUP, Melbourne, 1965, pp. 157–8.

3 Douglas Hay, Peter Linebaugh and Edward Thompson, *Albion's Fatal Tree*, Allen Lane, London, 1975, pp. 48–9, 62–3.

4 Karl Marx and Frederick Engels, *Collected Works*, Lawrence & Wishart, London, 1982, vol. 38, p. 461.

5 Frederick Engels, *The Condition of the Working Class in England in 1844*, Allen & Unwin, London, 1950 reprint, pp. 126, 128.

6 E. P. Thompson, *The Making of the English Working Class*, Penguin, London, 1981 reprint, pp. 59–60.

7 Kathleen Fitzpatrick, *Sir John Franklin in Tasmania, 1837–1843*, MUP, Melbourne, 1949, pp. 80–1.

8 Alan Atkinson, 'Four Patterns of Convict Protest', *Labour History*, 37, November 1979, p. 32.

9 John Ritchie (ed.), *The Evidence to the Bigge Reports*, Heinemann, Melbourne, 1971, vol. 1, p. 14.

10 E. G. Wakefield, *A Letter from Sydney*, Everyman edition, London, 1929, pp. 37–8.

11 Evidence of G. Druitt, in J. Ritchie, *The Evidence to the Bigge Reports*, vol. 1, p. 38.

12 Kathleen Fitzpatrick, *Sir John Franklin in Tasmania, 1837–1843*, p. 90.

13 John Williams, 'Irish Female Convicts and Tasmania', *Labour History*, 44, May 1983, p. 11.

14 A. T. Yarwood, *Samuel Marsden: The Great Survivor*, MUP, Melbourne, 1977, p. 277.

15 James Atkinson, *An Account of the State of Agriculture and Grazing in New South Wales*, [1826], facsimile reprint, SUP, Sydney, 1975, p. 116.

16 Alan Atkinson, 'Four Patterns of Convict Protest', *Labour History*, November 1979, pp. 38–9.

17 Evidence to Bigge Enquiry, in John Ritchie, *The Evidence to the Bigge Reports*, vol. 2, p. 73.

Chapter 4

1 Karl Marx, *Capital*, vol. I, Allen & Unwin edition, London, 1946, p. 791.

2 Ibid., pp. 791–6.

3 A. G. L. Shaw, *Convicts and the Colonies*, Faber, London, 1966, p. 231.

4 K. Buckley, 'E. G. Wakefield and the Alienation of Crown Land in NSW to 1847', *Economic Record*, XXIII, April 1957, p. 80.

5 M. F. Lloyd Prichard (ed.), *Collected Works of Edward Gibbon Wakefield*, Collins, Glasgow, 1968, p. 518.

6 Goderich to Governor Darling, 9 January 1831, *Historical Records of Australia*, I, XVI, p. 21.

7 An Emigrant Mechanic, *Settlers and Convicts*, ed. C. M. H. Clark, MUP, Melbourne, 1953, p. 226.

8 Wakefield's evidence to Select Committee on Disposal of Land in British Colonies, *British Parl. Papers*, 1836, Qq.875, 954.

9 R. B. Madgwick, *Immigration into Eastern Australia, 1788–1851*, SUP, Sydney, 1969, pp. 91, 105; A. J. Hammerton, '"Without Natural Protectors": Female Immigration to Australia, 1832–36', *Historical Studies*, 65, October 1975, p. 557.

10 S. Sidney, *The Three Colonies of Australia*, Ingram Cooke, London, 1852, p. 128.

11 Brian Fitzpatrick, *The British Empire in Australia, 1834–1939*, Macmillan, Melbourne, 1969 reissue, p. 66.

12 Macarthur's evidence to Committee on Transportation, *British Parl. Papers*, 1837, Qq.2491–2, 2498, 2503. Incidentally, the Macarthurs were able to employ more than the official maximum of seventy convicts, because there were three adult males (brothers) in the family.

13 Macarthur's evidence, Q.3321. Note the analogous quotation from James Burns in the preceding chapter of this book. There is a long lineage of conservative thought.

14 John M. Ward, *James Macarthur: Colonial Conservative, 1798–1867*, SUP, Sydney, 1981, p. 163.

Chapter 5

1 Copy of a letter from Bishop of Australia (a staunch Tory) to a friend in England, 17 February 1846, enclosed in Gipps to Stanley, 23 February 1846, *Historical Records of Australia*, Ser. I, XXIV, p. 786.

2 Elizabeth Macarthur rather than her husband John should be given most of the credit for improved breeding of sheep on the family estate. John Macarther was away in London between 1801 and 1806 and again between 1809 and 1817. Elizabeth had sole responsibility for the management of the estate at these times. She also reared eight children.

3 F. J. A. Broeze, 'Private Enterprise and the Peopling of Australasia, 1831–50', *Economic History Review*, XXXV, 2, May 1982, p. 240.

4 S. J. Butlin, *Foundations of the Australian Monetary System, 1788–1851*, MUP, Melbourne, 1953, p. 509.

5 Philip McMichael, 'Crisis in Pastoral Capital Accumulation', in E. L. Wheelwright and Ken Buckley (eds), *Essays in the Political Economy of Australian Capitalism*, vol. 4, 1980, p. 17.

6 *Sydney Morning Herald*, 23 April 1844. Hamilton's targets were the forerunners of today's 'Pitt Street farmers', although nowadays the prime motive for absentee investment in land through stockbrokers and the like is to benefit from tax lurks.

7 Michael Cannon, *Who's Master? Who's Man?*, Nelson, Melbourne, 1971,

p. 82. On the other hand, the staple topic of conversation among women of 'the higher orders' was 'bad servants' (p. 17).

8 Gipps to Russell, 13 September 1841, *Historical Records of Australia*, I, XXI, p. 505.

9 Elizabeth Windschuttle, 'Discipline, Domestic Training and Social Control: The Female School of Industry, Sydney, 1826–1847', *Labour History*, 39, November 1980, pp. 10–11.

10 Gwyneth M. Dow, *Samuel Terry: The Botany Bay Rothschild*, SUP, Sydney, 1974, p. 240. The author, herself a descendant of Terry, says frankly that her own father 'never had to work, and was even able to survive the Depression [of the 1930s] ... on what was cryptically but tediously referred to time and again as "living on our capital" ' (p. 232).

11 S. J. Butlin, *Foundations of the Australian Monetary System*, p. 541.

12 David S. Macmillan, *The Debtor's War*, Cheshire, Melbourne, 1960, p. 32.

13 *The Australian*, 28 October 1841.

14 Paul de Serville, *Port Phillip Gentlemen*, OUP, Melbourne, 1980, p. 40.

15 Douglas Pike, *Paradise of Dissent: South Australia, 1829-1857*, MUP, Melbourne, second edition, 1967, p. 131.

16 John Williams, 'Irish Female Convicts and Tasmania', *Labour History*, 44, May 1983, p. 7. Transportation of convicts to Tasmania continued until 1852 when Fitz Roy, Governor of New South Wales, remarked that there were then 'few English criminals who would not regard a free passage to gold-fields via Hobart town as a great boon'.

Chapter 6

1 V. I. Lenin referred to a merger of industrial and finance capital in his *Imperialism: The Highest Stage of Capitalism*, but the evidence was mainly applicable to the USA and Germany. In relation to Britain, see Peter Cain, 'J. A. Hobson: Financial Capitalism and Imperialism in Late Victorian and Edwardian England', *Journal of Imperial and Commonwealth History*, XIII, 3, May 1985; Y. Cassis, 'Bankers in English Society in the Late Nineteenth Century', *Economic History Review*, XXXVIII, 2, May 1985.

2 'British' here relates to capital and people based primarily in the United Kingdom, in contrast to people living or based in Australia. Most of the latter were also British in law.

3 *Age*, 24 February 1860. Quoted in J. A. La Nauze, *Political Economy in Australia*, MUP, Melbourne, 1949, p. 123.

4 Geoffrey Serle, *The Golden Age: A History of the Colony of Victoria, 1851-1861*, MUP, Melbourne, 1963, p. 239.

5 N. G. Butlin, in *Australia, 1938-1988: Bicentennial History Project, Bulletin*, no. 2.

6 G. Serle, *The Golden Age*, p. 143.

7 Geoffrey Serle, *The Rush to be Rich: A History of the Colony of Victoria, 1883-1889*, MUP, Melbourne, 1971, p. 269.

8 R. M. Crawford, *Australia*, Hutchinson, London, third edition, 1970, p. 79.

9 J. M. Powell, *The Public Lands of Australia Felix*, OUP, Melbourne, 1970, p. 85; Margaret Kiddle, *Men of Yesterday: A Social History of the Western District of Victoria, 1834-1890*, MUP, Melbourne, 1961, p. 468.

10 R. M. Crawford, *An Australian Perspective*, University of Wisconsin Press, Madison, 1960, pp. 24-5.

11 Graeme Davison, *The Rise and Fall of Marvellous Melbourne*, MUP, Melbourne, 1979, p. 96.

12 G. Serle, *The Golden Age*, p. 223.

13 H. Howitt, *Land, Labour and Gold*, facsimile of 1855 edition, SUP, Sydney, 1972, Vol. I, pp. 36, 43-4.

14 Humphrey McQueen, 'Convicts and Rebels', *Labour History*, 15, November 1968, p. 30.

Chapter 7

1 P. N. Lamb, 'Crown Land Policy and Government Finance in New South Wales, 1856-1900', *Australian Economic History Review*, VII, 1, March 1967, p. 50.

2 D. W. A. Baker, 'The Origins of Robertson's Land Acts', *Historical Studies*, 30, May 1958, p. 181; R. B. Walker, *Old New England: A History of the Northern Tablelands of New South Wales, 1818-1900*, SUP, Sydney, 1966, p. 65.

3 C. M. H. Clark (ed.), *Select Documents in Australian History, 1851-1900*, Angus & Robertson, Sydney, 1955, pp. 127, 133.

4 Geoffrey Serle, *The Rush to be Rich: A History of the Colony of Victoria, 1883-1889*, MUP, Melbourne, 1971, p. 5; D. B. Waterson, *Squatter, Selector and Storekeeper: A History of the Darling Downs, 1859-93*, SUP, Sydney, 1968, p. 99.

5 J. M. Powell, *Yeomen and Bureaucrats: The Victorian Crown Lands Commission, 1878-79*, OUP, Melbourne, 1973, pp. 27, 52, 68.

6 John McQuilton, *The Kelly Outbreak, 1878-1880*, MUP, Melbourne, 1979, pp. 4, 208; Max Brown, *Australian Son*, Georgian House, Melbourne, 1956, pp. 280-1. It is ironic that a high proportion of members of the Victorian Police were Irishmen.

7 D. B. Waterson, *Squatter, Selector and Storekeeper*, p. 277.

8 Adam Smith, *The Wealth of Nations*, ed. E. Cannon, University Paperbacks, London, 1961, vol. I, p. 56.

9 Robin Gollan, *Radical and Working Class Politics: Eastern Australia, 1850-1910*, MUP, Melbourne, 1960, p. 105. The words of this resolution were lifted directly from George's *Progress and Poverty*.

10 Robert Skidelsky, *John Maynard Keynes*, Macmillan, London, 1983, vol. I, 1883-1920, pp. 41, 48.

11 J. M. Keynes, *Essays in Biography*, Hart-Davis, London, 1951, pp. 129-30.

Chapter 8

1 D. B. Waterson, *Squatter, Selector and Storekeeper: A History of the Darling Downs, 1857-93*, SUP, Sydney, 1968, p. 151.

2 Patricia Grimshaw, Chris McConville and Ellen McEwen (eds), *Families in Colonial Australia*, Allen & Unwin, Sydney, 1985, pp. 129-30.

3 Desley Deacon, 'Political Arithmetic: The Nineteenth-Century Australian Census and the Construction of the Dependent Woman', *Signs: Journal of Women in Culture and Society*, II, 1, 1985; Katrina Alford, 'Colonial Women's Employment as seen by Nineteenth-Century Statisticians and Twentieth-Century Economic Historians', *Labour History*, 51, November 1986. See also the debate between Katrina Alford and Tony Endres in *Labour History*, 52, May 1987.

4 Kay Daniels, Mary Murnane and Anne Picot, *Women in Australia: An Annotated Guide to Records*, AGPS, Canberra, 1977, p. xiii. It is not suggested that wife-desertion is found only among rural dwellers.

5 Geoffrey Blainey, *The Rush that Never Ended*, MUP, Melbourne, 1963, p. 98.

6 Robin Gollan, *The Coalminers of New South Wales: A History of the Union, 1860-1960*, MUP, Melbourne, 1963, p. 15.

7 *Australian Town and Country Journal*, 27 November 1886, p. 1114.

8 W. G. Spence, *Australia's Awakening*, Worker Trustees, Sydney, 1961, p. 53; G. L. Buxton, *The Riverina, 1861-1891*, MUP, Melbourne, 1967, p. 281.

9 J. A. Merritt, 'W. G. Spence and the 1890 Maritime Strike', *Historical Studies*, 60, April 1973, p. 598. See also Merritt's comprehensive work, *The Making of the AWU*, OUP, Melbourne, 1986.

10 Doreen Bridges (ed.), *Helen Palmer's Outlook*, Edwards and Shaw, Sydney, 1982, pp. 167-9.

11 D. J. Murphy (ed.), *The Big Strikes: Queensland, 1889-1965*, UQP, Brisbane, 1983, p. 91.

12 G. L. Buxton, *The Riverina*, p. 260.

[13] Brian Fitzpatrick, *The British Empire in Australia, 1834–1939*, Macmillan, Melbourne, 1969 reissue, p. 228.

[14] One of them is said to have been the father of Shorty O'Neil, who was president of the Barrier Industrial Council at Broken Hill from 1957 to 1969.

[15] *Shearers' Record*, July 1888.

[16] Tom Collins (Joseph Furphy), *Such is Life*, Lloyd O'Neil, Melbourne, 1970 reprint, p. 107.

Chapter 9

[1] Karl Marx, *Manifesto of the Communist Party*, in *Selected Works*, Lawrence and Wishart, London, 1945, vol. 1, p. 216.

[2] Maurice Dobb, *Studies in the Development of Capitalism*, Routledge, London, 1963, pp. 265–6.

[3] J. A. Merritt, 'W. G. Spence and the 1890 Maritime Strike', *Historical Studies*, 60, April 1973, p. 595.

[4] *Labour History*, 40, May 1981, p.93. Incidentally, Monash, who later became a general in the Australian army, was the son of a merchant.

[5] P. G. Macarthy, 'Wages for Unskilled Work and Margins for Skill: Australia, 1901–21', *Australian Economic History Review*, XII, 2, September 1972, p. 154. See also Denis Rowe, 'The Robust Navvy: The Railway Construction Worker in Northern New South Wales, 1854–1894', *Labour History*, 39, November 1980.

[6] G. Serle, *The Rush to be Rich: A History of the Colony of Victoria, 1883–1889*, MUP, Melbourne, 1971, p. 91; R. E. N. Twopeny, *Town Life in Australia*, facsimile of 1883 edition, Penguin, Melbourne, 1973, p. 193.

[7] T. A. Coghlan, *Labour and Industry in Australia*, Macmillan, Melbourne, 1969 reprint, III, p. 1495.

[8] Bettina Cass, 'Women's Place in the Class Structure', in E. L. Wheelwright and Ken Buckley (eds), *Essays in the Political Economy of Australian Capitalism*, vol. 3, 1978, p. 28.

[9] Margaret Barbalet, *Far From a Low Gutter Girl: The Forgotten World of State Wards: South Australia, 1887–1940*, OUP, Melbourne, 1983, p. 27.

[10] Karl Marx, *Capital*, Allen & Unwin edition, London, 1946, vol. I, pp. 464–5.

[11] Ray Markey, 'Women and Labour, 1880–1900', in Elizabeth Windschuttle (ed.), *Women, Class and History*, Fontana, Melbourne, 1980, p. 91.

[12] Desley Deacon, 'Political Arithmetic: The Nineteenth-Century Australian Census and the Construction of the Dependent Woman', *Signs: Journal of Women in Culture and Society*, II, 1, 1985, pp. 42, 46.

[13] Henry Reynolds, *The Other Side of the Frontier*, Penguin, Melbourne, 1982, pp. 173, 200.

14 Andrew Markus, 'Talka Longa Mouth: Aborigines and the Labour Movement, 1890–1970', in Ann Curthoys and Andrew Markus (eds), *Who Are Our Enemies*, Hale & Iremonger, Sydney, 1978, p. 139.

15 Henry Reynolds, *The Other Side of the Frontier*, p. 189.

16 Andrew Markus, 'Divided We Fall: The Chinese and the Melbourne Furniture Trade Union, 1870–1900', *Labour History*, 26, May 1974, p. 10.

17 W. G. Spence, *Australia's Awakening*, Worker Trustees, Sydney, 1961, pp. 51–3. Paradoxically, Aborigines, Maoris and American Negroes were exempted from the union's colour bar.

18 Richard Broome, *Victorians Arriving*, Fairfax Syme & Weldon, Sydney, 1984, p. 102.

19 R. H. Tawney, *Religion and the Rise of Capitalism*, Penguin, London, 1983; Max Weber, *The Protestant Ethic and the Spirit of Capitalism*, Allen & Unwin, London, 1976, first published in 1930.

20 Patrick Ford, *Cardinal Moran and the ALP*, MUP, Melbourne, 1966, pp. xix-xxi and chapter 9.

21 Ibid., p. 83 (emphasis added).

22 R. N. Spann, 'The Catholic Vote in Australia', in Henry Mayer (ed.), *Catholics and the Free Society*, Cheshire, Melbourne, 1961, p. 119.

23 Ibid., pp. 119–20, 134.

24 Patrick Ford, *Cardinal Moran and the ALP*, pp. 284–5. Moran died in 1911.

25 Ross Fitzgerald, *From the Dreaming to 1915: A History of Queensland*, UQP, Brisbane, 1982, p. 327.

26 David Adams (ed.), *The Letters of Rachel Henning*, Penguin, Melbourne, 1979, p. 208.

27 S. H. Fisher, 'An Accumulation of Misery?', *Labour History*, 40, May 1981, p. 27.

28 Karl Marx, *Capital*, vol. I, pp. 564, 567.

29 K. D. Buckley, *The Amalgamated Engineers in Australia, 1852–1920*, Economic History Department, ANU, Canberra, 1970, p. 97.

30 J. Hagan & C. Fisher, 'Piece-Work and Some of its Consequences in the Printing and Coal Mining Industries in Australia, 1850–1930', *Labour History*, 25, November 1973, p. 22.

31 T. A. Coghlan, *Labour and Industry in Australia*, III, pp. 1239–40.

32 N. G. Butlin, 'Long-Run Trends in Australian per capita Consumption', in Keith Hancock (ed.), *The National Income and Social Welfare*, Cheshire, Melbourne, 1965, p. 8. For a comprehensive refutation of the notion of a workingman's paradise, see Jenny Lee and Charles Fahey, 'A Boom for Whom? Some Developments in the Australian Labour Market, 1870–1891', *Labour History*, 50, May 1986.

33 Graeme Davison, David Dunstan and Chris McConville, *The Outcasts of Melbourne*, MUP, Melbourne, 1979, 1985, p. 54.

34 Graeme Davison, *The Rise and Fall of Marvellous Melbourne*, MUP,

Melbourne, 1979, p. 269; G. J. R. Linge, *Industrial Awakening: A Geography of Australian Manufacturing, 1788 to 1890*, ANUP, Canberra, 1979, p. 483.

35 R. W. Connell and T. H. Irving, *Class Structure in Australian History*, Longman Cheshire, Melbourne, 1980, p. 171.

36 Shirley Fisher, 'Sydney Women and the Workforce, 1870–90', in Max Kelly (ed.), *Nineteenth-Century Sydney*, SUP, Sydney, 1978.

37 Ellen McEwen, 'Family, Kin and Neighbours: The Newcastle Coalmining District, 1860–1900', *Australia 1888, Bulletin* No. 4, May 1980, p. 81.

38 R. V. Jackson, 'Building Societies and the Workers in Melbourne in the 1880s', *Labour History*, 47, November 1984, p. 29.

39 Graeme Davison, *The Rise and Fall of Marvellous Melbourne*, pp. 177–8.

40 R. H. Tawney, *Equality*, Allen & Unwin, London, 1931, p. 151.

Chapter 10

1 Adrian S. Merritt, 'The Development and Application of Masters and Servants Legislation in New South Wales, 1845 to 1930', unpublished PhD thesis, ANU, 1981, p. 324.

2 Ibid., pp. 325–6.

3 K. D. Buckley, *The Amalgamated Engineers in Australia, 1852-1920*, Economic History Department, ANU, Canberra, 1970, p. 67.

4 D. P. Crook, 'Occupations of the People of Brisbane . . . in the 1880s',*Historical Studies*, 37, November 1961, p. 64.

5 J. Hagan and C. Fisher, 'Piece-Work and Some of its Consequences in the Printing and Coal Mining Industries in Australia, 1850–1930', *Labour History*, 25, November 1973, p. 27.

6 George Black, *A History of the NSW Political Labor Party*, Jones, Sydney, n.d., No. 1, pp. 20–1.

7 John Miller (William Lane), *The Workingman's Paradise*, SUP, Sydney, 1980, facsimile text, p. 110.

8 Jean O'Connor, '1890: A Turning Point in Labour History', *Historical Studies*, 16, May 1951, pp. 357, 361.

9 K. D. Buckley, *The Amalgamated Engineers*, p. 109.

10 K. Buckley and K. Klugman, *The History of Burns Philp*, Burns Philp, Sydney, 1981, p. 36.

11 G. Serle, *The Rush to be Rich: A History of the Colony of Victoria, 1883-1889*, MUP, Melbourne, 1971, p. 110; Robin Gollan, *The Coalminers of New South Wales: A History of the Union, 1860-1960*, MUP, Melbourne, 1963, pp. 71–2.

12 F. S. Piggin, 'New South Wales Pastoralists and the Strikes of 1890 and 1891', *Historical Studies*, 56, April 1971, p. 549.

13 Evidence to NSW Royal Commission on Strikes, 1891, Q.5247.

14 Robin Gollan, *The Coalminers*, pp. 79, 86.

15 *Argus*, 1 September 1890.

16 Australian Agricultural Co. papers, letter of 28 September 1890 (ANU Archives).

17 *Australian Workman*, 15 November 1890.

18 K. D. Buckley, *The Amalgamated Engineers*, p. 116.

Chapter 11

1 Brian Fitzpatrick, *The Australian People, 1788-1945* (1946), Macmillan reissue, 1969, p. 217.

2 N. G. Butlin, 'Company Ownership of NSW Pastoral Stations, 1865–1900', *Historical Studies*, 14, May 1950, including note by Fitzpatrick.

3 Graeme Davison, *The Rise and Fall of Marvellous Melbourne*, MUP, Melbourne, 1979, p. 154.

4 Michael Cannon, *The Land Boomers*, MUP, Melbourne, 1966, pp. 29–30.

5 *Sydney Morning Herald*, 2 March 1872.

6 K. Buckley and K. Klugman, *The History of Burns Philp*, Burns Philp, Sydney, 1981, p. 39.

7 Michael Cannon, *The Land Boomers*, pp.61, 122. A similar Act was passed in New South Wales in 1892, although it provided for less secrecy and more court control.

8 Stuart Macintyre, *The Oxford History of Australia*, vol. 4, OUP, Melbourne, 1986, pp. 1–5.

9 Luke Trainor, 'The Economics of the Imperial Connection: Britain and the Australian Colonies, 1886–1896', postgraduate seminar paper, Institute of Commonwealth Studies, London, November 1976.

10 Shurlee Swain, 'Charity Records as Sources for the Study of Social History', *Australia 1888*, Bulletin no. 2, August 1979, p. 116.

11 Tony Dingle, *The Victorians: Settling*, Fairfax, Syme & Weldon, Sydney, 1984, p. 170.

12 J. B. Hirst, 'Keeping Colonial History Colonial', *Historical Studies*, 82, April 1984, pp. 88–9.

13 R. N. Ebbels, *The Australian Labor Movement, 1850-1907*, Australasian Book Society, Sydney, 1960, p. 151.

14 Ray Markey, 'Labor and Politics in New South Wales, 1880–1900', unpublished PhD thesis, Wollongong University, 1983, p. 277. This congress was held in Ballarat.

[15] Terry Irving, 'Socialism, Working-Class Mobilisation and the Origins of the Labor Party', in Bruce O'Meagher (ed.), *The Socialist Objective*, Hale & Iremonger, Sydney, 1983, p. 37.

[16] Ray Markey, 'Labor and Politics', pp. 310–11.

[17] J. B. Hirst, 'Keeping Colonial History Colonial', p. 102. The quotation reflects the author's particular interest in South Australia but it is of general validity.

[18] R. N. Ebbels, *The Australian Labor Movement*, p. 232.

[19] K. D. Buckley, *The Amalgamated Engineers in Australia, 1852–1920*, Economic History Department, ANU, Canberrra, 1970, pp. 150, 152.

Chapter 12

[1] Karl Marx, *A Contribution to the Critique of Political Economy*, first published in 1859, Progress Publishers, Moscow, 1970, p. 21.

[2] John Merritt, *The Making of the AWU*, OUP, Melbourne, 1986, p. 34.

[3] Shirley Fisher, 'The Pastoral Interest and Sydney's Public Health', *Historical Studies*, 78, April 1982, p. 89.

[4] John Rickard, *Class and Politics: New South Wales, Victoria and the Early Commonwealth, 1890–1910*, ANUP, Canberra, 1976, p. 197.

[5] K. D. Buckley, *The Amalgamated Engineers in Australia, 1852–1920*, Economic History Department, ANU, Canberra, 1970, p. 164.

[6] Desley Deacon, 'Political Arithmetic: The Nineteenth-Century Australian Census and the Construction of the Dependent Woman', *Signs: Journal of Women in Culture and Society*, II, 1985, pp. 42–4; T. A. Coghlan, *Wealth and Progress of New South Wales, 1896–97*, Government Printer, Sydney, 1897, p. 488.

[7] W. Nicol, 'Women and the Trade Union Movement in New South Wales, 1890–1900', *Labour History*, 36, May 1979, p. 29.

[8] Geoffrey Serle, *The Rush to be Rich: A History of the Colony of Victoria, 1883–1889*, MUP, Melbourne, 1971, p. 76.

[9] G. J. R. Linge, *Industrial Awakening: A Geography of Australian Manufacturing, 1788 to 1890*, ANUP, Canberra, 1979, pp. 9, 250, 438, 463–5.

[10] B. R. Wise, *The Making of the Australian Commonwealth, 1889–1900*, Longmans, London, 1913, p. 356.

[11] Hugh Anderson (ed.), *Tocsin: Radical Arguments Against Federation, 1897–1900*, Drummond, Melbourne, 1977, pp. 63, 67.

[12] Sol Encel, Donald Horne and Elaine Thompson (eds), *Change the Rules: Towards a Democratic Constitution*, Penguin, Melbourne, 1977, pp. 52–3.

[13] Katrina Alford and Michelle McLean, 'Partners or Parasites of Men?

Women's Economic Status in Australia, Britain and Canada, 1850–1900', *Working Papers in Economic History*, ANU, 66, April 1986, p. 37.

14 K. D. Buckley, *The Amalgamated Engineers*, p. 176. This criticism was voiced in 1911.

15 Michael Cannon, *Life in the Cities*, Nelson, Melbourne, 1975, p. 290.

16 John Rickard, *Cass and Politics*, p. 154.

17 *Commonwealth Parl. Debates*, Session 1903, p. 3340.

18 *Commonwealth Parl. Papers*, Session 1907–8, IV, Part 2, Command Paper No. 147.

19 J. Lack, article on McKay, *Australian Dictionary of Biography*, 10, p. 292; P. G. Macarthy, 'Justice Higgins and the Harvester Judgement', in Jill Roe (ed.), *Social Policy in Australia: Some Perspectives, 1901–1975*, Cassell, Sydney/Melbourne, 1976, p. 45.

20 C. R. Hall, *The Manufacturers: Australian Manufacturing Achievements to 1960*, Angus & Robertson, Sydney, 1971, p. 225.

21 J. Lack, article on McKay.

22 Kees van der Pijl, *The Making of the Atlantic Ruling Class*, Verso, London, 1984, pp. 19 ff.

Chapter 13

1 Thomas More, *Utopia*, Clarendon Press, Oxford, 1895, p. 303: first published in 1516.

2 Mary Edwards to Royal Commission on Female Labour in Factories and Shops, *NSW Parl. Papers, 1911–12*, vol. II, part 2, Evidence, p. 39. The witness had worked as a dressmaker for thirty years.

3 K. D. Buckley, *The Amalgamated Engineers in Australia, 1852–1920*, Economic History Department, ANU, Canberra, 1970, p. 165.

4 N. Cain, 'Financial Reconstruction in Australia, 1893–1900', *Business Archives and History*, 6, 2, August 1966, p. 179.

5 K. Buckley and K. Klugman, *The History of Burns Philp*, Burns Philp, Sydney, 1981, p. 207.

6 H. L. Wilkinson, *The Trust Movement in Australia*, Critchley Parker, Melbourne, 1914, p. 40.

7 Andrew Hopkins, 'Anti-Trust and the Bourgeoisie, 1906 and 1965', in E. L. Wheelwright and Ken Buckley (eds), *Essays in the Political Economy of Australian Capitalism*, vol. 2, 1978, pp. 93, 97.

8 N. L. McKellar, *From Derby round to Burketown: The AUSN Story*, UQP, Brisbane, 1977, p. 220.

9 John Rickard, *Class and Politics: New South Wales, Victoria and the Early Commonwealth, 1890–1910*, ANUP, Canberra, 1976, p. 251.

[10] J. W. Turner, 'The Mechanisation of Coal Cutting in Pelaw Main Colliery, 1902–1905', *Labour History*, 18, May 1970, p. 65.

[11] Sidney and Beatrice Webb, *The History of Trade Unionism*, Longman Green, London, new edition 1920, p. 635.

[12] Stuart Macintyre, *Winners and Losers: The Pursuit of Social Justice in Australian History*, Allen & Unwin, Sydney, 1985, p. 54.

[13] Francis G. Castles, *The Working Class and Welfare*, Allen & Unwin, Sydney, 1985, p. 60.

[14] N. G. Napper, 'Mr Justice Heydon and the Living Wage: Industrial Arbitration in NSW, 1905–1914', unpublished B.Ec. Hons thesis, University of Sydney, 1983, p. 38.

[15] Ibid., p. 33. Heydon was a conservative member of the NSW Legislative Council in the 1890s.

[16] P. G. Macarthy, 'Victorian Wages Boards: Their Origins and the Doctrine of the Living Wage', *Journal of Industrial Relations*, 10, 2, July 1968, p. 128.

[17] David Plowman, 'Industrial Legislation and the Rise of Employer Associations, 1890–1906', *Journal of Industrial Relations*, 27, 4, September 1985, p. 307.

[18] Keith Hancock, 'The Wages of the Workers', *Journal of Industrial Relations*, 11, 1, March 1969, p. 17.

[19] John Merritt, *The Making of the AWU*, OUP, Melbourne, 1986, p. 363.

[20] K. D. Buckley, *The Amalgamated Engineers*, p. 212.

[21] Edna Ryan, *Two-Thirds of a Man: Women and Arbitration in New South Wales, 1902–08*, Hale & Iremonger, Sydney, 1984, pp. 173, 183.

[22] T. Mann, *Memoirs*, Labour Publishing Co., London, 1923, p. 224.

[23] K. D. Buckley, *The Amalgamated Engineers*, p. 190. Earsman, who worked in Melbourne, was later the first secretary of the Communist Party of Australia.

[24] E. C. Fry (ed.), *Tom Barker and the IWW*, Australian Society for Study of Labour History, Canberra, 1965, p. 16.

[25] D. J. Murphy (ed.), *The Big Strikes: Queensland, 1889–1965*, UQP, Brisbane, 1983, p. 124.

[26] K. D. Buckley, *The Amalgamated Engineers*, p. 200.

[27] Report of Royal Commission on Sugar Industry, *Commonwealth Parl. Papers*, 1912, III, pp. lvi, lix.

[28] K. Buckley and K. Klugman, *The History of Burns Philp*, p. 228. The 'cancerous institution' was the Sydney Trades Hall.

Chapter 14

[1] Stuart Rosewarne, 'Capital Accumulation in Australia and the Export of Mining Capital before World War II', in E. L. Wheelwright and Ken Buckley

(eds), *Essays in the Political Economy of Australian Capitalism*, vol. 5, 1983, p. 192.

2 K. Buckley and K. Klugman, *The History of Burns Philp*, Burns Philp, Sydney, 1981, pp. 247–9. In the event, the Wing Sang proposal was not adopted by Burns Philp.

3 Lorraine Phillips, 'Plenty More Little Brown Man! Pearlshelling and White Australia in Queensland, 1901–18', in E. L. Wheelwright and Ken Buckley (eds), *Essays in the Political Economy of Australian Capitalism*, vol. 4, 1980, pp. 71, 77.

4 Raymond Evans, K. Saunders and K. Cronin, *Exclusion, Exploitation and Extermination: Race Relations in Colonial Queensland*, ANZ Book Co., Sydney, 1975, p. 367.

5 Andrew Markus, 'Divided We Fall: The Chinese and the Melbourne Furniture Trade Union, 1870–1900 ', *Labour History*, 26, May 1974, p. 8.

6 A. A. Graves, 'The Abolition of the Queensland Labour Trade: Politics or Profits?', in E. L. Wheelwright and Ken Buckley (eds), *Essays in the Political Economy of Australian Capitalism*, vol. 4, p. 49.

7 Kay Saunders, 'Masters and Servants: The Queensland Sugar Workers' Strike, 1911', in Ann Curthoys and Andrew Markus (eds), *Who are Our Enemies? Racism and the Australian Working Class*, Hale & Iremonger, Sydney, 1978, p. 105. Relevant to this quotation is the fact that the entry of strikebreakers as immigrants was prohibited by the Contract Immigrants Act of 1905.

8 Derived from material which was housed in the CSR Library, Sydney, a number of years ago, mostly under the heading 'Political'. Presumably the material is now in the CSR records which have been transferred to ANU Archives, Canberra. Except where otherwise indicated, later CSR quotations in this chapter are similarly sourced.

9 K. L. Gillion, *Fiji's Indian Migrants: A History to the End of Indenture in 1920*, OUP, Melbourne, 1962, pp. 92, 129.

10 Michael Moynagh, *Brown or White? A History of the Fiji Sugar Industry, 1873-1973*, ANU, Canberra, 1981, p. 34.

11 Minutes of Evidence, Royal Commission on Sugar Industry, Commonwealth Parl. Papers, 1913, IV, Part 2, p. 825.

12 Report of Royal Commission on Sugar Industry, *Commonwealth Parl. Papers*, 1912, III, p. xxxviii.

13 Ibid., pp. xxii, xlii.

14 Ibid., p. ix; quoted approvingly in CSR, *South Pacific Enterprise*, Angus & Robertson, Sydney, 1956, p. 51.

15 *Sydney Morning Herald*, 25 December 1912.

16 Karl Marx and Frederick Engels, *Manifesto of the Communist Party*, in Karl Marx, *Selected Works*, Lawrence and Wishart, London, 1945, vol. 1, pp. 207–10.

17 Ibid., pp. 128–9.

Further Reading

Some works can be recommended as both useful and relevant to most of the ground covered in this book. In particular, there are Brian Fitzpatrick's *British Imperialism and Australia, 1783-1833* (Allen & Unwin, London, 1939) and *The British Empire in Australia, 1834-1939* (Macmillan re-issue, Melbourne, 1969); R. W. Connell and T. H. Irving, *Class Structure in Australian History* (Longman Cheshire, Melbourne, 1980); and the five volumes of *Essays in the Political Economy of Australian Capitalism*, edited by E. L. Wheelwright and Ken Buckley (ANZ Book Co., Sydney, 1975-83). The Australian journal, *Labour History*, has also published many good articles over the years; and the *Australian Dictionary of Biography* is a useful compendium of information. Readers interested in particular aspects may follow up by consulting the works listed in footnotes to each chapter of the present volume. It would be tedious to repeat those references here. Instead, we append a further list of authorities. It is arranged chapter by chapter, although of course some works are also relevant to other chapters.

Chapter 1

M. F. Christie, *Aborigines in Colonial Victoria, 1835-86*, SUP, Sydney, 1979

Mervyn Hartwig, 'Capitalism and Aborigines: The Theory of Internal Colonialism and its Rivals', in E. L. Wheelwright and Ken Buckley (eds), *Essays in the Political Economy of Australian Capitalism*, vol. 3, 1978

Peter Fitzpatrick, ' "Really Rather Like Slavery": Law and Labour in the Colonial Economy of Papua New Guinea', in E. L. Wheelwright and Ken Buckley (eds), *Essays*, vol. 3, 1978

Geoffrey Blainey, *Triumph of the Nomads*, Macmillan, Melbourne, 1975

Chapter 2

Margaret Steven, *Merchant Campbell, 1769-1846*, OUP, Melbourne, 1965

Chapter 3

George Rudé, *Protest and Punishment*, Clarendon, Oxford, 1978

J. B. Hirst, *Convict Society and Its Enemies*, Allen & Unwin, Sydney, 1983

Sandra Blair, 'The Felonry and the Free? Divisions in Colonial Society in the Penal Era', *Labour History*, 45, November 1983

Michael Sturma, 'Eye of the Beholder: Stereotype of Women Convicts, 1788–1852', *Labour History*, 34, May 1978

Katrina Alford, *roduction or Reproduction? An Economic History of Women in Australia, 1788-1850*, OUP, Melbourne, 1984

Russel Ward, *The Australian Legend*, OUP, Melbourne, 1958

Ken Buckley, *Offensive and Obscene: A Civil Liberties Casebook*, Ure Smith, Sydney, 1970

Chapter 4

Anne Summers, *Damned Whores and God's Police*, Penguin, Melbourne, 1975

Adrian Merritt, 'The Historical Role of Law in the Regulation of Employment', *Australian Journal of Law and Society*, I, 1, 1982

J. W. Turner, 'Newcastle Miners and the Masters and Servants Act, 1830–1862', *Labour History*, 16, May 1969

Peter Burroughs, *Britain and Australia, 1831-1855: A Study in Imperial Relations and Crown Lands Administration*, Clarendon, Oxford, 1967

Chapter 5

Philip McMichael, *Settlers and the Agrarian Question: Capitalism in Colonial Australia*, CUP, Cambridge, 1986

K. Buckley, 'Gipps and the Graziers of New South Wales, 1841–6', *Historical Studies*, VI, May 1955; VII, May 1956

Kelvin Rowley, 'Pastoral Capitalism', *Intervention*, 1, April 1972

A. Grenfell Price, *Founders and Pioneers of South Australia*, Martin, Adelaide, 1978

J. C. Belchem, 'The Spy-System in 1848: Chartists and Informers—An Australian Connection', *Labour History*, 39, November 1980

Chapter 6

E. J. Hobsbawm, *The Age of Capital, 1848-1875*, Weidenfeld & Nicolson, London, 1975

Michael Edelstein, *Overseas Investment in the Age of High Imperialism: The United Kingdom, 1850-1914*, Methuen, London, 1982

N. G. Butlin, *Investment in Australian Economic Development, 1861-1900*, CUP, Cambridge, 1964

A. R. Hall, *The Stock Exchange of Melbourne and the Victorian Economy, 1852-1900*, ANUP, Canberra, 1968

Chapter 7

S. H. Roberts, *History of Australian Land Settlement, 1788-1920*, Macmillan, Melbourne, 1924

D. N. Jeans, *The Historical Geography of New South Wales to 1901*, Reed, Sydney, 1972

Eleanore Williams, 'Through Eastern Eyes: Large Freehold Estates in South Australia', *Australian Economic History Review (AEHR)*, XVII, 1, March 1977

Chapter 8

J. B. Hirst, *Adelaide and the Country, 1870-1917*, MUP, Melbourne, 1973

Duncan Waterson, *Personality, Profit and Politics: Thomas McIlwraith in Queensland, 1866-1894*, Macrossan lecture, UQP, Brisbane, 1978

J. Hagan and K. Turner, 'The Origins of the Labor Party in the Illawarra', paper at Whitlam Conference of Labour Historians, Sydney, December 1985

Chapter 9

W. D. Rubinstein, 'The Distribution of Personal Wealth in Victoria, 1860–19674', *AEHR*, XIX, 1, March 1979

W. D. Rubinstein, 'The Top Wealth-Holders of New South Wales, 1817–1939', *AEHR*, XX, 2, September 1980

J. Hagan, *Printers and Politics*, ANUP, Canberra, 1966

R. T. Fitzgeralad, *The Printers of Melbourne: The History of a Union*, Pitman, Melbourne, 1967

Chapter 10

Glenn Withers and others, *Australian Historical Statistics: Labour Statistics*, ANU, Source Paper in Economic History, 7, 1985

G. E. Patmore, 'A History of Industrial Relations in the NSW Government Railways, 1855-1929', unpublished PhD thesis, University of Sydney, 1986

Ann Stephen and Andrew Reeves, *Badges of Labour, Banners of Pride*, Allen & Unwin, Sydney, 1985

G. R. Henning, 'Steamships and the 1890 Maritime Strike', *Historical Studies*, 60, April 1973

R. B. Walker, 'Media and Money: The London Dock Strike of 1889 and the Australian Maritime Strike of 1890', *Labour History*, 41, November 1981

Ray Markey, 'New Unionism in Australia, 1880–1900', *Labour History*, 48, May 1985

D. J. Murphy (ed.), *Labour in Politics: The State Labor Parties in Australia, 1880–1920*, UQP, Brisbane, 1975

Chapter 11

A. R. Hall, *The London Capital Market and Australia, 1870–1914*, ANUP, Canberra, 1963

E. A. Boehm, *Prosperity and Depression in Australia, 1887–1897*, Clarendon Press, Oxford, 1971

Alan Barnard (ed.), *The Simple Fleece*, MUP, Melbourne, 1962

Chapter 12

Bob Gollan, 'The Ideology of the Labour Movement', in E. L. Wheelwright and Ken Buckley (eds), *Essays*, vol. 1, 1975

W. A. Sinclair, 'Women and Economic Change in Melbourne, 1871–1921', *Historical Studies*, 79, October 1982

J. A. La Nauze, 'The Name of the Commonwealth of Australia', *Historical Studies*, 57, October 1971

B. K. de Garis, 'The Colonial Office and the Commonwealth Constitution Bill', in A. W. Martin (ed.), *Essays in Australian Federation*, MUP, Melbourne, 1969

C. Forster, 'Federation and the Tariff', *AEHR*, XVII, 2, September 1972

Chapter 13

Beverley Kingston, *My Wife, My Daughter and Poor Mary Anne*, Nelson, Melbourne, 1975

N. G. Butlin, A. Barnard and J. J. Pincus, *Government and Capitalism*, Allen & Unwin, Sydney, 1983

J. Iremonger, J. Merritt and G. Osborne, *Strikes: Studies in Twentieth Century Australian Social History*, Australian Society for Study of Labour History, Sydney, 1973

D. Phillips, 'The Trade and Commerce Power', in R. Else-Mitchell (ed.), *Essays on the Australian Constitution*, Law Book Co., Sydney, 1961

Ian Turner, *Industrial Labour and Politics: The Labour Movement in Eastern Australia, 1900–1921*, ANUP, Canberra, 1965

L. Soltow, 'The Census of Wealth of Men in Australia in 1915 and in the United States in 1860 and 1870', *AEHR*, XII, 2, September 1972

F. Lancaster Jones, 'The Changing Shape of the Australian Income Distribution, 1914-15 and 1968-9', *AEHR*, XV, 1, March 1975

Chapter 14

Hugh Tinker, *A New System of Slavery: The Export of Indian Labour Overseas, 1830-1920*, OUP, London, 1974

Kay Saunders, *Workers in Bondage: The Origins and Bases of Unfree Labour in Queensland, 1826-1916*, UQP, Brisbane, 1982

Ralph Schlomowitz, 'The Search for Institutional Equilibrium in Queensland's Sugar Industry, 1884-1913', *AEHR*, XIX, 2, September 1979

Geoffrey Sawer, *Australian Federal Politics and Law, 1901-1929*, MUP, Melbourne, 1956

Index